AMERICAN FAMILIES
AND HOUSEHOLDS

AMERICAN FAMILIES AND HOUSEHOLDS

James A. Sweet
and
Larry L. Bumpass

for the
National Committee for Research
on the 1980 Census

RUSSELL SAGE FOUNDATION / NEW YORK

The Russell Sage Foundation

The Russell Sage Foundation, one of the oldest of America's general purpose founda-
tions, was established in 1907 by Mrs. Margaret Olivia Sage for "the improvement of social
and living conditions in the United States." The Foundation seeks to fulfill this mandate by
fostering the development and dissemination of knowledge about the political, social, and
economic problems of America. It conducts research in the social sciences and public
policy, and publishes books and pamphlets that derive from this research.

The Board of Trustees is responsible for oversight and the general policies of the Foundation, while administrative direction of the program and staff is vested in the President,
assisted by the officers and staff. The President bears final responsibility for the decision to
publish a manuscript as a Russell Sage Foundation book. In reaching a judgment on the
competence, accuracy, and objectivity of each study, the President is advised by the staff
and selected expert readers. The conclusions and interpretations in Russell Sage Foundation
publications are those of the authors and not of the Foundation, its Trustees, or its staff.
Publication by the Foundation, therefore, does not imply endorsement of the contents of the
study.

Library of Congress Cataloging-in-Publication Data

Sweet, James A.
American families and households/James A. Sweet, Larry Bumpass.
    p.   cm.—(The Population of the United States in the 1980s)
"For the National Committee for Research on the 1980 Census."
Bibliography: p.
Includes index.
ISBN 0-87154-148-3
ISBN 0-87154-149-1 (pbk)
    1. Family—United States   2. Marriage—United States.
3. Households—United States. I. Bumpass, Larry L. II. National Committee for Re-
search on the 1980 Census. III. Title. IV. Series.
HQ 536.S88 1987
306.8-5-0793—dc19   87-32113

First Paperback Edition 1990

Cover and text design: HUGUETTE FRANCO

10 9 8 7 6 5 4 3 2

The National Committee for Research on the 1980 Census

The committee is sponsored by the Social Science Research Council, the Russell Sage Foundation, and the Alfred P. Sloan Foundation, in collaboration with the U.S. Bureau of the Census. The opinions, findings, and conclusions or recommendations expressed in the monographs supported by the committee are those of the author(s) and do not necessarily reflect the views of the committee or its sponsors.

87344

Foreword

American Families and Households is one of an ambitious series of volumes aimed at converting the vast statistical yield of the 1980 census into authoritative analyses of major changes and trends in American life. This series, "The Population of the United States in the 1980s," represents an important episode in social science research and revives a long tradition of independent census analysis. First in 1930, and then again in 1950 and 1960, teams of social scientists worked with the U.S. Bureau of the Census to investigate significant social, economic, and demographic developments revealed by the decennial censuses. These census projects produced three landmark series of studies, providing a firm foundation and setting a high standard for our present undertaking.

There is, in fact, more than a theoretical continuity between those earlier census projects and the present one. Like those previous efforts, this new census project has benefited from close cooperation between the Census Bureau and a distinguished, interdisciplinary group of scholars. Like the 1950 and 1960 research projects, research on the 1980 census was initiated by the Social Science Research Council and the Russell Sage Foundation. In deciding once again to promote a coordinated program of census analysis, Russell Sage and the Council were mindful not only of the severe budgetary restrictions imposed on the Census Bureau's own publishing and dissemination activities in the 1980s, but also of the extraordinary changes that have occurred in so many dimensions of American life over the past two decades.

The studies constituting "The Population of the United States in the 1980s" were planned, commissioned, and monitored by the National Committee for Research on the 1980 Census, a special committee appointed by the Social Science Research Council and sponsored by the Council, the Russell Sage Foundation, and the Alfred P. Sloan Foundation, with the collaboration of the U.S. Bureau of the Census. This committee includes leading social scientists from a broad range of fields—demography, economics, education, geography, history, political science, sociology, and statistics. It has been the committee's task to select the main topics for research, obtain highly qualified specialists to carry out that research, and provide the structure necessary to facilitate coordination among researchers and with the Census Bureau.

The topics treated in this series span virtually all the major features of American society—ethnic groups (blacks, Hispanics, foreign-born); spatial dimensions (migration, neighborhoods, housing, regional and metropolitan growth and decline); and status groups (income levels, families and households, women). Authors were encouraged to draw not only on the 1980 Census but also on previous censuses and on subsequent national data. Each individual research project was assigned a special advisory panel made up of one committee member, one member nominated by the Census Bureau, one nominated by the National Science Foundation, and one or two other experts. These advisory panels were responsible for project liaison and review and for recommendations to the National Committee regarding the readiness of each manuscript for publication. With the final approval of the chairman of the National Committee, each report was released to the Russell Sage Foundation for publication and distribution.

The debts of gratitude incurred by a project of such scope and organizational complexity are necessarily large and numerous. The committee must thank, first, its sponsors—the Social Science Research Council, headed until recently by Kenneth Prewitt; the Russell Sage Foundation, under the direction of president Marshall Robinson; and the Alfred P. Sloan Foundation, led by Albert Rees. The long-range vision and day-to-day persistence of these organizations and individuals sustained this research program over many years. The active and willing cooperation of the Bureau of the Census was clearly invaluable at all stages of this project, and the extra commitment of time and effort made by Bureau economist James R. Wetzel must be singled out for special recognition. A special tribute is also due to David L. Sills of the Social Science Research Council, staff member of the committee, whose organizational, administrative, and diplomatic skills kept this complicated project running smoothly.

The committee also wishes to thank those organizations that contributed additional funding to the 1980 Census project—the Ford Foundation and its deputy vice president, Louis Winnick, the National Science Foundation, the National Institute on Aging, and the National Institute of Child Health and Human Development. Their support of the research program in general and of several particular studies is gratefully acknowledged.

The ultimate goal of the National Committee and its sponsors has been to produce a definitive, accurate, and comprehensive picture of the U.S. population in the 1980s, a picture that would be primarily descriptive but also enriched by a historical perspective and a sense of the challenges for the future inherent in the trends of today. We hope our readers will agree that the present volume takes a significant step toward achieving that goal.

CHARLES F. WESTOFF

Chairman and Executive Director
National Committee for Research
on the 1980 Census

Acknowledgments

Support for the preparation of this book was provided by the Russell Sage Foundation through the National Committee for Research on the 1980 Census. Our work was also assisted by the facilities of the Center for Demography and Ecology of the University of Wisconsin. These facilities are funded in part by the Center for Population Research, National Institute of Child Health and Human Development of the National Institutes of Health (HD 05876). This project also benefited from NIH grant HD-15227 and contract NO 1-HD-02852, on which the authors were working at the same time that this monograph was being prepared.

We are deeply indebted to Cheryl Knobeloch and Barbara Witt for their skill, efficiency, and patience in managing data files and in coping with our complex, and often cryptic, computational instructions. Barbara Weston Corry was similarly invaluable in managing the editorial details of this project. Brian Lapec assisted in making and checking computations, and in keeping track of the thousands of tables that were created during the course of the project. Linda Jacobson participated in the early stages of this project, and assisted in preparing materials on single persons in Chapter 3.

Our thanks go to Charles F. Westoff, Arthur J. Norton, and Andrew J. Cherlin for reading earlier drafts and providing many useful comments.

We would also like to acknowledge the broad support for family and household demography provided by the Center for Population Research, particularly the leadership of Wendy H. Baldwin and V. Jeffery Evans. The interaction with our colleagues across the country that they have facilitated has contributed in many ways to our own work. The Center for Population Research is also currently funding our National Survey of Families and Households, a major project which will help to fill in many of the gaps in knowledge for which the present volume provides the descriptive skeleton. The unanticipated opportunity to spend much of the past several years developing this survey also deserves a great deal of the credit for delaying the completion of this volume until so late in the intercensal period.

JAMES A. SWEET
LARRY L. BUMPASS

Center for Demography and Ecology,
University of Wisconsin

Contents

List of Tables

List of Figures

1

INTRODUCTION

E VEN THOUGH family relationships extend beyond household boundaries, household living arrangements are among the most significant aspects of everyday life. Household membership defines a set of primary relationships, a pool of resources, and a number of persons with whom those resources are shared. These arrangements have a profound effect on the economic and social well-being of individuals, and the relative prevalence of different types of arrangements, with associated differences in resources and lifestyles, affects the very character of our society.

Changes in family and household composition are a normal part of the life course of individuals. Even a life history uncomplicated by marital disruption involves many transitions: as the size of the family of childhood expands and contracts with the birth and home-leaving of siblings, as the individual leaves home to set up an independent household, as he or she marries, has children, and then experiences the departure of adult children and ultimately the spouse's death. There is great diversity in family life cycle experience: many now experience divorce and remarriage, and this may occur at diverse ages in either childhood as the parental marriage is disrupted, in adulthood, or both. In addition, increasing proportions may never marry or have children.

In the aggregate, these individual histories both reflect and affect the character of a society. Norman B. Ryder has aptly used the label "demographic metabolism" to characterize the changing composition of society that results from the aggregation of the life histories of successive cohorts.[1] The prevalence of young single persons, of young families, of single-parent families, of remarriages, of elderly couples, or of elderly widows depends on the sizes of successive birth cohorts and on the rates at which they make various life course transitions. The "baby boom" has created an age structure characterized as analogous to a "pig in a python," which will affect the prevalence of successive life cycle stages—from unmarried singles to dependent elderly—as its members age, quite apart from whatever changes may occur in the rates of marriage or mortality. The life experiences of successive cohorts get translated into population experience in ways that reflect changes both in behavior and in the sizes of groups at risk of that behavior.

There have also been major transformations in the organization of the life course of individuals; rates of family transition have changed dramatically at virtually every stage. Rates of marriage and childbirth have declined markedly, rates of marital disruption have increased, and those who can are much more likely to maintain independent households.

In this volume we have set out to do several things with respect to family transitions and family and household structure:

1. To describe, as of around 1980, the family and household situation of the American population. This description includes several distinct components including:
   a. the rate at which family transitions are occurring—marriage, childbearing, marital dissolution, and "leaving home" as a young adult;
   b. the social and economic characteristics of persons in various family and household situations; and
   c. the prevalence and characteristics of various household and family types.

2. To describe recent changes in these family and household distributions, and in the processes underlying them. The temporal focus of these comparisons is primarily the period from 1960 through 1980, although in many cases we include data back to 1940 and earlier.

3. To describe differentials within the American population. We are concerned with differential family and household structures, differential rates of family transitions, and differential trends among major population subgroups. Among the population

---

[1]Norman B. Ryder, "Components of Temporal Variations in American Fertility," in Robert W. Hiorns, ed., *Demographic Patterns in Developed Societies*, vol. 19, Symposia of the Society for the Study of Human Biology (London: Taylor & Francis, 1980).

characteristics that differentiate family and household behavior and structure are age, sex, race and ethnicity, and education.

A brief comment on each of these characteristics may help in understanding the rationale for the structure of our analysis.

Differentials Among Racial and Ethnic Groups

In each chapter of this volume we compare and contrast the family and household situation of blacks and Mexican-Americans (the two largest minority groups in the United States) with that of majority (non-Hispanic) whites. We also devote an unusual amount of attention to other racial and Hispanic groups, such as American Indians, Asian-American groups, Puerto Ricans, and Cubans. Because of the relatively small size of these groups, the decennial census is the only source of comparative information on these groups, some of which are relatively affluent (Chinese and Japanese-Americans) and others quite disadvantaged (American Indians, Hawaiians, and Puerto Ricans), and each with a unique cultural tradition affecting their family structure. Except for a brief discussion of differential marriage patterns, we have not included comparisons of family and household characteristics of ancestry groups within the white population.

Differentials by Education

Although not a fixed characteristic like race, sex, or cohort membership, the educational level of adults rarely changes. Education plays an important role in differentiating the family and household patterns within the American population. Education is an indicator of long-term socioeconomic status, one which, unlike income, is not much affected by the current family situation. It is also an indicator of an individual's earning potential in the labor market. There are also value and "cultural" differences by level of educational attainment, which may affect such family transitions as childbearing or divorce.

Two other features of educational level are especially important to the analyses reported in this volume. First, going to school is an activity that is concentrated in the early adult (as well as pre-adult) years, during which family transitions—leaving the parental home, marriage, childbirth—are occurring at a high intensity. Education, especially college education, serves to delay the process of reaching full adulthood (emancipation from the parental household, economic independence, marriage, parenthood).

Second, there has been an extremely rapid educational upgrading. Each successive cohort has a larger proportion who have attended college and a smaller proportion who have not completed high school. An adequate understanding of recent change in the rate at which each of the family transitions is occurring and of changes in each of the dimensions of family and household structure, requires consideration of the effect of changing education composition. For example, educational upgrading implies rising marriage ages, quite apart from any change in education-specific marriage behavior. Note that differentials in education are also relevant to understanding differences in family behavior among racial and ethnic subgroups.

Differentials Between Men and Women

In many analyses we have included both men and women, and have contrasted the patterns of the two sexes. Much of the prior work in family demography, as well as family sociology and economics, has had an almost exclusive focus on women. This emphasis on women, and exclusion of men, probably derives from several sources, including: the dominant interest of social demographers in reproductive patterns, the idea that men are "breadwinners" and that women are "homemakers," and the fact that most of the data on family and household phenomena focus on women. Since there are identical census data for all persons, irrespective of sex, and since the family and household experience of men is of similar substantive interest, we pay much more attention to men than has been customary.

Differentials by Age

In order to make substantive interpretations, most comparisons of the incidence of family transitions and of the characteristics of persons in different family and household statuses must be age-specific or age-standardized. Particularly important is the effect of the large baby boom cohorts on aggregate marriage and household patterns.

Data Sources

For a volume in a census monograph series, it seemed reasonable to us to make the decennial censuses our primary source of data. We have made extensive use of the public use microdata tapes produced by the United States Bureau of the Census from the 1960, 1970, and 1980 censuses. With these data files, we have been able to construct identical tabulations at several points in time. We have been able to extend the analysis backward in time to 1950 and 1940, thanks to the microdata files created by a project directed by our Wisconsin colleagues Hal Winsborough, Karl Taeuber, and Robert Hauser (funded by the National Science Foundation), which has created comparable microdata files from the 1940 and 1950 decennial censuses. In a few instances we have also used the microdata file for 1900, created by a group at the University of Washington.

The major shortcoming of the census data for our purposes is that they include little information on the incidence of family transitions. In Chapters 2 and 5, which deal with the incidence of first marriage and marital disruption, respectively, we have made extensive use of two additional data sources: the vital registration system data on marriage and divorce and the June 1980 Current Population Survey (CPS), which gathered marriage histories of a large sample of American adults.

We have resisted the temptation to use other data sets such as the Panel Study of Income Dynamics, the National Longitudinal Survey of Labor Force Behavior, or various CPS supplements (such as those on child support and child care) and the temptation to update the analysis by replicating many of the tables and analyses with, for example, the March 1985 Current Population Survey. We have tried to maintain our focus on the general question, "What do recent decennial censuses tell us about American family and household structure?" We have departed from this principle only in Chapters 2, 5, and 7, where crucial parts of the picture were not available in the census.

Overview

This book takes advantage of the large samples provided by the decennial censuses and Current Population Surveys to document in detail the changing prevalence of different family and household living arrangements. Attention is given to the differences in both rates of transition and population composition that underlie these trends and differentials. Our intent is explicitly to provide a reference work that will be useful to persons desiring more detailed information than is generally available on some of the most important dimensions of these domains. In so doing, we have constantly had to make decisions about what variables, and what level of detail, to include. Within the limits of available data, such decisions have been informed by what we understand to be the major theoretical and substantive issues in family and household research. At the same time, statistical modeling and extensive theoretical discussions are beyond the objectives of this volume—not because we do not care about them but because we judge the present format most likely to be of value to a wide community of scholars over a substantial time period. This is a work in the social demography tradition that regards a careful understanding of what has happened as a necessary condition for explanation.

We begin in Chapter 2 with an examination of trends in the timing of marriage across successive birth cohorts, paying attention to marriage rates, median marriage age, and measures of the dispersion of marriage ages. Here, as throughout, differences by race, education, and ethnicity are documented. The changing composition of marriages is noted with respect to both previous marriage and prior fertility. For persons who first married in the year preceding the census, we examine homogamy with respect to a number of characteristics including marital history, race/ethnicity, education, and age.

Chapter 3 examines the consequences of these trends, in conjunction with changing cohort sizes, for the prevalence of single young adults in the population. Attention is given to the changing major activities of this population in terms of school enrollment, employment, and armed forces participation. Living arrangements are described with particular attention to the proportion living with their parents, in dorms or with roommates, or in their own households. Childbearing patterns of the single population are reviewed, and the living arrangements of never-married women with children are also described. Finally, we briefly consider the population that has still never married by ages 35–44 and is likely to remain unmarried throughout their lives.

The analysis then turns to the characteristics of currently married couples. Chapter 4 documents trends and differentials in the prevalence of married couples in the population, and examines the composition and circumstances of such couples. Particular attention is given to the changing family size that has resulted from variations in fertility. Fertility expectations are considered, and differentials in recent fertility are examined for small groups using census data on the number of own children. The presence of children at various durations of marriage is described as a critical factor affecting married life, including the prevalence of "empty nests" among middle-age and older couples who have had children. Other topics considered are the previous marital status of the spouses, current school enrollment, patterns of wife's employment, and trends and differentials in homeownership.

Thus Chapters 2, 3, and 4 attend to rates of marriage formation and then the prevalence and characteristics of the single and currently married populations, respectively. In a parallel fashion, Chapters 5 and 6 turn to rates of marital disruption, and then to the prevalence and composition of the formerly married population.

Chapter 5 begins with a discussion of alternative measures of marital disruption, and the advantages and disadvantages of various available data sources. Trends in marital disruption are documented for both periods and cohorts. Differentials by age at marriage, education, and race are examined using Current Population Survey data, with a measure that includes separations as well as divorces in the definition of disruption. In addition, a cruder measure from the census—proportion no longer in intact first marriages—makes it possible to consider differences for more detailed ethnic groups. Again based on the CPS, patterns of divorce and of remarriage after separation are described. Finally, patterns of widowhood by age, sex, race, and education are documented.

The prevalence and composition of the formerly married population is the subject of Chapter 6. Topics considered include the proportions currently separated, divorced, or widowed; duration since separation; and presence and ages of children. For formerly married women with children, attention is given to employment patterns, the receipt of public assistance, poverty levels, and whether living in own household or the household of others. There are also sections of this chapter concerned with smaller groups of interest such as those who are cohabiting and those who are married but report that their spouse is absent for reasons other than marital discord. The chapter concludes with a description of the population of formerly married men.

In Chapter 7 our attention turns to the implications of the previously described patterns of marriage, marital disruption, and childbearing for the family circumstances of children. The parental composition of children's families are detailed, and special attention is given to children in mother-only and father-only families. Other compositional variables considered are the number of children present in the household, the presence of nonnuclear relatives and whether or not the child's family lives in someone else's household. Differences in poverty, parental education, and mother's employment are described for children in various types of families. This section includes a description of family type differences in the high school dropout rate of 16–17-year-olds.

The elderly are the focus of Chapter 8. We begin by considering the age and educational composition of the population over age 60 and then turn to the proportions widowed or married and living with a spouse. Next, we discuss trends and differentials in the living arrangements of the elderly. Separately for the widowed and the currently married, we examine the proportions of men and women living alone, with a spouse, with relatives, or in institutions. Levels of homeownership, employment, disability, and receipt of social security and pension income are considered.

The unit of analysis shifts from persons to households in Chapters 9 and 10. Chapter 9 begins with a description of the changing number of households and their changing composition by type (married couples with and without children, one-parent families, other families, nonfamily households), and also by family life cycle stage of the householder. In addition, variation in average household size and its components are discussed. Chapter 10 examines a number of subtypes of households: female-headed families, male-headed families other than married couples, and nonfamily households. In addition, attention is given to secondary and subfamilies and to the population in group quarters.

The final chapter seeks to put the major trends and differentials described in this monograph into a broader perspective. Implications for future patterns are drawn from a perspective that sees the recent trends as continuous with long-term changes in Western society.

2

MARRIAGE

THIS CHAPTER is composed of three major sections. Trends in first marriage are examined, taking advantage of the potential of the census data to provide both cohort and period descriptions for major population subgroups. Following this, differentials in marriage patterns are examined in more detail for the cohort that has recently reached age 30. Finally, characteristics of recent first marriages (including early fertility, living arrangements, and patterns of intermarriage) are detailed for marriages in the year preceding the census enumeration. This chapter is concerned with first-marriage patterns; remarriage is discussed in Chapter 5.

Information on trends in marriage rates is usually obtained from the registration of marriages in the national vital statistics system. The number of marriages occurring during a given year is related to the size of the total population, or of the unmarried population, to yield a marriage rate for each year. Except for providing trends in aggregate rates, however, these data are very limited. Few characteristics of the persons marrying are recorded on the marriage certificate, and even these characteristics are available for only forty-two states, those that meet the data quality and reporting requirements of the Marriage Registration Area. Hence, for analysis of the variability of marriage patterns by social characteristics, we turn to information from the census. The large census sample makes it possible to consider trends for major population subgroups and to focus on marriages occurring in a single year for the analysis of characteristics at the time of marriage.

Trends

In spite of the ambiguity introduced by the recent emergence of widespread cohabitation, marriage still remains an important marker in the life course of individuals and a major factor affecting population composition. While the causes are not all well understood, the propensity to marry has fluctuated considerably over this century. Substantial deviations associated with the depression of the 1930s and the demobilization following World War II are evident in Figure 2.1. Three main

FIGURE 2.1

Total Marriages per Thousand Unmarried Women 15–44 Years of Age, 1940–80

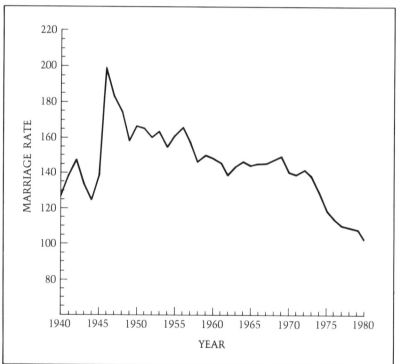

SOURCE: National Center for Health Statistics, *Monthly Vital Statistics Report*, "Advance Report of Final Marriage Statistics, 1983," DHHS, vol. 35, no. 1, Supplement, May 2, 1986.

trends are evident: (1) a steady increase in marriage rates from the low around 1930 to the postwar peak; (2) a steady decline from this peak around 1947 until the early 1970s; and (3) an acceleration in the rate of decline since then.

The marriage rate has now reached a level below that of 1930–32. This decline occurred for both first marriages and remarriages but was larger for first marriages. Further, the decline is understated in these data because the larger cohorts born during the baby boom were progressively moving into the prime marriage ages. The first-marriage rate at ages 20–24 declined by a very striking 53 percent (from 235 in 1969 to 110 in 1981). Indeed, the decline in the marriage rate has been concentrated in the 18–24 age range with little change at other ages. It remains to be seen whether rates will subsequently increase at older ages as delayed marriages are made up. In the absence of such an increase at older ages, age-specific marriage rates between 1975 and 1982 imply a total first-marriage rate of only about 70 percent: that is, if a cohort were to marry at recent age-specific first-marriage rates over the course of their lifetime, more than one-quarter would never marry.[1] While this must be an overestimate of the extent of nonmarriage for recent cohorts, it has persisted for a rather long time with no sign of an increase at the older ages.

We can examine these trends in more detail using the census reports on age and quarter of first marriage to construct first marriage dates.[2] We can combine this with information on age to represent both

---

[1]National Center for Health Statistics, *Monthly Vital Statistics Report*, "Advance Report of Final Marriage Statistics, 1983," DHHS, vol. 35, no. 1, Publication No. (PHS)86–1120.

[2]Although the 1980 United States census asked month and year of first marriage, the information provided on the public use data tapes is age at first marriage and calendar quarter of first marriage. This results in an ambiguity in identifying year of first marriage in cases where the calendar quarter of first marriage and calendar quarter of birth are the same. (Birth is treated the same way as marriage: we know the person's age as of April 1, 1980, and the calendar quarter of birth.)

Consider a person age 25 at the time of the census, who was born in the first quarter, who reported that they were married in the first quarter, and whose age at first marriage was 24 years. This person must have been born in 1955, since the census date is April 1. However, the year in which they were first married is not clear. They could have been married in the first quarter of either 1979 or 1980, depending on whether their birthdate precedes or follows their marriage date within the first quarter. If their birthdate was February 1 and their wedding anniversary was March 1, they would have been married in 1979; however if the birthdate were March 1 and the wedding date February 1, the marriage would have occurred in 1980.

This affects about one-quarter of the cases, since if date of marriage and date of birth are independent, the chances of marrying in the same calendar quarter are about one in four. We have randomly assigned these cases to each of the two possible years with a probability of 0.5. Hence, about one-eighth of all cases are incorrectly assigned to a prior single-year marriage cohort. We were unable to determine whether this same problem occurs for 1960 and 1970 as well. We believe that it does.

cohort and period measures of the timing of first marriage. For cohorts, we document the trend in the median and the first and third quartiles of the marriage distribution. This provides a useful description of the timing and distribution of marriage as experienced by successive cohorts. Change in marriage behavior, however, appears to be much more a period than a cohort phenomenon.[3] Obviously, if there is considerable period fluctuation in marriage propensities, the first and third quartiles of a cohort's marriage experience may occur in very different marriage environments.

We can examine the recent period changes in more detail than is possible with vital statistics data by using the census data to create synthetic measures based on the age-specific experience of different cohorts in particular years. While the amount of relevant social and economic information in the census is limited, the advantage of these data is evident when we consider, for example, that race is not reported for over one-third of the marriages in the Marriage Registration Area, which in turn covers only about 80 percent of all marriages in the United States.

Except for validation purposes, we will not use one of the most commonly reported measures of the timing of marriage, the median age at marriage for marriages occurring in a given year. This measure is affected by both the age-specific propensity to marry and the age structure of the unmarried population. It describes an important characteristic of marriages in a given period, but gives a misleading picture of the level or trend of marriage propensities.

Figures 2.2a and 2.2b superimpose the median ages at marriage for birth cohorts as calculated from the 1980 census[4] on those calculated by Thornton and Rodgers, using a pooled data set from the 1960 and 1970 censuses and the June Current Population Survey from 1971, 1975, and 1980. The match between these two series is very close for non-Hispanic whites in Figure 2.2a. The medians calculated from the 1980 census tend to be about .1 to .2 years above the other series, but the basic trends are identical. The difference is very likely a consequence of some disrupted first marriages not being reported at the later observation. Thornton and Rodgers note a similar difference between the census estimates for 1960 and 1970.[5]

---

[3]Arland Thornton and Willard L. Rodgers, "The Influence of Individual and Historical Time on Marital Dissolution," *Demography* 24 (February 1987):1–24.

[4]These quartiles are defined in relation to the entire cohort, including those members who never marry. The quartile values are somewhat higher than those of the ever-marrying population. Of course, the proportion of the more recent cohorts who will never marry is still unknown.

[5]Arland Thornton and Willard L. Rodgers, "Changing Patterns of Marriage and Divorce in the United States." Final Report, Contract NO1-HD-02840, National Institute for Child Health and Human Development, 1983, p. 182.

FIGURE 2.2

Median Age at Marriage for Birth Cohorts of 1880–1950: Whites and Blacks

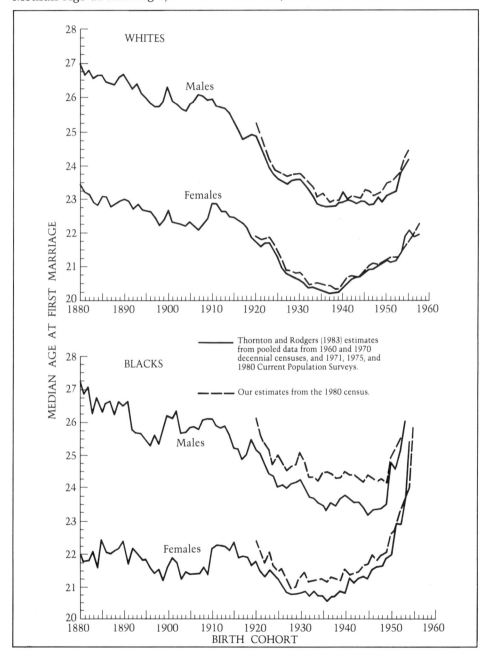

However, the discrepancy between the two series is very large for blacks (Figure 2.2b), especially for black men. The difference in estimated median age at marriage is often over a full year for men, and over half a year for women. Nonreporting of disrupted first marriages is probably the major factor in this difference, but other factors could contribute as well. To the extent that single blacks were less well enumerated in the earlier censuses, estimates of marriage ages would be downwardly biased; this would be particularly relevant to the larger difference among black males. Among black women, marriage ages would be downwardly biased in the earlier series if there was a greater tendency for a single mother to report herself as married in 1960 and 1970 than in 1980. Consequently, it is likely that the two series bracket the actual experience of blacks. While the underlying trends are similar, one must keep in mind that if nonreporting of first marriages is the major component of the difference between the series, the trends observed in the 1980 data may substantially understate the decline in marriage propensities among blacks.

Figures 2.2a and 2.2b reveal a long-term decline in median age at marriage between the cohorts born in 1880 and those born in the late 1930s: from a median age of 27 to about 23 years among men, and from 23.5 to slightly above 20 among women. Deviations from this trend are observed for both sexes, with later marriage for the cohorts marrying around the two World Wars and during the Great Depression. After the low for the cohorts born in the late 1930s, age at marriage rapidly returned to levels similar to those of the early 1900 cohorts among non-Hispanic white women and of the 1920 cohorts among non-Hispanic white men. Among recent cohorts of black men, median age at marriage is as high as it was for the 1880 cohort; among black women, recent cohorts are marrying at older ages than even this earliest cohort did.

It is instructive to reconcile the turning point in this cohort trend with the period trend observed earlier. The 1935–39 cohort entered the marriage market after the postwar decline in marriage rates was underway. How is it possible that they married at younger ages than preceding cohorts who married in the time of peak marriage rates? The answer is in the cumulative nature of a cohort's marriage experience and the differing trends by age in the postwar period. Figure 2.3 shows the trends in the probabilities of marrying at specific ages. It is clear from this graph that from 1947 to 1960, the "marriage boom" consisted entirely of rising marriage rates among women in their teens and early twenties. Rates at older ages rapidly declined, thus bringing down the overall rate for women 15–44.[6]

[6]Ibid., p. 17.

FIGURE 2.3

First Marriage Probabilities for White Females,
for Five-Year Age Groups, 1940–60

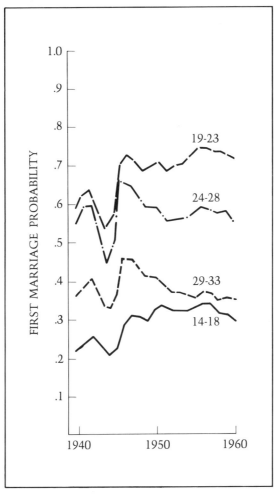

SOURCE: Willard L. Rodgers and Arland Thornton, "Changing Patterns of First Marriage in the United States," *Demography* 22 (1985):265–79.

We can observe in Figure 2.4 the trend in the quartiles of age at marriage for five-year birth cohorts since 1920 (based on the data in Table 2.1). One-quarter of the women born in the 1930s had already married by age 18.6. Of course, these cohorts not only married the earliest, they also had the highest fertility, giving us the baby boom. Subsequent cohorts have married at progressively later ages, with the median age at

FIGURE 2.4
Quartiles of Marriage Age Distribution, by Birth Cohort and Sex

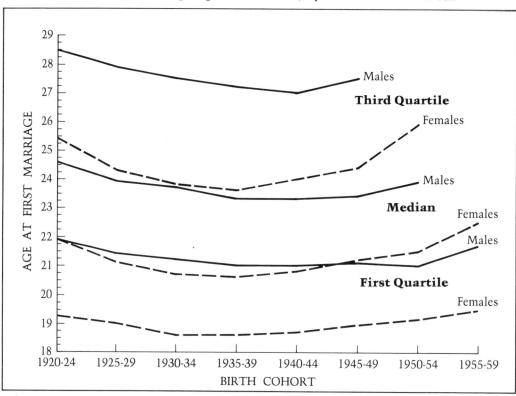

marriage increasing from the low of 20.6 to a high of 22.5 for the 1957 cohort.[7]

The accelerated increase over the last two cohorts reflects the sharp drop in first-marriage rates noted earlier. This drop is reflected as well in the change in the third quartile between the 1945–49 and 1950–54 cohorts from 24.4 to 25.9. This indicates the period, rather than cohort, nature of these changes. The marriage patterns of cohorts at various ages differ depending on the period in which each age was reached. The first quartile showed the least change, decreasing from 19.3 to 18.6 and then increasing again to 19.5.

We will return to subgroup differences in these trends and to a particular focus on the recent increase in age at marriage. First, however, it

[7]This is the last single-year cohort for which one-half of its members had married, that is, had reached its median age at marriage.

TABLE 2.1

Age at First Marriage Quartiles for Five-Year Birth Cohorts, by Sex and Race/Ethnicity

Birth Cohort	Total Quartile			Non-Hispanic White Quartile			Black Quartile			Mexican-American Quartile		
	1	2	3	1	2	3	1	2	3	1	2	3
MALES												
1920–24	21.9	24.6	28.5	21.9	24.5	28.1	21.6	25.6	32.7	21.4	24.7	29.8
1925–29	21.4	23.9	27.9	21.4	23.7	27.5	21.2	24.8	32.3	21.4	24.4	29.7
1930–34	21.2	23.7	27.5	21.1	23.5	26.9	21.2	24.5	30.8	21.0	24.3	29.0
1935–39	21.0	23.3	27.2	20.9	23.0	26.6	21.2	24.5	30.8	21.0	24.0	29.2
1940–44	21.0	23.3	27.0	20.9	23.1	26.4	21.4	24.7	31.0	20.9	23.8	28.1
1945–49	21.1	23.4	27.5	21.1	23.2	26.9	21.3	24.2	30.9	20.9	23.6	27.6
1950–54	21.0	23.9	—	21.0	23.7	—	21.7	25.5*	—	20.5	23.2	27.5*
1955–59	21.7*	—	—	21.6*	—	—	—	—	—	20.6*	—	—
FEMALES												
1920–24	19.3	21.9	25.4	19.4	21.8	25.2	18.5	21.9	28.1	18.6	21.8	27.0
1925–29	19.0	21.1	24.3	19.1	21.0	23.9	18.4	21.3	27.0	18.3	21.2	26.2
1930–34	18.6	20.7	23.8	18.6	20.6	23.4	18.3	21.3	26.7	18.3	21.2	25.9
1935–39	18.6	20.6	23.6	18.5	20.4	23.0	18.4	21.3	26.8	18.5	21.1	25.7
1940–44	18.7	20.8	24.0	18.7	20.7	23.4	18.6	21.5	27.4	18.5	21.2	25.9
1945–49	19.0	21.2	24.4	19.0	21.0	23.8	19.0	22.0	29.9	18.7	21.1	24.9
1950–54	19.2	21.5	25.9*	19.1	21.3	25.2*	19.6	23.4	—	18.6	21.0	24.7
1955–59	19.5	22.5*	—	19.4	22.2*	—	21.0	—	—	18.7	20.9*	—

*Based on single cohort in middle of five-year range; later cohorts not yet past quartile age.

is worth noting two dominant characteristics that have persisted in spite of fluctuations over these cohorts spanning more than half a century:

1. A substantial proportion of each cohort has married at young ages. One-quarter of the women have married by around age 19, and one-quarter of the men have done so by around age 21. Except for the most recent cohort, over a third of each cohort of women was married in the teenage years. Though men marry later than women, a substantial proportion, 10 to 15 percent, have married before age 20.

2. For each cohort, marriage has been relatively concentrated in a narrow age range. The interquartile range has been about five to six years, that is, half of each cohort married in this relatively narrow age range.

Racial and Ethnic Differences in Trends

The cohort trends are similar for blacks and whites with the exception that age at marriage has increased faster among black women: the difference in median age at marriage widened to .8 years for the 1935–39 cohort and then to two years for the 1950–54 cohort—women who reached age twenty in the early 1970s. This latter pattern emphasizes that the recent declines in marriage rates have been even greater among blacks (and may be understated, as noted previously). This accelerating divergence is a continuation of a long-term downward trend in black marriage rates.

Historical data on racial differences in marriage rates are very scant. Early in the century black females married about a year earlier than white females.[8] Marriage ages for males were similar by race for cohorts born around the turn of the century, but black men began to marry at later ages than white men beginning with the birth cohorts of about the 1920s. Figure 2.5 shows that the median age at marriage of black women was slightly above that of white women in the 1920–24 cohort. Even though the trends are similar among blacks and whites over these cohorts, black marriage age decreased less, and then rose more. Very different marriage patterns by race are emerging.

Because of substantial immigration in recent years, the data for Mexican-Americans more exactly describe the differences in marriage histories over age groups in the 1980 population than they represent trends over time within a well-defined population. In any event, the

[8]Thornton and Rodgers, "Changing Patterns."

FIGURE 2.5

Median Age at First Marriage, by Birth Cohort, Race, and Sex

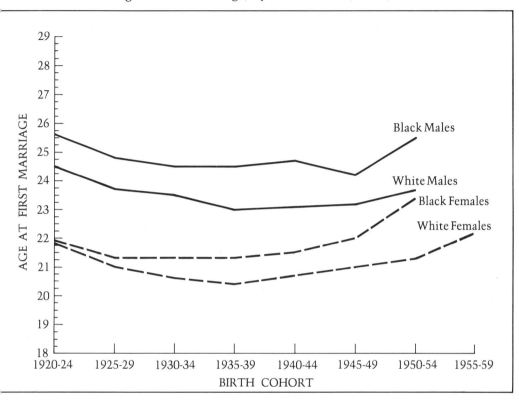

differences across cohorts do not reveal the recent upturn in age at marriage observed for non-Hispanic whites and blacks (see Table 2.1). Among Mexican-American men there is a continuous decline in median age at marriage from 24.7 among the oldest cohort to 23.2 among the youngest; and among the women age at marriage has remained at about 21.0 since the cohort of 1925–29.

The recent decline in marriage propensities observed at different ages for different cohorts is seen much more clearly when the data are rearranged to represent period experience. Table 2.2 presents the expected marriage distributions, and the probabilities of marrying over various age ranges, that would result if the age-specific first-marriage patterns of 1978–79 were to hold over a cohort's lifetime. (Lifetable procedures were used to combine the experience of the 1963 cohort at age

TABLE 2.2

Age at First Marriage Quartiles and Probabilities of Marrying Between Specific Ages by Sex, for Synthetic Cohorts Based on 1968–69 and 1978–79 First Marriage Probabilities: For Total, Non-Hispanic White, and Black Persons

	Quartile			Probability of Marrying*			
	1	2	3	Before 20	20–24	24–28	28–32
MALES							
Total							
1968–69	21.1	23.3	26.7	14.0	49.9	52.4	41.5
1978–79	22.0	24.9	30.6	10.3	36.6	42.0	37.3
Non-Hispanic White							
1968–69	21.0	23.1	26.3	14.5	52.4	55.3	43.4
1978–79	21.9	24.7	29.8	10.5	38.3	43.1	37.6
Black							
1968–69	21.4	24.2	29.8	13.0	41.1	40.6	35.2
1978–79	23.3	27.3	35.6	5.9	25.7	32.7	31.2
FEMALES							
Total							
1968–69	19.3	21.3	24.3	33.7	59.9	47.4	32.1
1978–79	20.1	23.0	28.0	23.8	43.1	41.3	31.2
Non-Hispanic White							
1968–69	19.2	21.1	23.7	35.3	64.0	51.5	33.6
1978–79	20.1	22.8	27.2	23.8	41.7	43.9	32.3
Black							
1968–69	19.5	22.3	28.5	29.7	44.5	33.3	27.3
1978–79	22.0	26.9	42.4	12.9	27.3	26.7	21.6

*Probability that a never-married person at the initial age will have married by the terminal age.

15 with those of the 1962 cohort at age 16, and so on.)[9] These figures imply even later ages at marriage than those observed for the most recent cohort. Whereas the median age at marriage for women increased by a full year between the cohorts of 1950–54 and 1955–59 (to 22.5), the

[9]For lifetable procedures, see Henry S. Shryock and Jacob S. Siegel, *The Methods and Materials of Demography*, ed. Edward A. Stockwell (New York: Academic Press, 1976).

1978–79 rates imply a distribution with a median of 23.0. For men the implied median is a year higher than that observed for the 1950–54 cohort (the 1955–59 cohort had not reached its median age at marriage by 1980). Table 2.2 also shows the same measures for 1968–69. Over the decade the median age at marriage increased by 1.6 years among men and by 1.7 years among women. For both men and women the decline in marriage propensities was greater at younger ages.

Quite apart from future trends in the propensity to ever marry, these numbers imply older first marriage age distributions for subsequent cohorts. However, there are two major stories in Table 2.2. The first concerns the changes and implied levels among blacks. The same contrast of implied medians over this decade reveals increases of 3.1 years among black males and 3.6 years among black females to median ages of 27.3 and 26.9, respectively. Even more important are the changes in the third quartiles of 5.8 years for black males and almost 14 years among females. The latter change, and the implied third quartile of 42.4, suggests that a substantial proportion of black women is unlikely ever to marry. The long-term decline in marriage propensities among blacks may be culminating in patterns that are different in kind rather than just in degree. This marked contrast in age-specific marriage rates can be seen in Figure 2.6. Marriage rates of black women are less than half those of white women throughout the peak marriage years. On the other hand, Mexican-American marriage rates are similar to, though slightly above, those of majority whites.

Even though the trend toward later marriage (or nonmarriage) revealed in the 1980 census data is very impressive, there is additional evidence that it is understated: First-marriage rates for women at ages 20–24 calculated from the 1980 census indicate a decline of 35 percent over the 1970s, in contrast to a decline of 48 percent reported for these ages from vital statistics data. Further examination reveals that the census data underestimate the vital statistics rate for female first marriages at ages 20–24 in 1969 by 11 percent but overestimate the 1979 rate by the same proportion. The underestimation of the earlier rates represents some deterioration with time in the quality of the reported marriage dates. One reason for such deterioration might be a tendency for some remarried persons to report their current marriage as their first. This would deflate estimates of first marriage for the earlier period and inflate them for the most recent period. This helps explain the overestimation of rates for 1979. It is also possible that this overestimation reflects the inclusion of some couples who are living together, but who represent themselves as married (perhaps to others as well as to the census), and report a marriage date consistent with that representation.[10]

[10]Data on marriages published in the annual Vital Statistics of the United States are based on data from the states that are in the Marriage Registration Area (MRA). States not in the MRA in 1979 were Arizona, Arkansas, Nevada, North Dakota, Oklahoma, Texas, and Washington. In 1978 in addition, Colorado was not in the MRA. These states included 20 percent of all marriages in 1980. All of them had age-specific marriage rates that were above the national average in 1980, when a more intensive effort was made to get national marriage data. Thus the MRA data understate age-specific marriage rates. The following table shows the degree of understatement at each age:

Age-Specific Marriage Rates: (All Orders): MRA and Total United States

	Males			Females		
	Total	MRA	Total: MRA	Total	MRA	Total: MRA
15–17	3.4	3.0	1.13	22.7	20.2	1.12
18–19	42.9	39.2	1.09	98.2	90.9	1.08
20–24	106.2	100.4	1.06	139.1	130.8	1.06
25–29	139.9	131.2	1.07	137.5	126.3	1.09
30–34	134.6	122.8	1.10	107.3	95.0	1.13
35–44	117.0	102.0	1.15	72.1	62.3	1.16

There is, however, a factor working in the opposite direction. The rates published in 1980 for 1971 through 1979 have been revised to take account of new intercensal population estimates that were made after the 1980 census, which enumerated 5 million more people than were expected. Evidently, because the denominators were based on intercensal population estimates that were too low, the vital statistics rates are too high by about 2 percent. The published 1979 marriage rates before and after adjustment to the 1980 census population counts were:

	Before 1980 Census	After 1980 Census
Crude Rate	10.6	10.4
Rate per 1,000 Unmarried Persons of age 15 +		
Males	28.7	28.1
Females	26.3	25.8

The following table reports the ratio of our census estimates to adjusted vital statistics estimates (The 1979 reported age-specific marriage rates have been adjusted to represent the total United States, on the assumption that the ratio of the total of the MRA is the same for first as for all marriages, and adjusted for the 1980 census count.):

	Census/Vital Statistics First Marriage Rates	
	Males	Females
14–17	1.70	1.02
18–19	0.99	1.01
20–24	1.11	1.13
25–29	1.08	1.07
30–34	1.17	1.09
35–44	1.16	1.23

FIGURE 2.6

Age-Specific First Marriage Rates, by Race/Ethnicity and Sex, 1978–79

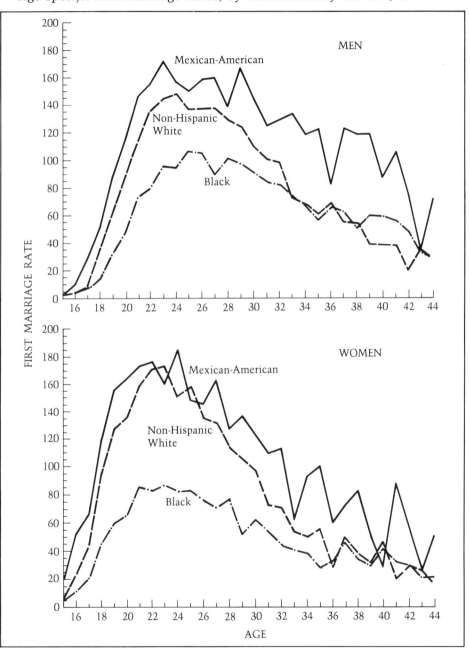

TABLE 2.3

Age at First Marriage Quartiles for Five-Year Birth Cohorts,
by Education and Sex: Non-Hispanic White Population

	Education—Years of School Completed											
Birth Cohort	0–11 Quartile			12 Quartile			13–15 Quartile			16+ Quartile		
	1	2	3	1	2	3	1	2	3	1	2	3
MALES												
1920–24	21.4	24.1	27.9	22.0	24.4	27.8	22.1	24.5	27.8	23.1	25.6	29.1
1925–29	20.8	23.0	26.9	21.3	23.5	27.1	21.7	23.9	27.4	22.7	25.0	28.7
1930–34	20.4	22.9	26.7	20.9	23.1	26.2	21.2	23.5	26.7	22.4	24.7	28.2
1935–39	20.0	22.2	26.3	20.5	22.5	25.7	21.1	23.1	26.4	22.3	24.4	27.9
1940–44	19.8	22.0	26.0	20.4	22.4	25.5	21.1	23.1	26.2	22.3	24.3	27.7
1945–49	19.6	21.9	25.8	20.4	22.5	25.5	21.2	23.3	26.9	22.3	24.3	28.8
1950–54	19.5	21.9	28.0	20.2	22.5	27.4	21.4	24.1	NA	22.8	25.7	NA
1955–59	19.8	NA	NA	20.9	NA	NA	NA	NA	NA	24.0	NA	NA
FEMALES												
1920–24	18.0	20.4	24.0	19.7	21.9	25.1	20.7	22.7	25.8	22.0	24.2	28.3
1925–29	17.9	19.8	22.7	19.3	21.0	23.6	20.1	21.8	24.5	21.6	23.4	26.7
1930–34	17.2	18.9	22.0	18.8	20.4	22.8	19.7	21.4	23.8	21.3	23.1	26.5
1935–39	17.0	18.6	21.4	18.6	20.1	22.3	19.5	21.1	23.3	21.2	22.9	26.3
1940–44	16.9	18.5	21.1	18.6	20.0	22.3	19.7	21.3	23.7	21.5	23.3	26.7
1945–49	17.0	18.4	21.0	18.7	20.1	22.4	19.9	21.4	23.8	21.7	23.4	27.4
1950–54	17.0	18.4	21.1	18.7	20.1	22.8	20.1	21.8	25.7	22.2	24.5	NA
1955–59	17.0	18.6	22.6	18.9	20.8	NA	21.6	NA	NA	22.9	NA	NA

Trends by Education

Tables 2.3 and 2.4 report the cohort marriage-age quartiles for separate education groups. We will not discuss these tables in detail but rather will note the most distinctive differences among education groups. The general trends discussed above are reflected within each educational category; however, the extent of change varies by education.

For the total and among non-Hispanic whites the increase in age at marriage is smaller and begins later among persons who did not complete high school: only a 0.2 year increase was registered among males and a 0.4 increase among females. Of course, persons with less than a high school education have become a smaller part of each successive cohort. Among males the increases in age at marriage were concentrated among those who attend college, whereas among females similar increases were experienced by both high school graduates and those who attended college. The changing educational composition of successive cohorts has contributed to the increased age at marriage, but decreases in marriage propensities within educational categories have played a major role as well, especially very recently.

Increases in median age at marriage of at least a year were experienced at all education levels among blacks, but they tended to be less among high school graduates who did not attend college. In contrast to the trend among whites, there were large increases in age at marriage among the least educated blacks, particularly for males: median age at marriage increased by almost three years between the least educated in the male cohorts of 1940–44 and 1950–54; it increased by over two years for the low education females from these cohorts.

Differentials

In this section we focus on age at marriage differences by education and by ethnicity and ancestry. For this analysis we will focus on the 1945–49 birth cohort, persons who had reached age 30 in the five years preceding the 1980 census.

Education

Looking first at the data for men in Figure 2.7, we find a nearly linear effect of education among non-Hispanic whites but not among blacks or Mexican-Americans. For majority white men, median age at

TABLE 2.4

Age at First Marriage Quartiles for Five-Year Birth Cohorts,
by Education and Sex: Black Population

Birth Cohort	Education—Years of School Completed											
	0–11 Quartile			12 Quartile			13–15 Quartile			16+ Quartile		
	1	2	3	1	2	3	1	2	3	1	2	3
MALES												
1920–24	21.2	25.1	32.7	22.0	25.8	33.0	22.3	25.7	31.3	23.6	27.0	32.7
1925–29	20.7	24.2	32.2	21.6	25.1	32.0	22.0	25.0	30.7	23.1	26.4	31.8
1930–34	20.7	24.2	31.9	21.3	24.6	30.5	21.7	24.6	29.6	22.8	25.7	30.5
1935–39	20.7	24.1	32.1	21.3	24.3	30.4	21.5	24.4	29.5	22.6	25.5	29.9
1940–44	20.7	24.2	32.5	21.2	24.1	29.7	21.5	24.4	29.0	22.6	25.1	29.4
1945–49	21.0	24.6	NA	21.2	24.0	30.1	21.4	24.0	29.4	22.3	24.9	30.4
1950–54	21.5	27.0	NA	21.2	24.8	NA	21.8	25.5	NA	23.2	26.8	NA
1955–59	NA	NA	NA	23.0	NA	NA	NA	NA	NA	NA	NA	NA
FEMALES												
1920–24	17.9	21.2	27.6	19.4	22.6	27.7	19.9	22.9	27.8	21.7	24.7	30.0
1925–29	17.6	20.6	27.0	19.0	21.5	26.8	19.5	22.0	26.5	21.1	24.1	29.1
1930–34	17.3	20.3	27.1	18.8	21.4	26.3	19.3	21.9	26.3	21.0	23.7	27.8
1935–39	17.4	20.3	27.3	18.9	21.3	26.1	19.2	21.6	26.4	21.1	23.6	27.9
1940–44	17.5	20.5	28.7	19.0	21.4	26.9	19.3	21.7	26.4	21.1	23.8	28.0
1945–49	17.6	20.7	31.4	19.1	21.5	28.1	19.7	22.1	28.3	21.7	24.3	33.7
1950–54	18.1	22.5	NA	19.3	22.3	NA	20.1	23.5	NA	22.5	26.4	NA
1955–59	19.4	NA	NA	20.2	NA	NA	23.6	NA	NA	23.9	NA	NA

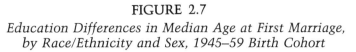

FIGURE 2.7

*Education Differences in Median Age at First Marriage,
by Race/Ethnicity and Sex, 1945–59 Birth Cohort*

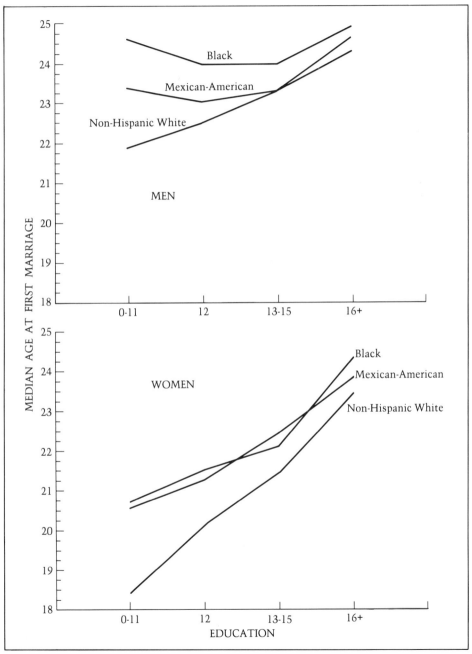

marriage increases regularly from 21.9 among high school dropouts to 24.3 among college graduates. In contrast, the pattern is U-shaped among both black and Mexican-American males. For both groups, but particularly for blacks, males with little education marry at later ages than high school graduates. This later age at marriage probably reflects the poor competitive position of such males in both the job and the marriage markets. The difference for the total population between the third quartile for high school dropouts and high school graduates (27.8 versus 26.0) is largely a consequence of the low marriage rates of those black males who had not married by their mid-twenties. Only two-thirds of these men had married before age 30 compared with three-quarters among other black men.

This U-shaped relationship between education and marriage age is not observed for women, although the relationship is again more clearly linear for the non-Hispanic whites. The education differences are much greater among non-Hispanic white women than among non-Hispanic white men, undoubtedly because marriage ages and typical ages for the completion of the schooling overlap more for women—whatever the causal ordering of the relationship.[11] Median age at first marriage differs by five years between the lowest and the highest education group among non-Hispanic whites (from 18.4 to 23.4) and by about 3.5 years among blacks and Mexican-Americans.

From a different perspective, the data for both males and females reveal much greater racial/ethnic similarity among college-educated persons than among those with less education. The race/ethnicity difference for persons with less education may reflect two different types of factors. First, as already noted, among men low education may interact with minority status to create a particularly poor competitive position in the job market that may then affect marriage prospects. In comparison to majority whites, low education among minority women may be less a consequence of (and hence less directly linked to) early age at marriage.

In Figure 2.8 we consider education differences in the age pattern of marriage probabilities for majority whites. For women who have not completed high school, marriage is heavily concentrated around ages 18–19; for men it is concentrated around age 21. Thereafter the marriage rate for this education group drops off rapidly, becoming lower than the rate for more highly educated persons. High school dropouts who do not marry young apparently are less competitive in the marriage market subsequently. At older ages a larger and larger share of the not-yet-mar-

[11]Margaret Mooney Marini,"Women's Educational Attainment and Parenthood," *American Sociological Review* 49 (1984): 491–511.

FIGURE 2.8

*Age-Specific First Marriage Rates for Non-Hispanic Whites,
by Education and Sex, 1978–79*

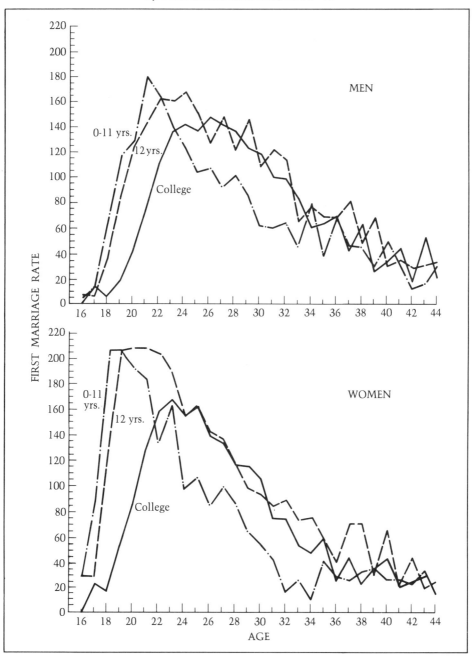

ried are persons with high levels of education, placing those never-married persons who did not complete high school in a more and more unfavorable position in the marriage market. On the other hand, differences in marriage rates between those who complete high school and those who attend college arise primarily before age 23 for women and before age 25 for men. This suggests that, among those who complete high school, education affects marriage more by sorting people according to when they enter the market than by creating characteristics and attitudes that affect marriage propensities thereafter. A similar, and related, argument has been made with respect to the effects of education on age at first birth.[12]

Ancestry

Cultural differences in marriage patterns may reflect historical adaptations to other aspects of the social and economic order. Such was the case with the differences between Western and Eastern Europe that have persisted over at least four centuries[13] and in the distinctive pattern of Asian marriages.[14] Do such cultural differences persist among descendants in other cultural settings, particularly among those whose ancestors may have immigrated several generations ago? There is a renewed interest in the persistence of differing "ethnic" perspectives in the United States.[15] Table 2.5 provides evidence of persisting cultural differences affecting the pace of marriage. However, the results with respect to the Western European pattern of late marriage are exactly the opposite of what we would expect. Persons with Western European heritage had a median age at marriage 1.1 year earlier than those with an Eastern European heritage. This may reflect the longer period of assimilation into the "American" pattern of earlier marriages for the Western European heritage group.

Further, there is considerable similarity among the values for specific national origins within these major groupings. (This table is based on persons born during the ten years from 1940 to 1949 to provide a larger number of cases to permit some detail by country.) Only one of

[12]Ronald R. Rindfuss, Larry L. Bumpass, and Craig St. John, "Education and Fertility: Implications for the Roles Women Occupy," *American Sociological Review* 45 (1980): 431–47.

[13]John Hajnal, "European Marriage Patterns in Perspective," in *Population in History*, ed. D. V. Glass and D. E. C. Eversley (London: Edward Arnold Publishing Co., 1965).

[14]Peter Smith, "Asian Marriage Patterns in Transition," *Journal of Family History* 5 (1980): 58–97.

[15]Richard D. Alba and Mitchell B. Chamlin, "Ethnic Identification Among Whites," *American Sociological Review* 48 (1983): 240–47.

TABLE 2.5

Age at First Marriage Quartiles, by Ancestry and Sex,
1940–49 Birth Cohort

	Male Quartile			Female Quartile		
	1	2	3	1	2	3
Western Europe	21.0	23.2	26.6	19.0	20.9	23.6
English	20.9	22.9	26.2	18.7	20.7	23.3
Scottish	21.2	23.3	26.9	19.2	21.3	24.0
Irish	21.0	23.3	26.9	18.8	20.9	23.8
French	20.8	22.9	25.8	18.7	20.4	22.8
German	21.0	23.0	26.2	19.1	20.9	23.4
Italian	21.7	23.9	27.5	19.8	21.6	24.4
Norwegian	21.3	23.4	26.8	19.3	21.2	23.6
Swedish	21.4	23.4	27.1	19.5	21.4	24.2
Dutch	20.8	22.8	26.2	18.6	20.4	22.9
Eastern Europe	22.1	24.3	28.4	20.0	21.9	25.0
Russian	22.6	24.9	29.7	20.6	22.5	25.8
Czech	21.7	24.0	27.6	19.6	21.6	24.4
Hungarian	22.0	23.8	27.7	19.7	21.6	24.3
Polish	21.9	23.9	27.6	19.8	21.7	24.8
Asian	24.8	27.5	31.1	22.0	24.8	28.3
Japanese	24.5	27.6	—	22.1	24.2	27.7
Chinese	25.4	28.2	33.3	22.3	25.0	28.8
Filipino	24.2	26.8	29.8	22.7	21.1	30.1
American Indian	19.9	21.9	25.0	17.9	19.5	21.9

the nine Western European countries of origin has a median marriage age that is higher than the lowest Eastern European country of origin.

Persons of Asian origin on the average marry about three years later than non-Hispanic whites. American Indians marry considerably younger than the majority population: one-quarter of the women from this cohort married before age 18, and one-half had done so before age 20.

Characteristics of Marriages

This section will examine characteristics of husbands and wives at marriage. It will begin with a brief overview of trends in the proportion of marriages involving previously married partners, and the proportion of first marriages to women who were already mothers. It will then consider the joint characteristics of husbands and wives who entered first marriages during the year preceding the 1980 census. Focusing on these very recent marriages minimizes the biases that may occur as a consequence of differential marital stability for various types of intermarriages.

Previous Marital Status

The proportion of first marriage (of at least one partner)[16] involving a previously married spouse has increased markedly from 15 to 24 percent between 1960 and 1980 (see Table 2.6). (The proportion of all marriages that were remarriages for both partners increased from 13 to 21 percent over these two decades. Almost half of all marriages occurring in 1982 involved a remarriage for at least one partner.) One factor in this trend is a simple demographic "market" effect: there is an increasing number of previously married persons as a consequence of the very rapid increase in the disruption of first marriages. A second, and related, factor may be a change in the normative climate. Traditional values have discouraged marrying a previously divorced person (and the Roman Catholic church is very explicit on this). However, the ascription of deviancy, or of undesirable characteristics, to those who have divorced has probably diminished as they represent an ever larger proportion of the population.

Premarital Birth or Pregnancy

Another characteristic of first marriage that has changed rapidly is the proportion of brides who have given birth before marriage. The trend in premarital fertility is discussed in more detail in Chapter 3. Table 2.7 arrays the data in a less familiar way to represent the experience of marriage cohorts.[17] In some proportion of these marriages, the baby was given up for adoption, perhaps in some cases without the groom even knowing about the birth. However, in recent years at least, most represent marriages that began with the presence of a child. Between 1955–

---

[16]Since the census includes only the date of *first* marriage of each spouse, we cannot use these data to describe intermarriage patterns in marriages that were remarriages for both spouses.

[17]This table is based on the June 1980 Current Population Survey and may underestimate the proportions slightly; comparison of birth cohorts indicates that the proportion of nonmarital births in the CPS is about nine-tenths of the level reported in the vital statistics.

TABLE 2.6

Previous Marital Status of Husbands and Wives,
Marriages of 1960, 1970, and 1979

	All Marriages		
	1960	1970	1979
First Marriage for Both	74.5	71.4	60.2
First Marriage Wife, Husband Previously Married	5.9	7.0	10.3
First Marriage Husband, Wife Previously Married	6.8	6.7	8.7
Both Spouses Previously Married*	12.8	15.0	20.8
Total	100.0	100.0	100.0

	First Marriages		
	1960	1970	1979
First Marriage for Both	85.4	84.0	76.0
First Marriage Wife, Husband Previously Married	6.8	8.2	13.0
First Marriage Husband, Wife Previously Married	7.8	7.9	10.9
Total	100.0	100.0	100.0

*Includes some cases where the marital status of one spouse is not known.

SOURCE: Vital Statistics of the United States: vol. III, Marriage and Divorce, 1960, 1970, 1979.

TABLE 2.7

Percent of Women with Premarital Births and Premarital Pregnancies,
for First Marriage Cohorts of 1955–59 to 1975–79

Marriage Cohort	Birth Before First Marriage			Birth in First Seven Months		
	Total	Non-Hispanic White	Black	Total	Non-Hispanic White	Black
1955–59	7.9	4.6	34.3	10.0	9.1	15.5
1960–64	8.4	5.5	30.6	13.9	12.5	24.8
1965–69	9.0	6.1	33.7	15.0	13.7	21.0
1970–74	10.5	7.0	39.7	13.9	13.4	16.8
1975–79	11.4	7.2	44.3	12.5	12.4	11.4

SOURCE: June 1980 Current Population Survey.

59 and 1975–79, the proportion of first marriages to women who were already mothers increased from 4.6 to 7.2 percent among whites, and from 34 to 44 percent among blacks.

For both racial groups there was an increase and then a decrease in the proportion of brides pregnant at marriage, that is, with a birth in the first seven months of marriage. These trends are the complex outcome of changing age-specific pregnancy rates, changing durations of exposure (as a consequence of later marriage), and changing probabilities of birth or marriage, given pregnancy. Among majority whites, the proportion pregnant at marriage increased from 10 percent for the 1955–59 marriage cohort to 14 percent and then declined to 12 percent for the most recent marriage cohort. Among blacks this proportion rose from 16 to 25 percent and then declined to 11 percent. As a joint consequence of these trends, the proportion of women who were either a mother or pregnant before marriage increased from 14 to 20 percent among whites and from 50 to 56 percent among blacks. These are underestimates to the extent that women report an earlier date of marriage to hide a premarital pregnancy or birth.[18] In any event, it is clear that at least one-fifth of white first marriages, and the majority of first marriages to blacks, begin with a baby present or soon to arrive. This is a significant aspect of contemporary marriage that needs to be taken into account in considerations of such issues as early marital roles and interaction.

Differences in premarital pregnancy and birth by education and age at marriage are shown in Table 2.8. Although persons who marry at later ages tend to have higher education, these variables are related quite differently to the proportion already a mother at marriage. Low education may be associated with both attitudes and fertility control practices that raise the likelihood of birth out of wedlock. On the other hand, older age at marriage means a longer risk period during which such a birth might occur, even if age-specific rates are no higher. Among women marrying in the 1970s, almost one-fifth of those who married after age 25 had given birth before marriage. In over one-quarter of the marriages of high school dropouts, the bride had already given birth. The pattern of premarital pregnancy offsets the age at marriage differences in premarital births. Either pregnancy or motherhood characterizes almost one-third of marriages of women under 20, one-sixth of those of women in their early twenties, and one-quarter of those of women over age 25. However, the probabilities of both premarital births and premarital pregnancy are inversely related to education, leading to large differences in the proportion mother or pregnant at marriage: almost one-half

[18]William F. Pratt, "A Study of Marriages Involving Premarital Pregnancies" (Ph.D. diss., University of Michigan, 1965).

TABLE 2.8

Percent of Women with Premarital Births and Pregnancies,
by Age at Marriage and Education, for First Marriages,
by Race/Ethnicity, 1970–79

	Birth Before Marriage			Pregnant at Marriage*			Either Birth Before Marriage or Pregnant at Marriage		
	Total	Non-Hispanic White	Black	Total	Non-Hispanic White	Black	Total	Non-Hispanic White	Black
Total	11.2	7.2	41.6	12.8	12.6	14.2	24.0	19.7	55.7
AGE AT FIRST MARRIAGE									
<20	8.9	6.2	33.9	21.6	21.6	21.7	30.6	27.8	55.0
20–21	9.9	6.6	33.6	9.4	8.9	13.7	19.2	15.4	47.3
22–24	11.5	6.4	52.5	5.0	4.9	6.8	16.5	11.3	59.3
25+	19.0	12.1	51.4	5.8	4.9	9.7	24.8	17.0	61.1
EDUCATION									
<12 Years	24.4	18.3	58.6	21.9	24.9	14.8	46.2	43.2	73.4
12	11.3	7.3	42.5	14.1	14.2	12.6	25.3	21.5	45.1
13–15	6.6	3.9	31.8	9.9	9.2	17.5	16.5	13.0	49.3
16+	3.0	1.8	20.7	3.6	2.9	14.3	6.6	4.7	34.9

*First birth in first seven months of marriage.
SOURCE: June 1980 Current Population Survey.

among high school dropouts compared to only 6 percent among college graduates. Among blacks, these proportions are three-quarters and one-third. Even though premarital birth is strongly related to education among blacks, it is still the case that one out of every five black college graduates were mothers when they married.

Characteristics of Recently Married Couples

By selecting persons who first married in the year preceding the census date, we are able to observe a number of things about first marriages in more detail than is possible with vital statistics. While it would be possible to describe the circumstances of these recent marriages with respect to employment, earnings, and an array of housing characteristics, we will limit our attention here to patterns of mate selection with respect to previous marital status, race, age and education, and living arrangements.

The advantage in focusing on recent marriages is that it allows us to use these census data to describe patterns of intermarriage. The high levels of marital disruption in recent decades make it likely that intact marriages from earlier marriage cohorts may misrepresent such patterns. This would occur to the extent that marital disruption is higher for some kinds of intermarriages than for others. Focusing on marriages that occurred no more than twelve months before the census date does not risk much bias from selective losses. Both spouses are present in the household for about 90 percent of the marriages that were a first marriage for at least one partner—and these are the cases that we will use to describe joint spousal characteristics.

Racial and Ethnic Intermarriage

Racial intermarriage is relatively rare in the United States. However, since we will examine subsequent tables by race or ethnicity, that objective will be easier if we first consider patterns of intermarriage by race/ethnicity. Table 2.9 provides the proportion of all first marriages (to both spouses) that were in each of the sixteen combinations of the four race/ethnicity categories used here. Only 0.5 percent involved intermarriage between blacks and non-Hispanic whites. As is well known,

TABLE 2.9

Race/Ethnicity of Husband by Race/Ethnicity of Wife,
First Marriages of Both Spouses,
April 1979–March 1980 (percent distribution of all first marriages)

	Husband				
	Non-Hispanic White	Black	Mexican-American	Other	Total
Wife					
Non-Hispanic White	77.8	0.4	1.0	1.5	80.8
Black	0.1	8.2	—	0.1	8.5
Mexican-American	0.7	—	4.0	0.2	4.9
Other	1.7	0.2	0.2	3.8	5.8
Total	80.3	8.9	5.3	5.6	100.0

marriages between white wives and black husbands are many times more common than marriages between white husbands and black wives. Marriages between non-Hispanic whites and Mexicans represent 1.7 percent of all first marriages.

Although interracial marriage is still very rare, it has increased at a rapid rate over the last two decades. Table 2.10 shows the proportion of first marriages to men or women of each race that are racial intermarriages. For non-Hispanic white women, this proportion increased from 0.1 to 0.6 over these two decades; intermarriages rose from 0.1 to 0.2 of all first marriages among white men. Thus in first marriages, one white bride out of two hundred marries a black husband. Because of population size differences, the same intermarriages represent a larger share of the first marriages of blacks: 1.4 percent for black brides and 5 percent for black husbands.

Because the census asks each person's date of first marriage, only marriages that were the first marriage for at least one of the partners can be considered. Marriages involving a remarriage for one of the partners are more likely to be interracial, in part because intermarriages of all kinds increase with age. For example, the proportion of white women marrying a black husband is 0.7 percent among previously married wives whose husband had not been married before, compared to 0.5 percent when the marriage was the first for both. Ideally, we would like to be able to include a description of all marriages (including remarriages to both partners), and we should be able to do so with data from the national vital statistics system. Unfortunately, since information on

TABLE 2.10

Percent of First Marriages of Men and Women That Are Interracial (between non-Hispanic whites and blacks), Persons Marrying in the Year Preceding Census 1960, 1970, and 1980

	1959	1969	1979
Percent of Non-Hispanic White Persons Marrying a Black Spouse			
Women	.12	.35	.59
Men	.10	.10	.16
Percent of Black Persons Marrying a Non-Hispanic White Spouse			
Women	.88	.92	1.42
Men	.80	3.27	5.10

race is missing from these data for over one-third of all marriages, the vital statistics are not very helpful on this point. Race is not reported for many large states (for example, California, Michigan, Ohio, and Illinois) and thus it is questionable to treat the vital statistics data as national estimates, given the geographical variation in racial composition and the important role of propinquity in rates of intermarriage. (As we would expect, the vital statistics estimates for all marriages are of the same order of magnitude as those in Table 2.10, but intermarriage is slightly lower than our estimates, when it should be higher given the inclusion of remarriages to both partners. For example, in all reported marriages the proportion of white women marrying a black husband is 0.5 percent, compared to the 0.6 percent we find from our data, which exclude marriages in which both spouses were previously married.)

Previous Marital Status of Spouse

About three-quarters of these recent first marriages were first marriages of both spouses: in 14 percent the husband had been married before and in about 12 percent the wife had been (Table 2.11). These proportions were similar for non-Hispanic whites and blacks, but 83 percent of the first marriages among Mexican-Americans were first marriages for both partners. The various race/ethnic intermarriage categories have a lower proportion with both partners marrying for the first time. The last two columns of this table express the same data in terms of the proportion of first marriages of one spouse that involved a previously married partner. Reflecting in part the fact that husbands are usually older, wives are slightly more likely than husbands to enter a first marriage with a previously married spouse (15 percent versus 13 percent). This contrast is larger among blacks and is particularly large in intermarriages between non-Hispanic white wives and black husbands: almost one-quarter of these first-marrying wives had previously married husbands. The general pattern of higher proportions with previously married spouses for persons with racial or ethnic intermarriages suggests that those who marry outside of the "normative" pattern on one dimension are likely to do so on others. This is undoubtedly due to a complex of both attitudinal and market characteristics. On the one hand, persons less influenced by conventional expectations in general may extend their search over a wider array of potential marriage partners. On the other hand, persons with difficulty finding mates within specific preferred markets may meet each other at the boundaries of these markets.

TABLE 2.11

Marriages by Number of Times Each Spouse Has Been Married,
by Race/Ethnicity, First Marriages of at Least One Spouse
Between April 1979 and March 1980

	Both Married Once	Husband Married Before	Wife Married Before	Total	Percent of Not Previously Married Marrying a Previously Married Spouse	
					Husbands	Wives
Total	74.9	13.5	11.6	100.0	13.4	15.3
Both Non-Hispanic White	74.9	13.3	11.8	100.0	13.5	15.1
Both Black	73.9	15.4	10.8	100.0	12.8	17.2
Both Mexican-American	83.3	9.0	7.6	100.0	8.4	9.8
Husband Non-Hispanic White, Wife Black	67.6	15.9	16.5	100.0	19.6	19.0
Husband Non-Hispanic White, Wife Mexican-American	69.9	16.4	13.6	100.0	16.2	19.0
Wife Non-Hispanic White, Husband Black	65.4	20.3	14.2	100.0	17.8	23.7
Wife Non-Hispanic White, Husband Mexican-American	71.1	13.5	15.5	100.0	17.9	16.0

Living Arrangements

Most newlyweds set up their own household at marriage, but there is substantial variation by age, education, and race/ethnicity in the proportion who do so. Overall, only 6 percent of these recent marriages were living in a relative's household (Table 2.12). Of these, 86 percent were living with a parent (roughly evenly divided between the bride's and the groom's), 9 percent were living with a sibling, and 5 percent were living with other relatives.

Persons marrying at very young ages and those with the least education are particularly likely to be living in someone else's household in the first year after marriage. More detailed analyses indicate that the differential is at the lower extreme in each case, and that the characteristics of husbands and wives are roughly equal and additive. Consequently, the differences are clearest when marriages are classified into those where both, one, or neither were under 20, and where both, one,

TABLE 2.12

Percent Not in Own Household,* and Relationship to Householder
for Those Not in Own Household, by Age
at Marriage, Education, and Race/Ethnicity,
First Marriages of Both Spouses, April 1979–March 1980

	Percent Not in Own Household	Householder for Those Not in Own Household			
		Parent	Sibling	Other	Total
Total	5.9	86.1	9.1	4.8	100.0
Spouses' Ages at Marriage					
Both <20	16.4	88.9	7.0	4.1	100.0
One <20	8.5	85.6	9.6	4.8	100.0
Both 20+	3.2	84.1	10.5	5.3	100.0
Spouses' Educational Levels					
Both <12	17.2	82.7	12.7	4.6	100.0
One <12	10.2	87.8	7.5	4.6	100.0
Both 12+	3.4	87.2	7.8	5.0	100.0
Both Non-Hispanic White	5.1	88.4	7.3	4.4	100.0
Both Black	8.0	84.5	8.0	7.6	100.0
Both Mexican-American	14.7	74.1	21.9	4.0	100.0

*Living in "subfamilies."

or neither were high school dropouts. In marriages where both spouses are under 20, or where neither has completed high school, approximately one in six do not have their own household; whereas when both are age 20 or older, or when both have completed high school, only about 3 percent are in subfamilies.

There are also substantial differences by race and ethnicity. The proportion living in the households of relatives was 5 percent among non-Hispanic whites, 8 percent among blacks, and 15 percent among Mexican-Americans. Among those in subfamilies, blacks are more likely to be living with other relatives (mostly grandparents), and Mexican-Americans are much more likely to be living with siblings (over one-fifth of those living in subfamilies). Hence these differences are consistent with the literature emphasizing the greater role of kin assistance in these communities. Detailed analyses within both education and age groups indicate that the ethnic differences persist at both extremes. When both spouses are young and neither has completed high school, the proportion in subfamilies is 25 percent among non-Hispanic whites,

34 percent among blacks, and 38 percent among Mexican-Americans. Conversely, when both spouses are over 20 and both have completed high school, the proportion in subfamilies is 2 percent among non-Hispanic whites, 5 percent among blacks, and 8 percent among Mexican-Americans. Of course, these differences may reflect substantial variation in economic conditions and housing options; that is, differential necessity may be more a factor than cultural differences in preferences.[19]

Age Differences Between Spouses

Spouses tend to be similar in age, with the husband older than the wife by about three years on average. There is considerable dispersion around the average three-year difference. Table 2.13 displays differences in the ages of husbands and wives in some detail for first marriages for both spouses. Very few husbands are younger than their wives by more than one year (about 8 percent); about one in six is older by five or more years. In the remaining three-quarters of marriages, the husband is between five years older and one year younger than his wife. The dispersion in ages is considerably greater among black and Mexican-American couples, and in intermarriages between these groups and the majority white population. Husbands are ten or more years older than their wives in about 2 percent of the marriages among non-Hispanic whites; this proportion is 5 percent among minority couples, and reaches 9 percent in marriages between black men and non-Hispanic white women. Wives are rarely ten years or more older than their husbands (0.2 percent among majority whites); this figure rises to 0.9 percent among minority couples, and is 3.5 percent in marriages between white wives and black husbands.

Table 2.14 considers variations in these patterns by age, education, and race/ethnicity, using a less detailed coding of differences. The first two panels show the expected dependency of age differences on the age at marriage of brides or grooms. The proportion of wives with husbands five or more years older than themselves varies only slightly with wife's age at marriage: it is around 15 percent for those who marry in their twenties, but is about one-fifth for teenage wives or those 30 or older. On the other hand, the proportion with husbands two to four years older declines monotonically from 47 percent among teenage wives to 18 per-

---

[19]Trends and differentials in the proportion of couples of all marriage durations living as subfamilies are discussed further in Chapter 4. The overall prevalence of subfamilies of all types is discussed in Chapter 11.

TABLE 2.13

Age Differences Between Spouses, by Race/Ethnicity of Each Spouse,
First Marriages of Both Spouses, April 1979–80

Age Difference	Husband: White* Wife: White*	Black Black	Mex-Amer Mex-Amer	White* Black	White* Mex-Amer	Black White*	Mex-Amer White*	Total
Husband Older by:								
10+ Years	2.3	5.3	5.1	5.2	3.3	9.1	2.1	2.8
6–9 Years	8.2	9.7	11.5	7.8	6.4	11.7	10.4	8.6
5 Years	5.4	5.8	5.9	2.6	6.4	4.4	7.1	5.5
4 Years	8.1	8.4	7.9	7.8	8.9	8.0	10.0	8.2
3 Years	12.0	11.1	10.7	12.2	12.6	10.9	13.1	11.8
2 Years	16.1	13.8	12.3	12.2	12.2	11.4	15.3	15.6
1 Year	17.8	15.5	14.8	10.4	15.5	12.7	15.2	17.3
Same Age	15.2	12.3	14.0	15.7	17.2	15.0	10.3	14.8
Wife Older by:								
1 Year	7.6	7.3	7.5	7.0	8.4	5.2	6.6	7.5
2 Years	3.3	3.8	3.6	4.3	3.1	3.4	4.2	3.4
3–9 Years	3.7	6.0	5.8	11.3	5.6	6.7	4.7	4.1
10+ Years	0.2	0.9	0.9	3.5	0.2	1.6	0.9	0.4
Total	100.0	100.0	100.0	100.0	100.0	100.0	100.0	100.0

*White is non-Hispanic white.

TABLE 2.14

Age Differences Between Spouses, by Age at Marriage, Education,
and Race/Ethnicity, First Marriages of Both Spouses
Between April 1979 and March 1980

	Husband Older by		Ages Within 1 year	Wife Older by 2+ yrs	Total
	5+ yrs	2–4 yrs			
WIFE'S AGE AT MARRIAGE					
<20	20.7	46.8	31.8	0.6	100.0
20–22	15.6	37.2	43.7	3.5	100.0
23–24	14.7	29.3	47.7	8.3	100.0
25–29	14.4	23.6	40.6	21.4	100.0
30+	19.0	18.3	26.4	36.3	100.0
HUSBAND'S AGE AT MARRIAGE					
<20	0.3	20.8	66.4	12.4	100.0
20–22	2.6	39.0	50.1	8.3	100.0
23–24	10.1	42.7	40.0	7.1	100.0
25–29	31.2	36.6	25.3	6.8	100.0
30+	58.9	21.3	14.0	5.8	100.0
WIFE'S EDUCATION					
<12 Years	24.9	40.6	28.1	6.4	100.0
12	16.3	37.1	39.7	6.9	100.0
13–15	15.3	33.9	42.7	8.1	100.0
16+	12.0	27.4	48.7	11.9	100.0
HUSBAND'S EDUCATION					
<12 Years	19.4	34.1	36.4	10.1	100.0
12	14.8	37.8	40.0	7.4	100.0
13–15	16.7	34.9	40.6	7.8	100.0
16+	19.6	32.8	40.7	6.9	100.0
RACE/ETHNICITY					
Both Spouses					
Non-Hispanic White	15.9	36.2	40.6	7.2	100.0
Black	20.8	33.3	35.1	10.7	100.0
Mexican-American	22.5	30.9	36.3	10.3	100.0
Husband Non-Hispanic White					
Wife Black	15.6	32.2	33.1	19.1	100.0
Wife Mexican-American	16.1	33.7	41.1	8.9	100.0
Wife Non-Hispanic White					
Husband Black	25.2	30.3	32.9	11.7	100.0
Husband Mexican-American	19.6	38.4	32.1	9.8	100.0

cent among wives over age 29. Of course, few wives under 20 are likely to be two or more years older than their husbands, but this proportion increases rather markedly with wife's age at marriage to over one-third for women ages 30 or over. By this older age at marriage, it is as common for the wife to be two or more years older than her husband as it is for the husband to be this much older than his wife. This reflects, in part, the rapidly changing market that single women face as they grow older. As women become older, there are proportionately fewer unmarried men older than themselves from whom they can select their husbands. In addition, there is less age segregation in the activities of persons at these ages, and the social significance of a year of age diminishes with each successive year. There is generally more of a "difference" between an 18-year-old and a 20-year-old than between a 28- and a 30-year-old. Note how rapidly the proportion marrying younger men jumps between ages at marriage of 23–24 and 25–29 (from 8 percent to 21 percent).

Similar processes affect the age distribution of partners chosen by men at various ages, but are reinforced by a tendency for men to prefer younger wives. Only 3 percent of the men marrying at ages 20–22 are five or more years older than their wives, compared to one-third of those 23–24 and three-fifths of those 30 and older. The proportion marrying a spouse within a year of their own age declines from two-thirds among men marrying under age 20 to 14 percent among grooms aged 30 and over. These patterns may in part reflect the market sorting functions of the educational system, which concentrates social interaction in a narrow age range.

Women who did not complete high school are particularly likely to marry men who are five or more years older then they are. More detailed analysis indicates that this is not a consequence of the fact that they tend to marry at younger ages. In fact, the effect is even larger when age at marriage differences are taken into account. Note that these are women who are outside of the age-segregated context of schools. The higher frequency of wives who are older than their husbands by two or more years among the most highly educated is a consequence of the fact that women with more education tend to enter the marriage market at older ages. Goldman et al. document how rapidly the preferred educational market contracts for more educated women, so that by ages 40–49, "there are fewer than three suitable men available for every ten college-educated women."[20]

[20]Noreen Goldman, Charles F. Westoff, and Charles Hammerslough, "Demography of the Marriage Market in the United States," *Population Index* 50 (1984): 5–25.

Age differences are not as strongly related to husband's education, but, as noted earlier for lower-education wives, there is a slight tendency for men with lower education levels to marry older women.

The racial and ethnic differences noted earlier in Table 2.13 are evident in the less detailed classifications here. Whereas among majority whites 16 percent of the husbands are five or more years older than their wives, this figure is over one-fifth among minority couples.

Education Differences Between Spouses

There is a high level of homogamy by education in the United States.[21] As can be seen in Table 2.15, over one-half of all brides and grooms were in the same major education category (summing along the main diagonal). (The data are organized this way rather than in terms of single years in the belief that a difference between having attended high school or college and having completed these levels is more important than the difference between completing one versus two years of college.) The further from the main diagonal, the lower the frequency of marriage—for example, 25 percent of all first marriages were between two partners with twelve years of schooling, about 14 percent were marriages between high school graduates and partners who had attended but not completed college (about one-half of whom have husbands in the higher education category), and only 4 percent were between high school graduates and a spouse who had completed college. Similar patterns are seen for minority couples, although because the education distribution of both Mexican-American men and women are concentrated in the three lower categories, a higher proportion of husbands and wives are in the same education category. Neither partner had completed high school in over two-fifths of the Mexican-American couples.

Table 2.16 rearranges the above information to focus on differences between spouses in major educational categories. The tendency of American women to marry up is apparent but not very large. The husband was in a higher education category than his wife in 25 percent of the marriages, compared to 20 percent where the wife was in a higher category than her husband. In comparison to whites, black wives are somewhat more likely to be better educated than their husbands, reflecting the slightly higher education distribution of black wives. As noted, Mexican-Americans are especially likely to be of the same edu-

---

[21]Richard Rockwell, "Historical Trends and Variations in Educational Homogamy," *Journal of Marriage and Family* 38 (1976): 1183–96.

TABLE 2.15

Education of Husband by Education of Wife, by Race/Ethnicity
for First Marriages of Both Spouses
Between April 1979 and March 1980
(percent distribution of all first marriages)

	Husband's Education				
Wife's Education	<12	12	13–15	16+	Total
TOTAL					
<12 Years	9.9	7.3	1.5	0.4	19.1
12	6.8	24.6	7.9	2.9	42.2
13–15	1.4	6.6	9.2	5.6	22.8
16+	0.2	1.6	3.5	10.5	15.9
Total	18.3	40.2	22.1	19.4	100.0
NON-HISPANIC WHITE					
<12 Years	7.7	6.9	1.3	0.3	16.2
12	6.2	25.3	8.3	3.1	42.9
13–15	1.0	6.7	9.4	6.2	23.3
16+	0.2	1.7	3.8	12.0	17.7
Total	15.1	40.6	22.7	21.6	100.0
BLACK					
<12 Years	11.3	8.4	1.9	0.4	22.0
12	9.6	25.2	6.5	1.5	42.9
13–15	3.3	8.2	9.6	3.5	24.6
16+	0.6	1.9	3.0	5.0	10.5
Total	24.8	43.8	21.0	10.4	100.0
MEXICAN-AMERICAN					
<12 Years	43.1	10.4	2.9	0.5	56.8
12	10.2	14.7	4.3	1.1	30.3
13–15	2.6	2.8	4.1	0.9	10.3
16+	0.4	0.3	0.8	1.0	2.5
Total	56.3	28.2	12.0	3.5	100.0

cational level as their partners (almost two-thirds). On the other hand, marriages between non-Hispanic white wives and black husbands are least likely to be between partners with similar education: compared to marriages between majority whites, these marriages have both a higher proportion in which husbands are considerably better educated than their wives, and a higher proportion in which the wife is the better educated by at least two education levels.

TABLE 2.16
Education Differences Between Spouses, by Race/Ethnicity
for First Marriages of Both Spouses Between April 1979 and March 1980

Education Category Difference†	Husband: White* Wife: White*	Black Black	Mex-Amer Mex-Amer	White* Black	White* Mex-Amer	Black White*	Mex-Amer White*	Total
Husband More								
2+	4.7	3.8	4.5	8.7	7.4	8.5	3.9	4.7
1	21.3	18.3	15.6	19.1	24.5	23.1	20.3	20.8
Same	54.3	51.2	62.9	53.9	49.9	46.4	53.7	54.3
Wife More								
1	16.8	20.9	13.8	13.9	15.4	16.3	18.5	16.9
2+	2.9	5.8	3.3	4.3	2.8	5.7	3.7	3.2
Total	100.0	100.0	100.0	100.0	100.0	100.0	100.0	100.0

*White is non-Hispanic white.

†Education grouped 0–11, 12, 13–15, and 16+ years.

TABLE 2.17

Education Differences Between Spouses, by Education and Age at Marriage for First Marriages of Both Spouses Between April 1979 and March 1980

| | Education Category Differences* | | | | | |
| | Husband More | | Same | Wife More | | |
	2+	1		1	2+	Total
WIFE'S EDUCATION						
<12 Years	9.7	38.3	52.1	—	—	100.0
12	6.9	18.7	58.3	16.1	—	100.0
13–15	—	24.7	40.3	29.1	6.0	100.0
16+	—	—	66.1	22.1	11.8	100.0
HUSBAND'S EDUCATION						
<12 Years	—	—	54.2	37.1	8.7	100.0
12	—	18.2	61.3	16.5	4.1	100.0
13–15	6.7	35.8	41.6	16.0	—	100.0
16+	16.9	29.0	54.2	—	—	100.0
WIFE'S AGE AT MARRIAGE						
<20 Years	4.3	25.2	56.5	13.3	0.7	100.0
20–22	4.2	20.7	52.9	19.7	2.7	100.0
23–24	4.8	18.7	52.5	18.7	5.2	100.0
25–29	5.8	16.4	54.1	17.6	6.2	100.0
30+	6.9	16.1	55.5	16.4	5.1	100.0
HUSBAND'S AGE AT MARRIAGE						
<20 Years	1.0	18.4	61.1	17.8	1.7	100.0
20–22	2.0	20.9	57.1	17.8	2.2	100.0
23–24	4.8	21.6	52.4	17.7	3.5	100.0
25–29	7.6	21.6	51.2	15.8	3.8	100.0
30+	8.6	19.5	52.2	14.6	5.1	100.0

*Education grouped 0–11, 12, 13–15, and 16+ years.

Table 2.17 considers these differences in more detail by education and age at marriage. There is an obvious necessary relationship between education as coded here and the direction and extent of differences between spouses. Nonetheless, there are interesting differences between brides and grooms in the proportion marrying a spouse with similar education. This is most common among brides who are college graduates, whereas it is most common among males who are high school graduates. The major difference is the contrast between the 66 percent of college-graduate brides who also marry college graduates, compared to 54 percent of college grooms married to college graduates. Some might be tempted to explain this difference in terms of traditional sex-role expectations: college-educated men are more willing to marry less-educated wives because many men hold the traditional view that husbands should be the primary earner and wives should be responsible for home and family.[22] A more parsimonious explanation would note that the earlier marriage schedule of women makes them more likely to be "in the market" while they are still in an educationally segregated social context (in college), whereas male college graduates may be more likely to consider marriage only after they have been out of school and in a more educationally diverse social setting.

Differences by age at marriage reveal two patterns of interest. First, from the perspective of either spouse, but particularly for males, the prevalence of large education differences in both directions increase for older ages at marriage. This might be interpreted from two different market perspectives. It may be that the later marriage occurs, the higher the proportion shopping outside of the segregated marriage market created by being in school. An even stronger pattern consistent with this explanation is the decrease in the proportion of women who are one education level lower than their husbands with increasing age at marriage: from 25 percent for teenage marriages to 16 percent for women marrying in their thirties. Second, however, marrying at a later age means that the field of potential eligibles has already been "picked over" by those who married earlier, with the consequence that the marriage search is likely to be over a more diverse range of prospects.

Summary

We have reviewed trends in marriage patterns with attention to both rates and the experience of successive birth cohorts. Except for a deviation associated with the Great Depression, ages at marriage declined over cohorts marrying in this century to a low among persons born in the late 1930s of 23.3 for males and 20.6 for females. The trend toward higher marriage rates was reversed after the postwar peak, and even during the baby boom marriage rates were declining at ages 24 and over. Declines in marriage rates have accelerated over the 1970s. De-

[22]Gary S. Becker, *A Treatise on the Family* (Cambridge, Mass.: Harvard University Press, 1981).

spite the historical variation in marriage rates, dominant features of the marriage patterns of this century include a substantial proportion of each cohort marrying at young ages (about one-quarter by age 19 among women and by age 21 among men) and a rather narrow interquartile range of five to six years.

The recent accelerated decline in marriage rates is particularly marked among black women, so that their age-specific marriage rates are now half those of whites during the prime years of marriage. These reduced marriage rates suggest a decline in the proportions ever marrying.

Recent trends are least evident at lower education levels among whites, but they are most pronounced for blacks with little education. Thus the racial difference in marriage propensities is concentrated at lower education levels and becomes more similar with increasing education. The well-known later age at marriage of more educated persons is seen to result primarily from differential rates during the early twenties, suggesting that the major impact of education on age at marriage is to sort persons with respect to the age at which they enter the marriage market.

The composition of marriages has shifted markedly, reflecting changing patterns of marriage, divorce, and fertility. One-quarter of all first marriages are now to a previously married spouse; in nearly half of all marriages at least one partner has been married before, and in one-fifth both were previously married. A child was either already born or on the way in one-fifth of recent majority-white first marriages and in over half of recent black first marriages.

We examined a number of characteristics of marriages for persons who first married in the year preceding the census date. Racial intermarriage remains very rare—0.5 percent of all marriages—although it has increased markedly over the last decade. While most newlyweds set up their own household at marriage, about 6 percent of recently married couples are living in a relative's household, and among those who did not complete high school or who married as teenagers, about one in six lives with relatives. Sharing a relative's household is higher among blacks (8 percent) and highest among Mexican-Americans (15 percent).

Homogamy and heterogamy are considered for first marriages to both spouses. The husband was two or more years younger than his wife in only 8 percent of marriages in 1979, and he is five or more years older than she in about 16 percent of these marriages. However, age patterns differ markedly depending upon race and ethnicity, education, and age at marriage. Interracial marriages, marriages to low education women, and those occurring after age 25 are particularly likely to have a greater age difference between spouses. For example, one-fifth of women first marrying in their late twenties are older than their husbands by two or more years.

Both spouses were in the same general educational category (high school dropout, completed high school, attended but did not complete college, completed college) in about one-half of first marriages in 1979. Extreme educational differences are very rare since most of the remainder are in adjacent categories. At the same time, however, the prevalence of larger education differences increases with age at marriage. We suggest that this may be because: (1) at older ages persons are less likely to spend most of their time in age- and education-segregated institutions (for example, schools); and (2) at older ages this pool of potential spouses of similar age is progressively depleted, and persons seeking a marriage partner must search a much more heterogeneous pool of potential spouses.

3

THE NEVER-MARRIED

W E DISCUSSED the trend in age at first marriage in Chapter 2. There was a post-World War II "marriage boom" as well as a "baby boom." Young men and women accelerated the timing of their first marriage, and almost everyone married. The median age at first marriage of women dropped from almost 22 to about 20.6 years. Beginning in the 1960s and continuing into the 1970s and 1980s there was a reversal of the trend in age at first marriage. Young women delayed their marriages, and about two years have been added to the median age at first marriage. (The trend for men has been similar, but the size of the fluctuations has been smaller.) It is not clear what fraction of young people now in their twenties and thirties will never marry, but it is almost certain to be larger than the 5 or 6 percent level of cohorts now in their forties and fifties. Rodgers and Thornton project that about 10 percent of both men and women born in the mid-1950s may never marry.[1]

In this chapter we will examine trends in the size, characteristics, and activities of the never-married population. The discussion will focus especially on persons between ages 18 and 29, most of whom will eventually marry. We will also discuss the prevalence and characteristics of

[1]Willard L. Rodgers and Arland Thorton, "Changing Patterns of First Marriage in the United States," *Demography* 22 (1985):265–79.

older persons who have never married, and who are likely to remain single throughout their lives.

Many significant life cycle transitions occur during the young adult years. Between ages 18 and 30 men and women typically complete their education, leave the parental household, enter the work force on a full-time basis, and change jobs and residence, often several times. Many serve in the armed forces. It is also within this age range that most people marry and begin having children. There are many paths that can be followed after leaving the parental household. Some individuals will leave their parents' household for the first time when they marry. Others may repeatedly leave and return to their parents' household while attending college, and then live alone or cohabit before eventually marrying. Still others may cohabit and/or have a child, and never marry at all. It is not only these various experiences and living arrangements that are important but also their timing and the amount of time spent in each. The occurrence, timing, and duration of these experiences affect the subsequent life experience of an individual. The character and duration of experiences during the "single" years are of special importance because of their substantial impact on the nature and timing of family formation. Depending on their experiences during this time, some individuals may decide never to marry, and still others to marry, but to forego childbearing. Women who work, get additional education, and live on their own during this interval are likely to have different notions about themselves, and possibly different expectations of marriage, than those who move directly from their parents' to their husband's household.[2] Experience as a single may also affect marital dissolution. Rising divorce rates may reflect the fact that more women feel they have reasonable options outside of marriage, and thus are less hesitant to end unhappy marriages than in the past.

In 1960, 37 percent of young adults age 18–29 had never married. By 1970, this figure rose to 42 percent, and by 1980, 52 percent of people in this age group were still single. The proportion of men who are single is substantially higher than that of women, although the gap has narrowed somewhat since 1960.

Figures 3.1 and 3.2 trace the fraction never-married by specified ages for each census since 1910. Between 1910 and 1940, about 80 percent of men age 21 had never married. By 1960, this fraction had fallen to 63 percent, but by 1980 it had returned to nearly 80 percent. This same general pattern is found for all ages—stability between 1910 and 1940,

[2]Karen O. Mason, "Women's Labor Force Participation and Fertility: Final Report 21U-662," prepared for the National Institutes of Health (1974). Glenna D. Spitze, "Role Experiences of Young Women: A Longitudinal Test of the Role Hiatus Hypothesis," *Journal of Marriage and the Family* 40 (1978): 471–79.

FIGURE 3.1

Percent of Men Never Married at Ages 17, 19, 21, 24, and 29, 1910–80

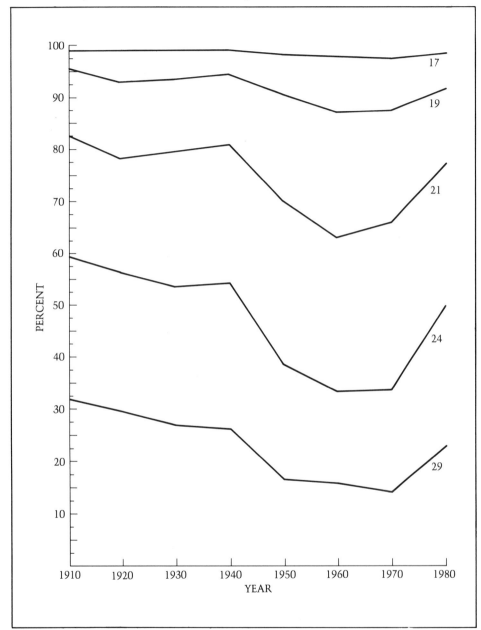

SOURCES: U. S. Bureau of the Census, *Census of Population: 1950,* vol. 2, "Characteristics of the Population, Part 1, United States Summary" (Washington, D. C.: U. S. Government Printing Office, 1953); 1940–1980 Census Public Use Samples.

FIGURE 3.2

Percent of Women Never Married at Ages 17, 19, 21, 24, and 29, 1910–80

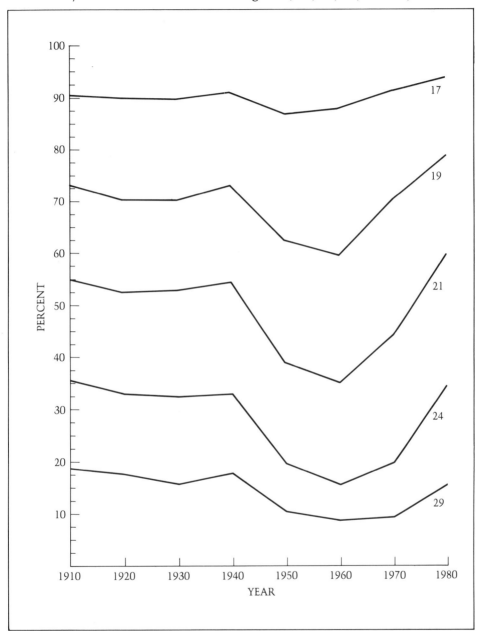

SOURCES: U. S. Bureau of the Census, *Census of Population: 1950*, vol. 2, "Characteristics of the Population, Part 1, United States Summary" (Washington, D. C.: U. S. Government Printing Office, 1953); 1940–1980 Census Public Use Samples.

rapid decline between 1940 and 1960, and a return to about the 1940 level by 1980. Although levels of singleness are lower for women at every age, the same general trend is observed as for men. Thus, young men and women are spending more of their young adult years single than they were twenty years ago. However, the pattern today is not a great departure from the past, but rather is essentially a return to the pattern of the past that was temporarily interrupted during the baby boom period. The only substantial difference between 1940 and 1980 is the higher 1980 fraction single among women at age 21 and under.

Changing Numbers of Young Singles

The number and age composition of singles at any point in time is a reflection of the demographic processes determining the age structure of a population, as well as the social and demographic processes affecting the marriage rates. The combined effects of the baby boom cohorts

TABLE 3.1

Number of Never-Married Persons 18–29, by Age, 1940–80

	18–19	20–24	25–29	Total 18–29
	Number (millions)			
1940	4.4	6.9	3.2	14.5
1950	3.5	5.2	2.3	10.9
1960	3.8	4.4	1.7	9.9
1970	6.1	7.3	2.1	15.6
1980	7.6	12.5	5.2	25.3
	Percent Change			
1940–1950	−19.5	−24.8	−31.1	−24.6
1950–1960	7.8	−17.2	−24.9	−10.8
1960–1970	61.9	67.7	24.9	58.1
1970–1980	24.6	70.7	144.6	62.6
	Percent of Total Adult Population (18+)			
1940	4.8	7.5	3.6	15.9
1950	3.4	5.0	2.2	10.6
1960	3.3	3.8	1.5	8.6
1970	4.6	5.5	1.6	11.7
1980	4.7	7.7	3.2	15.6

SOURCE: *1940–1950*: U.S. Bureau of the Census, *Historical Statistics of the United States, Colonial Times to 1970, Part 1, 1975; 1960–1980*: Public Use Samples.

reaching adulthood during the 1960s and 1970s and the delaying of marriage by these cohorts have resulted in a very rapid growth in the number of young single persons in the population. In 1960 there were 10 million single persons between ages 18 and 29 (see Table 3.1). By 1970 there were 15.6 million, and by 1980, 25.3 million. As a fraction of the total adult population, young singles increased from 9 percent in 1960 to 12 percent in 1970, and to 16 percent in 1980.

Socioeconomic Variation in Proportion Single

Racial and Ethnic Variation

As discussed in Chapter 2, blacks have historically married at younger ages than whites. Figures 3.3 and 3.4 show the fractions of blacks who had never married by specified ages. We will focus on the data for women. Between 1910 and 1960, about three-fifths of black women aged 19 had never married. This compared to about 70 percent of white women (through 1940). Slightly less than one-quarter of black women aged 24 were single. This is about 10 percentage points lower than for white women.

There was a postwar marriage boom for blacks, but its magnitude was small in comparison to that of whites and the subsequent decline was much greater than for whites. By 1960 the fraction of black women who were never married had begun to rise, and it has risen continuously since that time. Reflecting the trends discussed in Chapter 2, the fraction never-married at each age rose at a remarkable pace during the 1970s. For example, in 1970, 50 percent of 21-year-old black women were single; by 1980, 75 percent were single. At age 24, the fractions were 28 and 53 percent. At every age the percent of black women who are single is much higher in 1980 than at any earlier point in this century.[3]

Figure 3.5 compares the age-specific fractions of non-Hispanic white, black, and Mexican-American women who were never married in 1980. Non-Hispanic white women are 10 to 15 percentage points less likely to be single than black women. Up to age 25, Mexican-American women are 5 to 10 percentage points less likely to be single than majority white women. The same pattern of differentials is found for men (Figure 3.6).

There is considerable variation in the fractions of young adults who have never married among the more detailed racial and Hispanic groups.

[3]Andrew Cherlin, *Marriage, Divorce, and Remarriage* (Cambridge, Mass.: Harvard University Press, 1981).

FIGURE 3.3

Percent of Black Men Never Married at Ages 17, 19, 21, 24, and 29, 1910–80

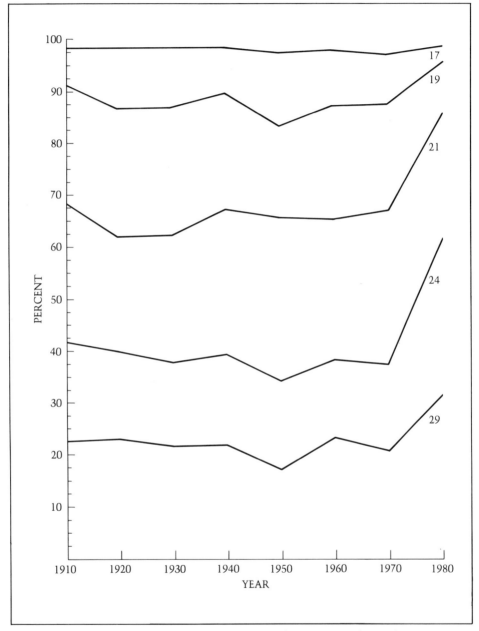

SOURCES: U. S. Bureau of the Census, *Census of Population: 1950*, vol. 2, "Characteristics of the Population, Part 1, United States Summary" (Washington, D. C.: U. S. Government Printing Office, 1953); 1940–1980 Census Public Use Samples.

FIGURE 3.4

Percent of Black Women Never Married at Ages 17, 19, 21, 24, and 29, 1910–80

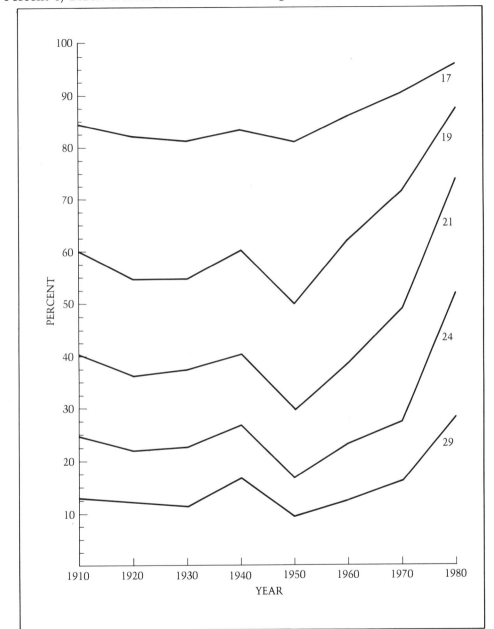

SOURCES: U. S. Bureau of the Census, *Census of Population: 1950*, vol. 2, "Characteristics of the Population, Part 1, United States Summary" (Washington, D. C.: U. S. Government Printing Office, 1953); 1940–1980 Census Public Use Samples.

FIGURE 3.5

Percent of Women Never Married, by Age and Ethnicity, 1980

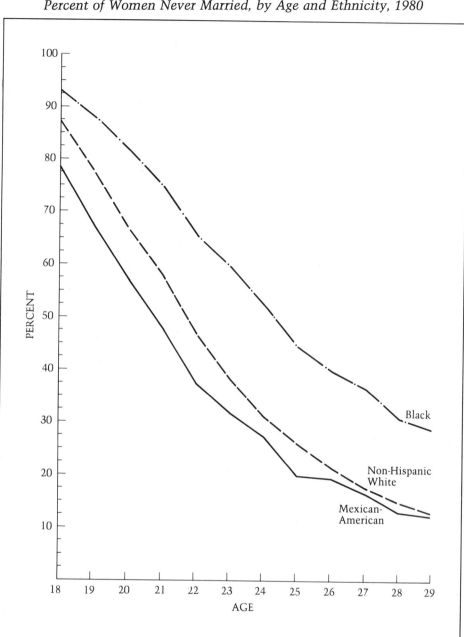

FIGURE 3.6
Percent of Men Never Married, by Age and Ethnicity, 1980

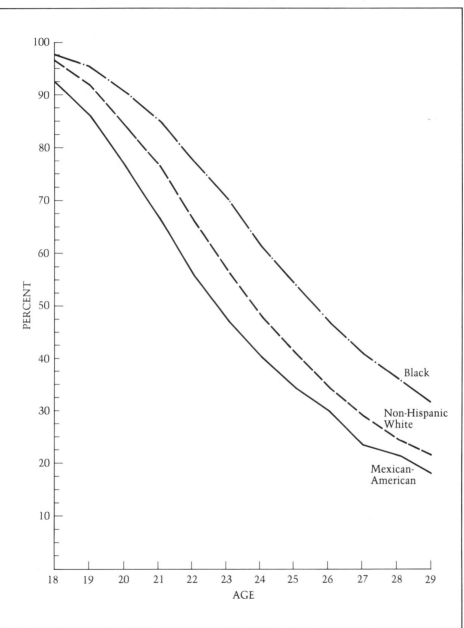

Table 3.2 shows the percent of 20–24- and 25–29-year-old men and women who were single. In 1980, 49 percent of the non-Hispanic white women aged 20–24 were never married. The group with the lowest proportion of women single at age 20–24 is Mexican-Americans (40 percent). Koreans, American Indians, and Puerto Ricans are next, with less than one-half married at age 20–24. About three-quarters of the Chinese and Japanese women are never married at ages 20–24. Only these two groups have a larger fraction never-married than do blacks—67 percent of women at age 20–24.

By age 25–29, 19 percent of non-Hispanic white women remain unmarried. Mexican-American women have only a slightly lower proportion single (17 percent). The lowest proportion single is found among Koreans (12 percent) and Asian Indians (10 percent). More than one-third of black women aged 25–29 are single. Other groups with very high proportion of singles are Japanese (34 percent), Chinese (30 percent), and Hawaiians (28 percent). The differentials among groups for men are very similar to those for women, but levels are higher.

Education Differences

Reflecting differences in age at marriage reported in the previous chapter, the fraction never-married increases with the level of education (see Figures 3.7 and 3.8). For example, in 1980 at age 21, 37 percent of

TABLE 3.2

Percent of Persons Who Have Never Married at Ages 20–24 and 25–29, by Sex, for Racial and Hispanic Groups, 1980

	20–24		25–29	
	Male	*Female*	*Male*	*Female*
Non-Hispanic White	66.7	48.6	30.3	19.0
Black	77.6	67.1	42.3	36.5
Chinese	91.6	77.8	55.8	30.5
Japanese	89.0	75.8	59.8	34.4
Filipino	77.4	52.6	35.1	26.3
American Indian	62.4	45.7	29.8	21.5
Korean	86.1	45.5	43.2	11.6
Asian Indian	81.9	38.8	41.7	9.9
Vietnamese	81.8	54.0	50.0	20.7
Hawaiian	74.5	53.1	34.6	28.5
Mexican	57.5	40.5	25.9	16.7
Puerto Rican	62.4	48.6	32.2	26.5
Cuban	67.5	51.8	31.7	23.9

FIGURE 3.7

Percent of Men Never Married, by Age and Education, 1980

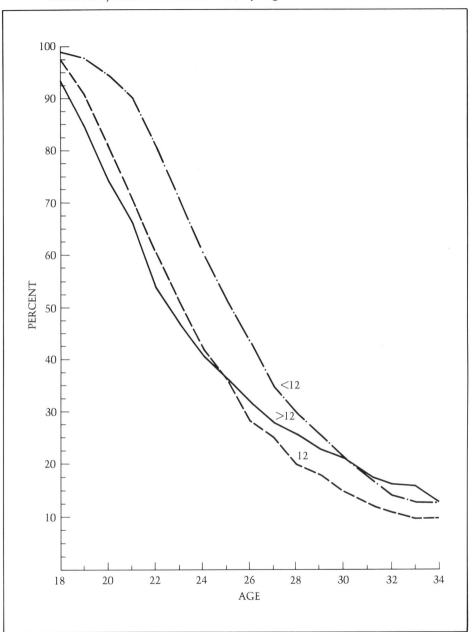

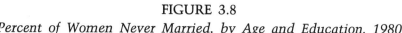

FIGURE 3.8

Percent of Women Never Married, by Age and Education, 1980

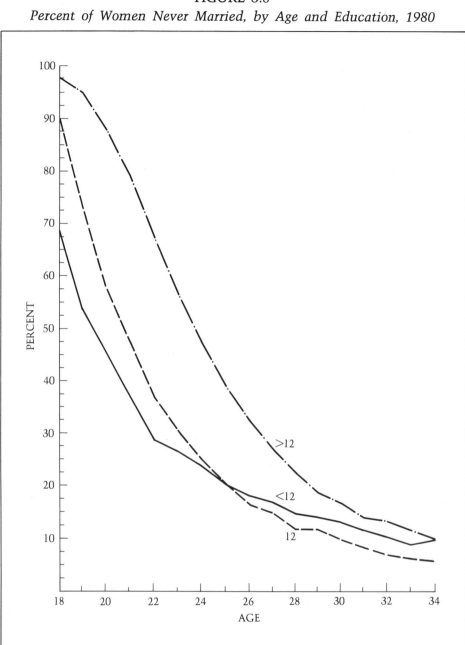

women who did not complete high school and 48 percent of high school graduates who never attended college had never married. Seventy-nine percent of women who had attended college were still single at age 21. At age 24, the fractions were 24, 26, and 47 percent, respectively.

It is clear from these differentials by education that the increase since 1960 in the overall proportion single at any given age was due in part, at least, to increased shares of women attending college and decreasing shares who did not complete high school. The cross-over observed for the lowest education group reflects the lower marriage rate at older ages of persons who did not complete high school (noted in Chapter 2). However, with the exception of ages over 30 for men, the proportion single remains lower for this group than for those who have attended college. The rapidity of the educational change is shown as Table 3.3, which gives the education composition of 25-year-olds at each census. However, the aggregate increase in fractions single may also be due to increased age-specific prevalence of being single for some

TABLE 3.3

Education Distribution of 25-Year-Olds,
by Sex and Race/Ethnicity, 1960–80

Years of Education	Male			Female		
	1960	1970	1980	1960	1970	1980
NON-HISPANIC WHITE						
<12	33.2	22.0	12.8	32.8	22.3	11.7
12	34.1	34.7	39.5	45.0	43.9	42.5
>12	32.6	43.4	47.8	22.2	33.8	45.9
Total	100.0	100.0	100.0	100.0	100.0	100.0
BLACK						
<12	65.1	44.0	25.9	58.6	42.1	22.7
12	24.1	36.4	40.6	29.0	39.0	41.7
>12	10.8	19.6	33.5	12.4	19.0	35.7
Total	100.0	100.0	100.0	100.0	100.0	100.0
MEXICAN-AMERICAN						
<12	63.3	56.5	47.9	65.6	57.0	47.8
12	17.0	27.6	27.5	27.7	31.3	30.4
>12	19.7	15.9	24.6	6.7	11.8	21.8
Total	100.0	100.0	100.0	100.0	100.0	100.0

TABLE 3.4

*Percent of Non-Hispanic White Women Never Married
at Selected Ages, by Education, 1940–80*

| | Years of Education | | | |
	<12	12	>12	Total
At Age 18				
1940	70.5	92.7	98.3	83.3
1950	51.3	81.2	94.4	73.6
1960	46.5	82.2	95.2	74.9
1970	53.1	83.8	96.2	82.1
1980	62.1	89.3	97.8	87.2
At Age 21				
1940	40.6	63.3	83.8	55.4
1950	21.4	37.8	62.6	37.1
1960	18.0	29.6	59.7	33.9
1970	20.3	31.8	64.1	43.3
1980	26.9	44.3	78.7	58.0
At Age 24				
1940	25.0	38.2	56.2	33.7
1950	13.0	19.5	32.5	19.1
1960	9.5	12.2	25.2	14.4
1970	12.7	13.3	27.9	18.5
1980	15.2	21.2	45.5	31.4
At Age 29				
1940	13.5	22.4	29.7	18.3
1950	7.2	9.4	14.6	9.3
1960	6.0	7.3	13.5	8.3
1970	6.9	5.9	12.7	8.2
1980	9.0	9.2	17.7	13.2
	Change			
1960–70				
18	6.5	1.6	1.0	7.2
21	2.3	2.2	4.4	9.4
24	3.2	1.1	2.7	4.1
29	0.9	−1.4	−0.8	−0.1
1970–80				
18	9.0	5.5	1.6	5.1
21	6.6	12.5	14.6	14.7
24	2.5	7.9	17.6	12.9
29	2.1	3.3	5.0	5.0

or all education categories.[4] To examine this question, we will look at the proportions single by education at four ages—18, 21, 24, and 29.

Among non-Hispanic white women a large share of the increase in the percent single that occurred between 1960 and 1970 was associated with educational upgrading (Table 3.4). There was a 6.5 percentage point increase in the fraction single at age 18 among high school dropouts, and a 4.4 percent increase in the fraction single at age 21 among college-educated women. Otherwise the age-by-education percentages single changed very little.

However, during the 1970s there were large increases in age-by-education-specific percentages single. At age 18 the fraction single rose for both high school dropouts (9 points) and high school graduates (6 points). At age 21 the fraction single increased for all educational levels, but especially for high school graduates and for college-educated women. At age 24 there was a sizable increase for college women (18 points), and less of an increase for high school graduates (8 points).

During the 1960s there was an increase at all ages in the age-specific fraction who were single among black women who did not complete high school. The increase was greatest at age 18 (Table 3.5). Among high school graduates there was a drop in the fraction single at age 18, but an increase of between 2 and 4 percentage points at the older ages. College-educated black women did not experience any increase in fractions single except at age 21, where there was a rise of 6 points. This may have been due to a larger fraction of 21-year-olds who were currently enrolled in college at the time of the census.

However, during the 1970s the age-specific fraction single among black women rose a great deal at all education levels. The increases were slightly larger for high school dropouts than high school graduates, and somewhat larger for high school graduates than for women who attended college. For black women there was also a great educational upgrading that tended to increase the overall percent single at each age.

For white men, fractions single changed very little during the 1960s. When they did change, the change was toward a *lower* fraction single (Table 3.6). However, in the 1970s there was a sharp rise in the education-specific fraction single at each age. The increase tended to be larger for college-educated men than for those with less education. Similar

---

[4]The education classification used here is somewhat unusual. Because the census is conducted in April near the end of the school year, persons currently enrolled in grade 12 are included with the high school graduates. This primarily affects 18-year-olds. Similarly, persons presently enrolled in grade 13 are included in the "greater than 12" category. For persons not currently enrolled, classification is based on highest grade completed.

TABLE 3.5

Percent of Black Women Never Married at Selected Ages,
by Education, 1960–80

	Years of Education			
	<12	12	>12	Total
At Age 18				
1960	65.1	88.3	96.1	76.6
1970	75.6	84.7	94.7	83.1
1980	88.8	93.7	97.6	93.3
At Age 21				
1960	32.0	42.7	63.6	39.5
1970	38.1	45.2	69.8	48.8
1980	67.5	69.4	83.8	74.8
At Age 24				
1960	21.6	23.1	36.9	23.9
1970	25.7	26.4	36.0	27.9
1980	51.8	47.3	58.6	52.5
At Age 29				
1960	13.1	10.8	17.4	13.0
1970	17.7	15.3	17.6	16.8
1980	32.3	26.5	29.8	29.0
	Change			
1960–70				
18	10.5	−3.6	−1.4	6.5
21	6.1	2.5	6.2	9.3
24	4.1	3.3	−0.9	4.0
29	4.6	4.5	0.2	3.8
1970–80				
18	13.2	9.0	2.9	10.2
21	29.4	24.2	14.0	26.0
24	26.1	20.9	22.6	24.6
29	14.6	11.2	12.2	12.2

changes occurred for black men—the fraction single tended to decrease at each age-education level between 1960 and 1970 (Table 3.7). However, between 1970 and 1980 there was a remarkable turnaround. The rise in fractions single during the 1970s was somewhat larger among high school dropouts than among men with more education.

TABLE 3.6

*Percent of Non-Hispanic White Men Never Married at Selected Ages,
by Education, 1940–80*

	Years of Education			
	<12	12	>12	Total
At Age 21				
1940	75.3	85.6	93.1	81.5
1950	60.4	69.2	84.6	69.2
1960	51.5	58.0	78.1	62.5
1970	47.6	57.3	77.3	66.2
1980	61.0	69.2	89.8	76.9
At Age 24				
1940	51.6	56.6	69.2	55.7
1950	31.1	35.2	48.5	36.9
1960	28.0	28.9	40.3	32.4
1970	27.7	27.1	39.9	33.0
1980	34.4	39.8	59.7	48.2
At Age 29				
1940	25.6	26.6	30.2	26.5
1950	16.0	14.9	17.1	15.9
1960	14.2	13.1	18.7	15.3
1970	13.6	10.6	14.1	12.8
1980	18.5	15.9	25.2	21.5
	Change			
1960–70				
21	−3.9	−0.7	−0.8	3.7
24	−0.3	−1.8	−0.4	0.6
29	−0.6	−2.5	−4.6	−2.5
1970–80				
21	13.4	11.9	12.5	10.7
24	6.7	12.7	19.8	15.2
29	4.9	5.3	11.1	8.7

Activities of Young Singles:
Working and Going to School

Although we cannot describe patterns and trends of enrollment and employment of young single men and women in great detail, some discussion is essential to an understanding of changing marriage and family patterns.

TABLE 3.7

Percent of Black Men Never Married at Selected Ages,
by Education, 1960–80

| | Years of Education | | | |
	<12	12	>12	Total
At Age 21				
1960	60.4	70.2	83.6	65.6
1970	64.5	62.3	76.6	66.4
1980	85.7	80.9	91.1	85.3
At Age 24				
1960	37.9	38.8	42.6	38.7
1970	37.2	35.9	41.7	37.6
1980	65.4	55.0	65.3	61.2
At Age 29				
1960	24.7	17.9	26.0	23.5
1970	24.0	18.3	18.6	21.2
1980	37.9	29.6	29.0	31.4
	Change			
1960–70				
21	4.1	−7.9	−7.0	0.8
24	−0.7	−2.9	−0.9	−1.1
29	−0.7	0.4	−7.4	−2.3
1970–80				
21	21.2	18.6	14.5	18.9
24	28.2	19.1	23.6	23.6
29	13.9	11.3	10.4	10.2

Enrollment

Table 3.8 shows the age pattern of school enrollment of single men and women at ages 18–29 for 1960, 1970, and 1980. In 1980 about one-third of the never-married men and 38 percent of the never-married women were enrolled in school, either full or part-time.[5] The fraction of singles enrolled varies by age. Among men, 55 percent of the 18–19-

---

[5]With decennial census data it is not possible to distinguish between full- and part-time enrollment, or between persons for whom going to school is the major activity or a secondary activity. School enrollment, however, is limited to "regular school or college"—schooling that "leads to a high school diploma or college degree." Persons in specialized vocational, trade, or business schools outside the "regular system" should not be included as enrolled.

TABLE 3.8

Percent of Never-Married Persons Who Are Enrolled in School,
by Age and Sex, for Total and Black Persons, 1960–80

	Total			Black		
	1960	1970	1980	1960	1970	1980
MALE						
18–19	49.2	58.2	54.8	42.0	42.7	50.9
20–21	32.6	42.8	38.2	19.4	21.7	28.2
22–24	22.0	25.7	26.1	11.6	14.6	18.1
25–29	15.2	12.3	15.9	8.6	6.2	13.2
30–34	6.6	5.6	9.9	4.6	3.7	8.8
Total	30.2	38.2	32.9	20.9	24.1	26.6
FEMALE						
18–19	51.2	58.8	61.1	46.2	46.2	57.0
20–21	34.1	43.2	45.4	23.5	28.3	36.9
22–24	14.9	18.8	26.0	11.0	12.0	20.9
25–29	9.9	8.6	16.4	6.7	5.0	13.1
30–34	6.2	6.0	11.2	5.2	4.4	9.0
Total	31.6	38.6	38.0	23.7	25.5	30.4

year-olds, 38 percent of the 20–21-year-olds, and 26 percent of the 22–24-year-olds are enrolled. The fraction drops to 10 percent by age 30–34. For women, the fraction enrolled is slightly higher at each age, especially at age 20–21. A larger fraction of all women has married at each age; these data refer to the fraction of those remaining single who are going to school.

Between 1960 and 1970 there was a rapid increase in the fraction of singles enrolled at ages 18–24, and a slight decline at ages 25–29. During the 1970s, the trends diverged for younger men and women. Whereas there was a continual, although slower, increase in enrollment among single women, there were slight declines in enrollment among single men under age 21. During the 1970s, however, there were substantial increases for both sexes at ages 25–34.

Single blacks are much less likely than single whites to be enrolled. This does not tell us anything about the relative fractions of the cohorts enrolled at any given age, since blacks of a given age are more likely to be single, and single persons of a given age are more likely to be enrolled. (In fact, by 1980, cohort enrollment differentials between blacks and whites had narrowed considerably, especially among women.) The fraction of single blacks who are enrolled has been generally upward since 1960, but there was a particularly large rise in enrollment in the 1970s. This is true at all ages, and for both men and women.

Employment

The majority of young single men and women are employed.[6] The fraction employed increases with age and is slightly higher for women than men at each age (Table 3.9). At age 18–19, one-half the singles are employed. The fraction increases to three-quarters by age 25–29.

There was a marked decline between 1940 and 1970 in the proportion employed among single men at all ages. The level for ages 20–21 in 1970 was 20 points lower than it was in 1940, and substantial declines occurred in each decade. While this trend is undoubtedly tied to increasing enrollment, there were marked *increases* over the 1970s to levels close to those of 1940. In spite of enrollment increases, employment among single women was remarkably stable over the forty years except for a peak in 1950. During the 1970s, however, while the employment rate of young single men increased sharply, the rates for women increased only slightly at most ages.

Employment rates of black singles are much lower than those of whites (Table 3.9). At age 18–19 only about 30 percent of single black men and women are employed, in comparison to over one-half of single whites. At ages 25–34, about three-fifths of single blacks and three-fourths of single whites are employed. These differences emerged among men when the employment rates of single black men under age 25 fell during the 1960s and 1970s. The trend varied by age among single black women. In general, there was a decline after 1940, followed by an increase peaking in 1970; employment rates declined considerably by 1980 for ages 20–24.

Employment rates of single young adults cannot be understood without considering their other activities. Rates of employment are heavily influenced by the fraction of single persons enrolled in school, by the fraction in the armed forces, and, for single women, by the fraction with children present.

The fraction of single persons in the armed forces has varied over time.[7] In 1960, 2.5 percent of single men aged 18–34 were in the armed

[6]The employment rate used here is the percent of all single persons employed in civilian jobs. Persons in the military are counted in the denominator, but are not included in the numerator. We use the employment rate rather than the labor force participation rate. The employment rate is the number of persons employed as a percent of the total population. The labor force participation rate would also include the unemployed in the numerator.

[7]The census counts only persons living in the United States. Since a portion of the armed forces is abroad, the fraction in the armed forces is understated in these data.

TABLE 3.9

Employment Rates of Never-Married Persons,
by Sex and Age, for Non-Hispanic Whites and Blacks, 1940–80

	1940	1950	1960	1970	1980
NON-HISPANIC WHITE					
Males					
18–19	50.0	51.4	46.7	47.2	54.2
20–21	66.8	60.7	55.0	46.8	61.1
22–24	75.8	66.4	61.5	61.2	71.6
25–29	80.2	73.1	74.7	75.1	79.1
30–34	78.3	77.0	77.6	76.0	79.9
Total	68.7	63.5	59.0	55.4	66.7
Females					
18–19	36.9	51.4	52.2	46.7	56.0
20–21	59.3	68.3	66.9	60.7	65.8
22–24	71.8	79.2	79.2	78.3	79.4
25–29	74.5	80.0	79.4	81.0	84.1
30–34	74.6	76.6	78.5	78.1	82.5
Total	59.9	65.2	65.7	63.1	70.0
BLACK					
Males					
18–19	60.8	56.0	43.4	35.6	31.1
20–21	68.8	60.9	54.0	42.8	42.6
22–24	71.6	61.6	58.4	54.2	52.7
25–29	71.2	63.6	62.4	63.4	57.8
30–34	69.6	66.5	61.3	62.0	58.3
Total	67.5	60.7	54.1	47.0	46.7
Females					
18–19	35.5	30.4	29.6	30.4	28.6
20–21	49.4	45.6	47.1	48.8	42.1
22–24	59.5	54.7	56.3	61.0	52.3
25–29	65.2	64.2	57.9	58.8	60.2
30–34	64.2	61.8	62.2	61.4	63.6
Total	51.8	47.8	46.6	47.5	47.1

forces. This rose to 9 percent in 1970, and fell to less than 4 percent in 1980 (Table 3.10). At age 20–21, participation in the military is greatest—14 percent in 1960, 15 percent in 1970, and 6 percent in 1980. By 1980, with the "all-volunteer" military, single black men were nearly twice as likely as single white men to be in the armed forces (Table 3.11).

TABLE 3.10

Percent of Never-Married Men in Armed Forces,
by Age, for Total and Black Population, 1950–80

	1950	1960	1970	1980
TOTAL				
18–19	8.4	11.0	7.1	4.3
20–21	9.2	13.9	15.2	5.7
22–24	4.0	13.2	11.2	3.5
25–29	3.1	4.1	3.7	1.8
30–34	2.5	2.0	1.8	1.0
Total	6.0	10.0	9.1	3.7
BLACK				
18–19	8.8	4.8	5.8	6.9
20–21	8.5	7.4	15.0	9.2
22–24	4.3	8.4	8.0	5.7
25–29	3.7	3.4	2.9	2.4
30–34	1.9	1.3	1.5	0.8
Total	6.1	5.4	7.6	5.6

Employment rates of students at all ages rose during the 1970s (data not shown). The rates of female students rose very rapidly. In 1980, 46 percent of enrolled males age 20–21 were employed; a decade earlier it was 41 percent. For women the employment rate rose from 40 to 50 percent. The picture for single blacks is very different. Rates of employment of black men who are students have remained more nearly constant since 1960. For women aged 18–21, however, employment rates have risen. For both men and women the rates of single black students are much lower than for non-Hispanic whites. At ages 20–21, for example, 37 percent of the black male students and 46 percent of the non-Hispanic white male students are employed. For female students the employment rates are 37 and 50 percent, respectively.

Nonenrolled persons have higher employment rates than students. In 1980, 76 percent of the single non-Hispanic white men and 81 percent of the single women were employed in civilian jobs. For men, there was a drop in employment between 1960 and 1970, and a rise during the 1970s. However, this change was associated with the rise and fall in the size of the armed forces.

Single black men who are not enrolled have a much lower rate of employment than do white men. At age 18–19, 36 percent are employed. The rate increases to 45 percent at age 20–21, and to nearly 60

TABLE 3.11

Percent of Never-Married Persons in the Armed Forces,
by Age, Race/Ethnicity, and Sex, 1980

	Non-Hispanic White	Black	Mexican-American	Total
MALES				
18–19	3.8	6.9	4.0	4.3
20–21	5.1	9.2	3.5	5.7
22–24	3.1	5.7	2.4	3.5
25–29	1.7	2.4	1.7	1.8
30–34	1.1	0.8	0.0	1.0
Total	3.3	5.6	2.8	3.7
FEMALES				
18–19	0.5	1.1	0.6	0.6
20–21	0.6	1.0	1.2	0.7
22–24	0.6	0.6	0.1	0.6
25–29	0.6	0.8	0.0	0.6
30–34	0.4	0.1	0.4	0.3
Total	0.5	0.8	0.5	0.6

NOTE: Census includes only persons living in the United States; armed forces abroad are not included.

percent at age 25–34. Nonenrolled single black women have employment rates very similar to those of black men. When we add the rate of armed forces participation to the rate of employment, there was a drop during the 1970s at every age, especially at ages 18–19 and 20–21. For ages 18–24 this was a continuation of a decrease during the 1960s. Expressed differently, by 1980 more than two single black men in five who were not in school were neither employed nor in the armed forces. This fraction was high in 1960 (one in three), but it has increased further during the last two decades.

This question is addressed from a different perspective in Table 3.12, which shows the percent of single men who are neither working, enrolled, nor in the armed forces, by age and race/ethnicity, at each of the past four census dates. Among non-Hispanic white men aged 18–34, about one never-married man in six is "idle," in the sense of not working, going to school, or being in the armed forces. The proportion does not vary much by age, nor has it changed much over the four census dates. The levels are much higher for black men—about 25 percent of the 18–19-year-olds, and nearly one-third of each of the older age groups.

Table 3.12

Percent of Men Aged 18–34 Who Are Not Employed, Not Enrolled,
and Not in the Armed Forces, by Age and Race/Ethnicity,
for Total and Never-Married Men, 1950–80

	1950		1960		1970		1980	
	Total	Never Married	Total	Never Married	Total	Never Married	Total	Never Married
NON-HISPANIC WHITE								
18–19	11.8	11.6	10.9	11.1	10.1	10.2	11.5	11.3
20–21	10.8	11.4	10.3	11.7	10.3	11.4	12.4	12.6
22–24	8.8	12.4	8.9	13.2	9.3	13.6	11.6	13.1
25–29	7.1	14.2	6.7	14.9	6.6	15.9	9.5	14.0
30–34	—	—	6.0	18.6	5.7	20.5	7.8	16.3
BLACK								
18–19	18.7	17.9	22.2	22.7	26.7	27.0	24.9	25.0
20–21	19.0	21.4	23.5	26.7	25.4	28.7	29.8	31.2
22–24	17.1	23.1	20.6	27.2	21.0	29.1	27.0	31.4
25–29	16.6	25.4	17.2	30.2	16.5	30.4	24.2	33.5
30–34	—	—	17.0	35.3	14.4	35.1	20.7	37.7
MEXICAN-AMERICAN								
18–19	21.5	21.2	18.9	20.2	16.6	16.9	18.1	18.1
20–21	19.4	22.3	21.4	23.2	17.7	19.4	18.0	18.9
22–24	15.8	18.5	15.1	23.9	15.2	20.1	15.6	20.6
25–29	15.0	17.8	12.6	25.7	10.6	21.7	14.0	18.6
30–34	—	—	11.0	31.4	10.2	21.2	21.2	23.3

NOTE: — Could not be calculated in 1950 because enrollment status was not asked of persons age 30–34.

Among young, single black men, there has been a slow increase in the proportion "idle" over the past three decades. For example, at age 22–24 it rose from 27 percent in 1960, to 29 percent in 1970, and to 31 percent in 1980.

Some have attributed part of the drop in the frequency of marriage, especially of young blacks, to the deterioration of their labor market position. This measure of inactivity would be an indicator of the most extreme employment difficulty. Addressing this question requires examining the trend in "inactivity" for the whole cohort, not just for those who have not yet married. The proportion who are "inactive" is over twice as high among black men as among non-Hispanic white men. A quarter or more of black men are not employed, enrolled, or in the armed forces at all ages below 30. Among white men the proportion "inactive" is about 12 percent under age 25, declining to 8 percent by age 30–34. There was a marked increase during the 1970s in the percent inactive, especially after the early twenties for both blacks and whites. Hence the underlying causes are likely not to be unique to the black population. At the same time, however, the initially higher levels among blacks may mean that a threshold was passed in the 1970s after which the likelihood of unstable employment of men has become more salient in marriage decisions. This may particularly be the case since these cross-sectional measures (one quarter among black men in the prime marriage years) imply even higher proportions that are likely to have substantial periods of inactivity during their adult years. This is a complex issue which the simple cross-sectional data in this table address only obliquely. What we are suggesting is that the rise in the level of inactivity during the 1970s is temporally consistent with the decline in marriage rates, and that the levels of inactivity of young black men are now high enough that they may be an important factor in the marriage delay.

Living Arrangements of Never-Married Persons

The living arrangements of single persons are very different from one age to another (Figures 3.9 and 3.10). In Table 3.13 the living arrangements of men and women at four ages (18, 21, 24, and 29) are summarized. At age 18, three-quarters of single persons are living with their parents. Many of these are persons still in high school, some are in college, and others are not in school. About one-tenth are living in college dorms (or other college housing such as sororities or fraternities). Very few are living on their own in nonfamily households (5 percent of the men and 8 percent of the women). The distribution of living arrangements of 18-year-old men and women is very similar. More women are in dorms and more men in "other group quarters," including military barracks. Slightly more women are in nonfamily households.

By age 21 only about half of the single persons are living with parents. Again, about 10 percent are in dorms. Seven percent of the men, but only 2 percent of the women, are living in other group quarters. One-quarter of the men and nearly 30 percent of the women are in nonfamily households. However, only one-third to one-quarter of these are living alone (in one-person households). More are in two or more person nonfamily households (that is, "other household heads" or "roommates," including cohabiting relationships). Five percent of the women are "family heads," many of whom are unmarried mothers living with their children.

FIGURE 3.9

Living Arrangements of Never-Married Men, 1980

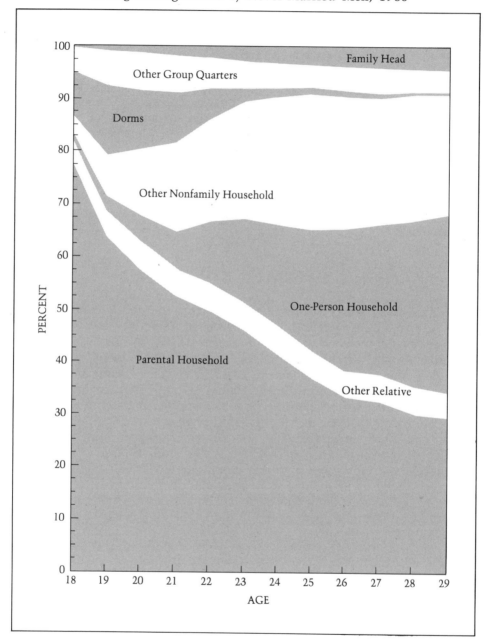

FIGURE 3.10

Living Arrangements of Never-Married Women, 1980

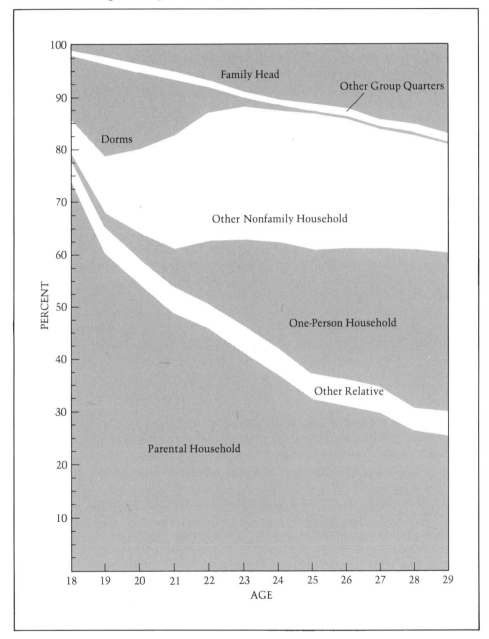

TABLE 3.13

Living Arrangements of Never-Married Persons Aged 18, 21, 24, and 29,
by Sex, for Total and Black Populations, 1980

	Age 18		Age 21		Age 24		Age 29	
	Men	Women	Men	Women	Men	Women	Men	Women
TOTAL								
In Household								
In Family								
Head	0.3	1.0	1.7	5.1	3.2	10.5	4.2	17.0
Child	76.9	74.0	52.3	48.7	41.1	37.1	29.1	25.3
Other Relative	4.8	4.3	5.2	5.0	5.6	5.1	4.9	4.7
Not in Family								
Alone	1.1	1.2	7.1	7.4	19.2	20.0	34.0	30.2
Other Household Head	0.8	1.1	6.5	6.5	10.7	8.6	10.5	7.0
Roommate*	1.7	3.1	8.6	12.2	10.8	13.4	9.2	11.0
Nonrelative†	1.3	2.1	2.0	2.9	3.0	3.1	3.5	2.6
In Group Quarters								
College Dorm	8.2	12.2	9.6	10.7	1.5	1.0	0.6	0.4
Other	4.8	1.0	7.0	1.6	4.8	1.1	4.1	1.6
Total	100.0	100.0	100.0	100.0	100.0	100.0	100.0	100.0

TABLE 3.13 (continued)

	Age 18		Age 21		Age 24		Age 29	
	Men	Women	Men	Women	Men	Women	Men	Women
BLACK								
In Household								
In Family								
Head	0.4	2.5	2.5	14.1	5.6	28.4	6.8	42.5
Child	73.8	74.0	54.1	53.0	43.3	38.6	32.0	22.3
Other Relative	9.0	9.7	9.9	9.7	10.4	8.0	10.9	6.9
Not in Family								
Alone	0.5	0.5	5.4	5.0	14.2	11.0	23.0	16.4
Other Household Head	0.3	0.4	2.8	1.9	4.9	2.9	5.3	2.5
Roommate*	0.7	1.4	3.3	4.4	5.3	5.9	6.8	4.7
Nonrelative†	1.5	1.9	2.6	2.9	3.6	3.0	5.3	3.2
In Group Quarter								
College Dorm	5.3	8.3	6.0	7.3	1.3	0.7	0.4	0.2
Other	8.6	1.4	13.5	1.6	11.3	1.4	10.6	1.3
Total	100.0	100.0	100.0	100.0	100.0	100.0	100.0	100.0

*Persons who checked "Partner or Roommate" box on census schedule.

†All other nonrelatives including "Roomer, Boarder," "Paid Employee," and "Other Nonrelative" on census form.

By age 24 the fraction living with parents drops to about 40 percent. It drops further to about one-quarter by age 29. Very few persons aged 24 and over live in dorms. By age 24 the fraction living in nonfamily households rises to about 50 percent of the men and 45 percent of the women, including about 20 percent of each sex living in one-person households. At age 29, 57 percent of the men and 50 percent of the women live in nonfamily households, the majority in one-person households. More than one-sixth of the single women age 29 are family heads.

The major differences in the living arrangements of single blacks as compared to the total population are (see bottom panel of Table 3.13):

1. Single black women at all ages are more likely to be family heads. This is the case because single black women are much more likely to have own children present (see discussion in next section).

2. Blacks, both men and women, are more likely at each age to be living in the household of relatives.

3. Blacks are less likely to be living alone or as "roommates."

4. Blacks are less likely to be living in college dorms.

5. Black men are more likely to be living in "other group quarters." As our later discussion will show, blacks are more likely to be in both military barracks and in correctional institutions.

Trend in Living Arrangements. Between 1960 and 1980 there was a decrease in the fraction of single men and women living with parents (Figures 3.11 and 3.12). Among men aged 18–21 the fraction in the parental household did not change very much. Beyond age 22, however, there was a sharp drop. For women there was a drop at all ages, but only beyond age 20 was the decrease very large.[8] Table 3.14 summarizes these changes in living arrangements in greater detail.

The major long-term trend for both age groups is the drift out of the parental household into being a household head. Among non-Hispanic whites of both sexes the proportion heading their own households increased about tenfold since 1940, to around two-fifths for those 23–29 years of age. For the younger group of men, there was a sharp drop in the fraction in group quarters (25 percent to 15 percent) during the 1970s. This reflects both a decrease in the fraction of men in the military and a decrease in college enrollment. There was an increase in the

[8]In censuses prior to 1960, persons who were single and living apart from their parents while attending college were counted as members of their parental household. Beginning in 1960 they were counted where they were actually living.

FIGURE 3.11

Percent of Never-Married Women Living in Their Parental Household, by Age, 1960–80

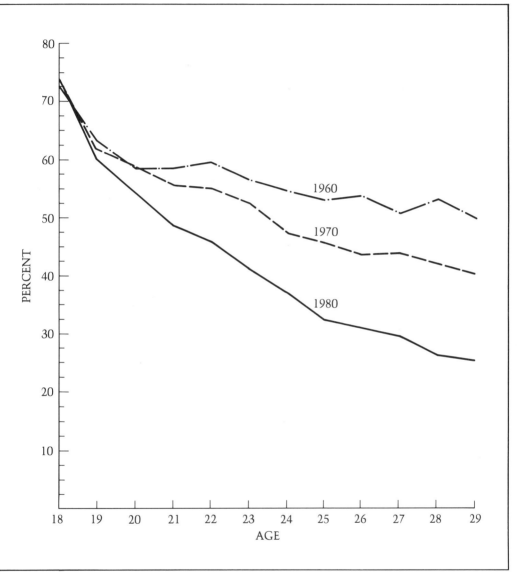

FIGURE 3.12

Percent of Never-Married Men Living in Their Parental Household, by Age,
1960–80

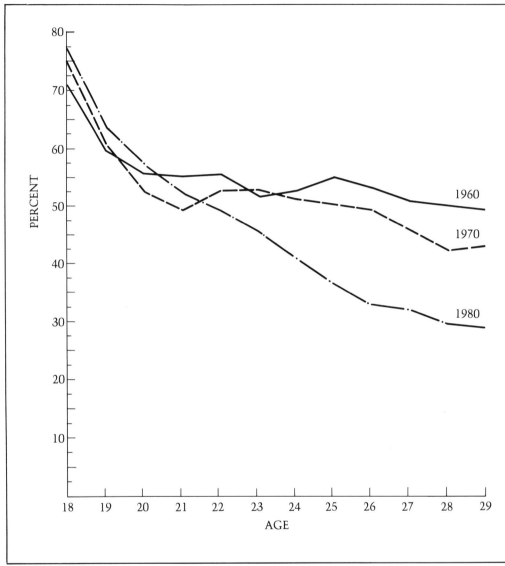

fraction of men who were householders (5 percent to 11 percent). There was very little change between 1960 and 1970 in the distribution of living arrangements.

Among women of both ages there was a rise in the fraction who are householders and nonrelatives of head, and a decrease in the percent living with parents and in group quarters (dorms primarily). These changes were more rapid during the 1970s than the 1960s.

The trend for blacks is similar to that for whites, except that the fraction living with parents has not declined as much, nor has the decrease in the fraction living in group quarters been as large. There has been a sharp drop for all groups of blacks in the fraction living with "other relatives."

Variation Among Racial and Hispanic Groups. The proportion of 18–24-year-old, never-married men and women who are living in their parental household depends on a number of factors, including the prevalence of college attendance, the degree to which persons attending college are doing so within the local community, the extent of military service, the pattern of marriage ages, the employment and economic opportunities of young persons of a specific racial or ethnic group, and a variety of other factors.[9]

We will look primarily at the pattern for females. The proportion living with parents is very similar for whites and blacks (55 and 56 percent), and most other groups have similar levels (see Table 3.15). However, a higher proportion of Mexican-Americans (64 percent) and Cubans (78 percent) are living in the parental household. The proportion is lower for American Indians (51 percent) and Vietnamese (48 percent).

Residence in group quarters is more common among young adults than among any other group. Table 3.16 shows the proportion of never-married persons 18–24 years of age who are living in group quarters. The proportion is generally higher among men than among women, and varies widely from group to group. Fourteen percent of the single majority-white men live in group quarters. Higher than average fractions of black (17 percent), Korean (17 percent), and Puerto Rican (16 percent) men are in group quarters. These groups have higher than average proportions in the armed forces. Black males have a larger than average fraction in prison (4 percent) as well, but a smaller proportion in college dormito-

---

[9]We are aware of, but have ignored, the fact that persons in this age group—particularly disadvantaged, minority males—are underenumerated in the census. The reason for ignoring it is that there is nothing we can do to "adjust" the data. The reason for mentioning it in a footnote is that it involves a potential bias. Persons omitted in the census enumeration would be disproportionately those living outside of the parental household. Because this problem is more serious for men than for women, we limit the discussion in the text to the patterns of women.

TABLE 3.14

Living Arrangements of Never-Married Persons,
by Age, Sex, and Race, 1940–80

	Age 18–22					Age 23–29				
	1940	1950	1960	1970	1980	1940	1950	1960	1970	1980
NON-HISPANIC WHITE MALE										
Household Head	1.0	1.1	2.9	5.4	10.9	4.7	5.9	13.8	24.8	39.6
Child of Head	82.4	69.2	60.8	60.3	61.4	68.4	61.3	54.1	50.6	37.2
Other Relative	6.5	5.5	4.8	3.0	4.3	7.7	7.1	6.5	4.0	4.1
Nonrelative	4.9	5.1	4.5	5.5	7.8	10.5	9.8	8.7	9.4	14.2
Inmate	1.1	1.1	1.5	1.2	1.1	1.8	2.7	2.9	2.5	1.7
Other Group Quarters	4.1	17.9	25.5	24.6	14.6	6.9	13.2	14.0	8.7	3.2
Total	100.0	100.0	100.0	100.0	100.0	100.0	100.0	100.0	100.0	100.0
NON-HISPANIC WHITE FEMALE										
Household Head	0.9	1.6	3.8	6.2	11.8	4.2	8.7	16.7	29.2	41.8
Child of Head	79.9	70.6	64.7	63.0	58.1	66.8	62.8	55.7	48.3	34.1
Other Relative	6.6	5.9	5.2	3.4	3.7	8.2	7.5	6.6	4.4	3.8
Nonrelative	7.9	6.5	5.7	6.2	11.5	13.5	11.1	12.6	13.0	18.1
Inmate	0.6	0.7	0.8	0.6	0.3	1.3	1.8	1.9	1.5	0.7
Other Group Quarters	4.1	14.8	19.9	20.5	14.6	6.1	8.0	6.5	3.7	1.5
Total	100.0	100.0	100.0	100.0	100.0	100.0	100.0	100.0	100.0	100.0

TABLE 3.14 (continued)

	Age 18–22					Age 23–29				
	1940	1950	1960	1970	1980	1940	1950	1960	1970	1980
BLACK MALE										
Household Head	2.9	1.7	2.5	3.8	6.7	9.1	7.2	10.2	20.6	27.7
Child of Head	68.2	59.9	61.3	61.6	61.0	45.2	40.8	41.9	43.5	40.2
Other Relative	14.9	14.8	16.3	10.2	9.7	13.1	13.8	15.9	12.3	10.2
Nonrelative	7.9	6.1	4.4	3.6	4.1	19.9	16.3	11.6	7.0	10.3
Inmate	3.4	3.9	4.4	5.1	4.4	7.0	8.1	9.6	10.3	7.0
Other Group Quarters	2.8	13.5	11.1	15.8	14.2	5.7	13.8	10.8	6.3	4.5
Total	100.0	100.0	100.0	100.0	100.0	100.0	100.0	100.0	100.0	100.0
BLACK FEMALE										
Household Head	2.0	2.2	4.7	8.3	14.1	9.6	9.7	19.9	37.1	49.1
Child of Head	67.4	64.1	63.3	64.8	60.8	44.1	49.4	44.4	41.1	32.9
Other Relative	15.6	15.3	17.0	12.1	9.3	15.5	15.5	18.3	12.2	8.0
Nonrelative	11.6	7.6	6.4	4.2	5.9	24.2	16.7	12.2	6.5	8.1
Inmate	1.1	1.6	0.8	0.6	0.5	1.6	1.1	2.1	1.6	0.6
Other Group Quarters	2.3	9.3	7.9	10.2	9.4	5.1	7.6	3.0	1.5	1.4
Total	100.0	100.0	100.0	100.0	100.0	100.0	100.0	100.0	100.0	100.0

NOTE: In censuses prior to 1960, persons who were single and living apart from their parents while attending college were counted as members of their parental household. Beginning in 1960 they were counted where they were actually living.

TABLE 3.15

Percent of Never-Married Persons
Aged 18–24 Living in Parental Household, 1980

	Male	Female
Non-Hispanic White	58.1	54.4
Black	58.4	56.4
Chinese	57.6	59.1
Japanese	56.0	57.6
Filipino	56.6	52.6
American Indian	53.4	50.7
Korean	55.4	46.8
Asian Indian	43.4	56.9
Vietnamese	30.1	48.2
Hawaiian	50.8	52.7
Mexican	54.7	63.4
Puerto Rican	54.5	53.2
Cuban	72.0	78.1

NOTE: In an attempt to eliminate foreign students, persons who are noncitizens and enrolled in college have been excluded. This exclusion was not made for Vietnamese and Cubans.

ries. Mexican-Americans, Vietnamese, and Cubans have low fractions of men in group quarters. Similar ethnic differences are found for women, except that black women have a much lower proportion in group quarters than white women (8 versus 13 percent).

A large fraction of never-married college students (age 18–22) lives in the parental household. In 1980, 45 percent of white men and 43 percent of white women were "children of the household head" (data not shown). Over 50 percent of black students of each sex are living in the parent's household. About one-third of the single white students were living in group quarters (dorms). There was no difference between men and women. Black college students were slightly less likely than whites to be living in group quarters. About one-fifth of the white men and women and about one-eighth of the black students are living in nonfamily households, either as household head or as a nonrelative of head.

Over the past two decades the fraction living with parents has risen for each of the four groups. Among whites the fraction living in dormitories has decreased—for men from 47 to 32 percent, and for women from 60 to 35 percent since 1960. The decrease was even more dramatic for black students. The share of single white students living in nonfamily households (alone or with roommates) has risen from 10 to 21 per-

TABLE 3.16

Percent of Never-Married Persons Aged 18–24 Living in All Group Quarters and in Specified Types of Group Quarters, by Sex and Race/Ethnicity, 1980

	Percent in All Types of Group Quarters		Male			Female
	Male	Female	Armed Forces	Jails, Prisons	College Dorms	College Dorms
Non-Hispanic White	14.1	13.4	3.3	0.7	9.2	12.1
Black	17.0	8.4	6.3	3.9	5.2	6.7
Chinese	14.8	15.0	0.6	0.2	13.1	13.5
Japanese	17.4	14.1	2.4	0.0	13.7	13.3
Filipino	13.2	7.1	8.2	0.2	4.0	4.6
American Indian	14.6	8.7	5.1	3.2	4.1	5.1
Korean	17.0	14.3	3.4	0.4	13.1	12.6
Asian Indian	15.8	13.7	0.8	0.6	13.8	13.5
Vietnamese	7.5	7.9	0.4	0.0	5.1	5.8
Mexican	8.7	3.9	2.8	1.6	2.2	2.4
Puerto Rican	16.2	5.9	7.9	2.8	3.5	4.0
Cuban	9.2	5.7	2.8	0.4	5.5	5.4

NOTE: In an attempt to eliminate foreign students, persons who are noncitizens and enrolled in college have been excluded. This exclusion was not made for Vietnamese and Cubans.

cent for men, and from 5 to 20 percent for women. There was also an upward trend for blacks, but it was not as large.

Cohabitation. The number of cohabiting couples increased very rapidly during the 1970s.[10] By 1980 about 5 percent of never-married men and 6 percent of never-married women (of all ages) were cohabiting (Table 3.17). The fraction cohabiting varies by age. At ages 25–34, about 9 percent of men are cohabiting. Only about 4 percent of the 20–24-year-old men and 1 percent of the 18–19-year-old men are cohabiting. For women the peak ages are 20–34. Eight percent of the 20–24-year-old, 10 percent of the 25–29-year-old, and 7 percent of the 30–34-year-old single women are cohabiting.

A slightly higher proportion of black men are cohabiting at young ages, but at ages beyond 30, the differential is quite large. Similarly, Mexican-American men have larger fractions at older ages, but have levels similar to whites at ages under 35. Young black women are less

[10]A person is a cohabitor if he or she is an adult member of a two-adult household consisting of unrelated, opposite-sex adults who are not classified as married, spouse present. This definition misses cohabitors who live in households including more than two adults, and also misses couples in which one partner is under age 18.

TABLE 3.17

Percent of Never-Married Persons Who Are Cohabitating,
by Age, Sex, and Race/Ethnicity, 1980

	Males			Females		
	Non-Hispanic White	Black	Mexican-American	Non-Hispanic White	Black	Mexican-American
18–19	0.9	0.8	1.0	3.3	1.9	3.1
20–24	4.4	5.0	4.5	7.8	6.6	6.0
25–29	9.2	10.7	7.9	11.2	8.2	6.6
30–34	8.0	11.0	8.1	7.3	7.5	6.3
35–44	4.0	9.0	9.7	3.1	5.2	3.1
45–54	2.4	6.7	3.9	1.4	4.4	3.4

likely than majority white women to be cohabiting, but at older ages they are more likely than white women to do so. Mexican-American women are generally less likely than non-Hispanic white women to cohabit.

Leaving Home

A related question, which the data on living arrangements which we have just discussed do not address, is how the timing of "leaving home" has changed in the past few decades. To examine this question, we need to look at the living arrangements of the entire cohort, and not just those of a given age who have never married. We know that there has been an increase in the age at marriage, which should tend to increase the fraction at any given age who are living with parents. On the other hand, there has been a decrease in the fraction of never-married persons living in the parental household. (One part of this decrease, for men, is the drop in the fraction of single persons in their late teens and early twenties who are in the armed forces. This would have the effect of raising the fraction of single men living with parents.)

Figures 3.13 and 3.14 plot the proportions of men and women aged 18–29 who are both single (never married) and living in the household of their parents by single years of age for 1960, 1970, and 1980. For both men and women at each age from 18 through the mid- to late twenties there was a large proportion single and living in the parental household in 1980 than in 1970. For women this is a continuation of the 1960–1970 trend, while for men there is little difference between 1960 and 1970. Hence, it appears that the effect of declining fractions married at

FIGURE 3.13

Percent of all Persons Living in Parental Household,
by Age—Men, 1960–80

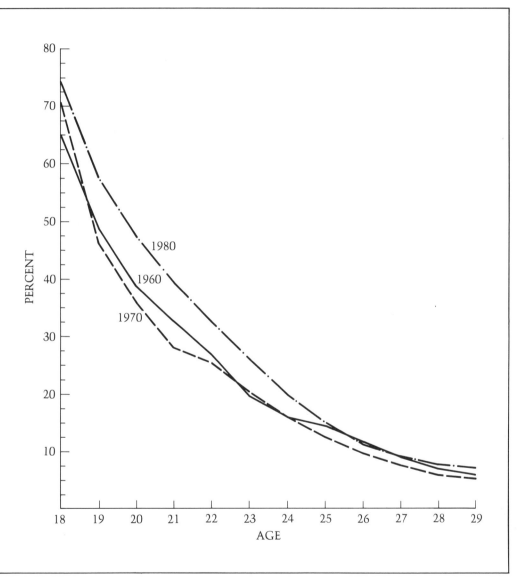

each age is greater than that of decreasing proportions of single persons living with parents. Recall that for women the decrease in age-specific proportions married began in the 1960s while for men marriage rates did not drop very much until the 1970s.

FIGURE 3.14

Percent of all Persons Living in Parental Household,
by Age—Women, 1960–80

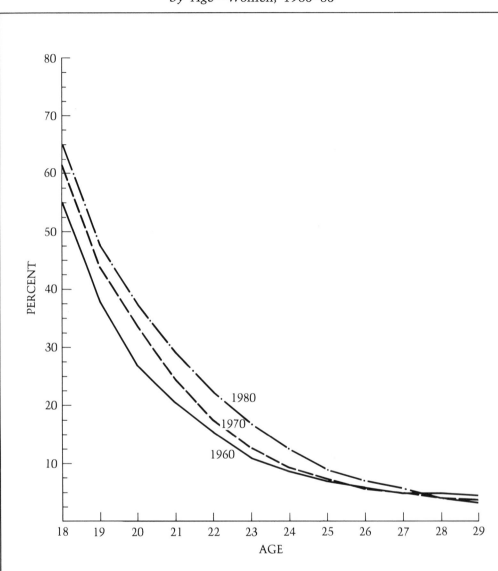

So what has happened is somewhat paradoxical. It is true that, at every age, more unmarried young adults are living "on their own." However, from the perspective of parents, who may be longing for the day when their "nest" is empty and they are again "on their own," it is also true that adult children are remaining in the parental household longer now than in the past. This is true because marriage, which has traditionally been the major "reason" for leaving home, has been significantly delayed.

Childbearing and Child-Rearing Among Single Women

In the previous chapter we noted that the bride has already had a child in an increasing proportion of first marriages. Consequently, childbearing and child-rearing by single women deserves some attention in our description of the changing experience of single persons in the United States. Such experience is the outcome of a complex of variables, including when sexual activity begins, ages at marriage, contraceptive use, and the likelihood of abortion, keeping a child, or marrying, given pregnancy.

Only a portion of women who have a baby while single raise the child. Some "give the baby up" for adoption. Evidently this has become less common in recent years. Hence we might find that fewer babies are born to single women, but more women are raising children while single. Marriage further complicates the analysis of childbearing and child-rearing of single women. A single woman who becomes pregnant may "legitimate" the birth by marrying before the child is born. This is what is often referred to by demographers as a "premarital pregnancy." Or the woman may marry the father or someone else after the birth. Then, although she was single when the child was born and the birth was "nonmarital," she is no longer a "single mother."

As age at marriage increases, women spend more years in a single state. Hence they have more of an opportunity to have a child while single. Even if the annual rates of childbearing by single women decrease, the fact that women are spending more years single may result in an increase in the fraction of single women with children or in the probability that a woman will eventually have a child while single.

Birthrates. In 1980 about 3 percent of unmarried women in their twenties gave birth to a child (Table 3.18).[11] The fraction is slightly lower among 15–19-year-olds, and considerably lower among women in their thirties. The fractions of unmarried black women giving birth are about five times as high as for white women. One out of ten single black women age 15–29 gave birth in 1980.

---

[11]Data on "illegitimacy" are not published separately by marital status. At the younger ages almost all unmarried women who give birth are never-married.

TABLE 3.18

Birthrates of Unmarried Women, by Age and Race, 1980
(births per 1,000 women)

	Total	White	Black
15–19	27.6	16.2	89.2
20–24	40.9	24.4	115.1
25–29	34.0	20.7	83.9
30–34	21.1	13.6	48.2
35–39	9.7	6.8	19.6
40–44	2.6	1.8	5.6
Total	29.4	17.6	82.9

NOTE: These data refer to all unmarried women, including the formerly married.

SOURCE: Vital Statistics of the U.S.: 1980, vol. III, Marriage and Divorce.

From 1940 until about 1965 the birthrates of unmarried women rose at every age (Figure 3.15). The increase was most rapid at ages 20–34. However, beginning around 1965, these rates began to decline, at about the same rate that they had previously increased. This decline occurred at all ages except 15–19. The rates for teenagers continued to increase. However, in about 1975, the birthrates of 20–24- and 25–29-year-old unmarried women also began to rise again, and have continued to rise into the mid-1980s.

The nonmarital birthrates of black women rose sharply from 1940 through about 1960 (Figure 3.16). Between 1960 and 1970 the rates of women in their twenties dropped at a very rapid rate. Since 1970 they have fluctuated somewhat, but there has not been much overall change. The birthrate of unmarried teens rose from the mid-1960s to the early 1970s, and has not changed much since that time. The recent increase in numbers of black illegitimate births is due to the increased amount of time women are spending unmarried, not to the increased rate at which unmarried women are having children.

Number of Never-Married Persons with Own Children. In 1980 there were 1.4 million never-married persons with own children under age 18. About 90 percent of these were women and 10 percent were men.[12] These never-married parents were predominantly in their

---

[12]It may seem surprising to find that in 1980 there were 129,000 never-married men with own children. More than half of these men were cohabiting at the time of the census (53 percent), and at ages 20–29, over 60 percent were cohabiting. In most of these cohabiting cases, the single man was designated as the householder and the child was probably the child of the couple, rather than a child that the never-married man had with another woman.

FIGURE 3.15

Birthrates of Unmarried White Women, by Age, 1940–83

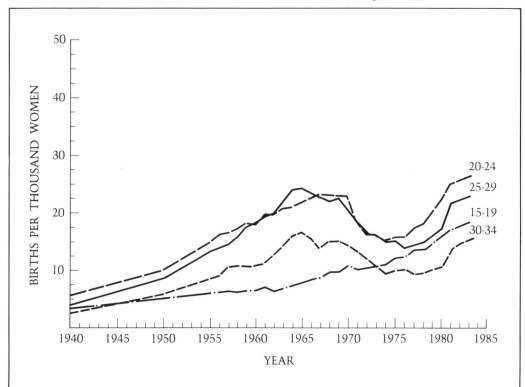

SOURCE: National Center for Health Statistics, *Monthly Vital Statistics Report*, "Advance Report of Final Natality Statistics, 1984," DHHS, vol. 35, no. 4, Supplement, July 18, 1986.

twenties. More than one-third were 20–24 years old, and an additional one-quarter were 25–29. Only 56,000, or 4 percent, were under age 18. The majority—833,000, or 61 percent—were black, and about 5 percent were Mexican-Americans (see Table 3.19).

There has been a rapid growth in the number of never-married mothers during the past two decades. In 1960, there were 73,000 never-married women age 18–34 with children.[13] This rose to 324,000 in 1970, and to 1,022,000 by 1980. In 1960, three-quarters were black women. The fraction who were black dropped to 66 percent in 1970, and to 63 percent in 1980.

[13]For the remainder of this section we will confine our discussion to women in the age range 18–34. Seventy-eight percent of all never-married adults with own children are women in this age range.

FIGURE 3.16

Birthrates of Unmarried Black Women, by Age, 1940–83

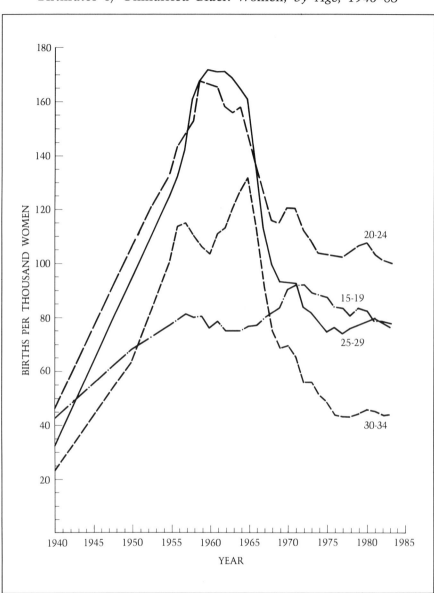

SOURCE: National Center for Health Statistics, *Monthly Vital Statistics Report*, "Advance Report of Final Natality Statistics, 1984," DHHS, vol. 35, no. 4, Supplement, July 18, 1986.

TABLE 3.19

Number of Never-Married Persons with Own Children Under 18,
by Age, Race/Ethnicity, and Sex, 1980 (in thousands)

	Total		Non-Hispanic White		Black		Mexican-American	
	Male	Female	Male	Female	Male	Female	Male	Female
<18	3	53	2	17	1	30	—	3
18–19	7	121	3	41	3	67	1	6
20–24	40	422	16	119	17	255	4	19
25–29	36	304	13	68	15	200	3	13
30–34	20	175	6	36	10	118	2	7
35–44	15	127	5	24	6	83	2	7
45–54	5	31	2	4	2	21	0	2
55–64	2	6	0	0	1	4	0	0
65+	1	1	0	0	0	1	0	0
Total	129	1240	47	293	54	779	11	57

The fractions of single women with own children and with children ever born have increased over the past two decades. In 1960, only 0.5 percent of single women aged 18–34 had a child present (Table 3.20). By 1980 it was 3 percent. Similarly, among blacks there was an increase from 8 percent in 1960 to 20 percent in 1970, and to 30 percent in 1980. The increase occurred at all ages and, as Table 3.21 shows, it has occurred at all education levels.

Single women with children are likely to be young, and their children are likely to be of preschool age (Table 3.22). Nearly half of the never-married women with own children have a child under age 3, and for an additional quarter the youngest child is age 3–5. Only one-sixth of the never-married mothers have a youngest child over age 8. Black mothers are more likely than whites to have older children. This suggests that single black women having had a child are less likely than white women to subsequently marry.

We have previously noted the remarkable rise in the age at first marriage of black women over the past decade. Now we have observed the rapid increase in the fraction of singles with children. The net effect of these two trends is shown in Figure 3.17, in which the age-specific percent of black women of all marital statuses who have no own children is shown for 1960, 1970, and 1980. Between 1960 and 1970 there was virtually no change in the fraction childless. During the 1970s the fraction with no own children rose by only a modest amount at each age. This is in sharp contrast to the extremely large increase in the fractions never-married at each age (see Figure 3.4).

TABLE 3.20

Percent of Never-Married Women Aged 18–34 with One or More
Own Children, and Percent with Children Ever Born, 1960–80

	With Own Children			With Children Ever Born*	
	1960	1970	1980	1970	1980
NON-HISPANIC WHITE WOMEN					
18–19	0.1	0.5	1.5	2.0	2.8
20–24	0.4	1.6	3.0	4.5	4.9
25–29	1.0	3.6	4.7	8.9	6.9
30–34	1.2	4.1	5.6	10.2	8.5
Total	0.4	1.5	3.1	4.3	5.0
BLACK WOMEN					
18–19	2.3	9.2	12.2	22.8	23.6
20–24	7.4	19.7	27.2	38.2	41.5
25–29	15.0	35.6	43.5	56.0	56.4
30–34	20.1	39.5	50.2	59.3	63.8
Total	8.5	20.4	30.2	37.7	43.6

*In 1960 the question on number of children ever born was not asked of never-married women.

TABLE 3.21

Percent of Never-Married Women Aged 18–34 with One or More
Own Children, by Race and Education, 1960–80

Years of Education	Non-Hispanic White			Black		
	1960*	1970	1980	1960	1970	1980
<9	2.0	5.7	10.6	14.2	31.6	41.2
9–11	1.0	6.6	7.4	11.8	35.4	39.2
12	0.2	1.8	3.6	5.2	18.2	30.7
13–15	0.1	0.4	1.3	2.7	7.5	19.8
16+	0.2	0.4	0.6	1.0	3.8	11.5
Total	0.4	1.5	3.0	8.5	20.4	29.2

*White except Spanish surname.

TABLE 3.22

Age Distribution of Youngest Own Child of Never-Married Mothers Under Age 60, by Race/Ethnicity, 1980

	Total	Non-Hispanic White	Black
0–2	46.3	52.6	43.4
3–5	23.1	23.1	22.8
6–8	13.5	11.6	14.5
9–11	9.1	7.2	10.2
12–14	4.9	3.3	5.7
15–17	3.1	2.1	3.4
Total	100.0	100.0	100.0
N(millions)	1.24	.31	.78

From census data we can examine both the number of births that never-married women report having had as well as the number of "own children" who are living with them. Table 3.23 shows the fraction of single women who have had at least one birth and the fraction with children living with them, by age and race. At age 18–19, one single woman in fifteen has had a birth; this increases to one in four by age 30–34. The fraction with own children present is 3 percent at age 18–19 and increases to 18 percent by age 30–34. These proportions are the weighted average of very different levels among blacks and whites. About 3 percent of never-married non-Hispanic white women aged 18–19 have borne a child, compared to 24 percent of blacks. At age 30–34, 8 percent of the never-married non-Hispanic white women have had a birth, while for blacks it is 64 percent. Similarly, the age-specific fraction of black women with own children present is nearly ten times as high as for non-Hispanic whites.

It is likely that some single women who have borne children (perhaps more often among whites than blacks) do not admit it when responding to the census. If, however, we take the data in Table 3.23 at face value, abut two-thirds of the single women who have given birth are raising a child. The fraction increases with age from half of the 18–19-year-olds to three-fourths of the 25–34-year-olds. It is somewhat higher for blacks than for whites beyond age 20 (see bottom panel of Table 3.23). Note, however, that this is not the fraction of single mothers who "keep their baby." That fraction is influenced by the number of mothers who give birth more than once, and by the rate at which single mothers marry after the birth, and the selectivity of marriage by presence of a child.

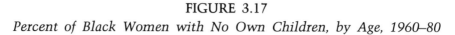

TABLE 3.23

*Percent of Never-Married Women with Children Ever Born,
and with Own Children, by Age and Race/Ethnicity, 1980*

Age	Total	Non-Hispanic White	Black	Mexican-American
		Percent with Children ever Born		
18–19	6.6	2.8	23.6	10.2
20–24	12.2	4.9	41.5	18.6
25–29	19.4	6.9	56.4	30.3
30–34	24.1	8.5	63.8	32.9
		Percent with Own Children		
18–19	3.4	1.5	12.2	4.1
20–24	7.8	3.0	27.2	10.4
25–29	14.4	4.7	43.5	21.4
30–34	18.2	5.6	50.2	24.8
		Ratio Own Child: CEB		
18–19	.518	.535	.515	.403
20–24	.638	.609	.655	.560
25–29	.743	.675	.772	.707
30–34	.754	.664	.786	.755

The higher the education level, the lower the proportion of women who have borne children (Table 3.24). Among single non-Hispanic whites ages 20–24, about one-quarter of those who did not complete high school have had at least one birth, and about one-sixth have a child present. The figures for high school graduates are 7 and 4 percent, respectively. Only about 1 percent of college-educated women have had a birth and only .5 percent have a child present. Among blacks, the same pattern exists, though at much higher levels. Two-thirds of the high school dropouts, nearly half the high school graduates, and about one-sixth of the college-educated women have had a birth.

The causal interpretation of this pattern by education is not obvious. In addition to a differential propensity to give birth, it may reflect differential propensity to raise a child born outside of marriage. It may also reflect a higher rate of educational continuation among women who do not choose to raise the child,[14] though there is disagreement

[14]Margaret Mooney Marini, "Women's Educational Attainment and Parenthood," *American Sociological Review* 49 (1984):491–511.

TABLE 3.24

Percent of Never-Married Women with Children Ever Born, and
Percent with Own Children, by Education, for 20–24- and 25–29-Year-Old
Black and Non-Hispanic White Women, 1980

	20–24				25–29			
	Non-Hispanic White		Black		Non-Hispanic White		Black	
	% with CEB	% with Own Child	% with CEB	% with Own Child	% with CEB	% with Own Child	% with CEB	% wit Own Child
<9	19.4	12.5	62.4	40.2	16.1	10.8	67.5	51.8
9–11	27.8	17.8	69.5	48.8	33.4	23.0	79.4	63.5
12	7.1	4.5	47.5	31.0	11.4	8.1	61.3	47.4
13–15	1.6	0.8	22.2	13.2	5.5	3.6	51.0	38.5
16+	0.6	0.2	11.8	5.7	1.2	0.6	20.4	14.3
Total	4.9	3.0	41.5	27.2	6.9	4.7	56.4	43.5

	20–24		25–29	
	Non-Hispanic White	Black	Non-Hispanic White	Blac
		Ratio Own Child: CEB		
<9	64.8	64.5	67.2	76.8
9–11	64.1	70.2	69.0	80.0
12	62.8	65.3	71.1	77.3
13–15	49.7	59.7	65.2	75.
16+	34.4	48.5	46.5	70.
Total	60.9	65.5	67.5	77.

about the extent to which early births actually affect educational attainment.[15]

Living Arrangements of Never-Married Women with Children. Two-thirds of never-married women with children maintain their own households, and about one-quarter live in the household of their parents. These fractions vary by age of the woman (Table 3.25). About one-third of the 18–19-year-old, three-fifths of the 20–24-year-old, and five-sixths of the 30–34-year-old mothers are family heads. A small minority of never-married mothers are classified as nonrelatives of householder.

[15]Ronald R. Rindfuss, Larry L. Bumpass, and Craig St. John, "Education and Fertility: Implications for the Roles Women Occupy," *American Sociological Review* 45 (1980): 431–47.

TABLE 3.25

Living Arrangements of Never-Married Women
with Own Children Present, by Age, 1980

	18–19	20–24	25–29	30–34	Total
Head	33.1	62.1	77.7	83.6	67.0
Child	55.1	29.1	16.5	10.8	25.3
Other Relative	6.5	3.8	2.3	2.2	3.4
Nonrelative	5.3	5.0	3.6	3.3	4.3
Total	100.0	100.0	100.0	100.0	100.0
Head	28.8	56.0	71.4	78.4	61.2
Child	55.1	29.1	16.5	10.8	25.3
Other Relative	6.5	3.8	2.3	2.3	3.4
Nonrelative	3.0	1.9	0.9	1.1	1.6
Cohabiting	6.6	9.2	9.0	7.4	8.5
Total	100.0	100.0	100.0	100.0	100.0

NOTE: Upper panel shows living arrangements without respect to cohabitation status; lower panel shows cohabitators as a separate category.

In the bottom panel of Table 3.25 we add a separate category for cohabitation to the living arrangements classification. Eight percent of the never-married mothers are cohabiting. The fraction does not vary much by age. Note that the cohabiting persons come out of two categories: 5.8 of the 8.5 percent are family heads, and 2.8 are nonrelatives. In some cases the woman's partner is the father of the child, and in other cases he is not, but it is not possible to distinguish these two cases.[16]

Slightly over two-thirds of never-married black mothers maintain their own households (Table 3.26). This is 8 percentage points higher than for non-Hispanic white mothers. For all groups, most of those who are not householders are living in the household of a parent. Non-Hispanic white women are more likely than blacks to be living with nonrelatives, which, as the lower panel shows, means that whites are more likely than blacks to be cohabiting. The distribution of living arrangements of Mexican-Americans is very similar to that of non-Hispanic whites. However, Puerto Rican mothers are very different. Nine-tenths

[16]The statistical system would not include among the never-married mothers those who are living with the father of the child, if he is designated as the householder. This is because the relationship of all persons in the household is specified with respect to the householder. The child would be a child of householder. The mother would be a nonrelative (or roommate or partner) of householder. The relationship of the child to its mother would not be specified.

TABLE 3.26

Living Arrangements of Never-Married Women Aged 18–34
with Own Children Present, by Race-Ethnicity, 1980

	Non-Hispanic White	Black	Mexican American	Puerto Rican	Total
Householder	60.2	68.8	62.1	89.9	67.0
Child of Householder	28.7	25.1	26.1	7.8	25.3
Other Relative	2.7	3.7	4.5	0.9	3.4
Nonrelative	8.4	2.3	7.4	1.5	4.3
Total	100.0	100.0	100.0	100.0	100.0
Householder	52.6	63.8	57.8	84.5	61.2
Child of Householder	28.7	25.1	26.1	7.8	25.3
Other Relative	2.7	3.7	4.5	0.9	3.4
Nonrelative	2.5	1.0	3.6	0.6	1.6
Cohabiting	13.5	6.4	8.0	6.3	8.5
Total	100.0	100.0	100.0	100.0	100.0

NOTE: Upper panel shows living arrangements without respect to cohabitation status; lower panel shows cohabitators as a separate category.

are householders. Only 8 percent live in the parental household. This may reflect a tendency for single Puerto Rican mothers to return to their parental household in Puerto Rico.

For both black and white single mothers there was a decline between 1960 and 1970 in the fraction maintaining their own household, and a corresponding rise in the fraction living with parents (Table 3.27). During the 1970s the trend reversed. However, by 1980 the proportion maintaining their own household was lower than in 1960.

TABLE 3.27

Living Arrangements of Never-Married Women Aged 18–34
with Own Children Present, by Race, 1960–80

	Non-Hispanic White			Black		
	1960	1970	1980	1960	1970	1980
Household Head	65.7	51.4	60.2	70.3	59.4	68.8
Child of Head	15.4	38.6	28.7	13.7	32.3	25.1
Other Relative	6.5	5.6	2.7	9.2	6.2	3.7
Nonrelative	12.4	4.5	8.4	6.7	2.1	2.3
Total	100.0	100.0	100.0	100.0	100.0	100.0

TABLE 3.28

Percent of Never-Married Mothers in Families Receiving
Public Assistance, and Percent in Poverty, by Race/Ethnicity, 1980

	Received Public Assistance Income	In Poverty
Non-Hispanic White	40.6	38.7
Black	45.2	55.8
Mexican-American	42.0	49.5
Total	44.8	52.2

Public Assistance and Poverty. Nearly half of the never-married mothers received public assistance income in 1979. The proportion receiving public assistance was slightly higher for blacks than for non-Hispanic whites. Slightly over half of the mothers were living in households with incomes below the poverty line. Black mothers were more likely (56 percent) than whites (39 percent) to be in poverty (see Table 3.28).

Persons Who Never Marry

Up to this point we have been observing the experience of the never-married population at young ages. We can think of this as a population that has not *yet* married. We now turn our attention to an older, single population, most of whom will remain permanently single. The lower age limit used in this section will vary depending on the topic being considered. In some sections, age 35 will be used. Although many persons marry for the first time at ages beyond 35, the population of single persons aged 35–44 consists primarily of those who will never marry.

The fraction of persons who never marry varies from one cohort to the next. For the birth cohorts for which data are available, the fraction of men not marrying by age 55–64 has varied between 5 and 11 percent. There was an increase from 7 to 11 percent between birth cohorts of 1835–44 and 1875–84, and a decrease to 5 percent for the cohort of 1915–1924. For women, there was the same general pattern of an increase from 7 to 9 percent, and a drop back to 5 percent. Table 3.29 shows age-specific percentages never-married for each census since 1900. We do not know what the fraction will be for the more recent

TABLE 3.29
Percent Never Married at Ages 35–64, by Age and Sex,
for Total and Black Populations, 1900–80

	1900	1910	1920	1930	1940	1950	1960	1970	1980
TOTAL									
Men									
35–44	17.0	16.7	16.1	14.3	14.0	9.6	8.1	7.9	7.8
45–54	10.3	11.1	12.0	11.4	11.1	8.5	7.4	6.4	5.9
55–64	7.6	8.3	9.8	10.1	10.7	8.4	8.0	6.5	5.4
Women									
35–44	11.1	11.4	11.4	10.0	10.4	8.4	6.1	5.7	6.1
45–54	7.8	8.5	9.6	9.1	8.7	7.8	7.0	5.5	4.5
55–64	6.6	7.1	8.4	9.0	9.0	7.9	8.0	6.8	5.0
BLACK									
Men									
35–44	17.3	12.2	14.2	13.0	13.4	8.6	11.0	12.4	13.5
45–54	10.2	6.8	8.6	8.1	10.5	6.1	8.0	8.9	9.6
55–64	7.3	5.0	7.0	6.0	8.0	5.2	7.3	7.4	7.9
Women									
35–44	7.8	7.1	6.9	6.4	7.6	5.9	6.9	8.8	12.9
45–54	5.0	4.7	4.8	4.6	4.9	4.4	5.9	6.7	7.9
55–64	4.1	3.9	4.2	4.0	4.4	3.7	5.4	6.4	6.4

SOURCE: *1900, 1920*: Irene B. Taeuber and Conrad Taeuber, *People of the United States in the Twentieth Century.* Washington, D.C.: Bureau of the Census, 1971; *1910: Population 1910*, vol. 1, chap. 5, table 6. Washington, D.C.: Government Printing Office, 1913; *1930: Population 1930*, vol. 2, chap. 11, table 5. Washington, D.C.: Government Printing Office, 1933; *1940–1980*: Public Use Samples.

cohorts who are in process of delaying marriage. It will undoubtedly increase, but it is not clear by how much.[17]

Up through the 1960 census the age-specific percent never-marrying was lower for blacks than for the total population. For example, in 1910 the percent never-married at age 45–54 was 10.3 for men and 7.8 for women, compared to 6.8 and 4.7, respectively, among blacks. However, since 1960 the differential has reversed. In 1980, 6 percent of all men and 10 percent of black men were single at age 45–54. For women, 4 percent of all, and 8 percent of blacks, were single at 45–54.

Nonmarriage by Education and Age. Persons with very high and very low levels of education are overrepresented in the population that never marries. At age 45–54, one person in seven with less than five years of schooling has never married. This compares to about one in twenty in the general population. There is very little difference between men and women. The relatively high level of nonmarriage among persons with very little education probably reflects the fact that a significant share of this population has mental and/or physical defects that have prevented their progression through the educational system. These same defects may reduce their marriage probability. A significant number are institutionalized. In a later section the differential prevalence of disability among never-married and ever-married persons will be discussed.

Nonmarriage is also common at the other extreme of education, particularly among women. In 1980, 13 percent of 45–54-year-old women with seventeen or more years of education had never married. This compares to 4.5 percent of the general population and 6 percent of women with sixteen years of education. There are a number of social processes operating to produce a high level of nonmarriage among very highly educated women. Women who forego marriage may find it easier to continue their education. There may also be a selectivity to the extent that women with high professional aspirations view marriage as detrimental to their careers. Some have suggested that it is difficult for highly educated women to find husbands, because men tend to avoid marrying women with more education than themselves. Further, as noted in the previous chapter, women who substantially delay marriage in order to obtain an advanced education face a reduced number of potential spouses when they enter the marriage market. Nothing in these data speaks directly to these processes.

There has been a change over the past two decades in the differential nonmarriage by education (see Table 3.30). By 1980 very few 45–54-

[17]Willard L. Rodgers and Arland Thornton, "Changing Patterns of First Marriage in the United States," *Demography* 22 (1985):265–79.

TABLE 3.30

*Percent Never Married, at Ages 45–54,
by Education and Race/Ethnicity, 1980 and 1960*

Years of Education	Women				Men		
	Total	Non-Hispanic White	Black		Total	Non-Hispanic White	Black
				1980			
<5	14.2	21.5	15.2		15.8	20.8	16.2
5–8	5.1	4.0	8.9		7.2	6.7	10.2
9–11	3.1	2.2	7.1		5.4	4.7	9.3
12	3.6	3.3	6.8		5.0	4.7	7.4
13–15	5.9	5.6	6.3		5.1	4.8	7.2
16	5.9	5.6	6.2		5.3	5.2	8.7
17+	12.7	13.0	11.1		6.2	6.2	8.3
Total	4.5	4.0	7.8		5.9	5.5	9.4
				1960			
<5	9.0	10.5	7.6		12.9	14.8	9.0
5–8	5.4	5.4	5.4		8.2	8.2	7.7
9–11	4.7	4.7	4.0		6.1	6.0	7.5
12	7.5	7.4	7.1		6.1	6.0	7.5
13–15	8.2	8.3	7.1		5.4	5.5	5.5
16	14.5	14.7	11.5		5.7	5.7	7.9
17+	28.5	29.6	5.6		8.2	8.4	4.2
Total	7.1	7.2	5.9		7.4	7.2	8.0

year-old white (or black) women had less than 5 years of education. Of those that did, a large share had never married. Persons with disabilities undoubtedly comprise a much larger share of this group in 1980 than in earlier decades.

Among highly educated persons, nonmarriage levels have also changed, especially for women. In 1960 over one-quarter of white women with postgraduate education had not married by ages 45–54. This compares to 13 percent of women with sixteen years of education. By 1980, women with postgraduate education continued to have a relatively high prevalence of nonmarriage, but the level was much lower than in 1960—13 percent had never married (compared to 4 percent of women with 16 years of education). In 1960, women who were college graduates with no postgraduate education had a much higher than average prevalence of nonmarriage. By 1980 their rate was about the same as that of high school graduates. These changes would be consistent with the marriage market explanation mentioned earlier and the marked delay in marriage that has generally occurred over this period, that is, the market is less depleted by the time these women enter it. They may also reflect a trend toward greater social acceptability and feasibility of combining marriage with schooling and professional achievement. Women who became adults in the 1920s and 1930s appear to have had to choose between marriage and family, on the one hand, and a professional career, or the other. More recently, a larger share of women appears to have been able to pursue both.

Variation Among Racial and Hispanic Groups. The fraction of 45–49-year-olds who have never married varies among race/ethnic groups. Virtually all Korean men and women have been married. Low rates of nonmarriage occur for Vietnamese, Filipino, Chinese, and Asian Indian men and Chinese women. Higher than average nonmarriage is found among Japanese (11.2 percent), black (9.7 percent), Hawaiian (9.2 percent), Puerto Rican (8.7 percent), and American Indian (8.6 percent) men, and among Filipino (9.0 percent), Puerto Rican (8.6 percent), and black women (8.5 percent) (Table 3.31).

Disability. In the 1980 census, questions were asked concerning work disabilities. Persons were asked if they had a disability that restricted or prevented working. Among 35–54-year-olds, 9 percent of the ever-married and 23 percent of the never-married men reported a work disability. For women the proportions were 9 percent of the ever-married and 20 percent of the never-married (Table 3.32).

TABLE 3.31

Percent of 45–49-Year-Olds Never Married,
for Racial and Hispanic Groups, 1980

	Males	Females
Non-Hispanic White	5.5	3.9
Black	9.7	8.5
American Indian	8.6	4.7
Japanese	11.2	4.5
Chinese	5.2	3.3
Filipino	4.7	9.0
Korean	1.5	2.6
Asian Indian	5.0	6.1
Vietnamese	3.3	5.1
Hawaiian	9.2	6.1
Mexican	6.0	5.4
Puerto Rican	8.7	8.6
Cuban	6.8	5.2

TABLE 3.32

Prevalence of Work Disability
of Never-Married and Total Population Aged 35–54,
and of Never-Married Black and Non-Hispanic White Population,
by Sex, 1980

| | 35–44 | | | | 45–54 | | | |
| | Male | | Female | | Male | | Female | |
	Never-Married	Total	Never-Married	Total	Never-Married	Total	Never-Married	Total
No Disability	80.0	92.2	83.2	93.2	72.4	86.9	76.6	87.7
Work Disability								
Prevents Work	12.2	2.9	11.2	3.4	18.4	6.1	17.2	7.7
Does Not Prevent Work	7.8	4.9	5.5	3.4	9.2	7.0	6.3	4.7
Total	100.0	100.0	100.0	100.0	100.0	100.0	100.0	100.0

| | Never-Married 35–54 | | | |
| | Male | | Female | |
	Non-Hispanic White	Black	Non-Hispanic White	Black
No Disability	77.0	73.0	81.1	76.8
Work Disability				
Prevents Work	14.3	18.3	13.4	16.2
Does Not Prevent Work	8.6	8.7	5.6	7.1
Total	100.0	100.0	100.0	100.0

There are wide differences by education. About two-thirds of the never-married men and 70 percent of the never-married women with less than five years of education have a work disability. Fifty-four percent of the men and 61 percent of the women report that they are prevented from working. These levels are several times higher than for ever-married persons with similar eduation. At all education levels disability is much higher for the never-married than for the ever-married (Table 3.33).

Living Arrangements. The modal living arrangement of never-married persons 35–54 is as a one-person household—37 percent of the men and 30 percent of the women. The next most common living situation is as a member of the household of parents—25 percent of the men and 22 percent of the women. About one-fifth of the women and one-tenth of the men are family heads. This would include never-married mothers with their own households and persons whose parents are living with them, as well as single persons in households including other

TABLE 3.33

Percent of Never-Married and Ever-Married Persons Aged 35–54
with a Work Disability, by Education

Education	Men		Women	
	Ever-Married	Never-Married	Ever-Married	Never-Married
	*Percent with a Work Disability**			
<5	20.6	67.7	20.9	70.2
5–8	17.2	38.0	18.4	37.0
9–11	12.8	26.1	13.5	24.5
12	8.3	18.0	6.9	13.8
13–15	8.3	15.6	6.3	10.6
16+	4.2	8.6	3.8	7.0
Total	9.3	23.0	8.9	19.5
	Percent Prevented from Working			
<5	12.6	54.3	15.5	60.6
5–8	9.0	26.4	12.7	28.3
9–11	5.7	18.1	8.3	17.0
12	2.8	9.7	3.5	9.2
13–15	2.4	7.3	2.6	5.0
16+	0.8	3.4	1.3	2.7
Total	3.6	14.7	5.0	13.6

*Person has a physical, mental, or other health condition that has lasted for six months or more and either:
  a. Limits the amount and kind of work the person can do at a job, or
  b. Prevents the person from working at a job.

kin. Only a small minority—8 percent of the men and 5 percent of the women—are in group quarters (Table 3.34).

Nearly half of the black women are family heads. Blacks are less likely to be living in one-person households, and black women are less likely to be living in their parental households. Black men are more likely to be living with other relatives.

The trend in the living arrangements of never-married persons age 35–44 since 1900 is shown in Table 3.35. There was a rise for both men and women in the fraction living in one-person households, and a sharp drop, especially for men, in the fraction living as nonrelatives. This was primarily a drop in the fraction of "boarders," and occurred prior to 1940. Surprisingly, there was little change in the fraction living with

TABLE 3.34

*Living Arrangements of Never-Married 35–54-Year-Olds,
by Sex, Total and Black Population, 1980*

	Total		Black	
	Male	Female	Male	Female
Householder				
Family Head	9.4	20.6	8.3	47.6
One Person Household	36.6	30.0	30.3	18.3
Other	6.1	4.6	5.0	1.9
Nonrelative	8.1	8.0	12.4	6.9
Relative of Head				
Child	24.7	22.5	21.0	14.2
Other Relative	7.6	8.9	12.5	9.0
Group Quarters	7.5	5.4	10.5	2.2
Total	100.0	100.0	100.0	100.0

parents, nor, for men, much of a change in the fraction living with other relatives. (The decrease that did occur in these categories was in the most recent period.) In 1900, a large share of women were living with relatives and a relatively small fraction of women were boarders. Between 1900 and 1940, the fraction of women living with other relatives dropped from 30 percent to 20 percent. There was a further decline to 9 percent following 1960.

TABLE 3.35

*Living Arrangements of Never-Married Persons Aged 35–54,
by Sex, 1900–80*

	Men				Women			
	1900	1940	1960	1980	1900	1940	1960	1980
Householder								
Family	7.8	9.2	11.5	9.4	6.9	9.1	12.3	20.6
One Person	9.9	11.0	20.6	36.6	3.4	9.3	20.1	30.0
Other	5.9	3.1	2.4	6.1	2.1	3.0	2.4	4.6
Relative								
Child	19.6	23.9	29.4	24.7	28.9	31.4	31.3	22.5
Other	9.9	14.6	14.1	7.6	30.3	20.4	16.8	8.9
Nonrelative	42.4*	19.4	8.8	8.1	21.7*	14.3	7.1	8.0
Group Quarters	4.2	18.8	13.3	7.5	6.5	12.6	9.9	5.4
Not Ascertained	0.3	—	—	—	0.1	—	—	—
Total	100.0	100.0	100.0	100.0	100.0	100.0	100.0	100.0

*37.8 percent of men and 9.7 percent of women were "boarders" in 1900.

Summary

The proportion single among young adults was relatively stable between 1910 and 1940, declined rapidly over the next two decades, and then returned by 1980 to the 1940 levels. For example, among men 18–29 the proportion single dropped from 80 to 63 percent and then returned to 80 percent. Thus more of the young adult years are being spent single than was true twenty years ago. As a fraction of the total adult population, young singles increased from 9 to 16 percent between 1960 and 1980.

As noted in the discussion of marriage in Chapter 2, recent declines in marriage rates have been particularly marked among black women. As a result, the proportion single at age 24 almost doubled during the 1970s. Mexican-Americans are somewhat less likely to be single than majority white women, while Chinese and Japanese-American women are even more likely than black women to be single in their early twenties.

Education differences in age at marriage are reflected in almost twice as high a proportion single at age 24 among women who have attended college as among those who did not complete high school—47 versus 24 percent. Change in educational composition accounts for much of the increase in the percent single over the 1960s among majority whites, but less for minorities. On the other hand, there were substantial education-specific increases in the proportions single for all groups during the 1970s.

About one-third of the never-married men and two-fifths of the never-married women were enrolled in school in 1980, either full or part-time. The fraction of singles enrolled varies from one-half at ages 18–19, to one-quarter at 22–24, and one-tenth at ages 30–34. There were diverse trends by age and sex.

Employment increases with age from half at 18–19 to three-quarters at ages 25–29. Among never-married males, employment declined between 1940 and 1970 but increased markedly by 1980 to near the 1940 level. In spite of enrollment increases, employment among single women was stable over the forty years except for a peak in 1950. Single blacks were less likely to be enrolled or employed in 1980. Armed forces participation is higher among single black men than among single white men: 9 versus 6 percent at the peak ages 20–21.

Three-quarters of single persons at age 18 are living with their parents, compared to one-quarter of those still single at age 29. About one-tenth of those in the prime college years are in college dorms. The proportion of young singles living with parents declined between 1960 and 1980, and there were particularly large increases in the proportion heading their own household. Single black women are more likely to be family heads, more likely to be living in the home of a relative, and less likely to be a roommate or living in a college dorm. Mexican-Americans and Cubans are particularly likely to be living in their parental household. Among college students, almost half live with their parents and one-third live in dorms. There has been a trend toward increased proportions of students living with parents, and a decrease in the proportion living in dorms. Cohabitation is highest at ages 25–34 among single men and at ages 20–34 among single women; about one-tenth are living with a partner of the opposite sex at these ages.

Childbearing by single women increased steadily between 1940 and the early 1960s, when rates turned downward for about ten years among women age 20 and over; rates have since begun to increase again. The patterns are very different between blacks and whites, with much higher rates among blacks (about six times as high). However, since 1965 rates of childbearing among unmarried blacks have decreased.

The number of never-married adults with children has increased dramatically since 1960. Increases occurred at all ages and education levels. There were 1.3 million never-married adults with children in 1980, mostly in their twenties. Nine-tenths of these were women and three-fifths were black women.

Two-thirds of the never-married women with children maintain their own households, and about one-quarter live in the household of their parents. The fraction maintaining their own household declined between 1960 and 1970 and then increased again in 1980. Eight percent of these women are cohabiting, compared to half of the never-married men with children. Nearly half of the never-married mothers received public assistance income in 1979; the proportion was slightly higher for blacks than for non-Hispanic whites. Never-married black mothers were more likely to be in poverty than never-married white mothers: 56 versus 39 percent.

The proportion who had not married by ages 35–44 was 8 percent for white men, 6 percent for white women, and 13 percent for black men and women. Most of these persons will remain unmarried through their entire lives. It is possible that delayed marriage will result in a considerably higher nonmarriage rate for more recent cohorts. Nonmarriage is most common at the extremes of the education distribution. The lowest extreme, those who did not complete elementary school, is highly selective of persons with severe handicaps, yet five-sixths of this population had married by ages 45–54. Among women, about one-sixth of those who went beyond college had not married by these ages.

4

MARRIED COUPLES

E VEN THOUGH both the ages at which people marry and the fraction of marriages ending in separation and divorce have increased considerably in recent years, Americans continue to spend the majority of their adult years living with a spouse. Nonetheless, recent social trends have altered the experience of married couples.

1. Fertility has decreased. There has been both a reduction in the total number of births per couple and an increase in the interval between births. Couples spend more of their married lives, particularly at younger ages, with no children in the household.

2. Increased rates of divorce, combined with continuing high rates of remarriage, mean that one or both spouses has been previously married in a large and growing share of marriages. Many of these families include children brought to the marriage by one of the spouses, as well as children of the couple.

3. A large and growing proportion of American women spend much of their married lives in the labor force, affecting both the economic situation and the very character of marriage.

4. In 1980, almost all American married couples maintained their own household. Very few were doubled up with other relatives, even early in marriage. Homeownership has continued to increase: more married couples own homes, and they become homeowners earlier in their marriages.

In this chapter we will focus especially on the experience of younger married couples, since this is where much of the significant change has occurred. The experience of elderly married couples is considered in Chapter 8, along with the experience of elderly persons in other marital statuses.

Prevalence of Marriage

Figures 4.1 and 4.2 display the percent of the population currently married (spouse present) at each age for men and for women in 1940, 1960, 1970, and 1980. For both men and women, the fraction currently married reaches over three-quarters by age 35–39, and persists at about that level through age 60. The peak is slightly lower for women than for men. Between 1940 and 1960 we see the result of the acceleration of marriage associated with the postwar baby boom (discussed in Chapter 2). For both men and women, the fraction currently married was higher at every age in 1960 than in 1940. Between 1960 and 1980 there was a sharp drop in the fraction currently married at every age up to age 50. Almost all of this decrease, especially for men, occurred during the 1970s. The levels for 1960 and 1970 were quite similar.

For men at ages under 35, the fraction currently married in 1980 was almost identical to that in 1940. At older ages it was midway between the 1940 and 1960 levels. For women at ages under 40 the fraction currently married was lower in 1980 than in 1940. Most of the change at these young ages resulted from the rise in age at first marriage, but it also reflects increased marital disruption and the recent decline in remarriage rates. At the older ages the downward trend in mortality, especially during the 1970s, affects the fraction who are widows, and therefore the fraction who remain married. These trends are discussed in Chapter 5.

This same information on proportions currently married by age can be used to assess the fraction of adult years spent in marriages and how this fraction has changed over time. According to the 1980 cross-sectional probabilities of being married, men would spend 70 percent of the time between ages 20 and 59 married and living with a spouse. Women would spend 68 percent of this time married. In 1960 these percentages were 77 and 76 for men and women, respectively (see Table 4.1), while in 1940 they were almost identical to the 1980 levels (69 and 70 percent).[1]

[1]These percentages are obtained by summing the age-specific proportions married, spouse present, over the age range 20–59, and dividing this number by the 40 years represented, assuming a person surviving from age 20–59 is subjected to the period age-specific proportions married, spouse present.

FIGURE 4.1
Percent of Men Who Are Married, Spouse Present, 1940–80

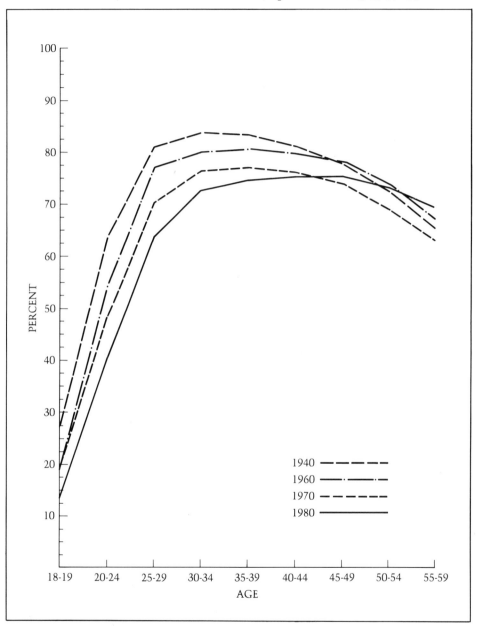

FIGURE 4.2

Percent of Women Who Are Married, Spouse Present, 1940–80

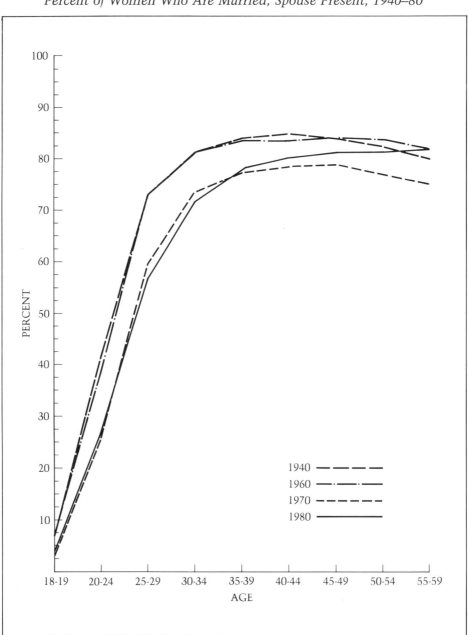

TABLE 4.1

Percent of Time Between Ages 20 and 59 That Would be
Spouse Present, Given the Age-Specific
Marital Status Distribution of a Given Year, 1940–80

	1940	1950	1960	1970	1980
TOTAL					
Male	68.6	74.4	76.9	76.7	70.1
Female	69.6	74.4	76.4	74.4	68.4
NON-HISPANIC WHITE					
Male	69.1	75.3	78.4	78.3	72.3
Female	70.7	75.9	78.7	76.9	72.1
BLACK					
Male	64.4	66.1	64.5	63.4	53.7
Female	58.4	59.6	58.2	53.7	44.1
MEXICAN-AMERICAN*					
Male	66.0	70.0	72.0	75.2	70.3
Female	68.5	71.4	73.1	72.0	68.3

*Spanish surname 1940–1960; Mexican origin or descent 1970–80.

Variation by Race/Ethnicity

There are substantial differences among major racial and ethnic groups in the fractions currently married at each age. Figures 4.3 and 4.4 plot these fractions for whites, blacks, and Mexican-Americans in 1980. At all ages, for both sexes, the percent currently married is much lower for blacks than for whites. For men aged 35–54, the majority-white level is over 80 percent, while for blacks it is just over 60 percent. For women the difference is even larger–80 percent for non-Hispanic white and 50 percent for black women.

As Figures 4.5 and 4.6 show, the proportion of blacks currently married was substantially lower in 1980 than in 1940 or 1960. This is especially true for women. There was a remarkable drop in fractions currently married during the 1970s as both the proportions divorced and single continued to increase rapidly. The pattern in 1980 implies that black men would spend 54 percent of the time between ages 20–59 in marriages, while black women would spend only 44 percent. These fractions fell from 63 percent for men and 54 percent for women in 1970 (Table 4.1).

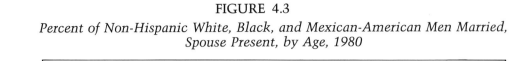

FIGURE 4.3

*Percent of Non-Hispanic White, Black, and Mexican-American Men Married,
Spouse Present, by Age, 1980*

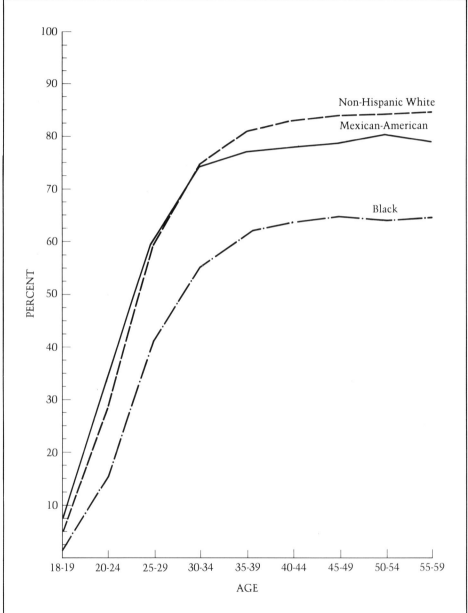

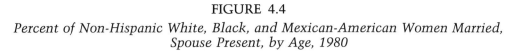

FIGURE 4.4

Percent of Non-Hispanic White, Black, and Mexican-American Women Married, Spouse Present, by Age, 1980

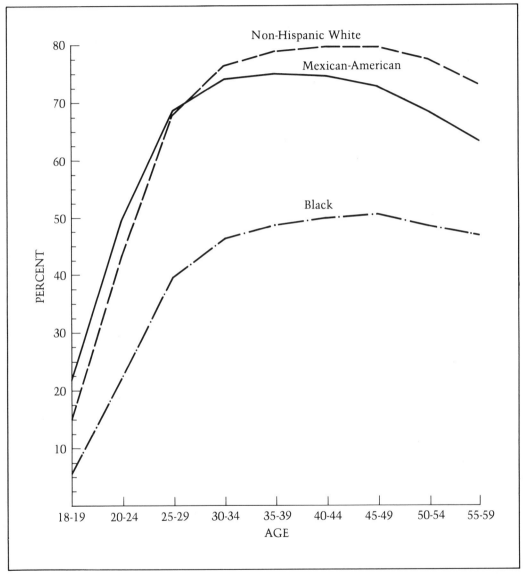

FIGURE 4.5

Percent of Black Men Who Are Married, Spouse Present, 1940–80

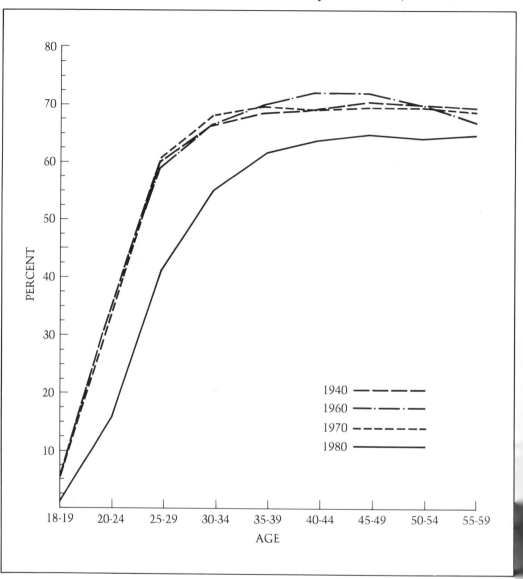

FIGURE 4.6

Percent of Black Women Who Are Married, Spouse Present, 1970–80

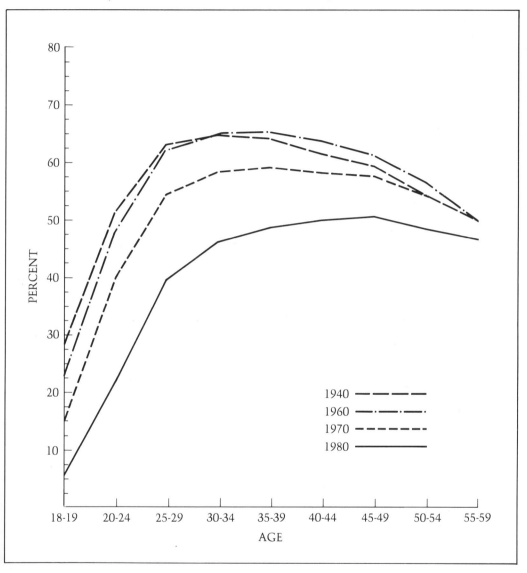

TABLE 4.2

Percent Married, Spouse Present, at Ages 35–39,
for Racial and Hispanic Groups, 1980

	Male	Female
Non-Hispanic White	80.5	78.9
Black	61.2	48.7
Chinese	81.6	84.5
Japanese	72.0	79.0
Filipino	81.0	77.3
American Indian	69.4	66.2
Korean	89.8	85.7
Asian Indian	89.5	89.6
Vietnamese	70.2	78.8
Hawaiian	72.9	68.0
Mexican	76.6	74.9
Puerto Rican	70.0	55.5
Cuban	75.6	76.6

Table 4.2 shows the percent of men and women who are currently married at age 35–39 for a number of racial and Hispanic minorities. We will describe differentials for women. The differentials for men are similar, but smaller.[2] Blacks have a much lower fraction currently married at age 35–39 than any other group (49 percent); only the level for Puerto Rican women comes close (56 percent). Other groups with lower than average levels are American Indians (66 percent) and Hawaiians (68 percent). All other groups have fractions of 35–39-year-old women who are currently married in the range from 75 percent to 90 percent. The Asian groups are at the high end of the range, and the Hispanic groups at the low end.

Reproductive Patterns and the Presence of Children

Fluctuations in fertility have been both cause and consequence of changes in household composition and family life. Trends in the proportion of couples having children, the number they have, and the ages at which they have them, are associated with differences in the composi-

---

[2]For most groups there is a fairly close correspondence between the levels for men and women. Among blacks and Puerto Ricans, however, the proportion of men who are currently married is considerably higher than the proportion of women. For both groups, this may reflect a high rate of underenumeration of unmarried men. For Puerto Ricans it may also reflect selective migration patterns.

FIGURE 4.7

Live Births and Fertility Rates, United States, 1910–80

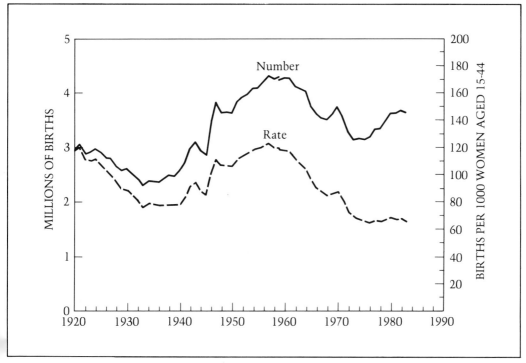

NOTE: Beginning 1959 trend lines are based on registered live births: trend lines for 1910–59 are based on live births adjusted for underregistration.

SOURCE: *Monthly Vital Statistics Report*, vol. 31, no. 8, Supplement, Advance Report of Final Natality Statistics, 1980. U. S. Department of Health and Human Services, November 30, 1982.

tion of households over time, and with the proportion of the life cycle individuals spend in parenting.

The trend in American fertility is characterized by a long-term decline, substantially interrupted by the period known as the "baby boom" (see Figure 4.7). Fertility declined from very high levels in the early 1800s to levels in the 1930s which were too low to maintain the population over the long run. Demographers and family sociologists at the time were convinced that the changing structure of society and the reduced functions of the family had made children too costly relative to other social goods.[3] The continuation of the low, and probably even lower, fertility level was seen as implicit in the structure of modern industrial society. Some modest recovery of fertility was expected with

[3]Warren S. Thompson and P. K. Whelpton, *Population Trends in the United States* (New York: Gordon & Breach, 1969).

demobilization after World War II, but nothing as large and as sustained as the baby boom. Because of this failure to predict a major fluctuation in the birth rate, the baby boom has held particular importance in attempts to understand the nature and future course of fertility in the United States and in other developed countries with low fertility.

An evaluation of the arguments that have been offered to explain the movement of fertility during the twentieth century is beyond the objectives of this volume, but we note several key points in passing.

1. Many of the most critical elements of the historical context of the baby boom seem to be captured in Easterlin's explanation.[4] These include: (a) the facilitation of earlier marriage and more rapid childbearing by an expanding postwar economy, including changes in the economic setting such as mortgage programs and the extension of consumer credit generally; (b) the enhancement of these economic gains for persons entering the labor force because of the reduced competition that resulted from their having been born in a time of low fertility; and finally, (c) the perception of relative economic well-being that came from the contrast of these conditions to the conditions these cohorts had experienced while being raised during the Depression. There is considerable debate about whether, in addition to being a useful explanation of an important demographic event, this constitutes a theory that would predict a new baby boom when recent low-fertility cohorts enter the childbearing years.[5]

2. Whatever the origin of the baby boom, it was characterized by three major demographic components: (a) an acceleration in the timing of marriage and first births[6]; (b) an increase in average family size that was largely a consequence of a greater proportion of women having at least two children[7]; and (c) a high level of "unwanted" fertility[8] among

[4]Richard A. Easterlin, "The American Baby Boom in Historical Perspective," National Bureau of Economic Research Occasional Paper #79, 1962; Easterlin, "Relative Economic Status and the American Fertility Swing," in Eleanor Bernert Sheldon, ed., Family Economic Behavior: Problems and Prospects (Philadelphia: Lippincott, 1973); Easterlin, Birth and Fortune: The Impact of Numbers on Personal Welfare (New York: Basic Books, 1980).

[5]Arland Thornton, "Fertility and Income, Consumption Aspirations, and Child Quality Standards," Demography 16 (1979):157–76; J. F. Ermisch, "Economic Opportunities, Marriage Squeezes and the Propensity to Marry: An Economic Analysis of Period Marriage Rates in England and Wales," Population Studies 35 (1981):347–56; D. P. Smith, "A Reconsideration of Easterlin Cycles," Population Studies 35 (1981):247–64.

[6]Norman B. Ryder, "Components of Temporal Variations in American Fertility," in Robert W. Hiorns, ed., Demographic Patterns in Developed Societies, vol. 19, Symposia of the Society for the Study of Human Biology (London: Taylor & Francis, 1980).

[7]Ibid.

[8]Unwanted births are those reported as having occurred after their mother wanted no more children.

women who had three or more children.[9] In fact, the level of wanted fertility reported by the women who gave birth to the baby boom was not far above that required for a stable population over the long run. A substantial part of the reduction over the 1960s was associated with the increasing prevention of accidental pregnancy.[10]

3. Recent low levels of fertility are consistent with the longer trend and are shared with almost all developed countries, including both socialist and capitalist, Catholic and Protestant countries.[11]

We will first review the trend in the size of completed families, and then describe the consequences of increasing delays in parenthood on family composition.

Completed Family Size

Figure 4.8 shows the distribution of completed family size for women born in successive five-year periods (for women who married by age 40). The increase in the proportion having at least two children is best seen in the contrast between the high and low fertility cohorts. The average number of births for the high fertility cohort, born in 1935–39, was 3.04 compared to 2.41 among the women born in 1905–1914. Only 7 percent were childless and 10 percent had one child in the high fertility cohort, compared to 18 percent childless and an additional 20 percent with one child in the earlier cohorts. However, the proportion having five or more was only somewhat greater, 18 versus 13 percent, and this difference resulted from the higher transitions at lower parities.[12] We know very little about how such a high proportion of these low fertility cohorts was able to live through approximately twenty years of married life and avoid having more births. Given what we know about the failure rates of the contraceptive methods then being used, it seems very likely that abortion played a substantial role in this accomplishment.

Figure 4.9 shows the distribution of children ever born for ever-married black women. For all cohorts the mean number of children ever born is higher for blacks than for the total. Black women born in 1930–34 had an average of 4.00 children, three-quarters of a child more than

[9]Charles F. Westoff and Norman B. Ryder, *The Contraceptive Revolution* (Princeton, N.J.: Princeton University Press, 1977).

[10]Charles F. Westoff, "The Decline in Unwanted Fertility 1971–76," *Family Planning Perspectives* 13 (1981):70–1.

[11]Ibid.

[12]The probability of having another child among women with four or more children actually went down during the baby boom.

FIGURE 4.8

Distribution of Completed Family Size, for Cohorts of 1895–99 and 1935–39, Women Married by Age 40

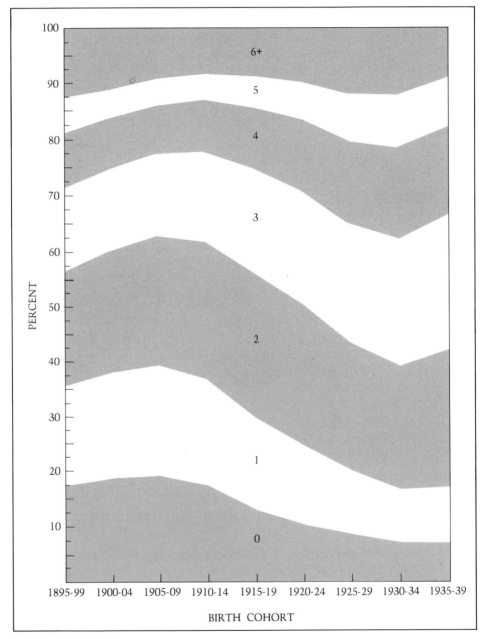

FIGURE 4.9

*Distribution of Completed Family Size, by Cohorts of Black Women
1895–99 to 1935–39, Married by Age 40*

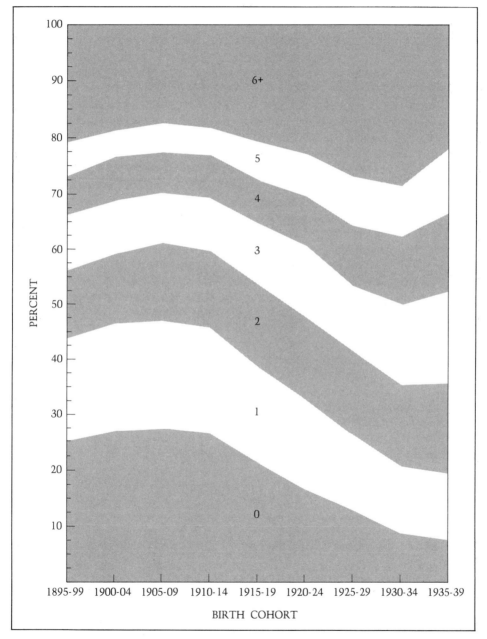

the average for the total population. For earlier cohorts the differential was smaller—closer to one-third of a child. This is a much higher level of fertility than that of the cohorts born earlier in the century. Black women in the birth cohort of 1905–09 had a mean family size of 2.76, with 28 percent childless and 20 percent with only one child. Thus the level of childlessness among black women was even higher than that for other women of these cohorts. Some have speculated that this may reflect impaired fecundity in addition to intentional factors.[13] Black women in these cohorts, as well as in all successive cohorts, also had a much higher fraction with very large families. Seventeen percent of the

TABLE 4.3

Distribution of Completed Family Size of Women Aged 40–44,*
by Education and Race/Ethnicity, 1980

Completed Family Size	Years of Education					
	<9	9–11	12	13–15	16+	Total
NON-HISPANIC WHITE						
0	6.0	4.6	6.1	7.1	11.5	8.7
1	9.5	8.3	9.5	9.4	11.8	12.1
2	19.4	20.5	27.2	29.5	34.0	27.8
3	19.9	23.2	26.6	27.8	25.8	23.4
4	17.7	19.0	16.9	15.3	11.0	14.0
5	11.6	12.8	8.0	6.4	3.8	7.0
6+	15.9	11.4	5.8	4.5	2.1	7.0
Total	100.0	100.0	100.0	100.0	100.0	100.0
Average	3.50	3.39	2.90	2.75	2.35	2.92
BLACK						
0	8.8	6.8	8.4	7.0	12.8	12.6
1	9.3	9.3	11.8	14.7	21.5	14.2
2	10.7	11.6	17.4	20.8	27.0	16.4
3	13.3	14.2	18.2	21.0	19.4	14.9
4	10.3	13.4	16.4	17.2	8.3	11.8
5	11.9	14.7	11.5	9.8	6.6	9.0
6+	35.8	30.0	16.2	9.6	4.3	21.2
Total	100.0	100.0	100.0	100.0	100.0	100.0
Average	4.59	4.27	3.40	3.07	2.27	3.66

*Women first married by age 40.

[13]Joseph McFalls, "The Impact of VD on the Fertility of the Black Population, 1880–1950," *Social Biology* 20 (1973):2–19; Reynolds Farley, *Growth of the Black Population* (Chicago: Markham, 1970).

cohort of black women born in 1905–09 had six or more children, compared to 9 percent for the total cohort. Twenty-seven percent of the black cohort of 1930–34 had six or more children versus 12 percent for all women in the cohort.

Completed family size is smaller, the greater the level of education (Table 4.3). Over 40 percent of the non-Hispanic white women who did not complete high school had four or more children. This compares with about 30 percent for high school graduates and 17 percent for college graduates. Nearly one-quarter of college graduates had fewer than two children, compared to 16 percent among the high school graduates and 13 percent among the high school dropouts. The differential by education is even larger for blacks.

Expected Completed Family Size

Some sense of the eventual completed family size distribution of younger women may be obtained from their stated birth expectations.[14] Questions on birth expectations have not been asked in the decennial censuses, but are routinely asked by the Census Bureau in the June Current Population Survey.

In June 1981, about one-tenth of women aged 18–34 expected to remain childless, and an additional 14 percent expected to have only one child (see Table 4.4). Slightly less than one-half expected to have two children, and nearly one-tenth expected to have four or more children. Thus, if these women fulfill their expectations, the fraction who are childless or have one child will not be much different from that of women who were reproducing during the baby boom. However, it is very likely that the proportion remaining childless will be much higher, as many who are delaying parenthood will eventually decide not to have a child after all.[15] Some estimates suggest that as many as one-quarter

[14]Women who are still in the reproductive ages are asked not only how many children they have already had, but also how many additional babies they expect to have. These two values are added together to get expected completed family size. In the Current Population Surveys these data on birth expectations are flawed by a fairly high level of nonreporting on birth expectation. Among 30–34-year-olds, 9 percent said they were uncertain with respect to whether they would have additional children, and another 9 percent did not report on their expectations. S. Philip Morgan has demonstrated that those who are uncertain are very likely in the process of deciding not to have any more children. Morgan, "Parity-Specific Fertility Intentions and Uncertainty: The United States, 1970–1976," *Demography* 19(1982):315–34. See also "Fertility of American Women: June 1985," Current Population Reports, Series P-20, No. 406, June 1986, pp. 7–8.

[15]Ronald R. Rindfuss and Larry L. Bumpass, "Age and the Sociology of Fertility," in Karl Taeuber, Larry Bumpass, and James Sweet, eds., *Social Demography* (New York: Academic Press, 1978); James A. Sweet, "Work and Fertility," in Greer Litton Fox, ed., *The Childbearing Decision: Fertility Attitudes and Behavior* (Beverly Hills, Calif.: Sage Publications, 1982).

TABLE 4.4

Distribution of Expected Completed Family Size of Women of All Marital Statuses, Aged 18–34 and 25–29, by Race/Ethnicity, 1981

| | Total Number of Children Expected | | | | | |
	None	1	2	3	4 +	Total
18–34						
White	11.2	13.8	48.8	17.4	8.7	100.0
Black	9.0	19.0	37.8	20.4	13.9	100.0
Spanish Origin	7.1	14.1	41.8	19.9	17.0	100.0
Total	10.9	14.4	47.5	17.8	9.3	100.0
25–29						
White	10.9	15.2	49.3	17.3	7.3	100.0
Black	8.5	16.7	38.1	22.7	14.1	100.0
Spanish Origin	4.8	15.3	39.3	22.8	17.8	100.0
Total	10.6	15.4	47.8	18.1	8.1	100.0

SOURCE: U.S. Census Bureau, *Fertility of American Women: June 1981*, table 9. Current Population Reports, Series P-20, #378. Washington, D.C.: Bureau of the Census, 1983.

of these cohorts will remain childless.[16] There will also be a sharp reduction in the fraction of four- or more-child families and a heavy concentration of families with two children.

The level of the "expected family size" of all women in the childbearing ages combines mostly past experience for the older women (including any unwanted births they may have had) with the projected experience of younger women. The number of children expected by women ages 18–24 in 1980 was 2.0. This level is slightly below that necessary to maintain long-run stability, but is still above the level of 1.8 implied by annual fertility rates that have persisted for over a decade.

Expected completed family size varies by race/ethnicity. A higher fraction of black women than white women expects to have only one child. Also, a higher fraction of blacks expects to have three- or more-child families. Persons of Spanish origin expect to have a larger proportion of families with four or more children and a smaller proportion of two-child families.

Education differences in expected family size are also apparent for these cohorts. Figure 4.10 shows the distributions in 1980 for women

[16]David Bloom and James Trussell, "What Are the Determinants of Delayed Childbearing and Permanent Childlessness in the United States?" *Demography* 21 (1984):613–23.

FIGURE 4.10

Distribution of Expected Completed Family Size, by Education,
All Women Aged 30–34, 1980

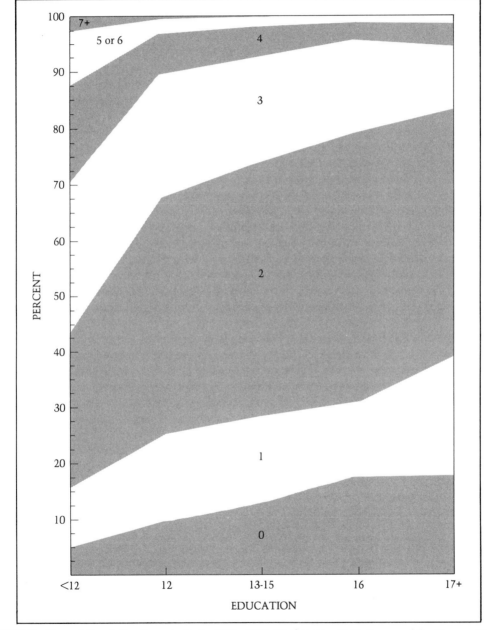

SOURCE: Current Population Reports, Series P-20, #375. Washington, D.C.: Bureau of the Census, 1982.

aged 30–34. Women with a college degree are more likely to expect to remain childless than those with less education. Women who did not complete high school are much more likely to expect three or more children than those with more education. Among whites, 40 percent of the high school dropouts, 30 percent of the high school graduates and college dropouts, and about 20 percent of the women with college degrees expect to have three or more children. Among blacks the same pattern prevails—50 percent of the high school dropouts, 35 percent of the high school graduates, and 25 percent of the college-educated women expect to have three or more children.[17]

Another way of getting a more current picture of group differences in fertility is to examine births in the last few years. This can be approximated with census data by the number of own children under age three. Racial and ethnic differences in this measure are shown in Table 4.5.

TABLE 4.5

Fertility Measures for Racial and Hispanic Groups, 1980

	Children Ever Born per Women Age 40–49†	Recent Fertility*	
		Crude	Age Standardized‡
Non-Hispanic White	3.01	333	334
Black	3.83	365	366
American Indian	4.13	416	397
Japanese	2.20	318	331
Chinese	2.82	356	350
Filipino	3.03	412	433
Korean	2.42	369	384
Asian Indian	2.72	382	371
Vietnamese	4.62	448	449
Hawaiian	4.09	406	406
Mexican	4.46	491	460
Puerto Rican	3.59	414	397
Cuban	2.18	294	312

*Number of own children under age 3 per thousand married, spouse present women under age 40

†First married by age 40.

‡Standardized on the age distribution of the total population of married women in 1980.

[17]These data on birth expectations are computed for all women, not just the ever-married. A large, but unknown, fraction of the never-married women aged 30–34 will marry by the time they are 40.

TABLE 4.6

Recent Fertility* of Married, Husband Present, Women Under Age 40,
by Education, for Total, Black, and Mexican-American Women, 1980

Years of Education	Crude			Age Standardized†		
	Total	Black	Mexican-American	Total	Black	Mexican-American
< 9	395	370	551	413	414	581
9–11	368	382	520	353	371	481
12	335	374	460	330	366	451
13–15	340	359	406	326	347	388
16	358	385	385	320	361	346
17 +	328	356	—	283	338	—

*Number of own children under age 3 per thousand married, spouse present, women under age 40.

†Standardized on the age distribution of the group.

Because the various groups may have very different age distributions, age-standardized comparisons are shown in the second column. The highest fertility levels (age standardized) are found for Mexican-Americans (.460), Vietnamese (.449), and Filipinos (.443). Very low levels of recent marital fertility are found among Cubans (.312), Japanese (.331), non-Hispanic whites (.334), and Chinese (.350).

Education comparisons are presented in Table 4.6. Since the education groups also may have very different age distributions, the comparisons are again standardized on age. There is an inverse relationship between recent fertility and education, but the differences are slight except at the extremes of the distribution. Recent fertility is 25 percent higher than average among women who have not gone beyond the ninth grade, and 14 percent lower than average among those who have gone beyond college graduation. There is almost no difference, however, among the majority whose completed education is high school graduation, some college, or college graduation. For blacks, women at both extremes of the education distribution have *lower* than average fertility, but there is little variation in between. The Mexican-American population continues to show a sharp inverse relationship between education and fertility.

Delayed Childbearing

The timing of a couple's first child is very important for the family composition of a population and for the life cycle experience of individuals and couples. The interval between marriage and first birth is hard to measure, however, because, until many years after marriage, it is difficult to distinguish couples who are delaying a first birth from those who will never have one. For example, a woman who marries at age 24 and who has not had a child by age 35 may never have a child or may have a very long first birth interval. Furthermore, although it is customary to think about child spacing *within marriage,* and to compare the average interval between marriage and first birth, it is clear that many women begin childbearing prior to marriage. The prevalence of both premarital pregnancy and premarital birth have been discussed in Chapter 2.

Despite these ambiguities, the data show that couples are delaying their first births longer after marriage. Table 4.7 presents the percent of women in successive marriage cohorts who have borne a child between the eighth and eighteenth month of marriage. (These are early marital births, excluding both premarital births and premarital conceptions. These data have been limited to women who did not give birth prior to or within the first seven months of marriage.) The proportion of such couples who had a pregnancy and birth in the first year and a half of marriage rose to 44 percent for the 1955–59 cohort and has since been cut almost in half, to 22 percent.

As a result of these changes in reproductive behavior within marriage, and the changes in premarital births and pregnancies noted in Chapter 2, more young couples in the 1980s spend more of the early years of their marriage with no children present.

Among majority-white couples, about 15 percent of those married

TABLE 4.7

Percent of Marriage Cohorts Having First Birth
Between the 8th and 18th Month of First Marriage

Marriage Cohort	Percent
1940–44	32.3
1945–49	36.9
1950–54	39.2
1955–59	44.3
1960–64	41.2
1965–69	31.9
1970–74	22.5

NOTE: Base excludes women who had birth prior to, or within first 7 months of marriage.

SOURCE: U.S. Census Bureau, *Childspacing Among Birth Cohorts of American Women: 1905 to 1959,* table 7. Current Population Reports, series P-20, no. 385. Washington, D.C.: Bureau of the Census, 1984.

TABLE 4.8

Percent of Married Couples Married 12–23 Months and 24–35 Months With Own Children Present (both spouses married once, wife under 40 at marriage), by Selected Characteristics, 1960, 1970, and 1980

	Percent with Own Children At:					
	12–23 Months			24–35 Months		
	1960	1970	1980	1960	1970	1980
WIFE'S EDUCATION (Years)						
< 9	67.5	61.8	65.7	77.2	76.0	80.8
9–11	69.5	67.4	65.7	80.1	81.3	77.7
12	62.2	51.1	43.0	74.7	66.7	57.0
13–15	57.3	37.0	30.6	70.9	58.0	45.2
16	46.3	24.1	18.4	62.6	39.5	30.5
17 +	44.9	17.1	16.7	56.4	37.7	26.1
Total	62.5	47.4	39.4	74.4	64.0	52.6
RACE AND ETHNIC GROUPS						
Non-Hispanic White	61.1	44.8	34.9	74.9	62.0	48.8
Black	71.1	61.4	66.1	71.3	73.0	69.9
Mexican-American	78.5	69.6	60.9	84.3	77.6	72.5

less than six months have children present (see Table 4.8).[18] This proportion increases to 36 percent by 12–17 months, one-half by 27–36 months, and three-quarters by 60–71 months.

The pattern for blacks is very different. Nearly one-half of the black couples have children present at the time of their first marriage (see Chapter 2), and three-quarters have children present by 36–47 months after marriage. By seven to eight years of marriage, nine-tenths of both black and white couples have own children present.

There has been a tremendous decrease since 1960 in the fraction of recently married couples with children at a given duration of marriage. Among non-Hispanic white couples married 12–17 months, 54 percent had children in 1960, 43 percent in 1970, and 36 percent in 1980. At 24–35 months the fraction with children dropped from 75 percent in 1960 to 62 percent in 1970, and to 49 percent in 1980 (see Figure 4.11). There has been very little change for blacks (Figure 4.12).

[18]The numbers in Table 4.8 are biased upward by an unknown amount. For reasons discussed in footnote 2 of Chapter 2, year of marriage is ambiguous and had to be randomly assigned when quarter of birth and quarter of marriage were the same. This means that some persons in the 12–23 months interval had actually been married 24–35 months. We believe that the trend and differentials are represented adequately in these data, but that levels are overstated.

FIGURE 4.11

Percent of Non-Hispanic White Couples with Own Children Present,
by Marriage Duration, 1960–80

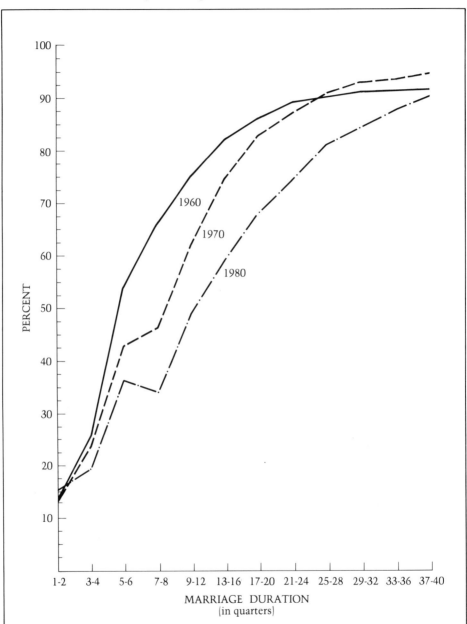

FIGURE 4.12

Percent of Black Couples with Own Children Present,
by Marriage Duration, 1960–80

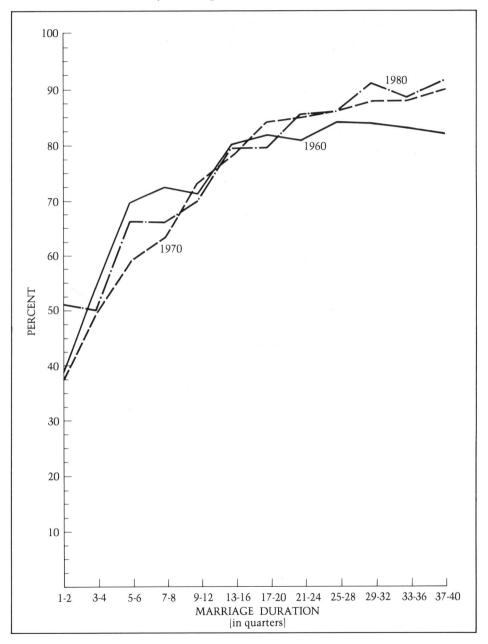

Table 4.8 shows that this change in early child spacing occurred earliest and most rapidly for the better educated couples. There has been little or no change since 1960 in the duration-specific fractions with own children for couples with wives who did not complete high school. For couples with wives who were high school graduates, the fraction with children at 12–17 months decreased by 20 points, while those with college educated wives experienced a 30 point decrease. At 24–35 months, the decrease was 18 points for high school graduates and 31 points for college graduates.

Family Composition

Changing patterns of marriage and childbearing have resulted in changes in the probability that a married person of a given age will have young children in the household. In 1960, 78 percent of married couples with 25–29-year-old husbands had a preschool-age child (Table 4.9). By 1980 the percentage had declined to 60. At age 35–39, over one-half of the married men had a preschool-age child in 1960; by 1980 it was slightly over one-third. The proportion of 45–49-year-old married men with a preschool-age child decreased from one-sixth in 1960 to less than 7 percent by 1980.

These changes are the result of several trends. Parents have fewer children, and, as we have seen, very large families are very rare. How-

TABLE 4.9

Percent of Married Couples with a Preschool Child (under age 6) in the Household, by Age of Husband, 1940–80

Age of Husband	1940	1950	1960	1970	1980
< 25	46.3	53.8	62.6	52.1	49.4
25–29	56.8	67.6	78.3	70.5	59.7
30–34	53.8	66.6	71.6	64.8	57.5
35–39	41.6	50.1	53.0	45.0	34.9
40–44	27.2	33.3	32.5	24.9	16.2
45–49	16.4	17.5	16.6	11.4	6.6
50–54	8.7	7.6	6.9	4.4	2.5
55–59	4.1	3.3	3.2	2.0	1.0
Total	32.7	39.2	40.6	34.3	29.9

ever, parents are now older on average at the birth of the first child because of delayed marriage ages, and children tend to be born at longer intervals.

The Empty Nest

Family demographers have labeled the period of the life cycle between parenting and retirement or widowhood as the "empty nest" stage.[19] There has been little effort empirically to describe this stage beyond Glick's and others' efforts to summarize its average duration.[20]

In Figure 4.13 are data from the 1980 census on the percent of women at each age between 30 and 64 with no children present in the household. The universe for this measure is ever-married women who have borne at least one child. The upper curve shows the percent of such women who have no own children under the age of 18 living with them. The lower curve shows the percent who have no sons or daughters of any age living with them. (If the woman is living in the "child's" household, she is regarded as not having a child present. She must be the householder or wife of the householder in order to be regarded as having children present.)

There is great variation in the age of entry into the empty nest stage. By age 40, about 10 percent of the women have no sons or daughters living with them, and 20 percent have no children under age 18. At age 55, about 12 percent still have a minor son or daughter living them, and 40 percent have at least one of their offspring still at home. Even at age 65, one woman in six still has a son or daughter at home.

Table 4.10 summarizes these data differently, showing selected decile and quartile values. By age 53, one-half of the women have no children (of any age) living with them, and by age 60, one-quarter of women still have at least one of their children living with them.

There is surprising little variation by education in the age of mothers when the last child has left home (bottom panel of Table 4.10). Although women with less education have more children, they tend to begin having them earlier. It is not clear how the ages of children when they leave home may vary by education of mother.

[19]Paul Glick, "Updating the Life Cycle of the Family," *Journal of Marriage and the Family* 39 (1977):5–13; Arthur Norton, "The Influence of Divorce on Traditional Life Cycle Measures," *Journal of Marriage and the Family* 42 (1980):63–9.
[20]See James A. Sweet, "The Timing and Duration of the 'Empty Nest' Stage of the Family Life Cycle," University of Wisconsin Center for Demography & Ecology Working Paper 81–25, 1981, for a discussion of some conceptual and operational problems with the "empty nest" idea.

FIGURE 4.13

Percent of Ever-Married Mothers with No Children in Household, by Age, 1980

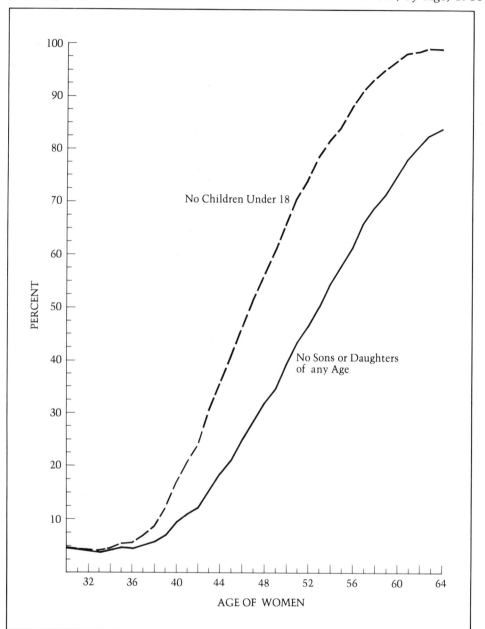

TABLE 4.10

Age at Which Specified Percent of Women No Longer Have
Children at Home: 1980 (universe limited to
ever-married women with one or more children ever born)

Percent	No Children Under 18	No Sons or Daughters of Any Age
10%	38.4	40.3
25%	42.2	46.0
50%	46.8	53.0
75%	52.3	60.1
90%	56.7	*

No Sons or Daughters of Any Age

Education of Mother (Years)

	<9	9–11	12	13–15	16+
25%	46.2	44.4	46.0	46.0	47.5
50%	53.7	52.0	53.0	52.7	53.6
75%	61.4	60.1	60.0	59.4	59.6

*The 90th percentile is over age 65, but was not computed. At age 65, 18 percent of never-married mothers have children living in their household.

Couples with Spouses Married More Than Once

In Chapter 2 we focused on the spouse's previous marital status among persons who were recently married for the first time. Here we examine the fraction of all existing marriages involving remarried spouses. A large and growing fraction of married couples includes spouses who have previously been married. Of the 49.5 million married couples in the United States in 1980, 11.2 million (22.6 percent) have one or both spouses who were previously married. Seventeen percent of the couples have husbands who have been married more than once and 16 percent have wives who have been married more than once. These two numbers add to considerably more than 22.6 percent because 10 percent of all married couples have both spouses who are remarried (see Table 4.11). As noted in Chapter 2, this proportion reached about 40 percent for recent marriages. The fraction of couples with one or both spouses in a second or higher-order marriage is somewhat higher for blacks (28 percent) than for whites (22 percent). It is somewhat lower for Mexican-Americans (17 percent).

TABLE 4.11

Distribution of Married Couples, by Whether or Not Each
Spouse Has Been Married More Than Once, 1980

Number of Times Each Spouse Has Been Married	Total	Ethnicity of Husband		
		Non-Hispanic White	Black	Mexican-American
Husband Married More Than Once				
Wife Married Once	6.7	6.4	9.7	6.4
Wife Married More Than Once	10.2	10.5	10.7	5.4
Wife Married More Than Once				
Husband Married Once	5.7	5.7	7.0	5.4
Both Spouses Married Once	77.4	77.5	72.5	82.8
Total	100.0	100.0	100.0	100.0

FIGURE 4.14

Percent of Couples with One or Both Spouses Married More Than Once,
by Age of Husband, 1960–80

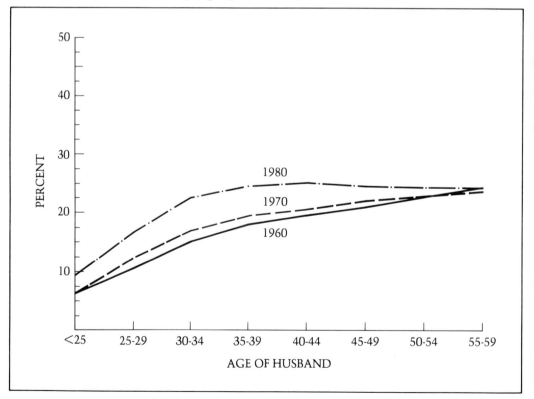

The fraction of couples with at least one spouse who has previously been married increases with age from about 10 percent for husbands under age 25, to 25 percent at ages 35–39. Beyond 35–39 the fraction does not increase further. (See Figures 4.14 and 4.15.) These cross-sectional age differences reflect the complex effects of rapid increase in marital disruption and age patterns of marriage, marital disruption, and remarriage. Among blacks the fraction continues to increase beyond ages 35–39, and reaches 35 percent by ages 55–59. As we will discuss in Chapter 5, blacks have a higher rate of separation and divorce but a lower rate of remarriage.

The fraction of married couples with at least one spouse in a remarriage increased only slightly during the 1960s, but during the 1970s the increase was very rapid. For example, in 1960, 18 percent of couples with husbands aged 35–39 included a remarried spouse. The fraction

FIGURE 4.15

Percent of Black Couples with One or Both Spouses Married More Than Once, by Age of Husband, 1960–80

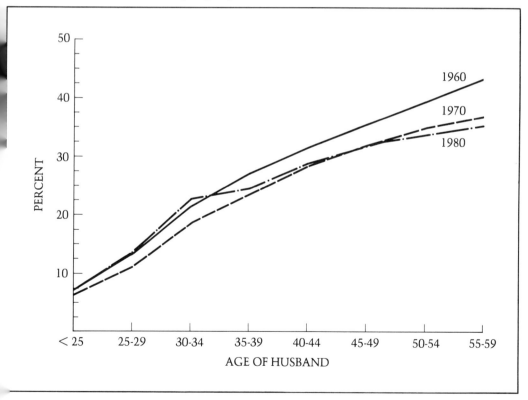

increased to 20 percent in 1970, and to 25 percent in 1980. Among black couples, however, the trend at ages beyond 30 has been in the opposite direction, with *lower* fractions of couples with a remarried partner in 1970 than in 1960, and little change during the 1970s. This reflects the low, and declining, level of remarriage among blacks.

Employment

Among the most significant changes in American society in the period since World War II has been the increasing participation of women in the labor force. To provide more of a context for considering the employment trends of married women we begin with an overview of changing life course patterns of employment of American women of all marital statuses. In 1980, 51 percent of all women age 16 and over were in the labor force. This compares to 77 percent for men. There has been a more or less continuous rise in the employment rate of women during the past century. At about the turn of the century it is estimated that about 20 percent of American women were in the labor force. By 1940, this figure had risen to about 26 percent. Following World War II there was an acceleration in the trend, and by 1950, 34 percent of all women were in the labor force. Ten years later, 38 percent were in the labor force, and by 1970, 43 percent. In the next decade the rate rose to the level of 51 percent.[21]

Associated with this rise in the overall rate of employment, there have been significant changes in the life cycle patterns of employment of American women. Before World War II working women tended to be young, single women; widows or women abandoned by their husbands; or impoverished immigrant or black wives.[22] In the period from World War II to the mid-1960s there was a rapid increase in employment of middle-aged married women whose children were of high school age or beyond. Since 1960 there has been a rapid rise in the rate of employment of married women with preschool-aged children.

[21]Gertrude Bancroft, *The American Labor Force: Its Growth and Changing Composition* (New York: Wiley, 1958), and John Durand, *The Labor Force in the United States: 1890 to 1960* (New York: Social Science Research Council, 1948), provides reviews of employment patterns through the 1940s. Other studies of patterns and trends of the employment of women include Glen Cain, *Married Women in the Labor Force: An Econometric Analysis* (Chicago: University of Chicago Press, 1966); William Bowen and T. Aldrich Finegan, *The Economics of Labor Force Participation* (Princeton, N.J.: Princeton University Press, 1969); James A. Sweet, *Women in the Labor Force* (New York: Seminar Press, 1973); Valerie K. Oppenheimer, *The Female Labor Force in the United States: Demographic and Economic Factors Governing Its Growth and Changing Composition* (Westport, Conn.: Greenwood Press, 1970); and Ralph E. Smith, ed., *The Subtle Revolution: Women at Work* (Washington, D.C.: The Urban Institute, 1979).

[22]Robert Smuts, *Women and Work in America* (New York: Columbia University Press, 1959).

FIGURE 4.16

Age Patterns of Employment for Birth Cohorts of Women

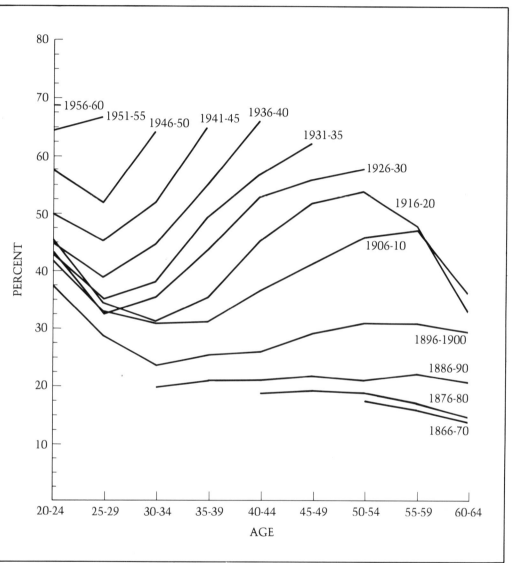

NOTE: Dates on lines refer to the years of birth of women whose experience is being followed.

In Figure 4.16, the age patterns of employment for various birth cohorts of women are plotted. The first cohort for which we have complete information are women born in 1896–1900. This cohort experienced a drop in employment between ages 20–24, 25–29, and 30–34, and then a slow rise in employment from ages 30–34 through ages 55–59. The later cohorts experienced the same pattern of decline at the marriage and childbearing ages. Each successive cohort shows a steeper and steeper rise in the thirties and forties.

There is very little change in labor force participation rates at ages 20–24 for the cohorts of 1906–10 to 1936–40. The rates of employment of later cohorts at age 20–24 have been much higher. The cohort born in 1954–56 had a rate of employment at age 20–24 of nearly 70 percent. Thus, the more recent cohorts have experienced sharper rises in employment at the ages beyond 30, and the very recent cohorts also have much higher rates at ages 20–24 and 25–29. These recent cohorts are the ones who have married later and have had very low fertility.

The age pattern of employment of women reflects, in large part, changing marital and family status. Women in their late teens and early twenties are often unmarried and in school. Through the twenties a growing share of women are married and have young children present. As women age through the thirties, fewer and fewer have preschool children. Through the forties and fifties children begin to leave the parental household and form families of their own.

Family Composition and the Employment Rates of Married Women

Employment rates of married women increase as their children get older. Although it does not represent the actual experience of a cohort over time, the best way to see this is to classify women by the age of their youngest child. In 1980, 38 percent of women with a child under age 1 were employed (see Figure 4.17). This rate increases by 7 points to 45 percent for women with youngest child age 1, and by an additional 5 points to 50 percent for women with a youngest child age 2. Between age of youngest child 2 to 7 years there is a gradual increase to about 60 percent. Beyond age 7 there is no further increase through age 17. The number of children in the household also affects the employment rate of married women, independently of its correlation with age of youngest own child. Childless women are much more likely to be working than women who have children, and at any age of youngest child, women with more children have lower employment rates.

Variation by Education and Family Economic Need

The greater the level of family economic need, the higher the rate of employment of the wife (Figure 4.18). Specifically, if a married wom-

FIGURE 4.17

*Employment Rates of Married Women, Husband Present,
by Age of Youngest Own Child, 1940–80*

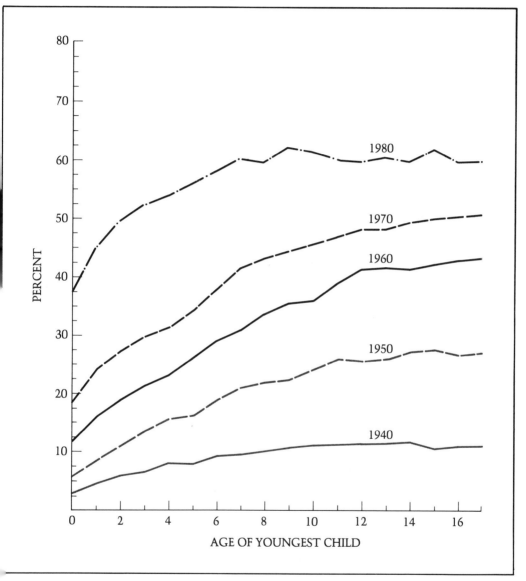

FIGURE 4.18

Employment Rates of Married Women, by Education and Husband's Income, 1980

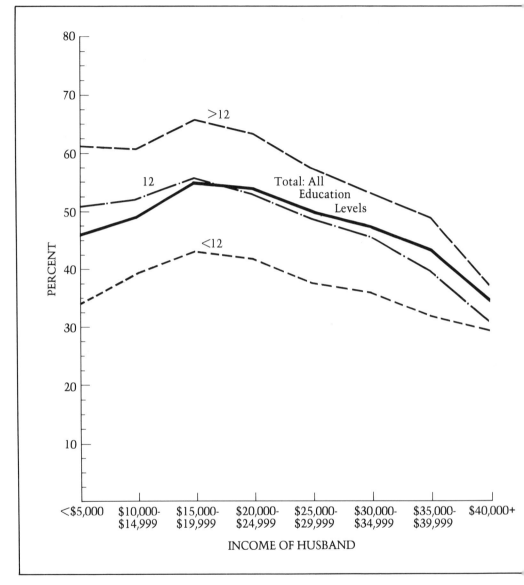

an's husband earns a great deal, the probability that she will be working is lower than if he earns relatively little. This relationship holds within levels of education and family status.

The greater the level of education, the higher the rate of employment. Several things contribute to this positive relationship between education and employment. Women with higher levels of education are:

—more likely to seek work because of socialization into work roles;

—more likely to have skills for which there is market demand;

—more likely to have access to more satisfactory job opportunities—clean, light, generally interesting, or at least tolerable, jobs;

—more likely to earn enough to make it worthwhile to seek work and continue working.

About one-half of married women with children were employed in 1980. The rate varies from slightly over one-third for women who did not attend high school to 60 percent for women with a college education. The relationship is even stronger for black women than for majority-white women (see Figure 4.19). Black women who are college graduates have a rate of employment of 84 percent compared to 58 percent for majority whites. Among high school graduates the employment rate is 63 percent for non-Hispanic whites and 49 percent for blacks. Mexican-American mothers have employment rates about equal to those of majority whites at education less than twelve years, but considerably higher rates than whites among the college-educated. A positive relationship between education and employment, with approximately the same slope, occurs at all ages of youngest child (Figure 4.20). These differences among education groups would be even larger were it not for the fact that low-education wives are likely to have husbands with relatively low incomes. Thus, while their probability of employment is depressed by low education, it is raised by greater family economic need. The observed level is the net result of these two countervailing forces.

Variation in Employment by Race and Ethnicity

Figure 4.21 shows that employment rates of black mothers are higher than those of majority-white mothers at all ages of youngest child. The differential is largest in the preschool ages.[23] Employment rates of black women have been higher than for white women for the

---

[23]Sweet, *Women in the Labor Force.*

FIGURE 4.19

*Employment Rate of Married, Spouse Present, Women with Children,
by Education, 1980*

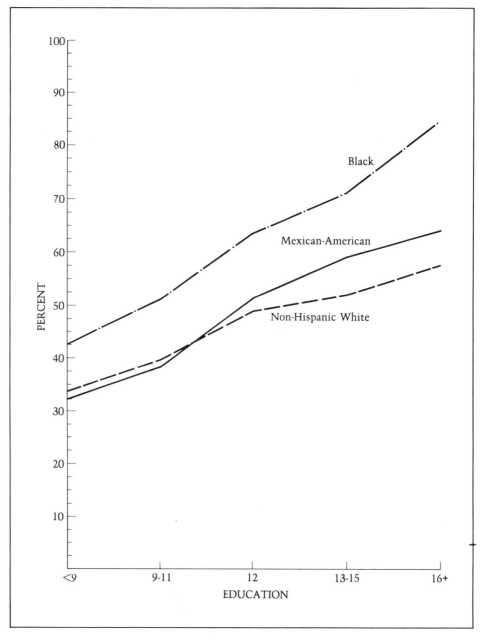

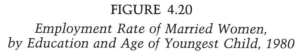

FIGURE 4.20

Employment Rate of Married Women,
by Education and Age of Youngest Child, 1980

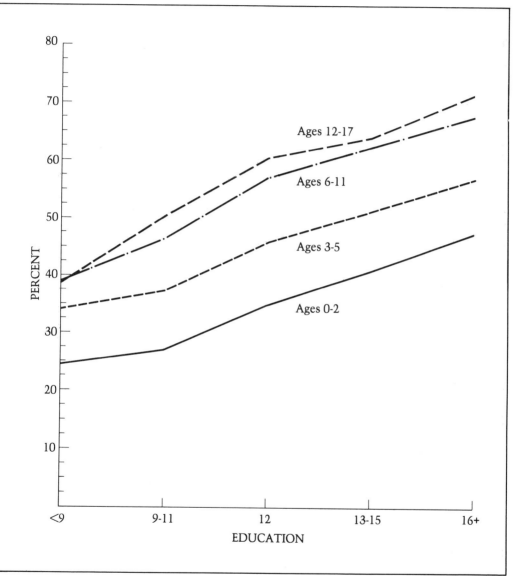

FIGURE 4.21

Comparison of Employment Rates of Currently Married Non-Hispanic White,
Black, and Mexican-American Women, by Age of Youngest Child, 1980

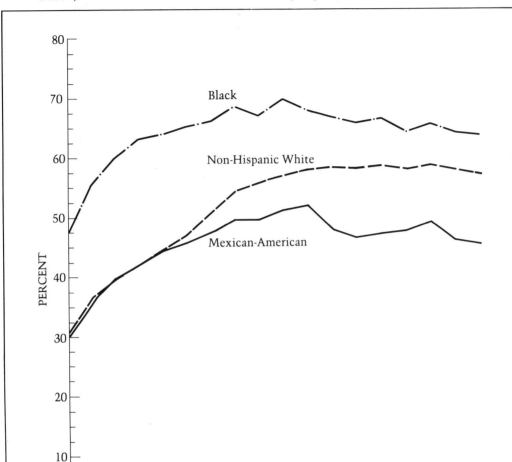

past several decades. There is no adequate explanation of this differential. It persists even after controlling for education and husband's income. This differential has been attributed to differences in attitudes or values with respect to the needs of young children for continuous care by the mother, different attitudes with respect to work, greater instability of husband's earnings, and greater access to child care within the household and in the community.[24]

The rates for Mexican-American mothers of preschool age children are almost identical to those of majority-white mothers, but Mexican-American rates are much lower among mothers of adolescent children. Overall, Mexican-American women have lower rates of employment than majority-white women. Again, explanations have been largely in terms of cultural differences in sex role attitudes and familial values. It would also appear that low education, inaccessibility to jobs, and difficulties with English may contribute to the lower rate of employment. In fact, as we showed in the previous section, Mexican-American women with a high school education or more have higher employment rates than comparably educated non-Hispanic white women. Of course, the Mexican-American population is much more heavily concentrated in the very low education categories than either the majority-white or the black population.

TABLE 4.12

Employment Rates of Married Women, by Age of
Youngest Own Child for Racial and Hispanic Groups, 1980

	Age of Youngest Child				
	<3	3–5	6–11	12–17	Total
Non-Hispanic White	35.0	44.4	55.6	58.1	48.6
Black	53.4	63.9	67.6	65.2	62.3
American Indian	34.8	45.4	52.5	51.7	45.1
Chinese	45.7	53.3	66.5	71.0	58.3
Japanese	37.8	43.4	53.5	63.4	51.4
Filipino	62.2	72.3	75.4	77.2	70.4
Korean	35.6	51.0	63.5	69.9	52.6
Asian Indian	40.0	49.4	57.9	59.0	49.2
Vietnamese	36.6	47.0	60.4	56.0	47.6
Hawaiian	38.8	60.4	60.5	68.6	55.5
Mexican	34.2	43.7	49.5	47.1	42.0
Puerto Rican	29.9	39.3	40.6	46.0	37.6
Cuban	45.1	51.3	57.6	65.9	56.8

[24]Sweet, *Women in the Labor Force*, chap. 2

Employment rates of married women with children are very high among Filipinos (70 percent), blacks (62 percent), Chinese (58 percent), Cubans (57 percent), and Hawaiians (56 percent). They are lowest among Puerto Ricans (38 percent), Mexican Americans (42 percent), American Indians (45 percent), and Vietnamese (48 percent) (see Table 4.12). The rank orderings of the groups are very similar for each of the four age-of-youngest-child categories. These groups vary widely in many different dimensions—English language ability, geographic concentration, education, family economic need, and culture. Without a more detailed analysis it is not possible to say much about the sources of these racial/ethnic differentials.

School Enrollment of Married Persons

An increasingly important fact of married life for American couples is the continuation of education after marriage.[25] This is especially relevant for the growing share of couples with partners who have attended college. Table 4.13 shows the percent of married couples in which one or both spouses were currently enrolled at each of the three census dates. The bottom panel shows the same data for couples with college-educated husbands (that is, with thirteen or more years of education).

In 1980, 12 percent of all couples with husbands aged 20–35 had at least one spouse enrolled in school. Surprisingly, there is little variation by age. In 8 percent of the couples the husband is enrolled, and in 6 percent the wife is enrolled. This adds to more than 12 percent because both spouses are students for 2 percent of the couples. For blacks the proportions enrolled are very similar to those of whites. The proportions of black wives enrolled is slightly higher than for whites, and the proportions of husbands are about the same.

The reason for restricting the universe to the college-educated in the lower panels is because almost all of the enrollment at these ages is in college. Only persons with more than twelve years of education can

[25]In the 1980 census persons were asked "Since February 1, 1980, has this person attended regular school or college at any time? Count . . . schooling which leads to a high school diploma or college degree." There is no information on whether the person is attending part- or full-time, nor do we know if the school attendance is the person's "major activity." Enrolled persons include those enrolled full- or part-time in pursuit of a college degree, as well as persons such as school teachers who may be taking a course or two at a time to improve their professional competence and/or qualify for a higher rate of pay. For more detailed analysis of education after marriage, see Nancy Davis and Larry Bumpass, "The Continuation of Education After Marriage Among Women in the United States," *Demography* 13 (1976):351–70; Larry L. Bumpass, "Recent Trends in Women's Education After Marriage," University of Wisconsin, Center for Demography & Ecology Working Paper 85–28, 1985.

TABLE 4.13

*Percent of Married Couples with Husband, Wife, or Either Spouse
Enrolled in School, by Age and Ethnicity, 1980*

Husband's Age	Non-Hispanic White			Black		
	Wife	Husband	Either	Wife	Husband	Either
ALL COUPLES						
20–21	8.5	7.8	13.8	8.0	8.9	14.5
22–23	7.5	10.1	14.8	8.4	9.0	14.8
24–25	7.1	10.5	14.8	9.3	9.2	15.0
26–27	6.9	9.4	13.9	8.2	8.1	14.2
28–29	6.3	8.8	13.0	9.4	8.4	15.0
30–31	6.1	7.5	11.8	8.3	9.5	15.2
32–33	5.6	6.2	10.4	8.8	7.1	13.4
34–35	5.0	4.5	8.4	7.3	6.7	11.9
Total	6.4	7.9	12.2	8.5	8.2	14.2
COUPLES WITH HUSBAND'S EDUCATION > 12 YEARS						
20–21	18.1	36.9	42.9	13.9	41.8	45.6
22–23	14.6	29.8	36.2	16.9	28.7	37.8
24–25	12.8	24.2	30.4	17.2	25.2	33.7
26–27	11.2	18.1	24.5	13.2	20.0	28.5
28–29	9.3	15.0	20.6	14.4	19.2	27.4
30–31	8.7	12.5	18.3	12.8	21.4	28.5
32–33	7.8	10.4	15.7	14.2	14.8	23.8
34–35	7.5	8.3	13.8	12.0	16.7	24.4
Total	9.6	15.1	20.9	14.0	20.2	28.3

be enrolled in college, and the ages and racial groups differ in the fractions with twelve or more years of education. Over one-fifth of the couples with college-educated husbands have at least one spouse enrolled. For blacks it is 28 percent. The fraction decreases with age, but even at husband's age 34–35, 14 percent of the white and 24 percent of the black couples have one spouse enrolled in school.[26]

Over the past two decades the fraction of young couples with at least one spouse enrolled in school has increased from 8 percent to 12 percent. The increase has occurred at all ages. As Table 4.14 shows, the

[26]It is deceptive to draw any conclusions about differences in levels of enrollment of husbands and wives from the data in the second panel, because we have restricted the comparison to couples with college-educated husbands, many of whom have wives with less education. When we restrict the comparison to couples with college-educated wives, we include many couples with husbands who have less education. In that case we find slightly more couples with wives enrolled than with husbands enrolled.

TABLE 4.14

Percent of Married Couples with Either Husband or Wife Enrolled in School, by Husband's Age, for All Couples and for Couples with Husbands Having More Than 12 Years of Education, 1960–80

Husband's Age	All Couples			Husband's Education > 12 Years		
	1960	1970	1980	1960	1970	1980
20–21	15.2	19.4	13.5	47.0	50.9	42.5
22–23	13.6	16.9	14.6	36.7	39.0	36.9
24–25	12.2	13.0	14.9	30.2	30.0	31.2
26–27	10.0	10.6	13.9	25.0	23.9	25.1
28–29	8.0	7.7	13.3	17.9	17.3	21.8
30–31	5.9	6.4	12.2	12.8	14.5	19.4
32–33	4.8	5.3	10.7	9.6	11.8	16.6
34–35	3.0	4.5	8.2	5.5	10.0	14.8
AGES 20–35						
Husband Enrolled, Wife Not	5.2	6.3	5.9	14.1	16.0	11.7
Both Enrolled	0.9	1.2	2.1	2.0	3.2	4.2
Wife Enrolled, Husband Not	1.8	2.0	4.4	2.2	3.0	5.9
Total	7.8	9.5	12.4	18.2	22.2	21.8

increase was due primarily to the shift in education composition. Enrollment after marriage is primarily enrollment of the college-educated, and more young married persons have college educations in 1980 than in 1960. The right panel of Table 4.14 shows that there was little change during the 1960s in the enrollment rates in couples with college-educated husbands. During the 1970s the enrollment rate in married couples with husbands under 24 decreased, while that for couples with husbands aged 24–35 increased. Among couples with college-educated husbands aged 20–35, the percent with at least one spouse enrolled rose from 18 to 22 percent during the 1960s and remained at 22 percent in 1980. During the 1970s the fraction of couples with enrolled wives increased from 3 to 6 percent for all couples, and from 6 to 10 percent for couples with college-educated husbands. The fraction with enrolled husbands decreased.

Living Arrangements of Married Couples

In the final section of this chapter we consider three aspects of the living arrangements of married couples. First we examine levels and trends in homeownership in relation to marriage duration and presence of children. We then discuss levels and trends in "doubling up," focusing especially on recently married couples. The final section examines variation in the presence of other relatives in married-couple households in relation to life cycle stage and race/ethnicity.

Homeownership

A substantial share of married couples own their own homes. This share increases with age and marriage duration. Figure 4.22 shows that the homeownership rate of non-Hispanic white married couples has increased very rapidly during the past two decades. (For these marriage duration comparisons the sample is limited to couples with both spouses married only once.) For example, at a marriage duration of ten years, 82 percent of couples were homeowners in 1980, compared to 72 percent in 1970 and 68 percent in 1960. By 1980 nearly one-third of couples in their first year of marriage were homeowners. In 1960 and 1970 the fraction was about one-sixth. By twenty years of marriage the fraction reaches a peak at about 90 percent homeowners, up from 85 percent in 1970 and 78 percent in 1960. Married couples are more likely to become homeowners than they were a decade ago, and they are likely to become homeowners earlier in their marriages.

The rate of homeownership has risen very rapidly for couples with children all of whom are preschool age—from 51 to 64 percent between 1960 and 1980 (data not shown). However, the fraction of young (husband under age 36) childless couples who are homeowners has grown even more rapidly—from 29 to 51 percent between 1960 and 1980.

The trend toward increasing homeownership has been even more pronounced for blacks than for majority whites (Figure 4.23). At five years of marriage, about 40 percent of blacks were homeowners in 1980. This compares to 30 percent in 1970, and to slightly over 20 percent in 1960. By 1980, 70 percent of black couples married twenty years were homeowners, up from 60 percent in 1970 and 50 percent in 1960. There has been very little change in homeownership rates of Mexican-American married couples (data not shown).

Despite the rapid increase in rates of homeownership of blacks there remain large differentials between majority whites and blacks and Mexican-Americans (see Figure 4.24). Whites begin marriage with a much higher rate of homeownership (30 percent for whites versus less than 20 percent for blacks and Mexican-Americans). Homeownership increases more rapidly early in marriage for whites, and by five years over 60 percent of whites and less than 40 percent of the two minority groups are homeowners. There are only small differences in homeownership between blacks and Mexican-Americans.

FIGURE 4.22

Percent of Non-Hispanic White Married Couples Who Are Homeowners,
by Duration of Marriage, 1960–80

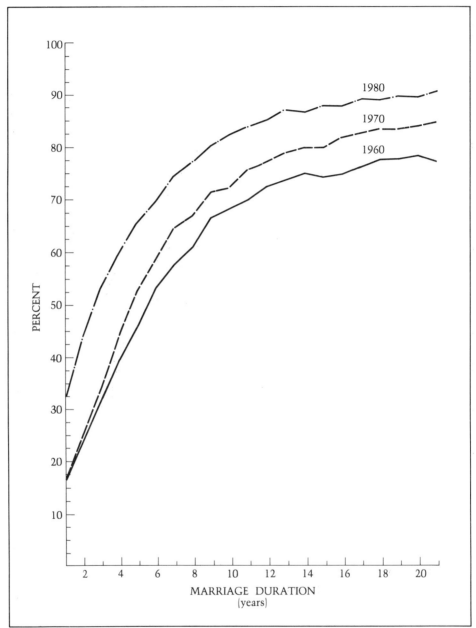

NOTE: Sample limited to couples with both husband and wife married only once.

FIGURE 4.23

Percent of Black Couples Who Are Homeowners, by Duration of Marriage, 1960–80

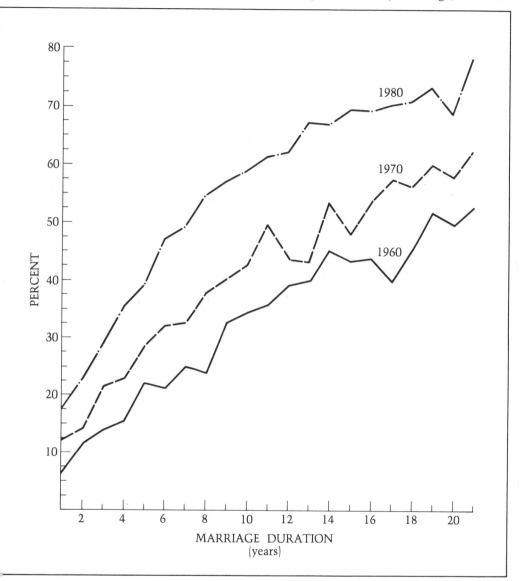

NOTE: Sample limited to couples with both husband and wife married only once.

FIGURE 4.24

Comparison of Homeownership Among Non-Hispanic White, Black, and Mexican-American Married Couples, by Marriage Duration, 1980

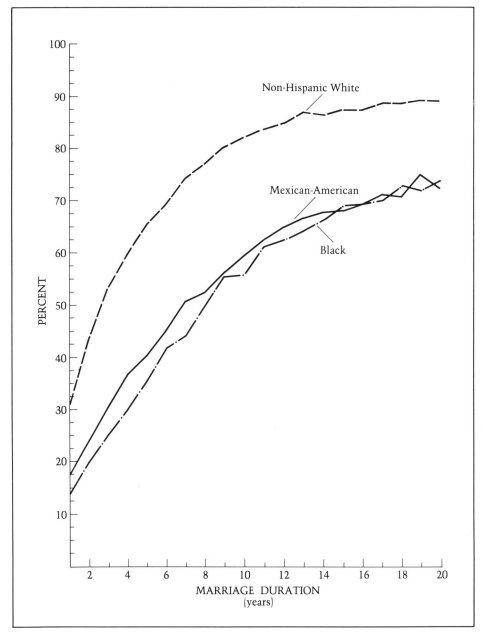

NOTE: Sample limited to couples with both husband and wife married only once.

FIGURE 4.25

*Percent of Married Couples with No Own Children, Who Are Homeowners,
by Age of Husband, 1940–80*

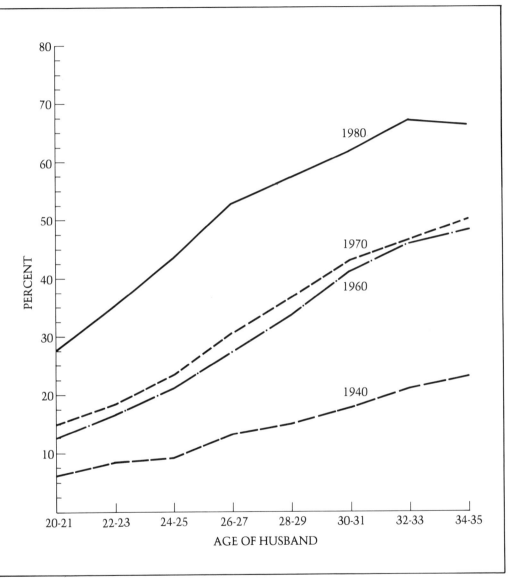

FIGURE 4.26

Percent of Married Couples Who Are Homeowners, with Preschool-Age Children,
by Husband's Age, 1940–80

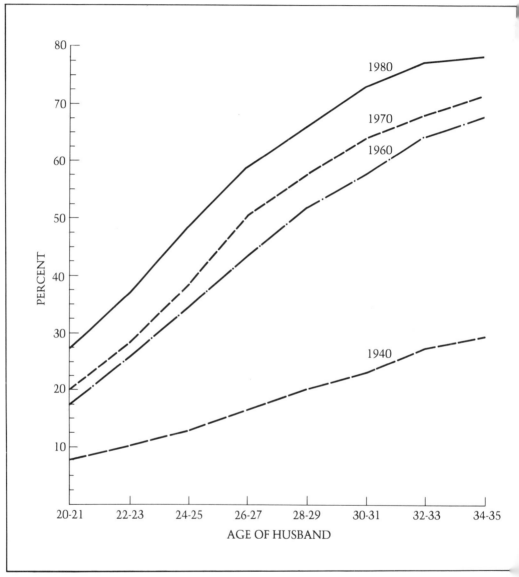

Fraction of Married Couples with Their Own Households

The great majority of married couples maintain their own households. In 1980, 99 percent of all married couples had their own households; only 1 percent lived in households maintained by others. (Living with relatives for recent marriages is examined in more detail in Chap-

TABLE 4.15

Percent of Married, Spouse Present, Couples Who Did Not Have Their Own Households, by Age of Husband, for Total, Black, and Mexican-American Couples, 1940–80

	1940	1950	1960	1970	1980
TOTAL					
< 20	41.8	37.4	24.5	17.6	15.7
20–24	22.7	18.6	8.9	5.6	4.3
25–29	12.7	10.5	3.5	2.1	1.8
30–34	7.7	6.4	1.9	1.0	0.9
35–39	5.0	4.4	1.2	0.6	0.6
40–44	3.2	3.1	1.0	0.5	0.4
45–49	2.1	2.4	0.8	0.5	0.4
50–54	1.9	2.1	0.8	0.4	0.4
50–59	2.0	1.8	0.9	0.5	0.4
BLACK					
< 20	46.6	54.2	45.0	29.0	22.6
20–24	27.1	33.7	20.6	11.4	6.4
25–29	15.9	20.6	7.6	4.9	2.7
30–34	11.3	12.2	4.0	2.2	1.3
35–39	7.6	8.6	2.5	1.4	0.8
40–44	5.1	6.4	2.0	1.3	0.7
45–49	3.3	5.0	1.6	1.1	0.7
50–54	3.5	4.0	1.4	0.8	0.6
55–59	2.0	3.1	1.2	0.7	0.5
MEXICAN-AMERICAN*					
< 20	NA	NA	39.8	29.7	25.3
20–24	NA	NA	12.2	10.4	8.3
25–29	NA	NA	5.6	3.9	3.7
30–34	NA	NA	1.8	1.6	1.9
35–39	NA	NA	1.7	0.6	0.9
40–44	NA	NA	1.0	0.3	0.5
45–49	NA	NA	1.0	0.7	0.7
50–54	NA	NA	0.8	0.7	0.7
55–59	NA	NA	0.9	0.5	0.8

*1960 Spanish surname.

ter 2.) By 1980 almost all married couples not maintaining their own households were very young. About 5 percent of the couples with husbands under age 25 were doubled up. By age 25–29 it was less than 2 percent, and between ages 30 and 64 it was less than 1 percent.

Black couples are nearly twice as likely to be doubling up as white couples, and Mexican-Americans are about three times as likely as majority whites to do so. For couples with husbands under age 25, 4.3 percent of non-Hispanic whites, 7.2 percent of blacks, and 9.4 percent of Mexican-American couples are doubling up.

The fraction of young couples doubled up (usually with parents) was quite high in the 1940s. In both 1940 and 1950, about one-fifth of couples with husbands aged 20–24 and about one-tenth of couples with 25–29-year-old husbands did not maintain their own households. This reflects the housing shortage that developed during the Great Depression and World War II, when there was little new residential construction (see Historical Statistics of the United States, Series N 1–6). For younger couples the fraction was about two-fifths. Even at age 35–39, about 5 percent were living in someone else's household. All of these fractions dropped in the 1950s, and by 1960 doubling up was very rare, except among couples with very young husbands. The trend is quite similar for blacks and Mexican-Americans (Table 4.15).

To compare the levels of the other racial and Hispanic groups, the percent of couples married less than five years who do not have their

TABLE 4.16

Percent of Married Couples, Married Less Than Five Years,
Who Did Not Have Their Own Households,
for Racial and Hispanic Groups, 1970 and 1980

	1970	1980
Non-Hispanic White	4.1	2.8
Black	9.5	4.8
American Indian	11.9	8.2
Chinese	5.6	5.1
Japanese	7.0	5.0
Filipino	13.8	10.0
Korean	NA	3.7
Asian Indian	NA	5.7
Vietnamese	NA	9.1
Hawaiian	NA	8.9
Mexican	9.4	7.4
Puerto Rican	5.7	4.2
Cuban	6.5	6.4

own households is shown in Table 4.16. Each of the groups shown has a higher prevalence of doubling up than non-Hispanic whites (2.8 percent). All except Koreans are higher than the blacks (4.8 percent). The highest prevalence of doubling up is found among Filipinos (10.0 percent), Vietnamese (9.1 percent), Hawaiians (8.9 percent), and American Indians (8.2 percent). All groups experienced a drop in doubling up during the 1970s. The most dramatic drop occurred for blacks, from 9.5 percent to 4.8 percent.

Presence of Other Relatives in Married-Couple Households

Table 4.17 presents the percent of all married-couple families that include one or more "other relatives," that is, relatives other than the couple and their children of any age. Looking first at the 1980 data in the last column, we find that very few couples with preschool age children have relatives present in the household (only 5 percent in 1980). Among couples with youngest child aged 6–11, the percentage is only slightly higher (about 6 percent), and among couples with youngest child aged 12–17, the fraction is about 8 percent. Only 3 percent of childless couples with husbands under age 30 have relatives present. The fraction peaks at about 10 percent for childless couples aged 45–59. This is the age at which persons are most likely to have elderly parents who are unable to care for themselves. About 7 percent of elderly couples have other relatives present in their household.

Black couples are more than twice as likely as whites to have relatives in the household. Eight percent of the couples with children under age 6 have relatives present. The fraction increases to over one-fifth for couples with youngest child aged 12–17. Over one-fifth of the couples with husbands aged 45–59 with no children have relatives present.

Other racial and Hispanic minorities have much higher proportions with relatives than majority whites (Table 4.18). Compared to 5 percent among non-Hispanic whites, the proportions are over 10 percent for all groups except Japanese (8.5 percent). Groups with very large fractions with relatives present include Vietnamese (32 percent), Filipinos (25 percent), Cubans (18 percent), and blacks (16 percent).

Over time the percent of married-couple families with relatives present decreased. In 1900, one-sixth of all, and one-fifth of black, married-couple families had relatives living with them. For blacks, the proportion rose to about one-quarter in 1940 and 1950. The rate of decline in presence of relatives was highest from 1950–60 and 1960–70 for the total population, with little decrease in the 1970s. For blacks the decrease began later, during the 1960s.

TABLE 4.17

*Percent of Married-Couple Families
with Other Relatives* in the Household, 1900–80*

	1900	1940	1950	1960	1970	1980
TOTAL——ALL COUPLES						
With Own Children						
Youngest < 6	14.6	12.2	10.3	7.8	5.4	5.1
6–11	14.5	12.2	13.4	10.2	7.4	6.2
12–17	16.7	15.9	15.6	12.3	9.5	8.1
No Children†						
< 30	16.2	9.8	7.0	4.8	3.3	3.3
30–44	18.0	15.6	14.3	13.0	9.2	6.5
45–59	22.4	19.8	18.4	15.0	10.3	9.5
60 +	28.6	20.2	16.7	11.5	6.5	6.6
Total	16.7	15.4	13.7	10.5	7.6	6.6
BLACK COUPLES						
With Own Children						
Youngest < 6	15.4	17.5	18.0	15.8	11.3	8.3
6–11	18.3	22.9	25.2	21.7	15.4	12.6
12–17	29.7	27.6	33.0	30.5	23.2	21.6
No Children†						
< 30	20.0	17.5	16.2	14.6	10.6	7.8
30–44	16.1	22.1	22.6	22.5	16.9	14.1
45–59	36.6	31.1	32.1	32.3	24.9	23.3
60 +	—	37.4	34.1	31.3	21.0	21.3
Total	20.8	24.0	25.0	23.2	17.4	15.6

*Related persons other than husband, wife, and their sons and daughters of any age.

†Couples with no own children under 18 are classified by age of husband.

Summary

The proportion of the population married and living with a spouse increases with age to about three-quarters at age 35 and remains at this level through age 60. Mirroring the trends in marriage rates and proportions single discussed in the preceding chapters, this proportion rose between 1940 and 1960 and subsequently dropped sharply. The proportion married, spouse present, is also much lower among blacks than among majority whites—the difference implying that black women will spend

TABLE 4.18

Percent of Married-Couple Households at
Selected Life Cycle Stages with "Other Relatives"* Present

	Total	Age 45–59, No Children < 18	Youngest Child < 6	Youngest Child 6–11
Non-Hispanic White	5.3	8.1	3.5	4.6
Black	15.6	23.2	8.4	12.6
American Indian	12.6	14.8	9.3	11.8
Japanese	8.5	12.4	4.8	7.9
Chinese	15.3	15.5	17.5	16.0
Filipino	25.4	27.2	29.8	21.9
Korean	14.8	16.2	18.0	14.0
Asian Indian	12.4	16.5	14.4	11.4
Vietnamese	31.8	28.6	34.0	27.1
Hawaiian	14.9	19.6	9.4	14.1
Mexican	14.3	19.5	12.9	12.9
Puerto Rican	12.9	19.1	10.9	11.4
Cuban	18.4	24.2	14.8	18.7

*Other relative means a related person living in the household other than spouse or child (of any age) of head.

only 44 percent of the time between ages 20 and 59 in this status compared to 70 percent among whites. Ethnic variations reveal high proportions currently living with a spouse among Asian-Americans and low proportions among Hispanic groups.

The composition and circumstances of the currently married population have been substantially altered by trends in fertility, marital stability and remarriage, women's labor force participation, and living arrangements. Trends in completed family sizes, expected fertility, recent fertility, childbearing early in marriage, and the presence of children in the household have been reviewed. Average family size increased from 2.4 to 3.0 over the cohorts producing the baby boom, with large increases in the proportion having at least two children at the same time that the prevalence of very large families continued to decline. Low-education women and blacks had larger families, and blacks experienced larger period variation and a much wider dispersion in family sizes. Family size expectations have become heavily concentrated on the two-child family with one-tenth intending childlessness and one-tenth intending four or more children. Racial and education differences in fertility expectations persist.

Differentials in recent fertility are examined for smaller population groups using census data on the number of own children under 3. Highest rates are found among Hispanics and American Indians and lowest rates among Asian-Americans and majority whites. Education differences are slight except for the extremes of the educational distribution.

Illustrating the contribution of timing fluctuations to the baby boom and subsequent fertility decline, early marital fertility (births between months 8 and 18) first increased by 37 percent and then declined by one-half. Less than a quarter of recent marriage cohorts became pregnant in the first ten months of marriage. Differences in premarital and early marital fertility are reflected in the proportion of married couples with children present at various marital durations. There was about a one-third decline in this proportion between 1960 and 1980. For example, children were present in 49 percent of marriages in their third year in 1980 compared to 75 percent of such marriages in 1960. These changes occurred earliest and were most rapid among better educated couples. The change since 1960 was almost twice as great among college graduates as among high school graduates. There was very little change among blacks.

Among ever-married women who have borne a child, 10 percent have no child present by age 40. This proportion rises to 60 percent by age 55 and to over 80 percent by age 65. Even at age 65, one woman in six still has a child at home (some of whom may have returned after being away). There is little variation by education in the proportion with an "empty nest" at each age.

A growing proportion of all married couples includes at least one spouse who has been married before, almost one-quarter in 1980. In about one of every ten marriages, both spouses have been married more than once.

School enrollment after marriage has become increasingly common among American couples. Twelve percent of couples with husbands aged 20–35 had at least one spouse enrolled in school in 1980. One-fifth of the couples with a college-educated husband had one partner enrolled. This experience has doubled over the last two decades.

Enormous changes have occurred in the distribution of women's employment within marriage. Employment rates first increased in the later years of marriage, and then progressively increased at younger ages of children and earlier marriage durations. The likelihood that a wife is employed still varies with the ages and number of children but much less so than in the past. Forty-five percent of mothers of 1-year-olds are employed, compared to 60 percent of mothers of children over age 6.

Wife's employment increases with the level of education and with the level of family economic need (each of which tends to mask the effect of the other because of their inverse correlation). Among married women with children in 1980, 60 percent of women with a college education were employed, compared to slightly over one-third of those who did not complete high school.

Blacks are more likely to be employed than whites, especially among mothers who are college graduates (84 percent versus 58 percent) and among mothers of children under age 3 (53 percent versus 35 percent). The rates for Mexican-American mothers are lower than those of majority whites although they are identical among mothers of preschool age children. There is considerable variation in mother's employment among racial and Hispanic groups, ranging from 70 percent among Filipinos to around 40 percent for Puerto Ricans and Mexican-Americans.

Homeownership among married couples has increased rapidly over the last two decades, from 68 to 82 percent among majority whites. The proportion owning their own home in the first year of marriage doubled from one-sixth to one-third. These trends were even more pronounced among blacks, although homeownership among black couples is still only about two-thirds the level of majority whites. Only 1 percent of married couples did not have their own household in 1980, a marked decline from the levels of the 1940s. For example, among couples with husbands aged 20–24, only 4 percent did not have their own household compared to about one-quarter in 1940 and one-third in 1950. Living in a household maintained by others and sharing one's household with others are both about twice as likely among blacks as among majority-white couples; such doubling up is also higher for most other racial and Hispanic groups.

5

INCIDENCE OF MARITAL DISRUPTION

T HIS IS the first of two chapters dealing with disrupted marriages. This chapter deals with the *incidence* of marital disruption—the rate at which marriages are being disrupted. The next chapter deals with the *prevalence* of formerly married persons in the population—the number and characteristics of persons who are no longer married. Incidence and prevalence are often confused. Incidence refers to a "flow" or a rate at which a particular marital status transition occurs, whereas prevalence refers to the "stock" of persons who at a given point in time are in a disrupted marital status. We will focus primarily on patterns of separation, divorce, and remarriage, although some consideration is also given to widowhood.

Rates of Marital Disruption

The incidence of marital disruption can be considered in either absolute or relative terms. That there were 1.2 million divorces in the United States in 1980 is a statement about the absolute incidence of divorce. However, it is usually of greater interest to know the divorce rate, and this requires an appropriate base. The number of currently married persons is typically used; for example, there were 23 divorces per 1,000 married couples in 1980.

Divorce rates vary greatly by duration of marriage (or age) from very high rates during the first few years of marriage (or at young ages), to quite low rates after twenty years or so of marriage. For this reason, rates standardized for marriage duration or age are more informative than crude comparisons, although this is rarely done. Some of the rise in divorce rates during the 1970s was due to the fact that there were relatively more short-duration marriages because of the baby boom. This was offset to some extent by the rise in the age at marriage of baby boom cohorts, given the tendency for marriages begun at young ages to be less stable than marriages occurring at older ages.

The ratio of divorces to marriages in a given year is commonly used in popular discussions as an indicator of the level of divorce. However, this ratio can be very misleading in some circumstances, since divorces in a given year occur to persons marrying over a long range of earlier years.

Incidence of What?

It is a relatively simple matter to identify a divorce, since it may occur only by an action of a court of law. Some separations, so-called legal separations, also are recognized by a court decree, but most separations occur without official recognition when one spouse establishes a residence apart from the other. No statistical agency regularly counts such events. Although we do regularly count the number of persons who are separated at a point in time, the net change in the separated population from one time to another provides little help in estimating the incidence of separation because the net change results from three types of transition: from separated to divorced, from separated to married (reconciliation), and from married to separated.

Ideally, a rate of marital disruption ought to relate the number of separations to the married population exposed to the risk of separation. But what should be regarded as a "separation"? Persons may "separate" for a week, and then reconcile, and they may do this ten times before terminating their marriage. Should we count this as one event or ten events? If the marriage is not subsequently terminated, should we count the brief separations at all? Perhaps an appropriate rule would be to count all separations lasting at least six months, or some other arbitrary period. Because of data limitations, very little is known about the incidence of separation followed by reconciliation, so it is impossible to determine whether or not this is an important issue. Nonetheless, we must include some measure of separation in our discussion of marital disruption in making comparisons of marital disruption among social groups, or at different points in time. The use of the divorce rate to make comparisons of levels of marital disruption is inappropriate to the extent that groups being compared vary in:

1. the conditional probability of divorce, given separation;
2. the length of time between separation and divorce; or
3. the degree to which separations are followed by reconciliation.

In general, divorce rates tend to understate social status differentials in marital disruption, since low-status persons tend to have a lower probability of divorce given separation and a longer average interval between the events.[1]

Data on Separation and Divorce

There are several sources of data on the incidence of separation and/or divorce. The first, divorce registration data collected as a part of the vital statistics system, is of very limited value for analysis for a number of reasons:

1. Although divorces are registered and compiled in all states, no information on separations is collected.
2. As of 1980, only thirty of the fifty-one states (including the District of Columbia) participated in the Divorce Registration Area for which detailed statistics are compiled. These states represented only 49 percent of all divorces in the United States in 1980. Although the number of states in the Divorce Registration Area increased during the 1970s, coverage deteriorated because California, which accounts for over one-eighth of all divorces in the United States, left the Divorce Registration Area. States not in the Divorce Registration Area do not maintain divorce records in a central location and/or do not meet quality or reporting standards set by the National Center for Health Statistics. There is a great deal of missing information even within the Divorce Registration Area. In 1970 and 1980, for ex-

---

[1]James Sweet and Larry Bumpass, "Differentials in Marital Instability of the Black Population: 1970," *Phylon* 35 (1974):323–31.

ample, the levels of nonreporting on several key characteristics were:

	1970	1980
Husband's Age	21%	15%
Husband's Age at Marriage	21%	14%
Race of Husband	24%	27%
Marriage Order of Husband	24%	13%
Marriage Duration	2%	1%
Number of Children	4%	3%

3. Quite apart from these problems, there is very little information about the spouses and their marriage. The standard divorce certificate includes only the following information:

    Age—both spouses

    Place of Residence—both spouses

    State of birth—both spouses

    Place of marriage

    Date of marriage

    Approximate date of separation

    Number of living children and number under age 18

    Race—both spouses

    Order of this marriage—both spouses

    How previous marriages ended—both spouses

    Education—both spouses

4. It is often difficult to get information on comparable characteristics of all currently existing marriages for the same geographic units, and thus difficult to estimate rates of divorce.

A second source of information on the incidence of separation and divorce is the retrospective marriage histories that have been collected from time to time in the Current Population Survey (CPS). The marriage history information collected in the June 1980 CPS is reproduced in Appendix 5.1. Even with a large sample of over 63,000 interviewed households, there are often too few cases to estimate marital transitions for many subpopulations of interest. The quality of these data is generally very good,[2] except for events that occurred more than ten years or so

---

[2]Larry Bumpass, "Children and Marital Disruption: A Replication and Update," *Demography* 21 (1984):71–82.

prior to the survey. Andrew Cherlin and James McCarthy find annual divorce rates estimates from the June CPS to be about 20 percent lower than those reported by the vital statistics system.[3] We find a much closer agreement when comparisons are made specific to marriage cohorts (see Appendix 5.1). No information on reconciliations is obtained in the CPS or any of the other data sources.

A third type of data on the experience of marital disruption has been gathered in recent decennial censuses. This is information on whether or not an individual has ever experienced marital disruption. In the 1980 census, in addition to current marital status, the following questions were asked:

Has this person been married more than once?

_____ Once   _____ More Than Once

Month and   Month and Year
Year of   of First
Marriage _____   Marriage _____

If married more than once:

Did the first marriage end because of the death of the husband (or wife)?

_____ Yes   _____ No

The same information was collected in the 1970 census, and all except the question on how the first marriage ended was gathered in 1960. Persons who have experienced marital disruption can be identified from these questions and from information on current marital status. This would include all those who are married once and are currently separated, widowed, or divorced, plus all those who are currently married and have been married more than once. We can further distinguish between persons whose first marriage ended in widowhood. Even though they do not provide information on when a marriage ended, these data are still very useful. By making comparisons specific to duration since first marriage, we can approximate differences in the incidence of marital disruption for various subpopulations, using the much larger samples provided by the census.

We will use all three of these data sources in this chapter. The primary source of data on *trends* in marital disruption and remarriage will be the vital registration system, supplemented by data from the successive censuses. Most of the analysis of *differentials* in marital disruption

[3]Andrew Cherlin and James McCarthy, "Final Report, Demographic Analysis of Family and Household Structure." Center for Population Research, 1984.

and remarriage will be based on data from the June 1980 CPS, supplemented by data from the decennial censuses for relatively rare population subgroups.

Trend in Divorce

In 1980 there were 1.2 million divorces in the United States. This amounted to 5.2 divorces per 1,000 population or 23 divorces per 1,000 married couples. Figure 5.1 shows the trend in the number and rate of

FIGURE 5.1

Number of Divorces (thousands) and Rate of Divorce per 1,000 Marriages, 1860–1980

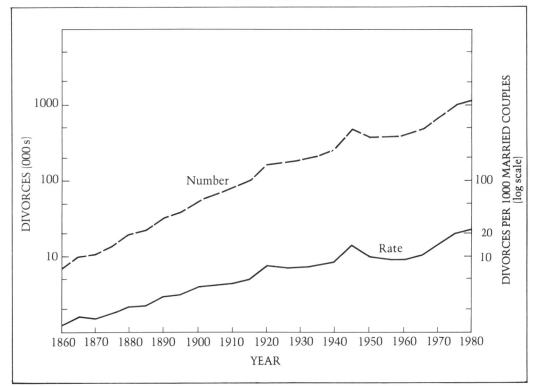

SOURCES: National Center for Health Statistics, U.S. Department of Health and Human Services, Monthly Vital Statistics Report, vol. 32, no. 3, Supplement, June 27, 1983.

U.S. Department of Health, Education and Welfare. DHEW Publication No. (PHS) 78–1907, 1978, "Divorces and Divorce Rates: United States." Vital and Health Statistics, series 21, no. 29.

Paul H. Jacobson, *American Marriage and Divorce* (New York: Rinehart & Co., Inc., 1959).

divorce from the mid-1800s to the present. We will focus on the rate. The divorce rate rose from about 1 per 1,000 in the mid-nineteenth century to over 8 per 1,000 just prior to World War II. During this period, the rate fluctuated from year to year, with an "excess" of divorces around 1920 associated with World War I and a "deficit" of divorces in the mid-1930s associated with the Great Depression. In the mid-1940s there was a divorce boom of unprecedented magnitude, with the rate doubling from about 9 per 1,000 in 1940 to 18 per 1,000 in 1946. Part of this increase at the end of World War II was simply the effect of the postwar marriage boom; part of it was due to the legal termination of marriages of persons who had actually separated during the war and depression years; and perhaps part was due to a somewhat higher rate of termination of marriages of persons who had rushed into marriage during the war and/or who had been living apart because of military service.

After the war, the rate dropped to below 10 per 1,000 for the entire decade of the 1950s and through the mid-1960s. Then, beginning in about 1965, there was a sharp rise in the rate, which by 1979 reached a level of 23 divorces per 1,000 existing marriages.

The rate leveled off and then declined by 4 percent between 1979 and 1982. While it is possible that this indicates a plateauing, or even reversal, of the trend toward increasing marital disruption, it is too early to reach that judgment from this brief deviation from the trend. Even this observed deviation has to be understood as, in large part, a product of compositional changes. The age composition of the married population has become older with the substantial delay in marriage discussed in Chapter 2. Indeed, we would have expected a 3 percent decline in the rate between 1979 and 1982 just based on the change in the age composition of the married population.[4]

An alternative way of describing the trend in divorce is in terms of the fraction of marriages occurring in a given period that ultimately end in divorce. Preston and McDonald have prepared estimates for earlier marriage cohorts.[5] About 7 percent of marriages begun in the 1860s ended in divorce. This fraction gradually moved upward to about one-sixth of marriages begun in the 1920s. According to projections made by the National Center for Health Statistics and by Cherlin, about one-half of marriages contracted in recent years will end in divorce.[6] (The major

[4]Calculated by applying the age composition of the married population in 1979 to the age-specific rates of 1982 (the first year for which age-specific rates were reported).

[5]Samuel Preston and John McDonald, "The Incidence of Divorce Within Cohorts of American Marriages Contracted Since the Civil War," Demography 16 (1978):1–25.

[6]James Weed, "National Estimates of Marriage Dissolution and Survivorship: United States." DHHS Publication (PHS) 81 1403, series 3, no. 19, 1980; Andrew Cherlin, Marriage, Divorce, and Remarriage (Cambridge, Mass.: Harvard University Press, 1981). See also Preston and McDonald, "The Incidence of Divorce."

TABLE 5.1

Proportion of Women Separated* Within a Specified Interval
Since First Marriage, by Marriage Cohort

Marriage Cohort	Years Since First Marriage				
	2	5	10	15	N
1977–79	9				3572
1974–76	9	21			3566
1971–73	8	20			3902
1968–70	8	17	30		3889
1965–67	5	14	26	35	3240

*Life Table Estimates (see Appendix 5.1).
SOURCE: June 1980 Current Population Survey.

assumption underlying these projections is that marriage cohorts will experience current duration-specific divorce rates through the remaining years of their marriages. For example, 25 percent of the cohort married in 1970 had experienced divorce by their seventh year of marriage (in 1977, the most recent data available when these estimates were made). Since the future divorce trajectory of this cohort was unknown, it was assumed that the marriage duration-specific rates of 1977 will apply to them at longer durations. When this was done, it is estimated that 49 percent of the 1970 marriages will ultimately end in divorce.)

A more complete picture of the process for recent marriage cohorts can be obtained from the June 1980 CPS. Table 5.1 presents the proportion who had separated by successive durations since first marriage for women marrying since 1965. Over one-third of the 1965–67 marriage cohort had separated before their fifteenth anniversary, while only 5 percent of this cohort had separated within two years; this proportion is 9 percent for the 1977–79 cohort. There was a one-third increase in the proportion separated after five years between the 1965–67 and 1974–76 marriage cohorts.

Fraction of Divorces to Couples with Children Present

The fraction of divorces in which children are involved has increased over time. It rose from less than 40 percent in the 1920s to about 45 percent in 1950. Between 1950 and 1960 the fraction increased further to 60 percent, where it remained until 1972. Since then it has begun to fall slowly, reaching about 56 percent in 1980. In 1960, 22 percent of divorcing couples had three or more children. By 1980 this fraction had fallen to 10 percent. These trends depend on the age and marriage-duration patterns of divorce, on trends in fertility, and on the effect of children on divorce probabilities. Divorcing black couples were slightly more likely to have children present than white couples (57 percent versus 54 percent in 1979).

Timing of Marital Disruption

There are many ways of summarizing the timing of marital disruption within marriages. The most commonly cited measure is the median duration of marriages that end in divorce within a given year. Currently the median interval is about seven years—one-half of all divorces in 1980 occurred in marriages less than seven years in duration. In the nineteenth century the median was about eight years.[7] It dropped to about six years by 1950, rose to over 7.5 years in the mid-1960s, and has fallen to seven years since then. This measure is not very satisfactory because it depends not only on changes in the timing of divorces within marriages but also on the distribution of existing marriages by duration. In a period following a rise in the number of marriages, the median duration at divorce will fall. If the number of marriages falls, the average interval to divorce will tend to increase.

A better representation of the timing of divorce is the pattern of duration-specific rates of divorce, as shown in Figure 5.2. This figure shows the rate at which first marriages and remarriages terminated in divorce at various marriage durations in 1975. The rate of divorce is very high early in marriage. For example, over 40 marriages per 1,000 (4 percent) end in divorce each year over the second through fifth years of marriage. Beyond five years, there is a gradual decrease to about 15 per 1,000 by fifteen years' duration, and to less than 10 per 1,000 by twenty-five years. If we had data on separation rates, they would be higher at the very short durations of less than one or two years, since many of the divorces that occur in years two and three, for example, were separations in years one and two.

Very high rates of divorce are also characteristic of the early years of remarriages. In fact, the duration-specific rates are much higher for remarriages than for first marriages—over 60 per 1,000 at two and three years. This is half again as high as for first marriages. Especially striking is the very high rate at a duration of less than one year for remarriages.

---

[7]National Center for Health Statistics, "Monthly Vital Statistics Report. Duration of Marriage Before Divorce," series 21, no. 38, 1981.

FIGURE 5.2

*Divorce Rates by Marriage Duration, for First Marriages and
Remarriages, 1975 (rate per 1,000 marriages)*

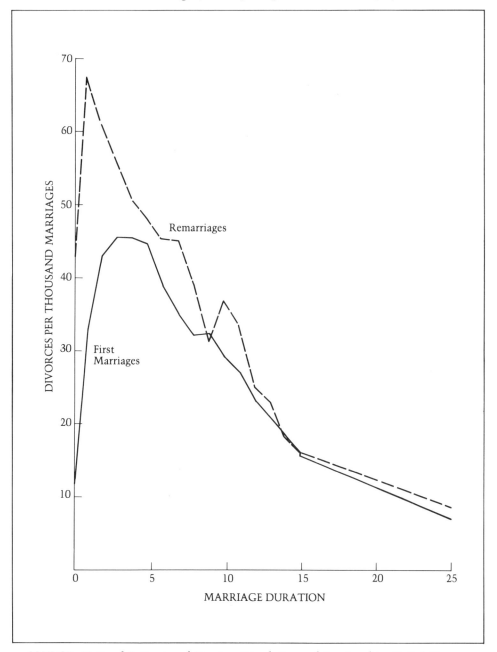

SOURCE: National Estimates of Marriage Dissolution and Survivorship: United States.
Analytical Studies, series 3, no. 19. DHHS Publication No. (PHS) 81-1403.

Evidently a substantial number of remarriages end almost immediately in separation.

Differentials

Differentials in duration-specific rates of divorce are best analyzed using the retrospective marriage history data from the June 1980 CPS. As noted earlier, one advantage of these data is the ability to include the currently separated in the measure of disruption. Because of greater statistical reliability, the cumulative proportion separated by a given anniversary is used as a summary measure. Table 5.2 presents these proportions for first marriages. (These estimates are based on persons under age 65 in 1980 who were married before age 40.)

Marriages since 1965 have been combined in Table 5.2 to provide a large enough sample to permit the estimation of differentials. Life-table procedures were used to take into account the truncation of exposure by interview. (This is discussed in Appendix 5.1.) Overall, the experience of the cohorts represented indicates a dissolution rate of 30 percent by ten years of marriage for first marriages of females and 27 percent by this time for first marriages of males. Given the rapid increase in the rate of separation over this period, the focus should be on subgroup differences rather than on the precise levels.

The rates may differ by sex for several reasons. The first marriage for one spouse may be a remarriage for the other. The somewhat lower stability of female first marriages may reflect the higher proportion that are to previously married spouses.[8] In 1979, 17 percent of female first marriages were to remarried men, whereas 14 percent of male first marriages were to remarried women. This difference arises in part because men tend to be older than their spouses at marriage. Differences between the sexes may also be due to differential reporting error (it is easier for a man without children present to fail to report a previous marriage than for his ex-wife with their children). Similarly, coverage in the CPS of formerly married men may be worse than coverage of formerly married women. In the CPS data there are fewer men than women who report a separation from a first marriage during the period 1965–79.[9] For non-Hispanic whites the ratio of men to women is .85, while for blacks it is .55. Whatever the source of the sex differential, it is a much more serious problem for blacks than for majority whites.

[8] Larry Bumpass and James Sweet, "Differentials in Marital Instability," *American Sociological Review* 37 (1972):754–66.

[9] There are fewer separated men than separated women in the decennial census. This is discussed in Chapter 6.

TABLE 5.2

Differentials in Separation* Within Specified Intervals After First Marriage, for Marriages, 1965–79

Characteristics	Females Years After Marriage				Males Years After Marriage			
	2	5	10	N	2	5	10	N
TOTAL	8	19	30	18,670	7	16	27	16,841
ETHNICITY/RACE								
Non-Hispanic White	8	18	28	15,858	7	16	26	14,537
Mexican-American	6	16	26	745	6	12	22	680
Black	12	29	47	1,629	10	22	34	1,276
AGE AT FIRST MARRIAGE								
<18	14	32	48	2,594	19	32	54	515
18–19	9	22	35	5,110	10	22	36	2,476
20–21	6	16	27	4,449	7	18	28	3,968
22–24	6	13	22	3,969	6	14	23	5,081
25–29	6	12	20	1,817	6	13	21	3,298
30–34	7	10	16	406	6	12	21	856
35+	4	8	15	325	5	12	21	647
EDUCATION								
0–8	9	20	31	843	9	16	24	888
9–11	13	29	43	2,171	10	23	34	1,841
12	9	19	31	8,680	8	19	29	6,515
13–15	7	18	30	3,620	7	17	29	3,456
16	4	10	18	2,218	4	10	20	2,272
17+	4	13	23	1,106	3	9	17	1,843

*Life-Table Estimates.
SOURCE: June 1980 Current Population Survey.

Age at First Marriage and Education

One finding that is consistent across all studies of marital disruption is that rates of disruption are very high for persons marrying at young ages. About half of both men and women who married under the age of 18 experienced marital disruption within ten years of first marriage. The rate was substantially lower for persons marrying at age 18–19 (about one-third), and even lower for persons marrying in their early twenties (about one–quarter). There was further decline, especially for women marrying in their late twenties and thirties. About one woman in six, and one man in five, marrying in their thirties experienced separation within ten years of marriage.

There was very little difference in the stability of first marriages among women with less than a high school education, high school graduates, and those with some college experience. High school dropouts had considerably higher rates than other groups, and college graduates had considerably lower rates. As noted by others, among women who completed college, those who went on to further education have higher disruption rates than those who did not (23 percent versus 18 percent by ten years).

One reason that persons with low levels of education have higher than average rates of marital disruption is that they tend to marry at very young ages. This high-level marital disruption may be due to the early marriage age rather than the low level of education.[10] We will not report the details of a similar analysis here, but only note that after adjusting for the confounding effects of other characteristics, especially age at first marriage, the only remaining educational differentials are a slightly higher rate of marital disruption for high school dropouts (4 percent above the other education groups)[11] and a slightly lower than average rate for college graduates.

---

[10]Bumpass and Sweet, "Differentials in Marital Instability."

[11]Paul Glick and Arthur Norton, "Frequency, Duration, and Probability of Marriage and Divorce," *Journal of Marriage and the Family* 33 (1971):307–17, and Glick, "Marriage, Divorce, and Living Arrangements: Prospective Changes," *Journal of Family Issues* 5(1984):7–26, offered an interpretation of the tendency for rates of marital disruption to be higher for high school and college dropouts than for persons who went on to obtain their degrees. They suggest that the kind of "personality and social background" that might be favorable to persevering and completing the desired level of education might also be favorable to persevering in marriage. Conversely, persons who are unable to "get their act together" and finish their schooling may be equally unable to maintain a marital relationship. Bumpass and Sweet, "Differentials in Marital Instability," however, find that this pattern is eliminated when other demographic and social characteristics, especially age at first marriage, are controlled, and this was also the case in the analysis of the June 1980 CPS reported above. We do not know whether this is true for blacks.

We can get a clearer picture of the combined effects of age at first marriage and education on marital disruption with 1980 census data on the percent of persons first married 10–14 years ago still in intact first marriages. Since patterns are so similar for men and women, we will look only at rates for women. We will use this same measure to examine levels of marital disruption for detailed racial, ethnic, and ancestry groups, as well as to examine subgroup trends.

Data from the 1980 census closely replicate the education patterns of marital disruption reported above (Figure 5.3). On the other hand, the census and the CPS estimates for ages at marriage over age 25 are not consistent. Whereas the CPS estimates revealed a continuous decline in the risk of separation or divorce over these older ages, the census data show a large increase—with the result that the risk for marriages over age 35 is similar to that of the teenage marriages. This is an important discrepancy, and despite considerable exploration, we are unable to determine why it occurs. Several points are relevant, however: (1) for ages at marriage under 25, the two sources agree very closely on the negative relationship between age at marriage and marital disruption; (2) first marriages of women at ages 25 and over represent only 14 percent of all first marriages for the cohorts represented, so whichever data source is correct, the differences should have little effect on other variables; (3) if some error in the census is generating the U-shaped pattern, it has been systematic over the last three censuses, since the same pattern is found in each.

The U-shaped pattern in the census data lends itself readily to a post hoc interpretation that many life-course sociologists might find appealing: that marrying outside of the normative range is associated with lower marital success. From a demographic perspective, it might be expected that the pool of eligible spouses becomes depleted in such a way that later marriages reflect greater compromise in mate selection. We do not know which of these patterns is correct. It is a puzzle that warrants further investigation.

Figure 5.4 shows the percent of women no longer in intact first marriages after 10–14 years within categories of education and age at first marriage jointly. The U-shaped relationship with age at marriage is found, to a varying degree, at all education levels. The lowest rate of instability occurs among college graduates who married at age 22–24. Marrying at advanced ages is less associated with increased marital instability for college-educated women than for women with less education, though there is still a modest increase at these ages. High school dropouts have an extremely high rate of marital instability, which is not much differentiated by age at first marriage.

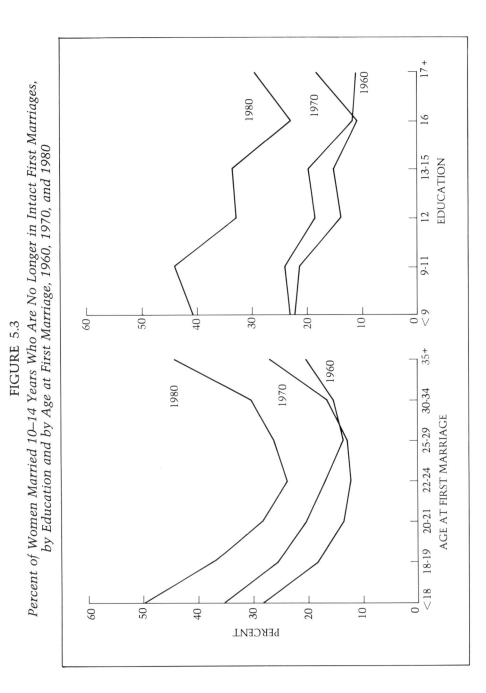

FIGURE 5.3

Percent of Women Married 10–14 Years Who Are No Longer in Intact First Marriages, by Education and by Age at First Marriage, 1960, 1970, and 1980

FIGURE 5.4

*Percent of Women Married 10–14 Years Who Are No Longer
in Intact First Marriages, by Education and Age at First Marriage, 1980*

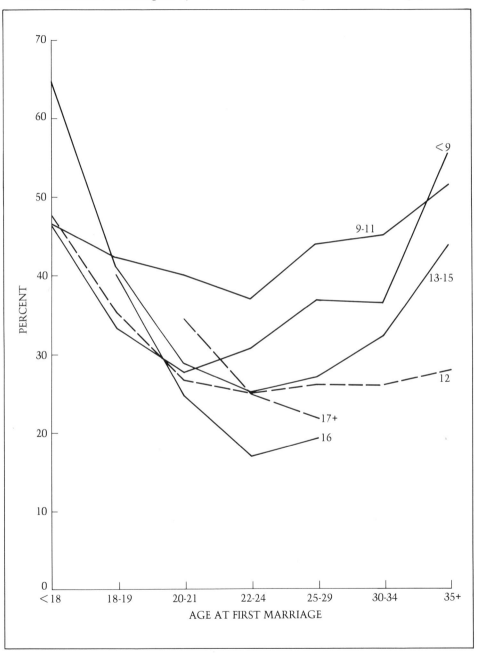

Variation among Racial and Hispanic Groups

About one-half of the first marriages of black women disrupted within ten years. This is about twice the level of majority-white or Mexican-American women. The much lower rate among black males compared to black females suggests an underreporting of disruption by black men or a serious problem of underenumeration of black men who have experienced marital disruption.

With decennial census data we can also make comparisons of levels of marital disruption among the smaller racial and Hispanic minority groups, as well as comparisons among subgroups within the black and Mexican-American populations. The percent of persons no longer in intact first marriages after 10–14 years of marriage is shown for racial and Hispanic groups in Table 5.3. Data are shown for both men and women, but we will discuss only the pattern for women. The pattern for men is almost identical, although the levels tend to be higher.

Blacks have the highest fraction no longer in their first marriage after 10–14 years of marriage—53 percent of women. Three other groups have very high proportions—American Indians (48 percent), Puerto Ricans (46 percent), and Hawaiians (39 percent). Extremely low levels of marriage instability are found for Asian Indians (7 percent), Chinese (15 percent), Filipinos (21 percent), Koreans (22 percent), and Japanese (22 percent).

TABLE 5.3

Percent of Persons First Married 10–14 Years Ago
Who Are No Longer in Intact First Marriages, by Sex,
for Racial and Hispanic Groups, 1980

	Males	Females
Non-Hispanic White	30.7	37.4
Black	43.5	52.7
Chinese	14.8	14.4
Japanese	19.4	21.8
American Indian	43.2	47.9
Filipino	19.6	21.4
Korean	13.2	21.7
Asian Indian	11.6	7.3
Vietnamese	24.2	28.1
Hawaiian	38.3	39.2
Mexican	27.8	30.5
Puerto Rican	31.2	45.5
Cuban	31.6	33.0

Table 5.4 presents the 1960–1980 trend in marital disruption by education for non-Hispanic white, black, and Mexican-American women. Patterns for men are quite similar. As expected, majority whites reflect the national trend, with an increasing proportion whose first marriage disrupted. During the 1960s there was an increase in the percent with disrupted marriages for all groups with less than sixteen years of education (ranging from 4 to 6 points), but no increase for persons who had

TABLE 5.4

Percent of Women First Married 10–14 Years Ago Who Are
No Longer in Intact First Marriages, by Education, for
Non-Hispanic Whites, Blacks, and Mexican-Americans, 1960–80

Years of Education	1960	1970	1980	Difference 1960–70	1970–80
NON-HISPANIC WHITE					
<9	26.5	30.9	40.8	+ 4.4	+ 9.9
9–11	24.4	30.8	44.1	+ 6.4	+13.3
12	15.2	19.2	32.9	+ 4.0	+13.7
13–15	16.3	20.1	33.6	+ 3.8	+13.5
16	12.3	12.4	23.0	+ 0.1	+10.6
17+	20.4	21.0	29.8	+ 0.6	+ 8.8
Total	19.8	22.3	33.4	+ 3.5	+11.1
BLACK					
<9	43.2	48.9	55.6	+ 5.7	+ 6.7
9–11	44.2	47.1	59.9	+ 2.9	+12.8
12	39.8	39.6	40.9	− 0.8	+ 1.3
13–15	34.6	41.0	54.5	+ 6.4	+13.5
16	34.0	36.8	43.8	+ 2.8	+ 7.0
17+	41.9*	37.9*	39.4	− 4.0	+ 1.5
Total	42.1	44.0	53.1	+ 1.9	+ 9.1
MEXICAN-AMERICAN					
<9	24.9	24.7	26.9	− 0.2	+ 2.2
9–11	27.0	26.4	29.4	− 0.6	+ 3.0
12	18.9	25.5	33.0	+ 6.6	+ 7.5
13–15	—	—	35.8	—	—
16	—	—	—	—	—
17+	—	—	—	—	—
Total	24.0	25.0	30.4	+ 1.0	+ 5.4

*Less than 150 cases.

—Less than 100 cases.

graduated from college. During the 1970s increases were similar at all educational levels.

The pattern of change is more irregular among blacks. During the 1960s, there was only a 2-point increase in the proportion whose first marriage had disrupted. There was little change for high school graduates, a decline for the small minority of black women with postcollege education, and an increase for the other groups, especially for those who did not attend high school and those who attended, but did not complete college. During the 1970s there was a 9-point aggregate increase, with higher than average rates of increase for high school and college dropouts. Again there was a lower than average increase for the high school graduates and women with postgraduate education.

Education differentials in marital disruption were very small among blacks in 1960, but by 1980 they had become sizable. Rates for persons with less than a high school education, and for persons who attended but did not complete college were well over 50 percent, while those of high school graduates and persons who completed college were around 40 percent.

Rates of marital disruption among Mexican-Americans increased very little in the 1960s and by only 5 points in the 1970s, much more slowly than for blacks or majority whites. In both decades, the increase was greater for high school graduates than for women with less education. By 1980 there was a *positive* relationship between education and marital disruption among Mexican-Americans. In the 1960s, in fact, there was a 6-point increase for the high school graduates, but no increase at all for those with less education. There are too few sample cases of Mexican-Americans with college education to make reliable estimates.

Divorce After Separation from First Marriage

Relatively little is known about the rapidity with which divorce follows separation. Registration data provide the interval since separation for divorces in a given year. However, relatively few states provide usable information on date of separation, and the data that do exist represent only those intervals of separation that are ended by a divorce. Furthermore, the divorces occurring in a single year are drawn from many different separation cohorts. In the June 1980 CPS marriage histories, date of separation was asked for the currently separated and for those who divorced. Here we use these data to examine patterns of divorce following separation. As can be seen in the first row of Table 5.5, the majority of separations are followed very rapidly by divorce, three-

TABLE 5.5

Differentials in the Proportion Divorced* Within Specified Intervals After Separation from First Marriage, for Separations Occurring Between 1965 and 1979

Characteristics	Females					Males				
	Years After Separation					Years After Separation				
	1	2	3	4	N	1	2	3	4	N
TOTAL	58	77	84	88	6,407	63	82	88	92	5,139
RACE/ETHNICITY										
Non-Hispanic White	63	84	91	94	5,197	66	85	92	94	4,402
Mexican-American	51	73	77	78	202	67	79	86	88	162
Black	28	42	49	55	884	39	53	61	67	483
AGE AT SEPARATION										
<20	59	78	86	89	815	67	84	90	93	1,708
20–24†	61	79	85	88	2,281					
25–29	58	79	85	89	1,675	64	82	89	93	1,521
30–34	55	76	83	85	954	58	78	87	90	946
35+	49	68	77	81	682	60	79	86	90	962
EDUCATION										
<9	45	57	63	68	376	62	78	84	87	359
9–11	51	70	76	79	1,119	59	76	83	87	747
12	60	79	86	89	3,015	64	83	89	92	2,060
13–15	61	82	88	91	1,143	66	84	91	95	1,043
16	62	84	90	95	430	63	81	90	93	482
17+	56	83	92	97	314	60	84	93	96	441

*Life-Table Estimates

†For men, under age 25

SOURCE: June 1980 Current Population Survey.

fifths within the first year. But it is precisely because there is substantial variation in the rapidity of divorce following separation, and in the proportions likely ever to divorce, that the topic is important and that separation is a preferable variable to divorce in the study of marital disruption.

The difference between blacks and whites in the rate of divorce following separation is large. Whereas 63 percent of the whites divorced within one year and 84 percent within two years of separation, the comparable proportions for blacks are 28 and 42 percent. Even after four years, almost one-half of the separated black women have not divorced. While these differences might be thought to reflect differing proportions able to afford the cost of a divorce or differences in the proportion with substantial economic assets to be divided, the black–white differential is unaltered when education and the other variables are controlled. Whatever the other origins of racial differences in the probability of divorce given separation, they are probably complexly interwoven with differences in the likelihood of remarriage. Persons who are not anxious to remarry may have less motivation to finalize a marital separation with a divorce.

Mexican-Americans were substantially less likely than non-Hispanic whites to divorce after separation (50 percent versus 63 percent in the first year), though they are closer to majority whites than to blacks in this regard.

The probability of divorce among women who separate declines with age at separation after age 30, perhaps reflecting the lower propensity to remarry. (Remarriage patterns will be described in a later section of this chapter.) This age difference is reduced, but not eliminated, after other variables are controlled.

Among separated women, the divorce probability is positively related to education, with the exception of a lower rate in the first year for the highest education group. Only 45 percent of those who did not attend high school obtained a divorce in the first year after separation, and only two-thirds did so within four years, compared to 62 percent in one year and 95 percent in four years among college graduates. Although this difference partially reflects differences in racial composition, the majority of the educational difference remains with multivariate controls. The lower rate of divorce of the most highly educated women in the first year or two after separation is a matter of timing rather than the likelihood of ever divorcing, since they had the highest proportion divorced after four years. There are no clear educational patterns in the data for males.

The data by year of separation (Table 5.6) suggest a modest increase in the proportion divorcing during the first year, from 51 to 58 percent between the late 1960s and the late 1970s.

TABLE 5.6

Proportion of Women Divorced* Within Specified Intervals After Separation from First Marriage, by Separation Cohort

Separation Cohort	Years After Separation				N
	1	2	3	4	
1975–79	58	76	84	88	2,782
1970–74	56	77	84	87	2,116
1965–69	51	74	81	84	1,229
1960–64	54	76	83	87	609

*Life-Table Estimates.

SOURCE: June 1980 Current Population Survey.

Remarriage

The sources of data on remarriage are the same as those on divorce:

1. The vital registration system compiles information on marriages by marriage order. This information provides characteristics of the population entering second and higher-order marriages, and provides numerators from which to compute rates of remarriage. However, little else can be done with these data.

2. The retrospective marriage histories collected in the June 1980 CPS can be used to compute rates of remarriage, in much the same way as these data are used to examine rates of separation. Since separation and divorce occur to only a fraction of the population, and remarriage to a subset of them, the number of sample cases for analysis is often small and estimates of rates are more unstable than divorce or separation rates.

3. The census provides information on number of times married from which the cumulative experience of remarriage up to the census date can be inferred. The census provides no information on the timing of remarriage. The situation is even worse for analysis of remarriage than for marital disruption, because we do not have information on the date of disruption, so we know nothing about how long a person has been "exposed to the risk" of remarriage.

It is clear that a great majority of persons whose first marriage ends in separation and divorce eventually remarry. Similarly, a large share of persons who are widowed in the prime adult years also remarry. Table 5.7 shows remarriage rates by age for 1960, 1970, and 1980 for men and women by marital status and age.

TABLE 5.7

Remarriage Rates (per 1,000 persons)
of Widowed and Divorced Men and Women, 1960, 1970, and 1980

	Men			Women		
	1960	1970	1980	1960	1970	1980
DIVORCED						
14–24	360	402	218	433	413	236
25–44	265	325	188	172	179	122
45–64	96	108	79	44	42	30
65+	30	23	23	8	6	5
WIDOWED						
14–44	134	107	107	62	54	51
45–64	68	79	59	14	17	12
65+	15	19	18	2	2	2

SOURCE: National Center for Health Statistics, Vital Statistics of the U.S., vol. III, Marriage and Divorce, 1960, p. 1–28; 1970, p. 1–22; 1980, p. 1–23.

Remarriage rates are very high at the young ages and decrease with increasing age. Among divorced men and women the rate at ages less than 25 was over 200 remarriages per 1,000 population per year in 1980. This was down from over 400 a decade earlier. At age 25–44 the rate was 188 for men and 122 for women. At all ages over 25 the rate is higher for men than for women. The rates for widowed persons are lower than for divorced persons, but this is deceptive. Within these broad age ranges widowed persons would be older than divorced persons, and remarriage decreases sharply with increasing age.

Rates of remarriage were higher in 1970 than in 1960, but lower in 1980 than in either 1970 or 1960. This is true for both sexes, both marital statuses, and for all ages except for the oldest. For persons 65 and over there was little change. Because of the broad age groups, the trend may be confounded by changes in the age distribution of the divorced and widowed populations. These data from the vital statistics system are extremely crude, and do not provide a very good basis for understanding either the trend or differentials in remarriage. The age groups are very broad, and age is really not a good control for exposure to risk. Both the rate and number of divorces have changed markedly over time.

A better idea of the level and trend in remarriage comes from the retrospective marriage histories of the June 1980 CPS. The procedure we used to analyze remarriage is identical to that used to analyze separation. The date of separation is regarded as the beginning of "exposure to risk" of remarriage. While it is not true in a legal sense, we think that this definition better captures the social reality. Separation marks the termination of a marriage. Divorce follows after a variable period of time. As noted above, for many persons there is little need to become divorced until another marriage is contemplated.

Tables 5.8 and 5.9 present the proportion remarried within specified intervals following the date of separation from first marriage. Based on separations between 1965 and 1979, about two-thirds of separated women and three-quarters of separated men remarry within ten years (first row of Table 5.9). This difference arises from a lower rate of later remarriages among women since the proportions remarried in the first two years after separation are very similar for men and women.

Comparison of the remarriage experience of successive separation cohorts of women suggests that there was a drop in remarriage rates between the separation cohorts of the 1960s and those of the 1970s (Table 5.8).[12]

Race and ethnic differences in remarriage are very large, just as they were for separation and divorce (Table 5.9). The proportion of women remarried within ten years of separation is almost three-quarters among non-Hispanic whites, compared to one-half among Mexican-Americans and one-third among blacks. Not remarrying is clearly the modal pattern for black women whose marriages disrupt. These differences are not at all affected by controls for the other relevant characteristics (data

TABLE 5.8

Trend in the Proportion of Women Remarried* Within Specified Intervals After Separation from First Marriage, by Separation Cohort

Separation Cohort	Years After Separation				
	2	5	10	15	*N*
1975–79	19	45			2,782
1970–74	20	45	65		2,116
1965–69	20	48	65	72	1,229
1960–64	25	52	69	79	609

*Life-Table Estimates.

SOURCE: June 1980 Current Population Survey.

[12]T. Espenshade, "Marriage Trends in America: Estimates, Implications, and Underlying Causes," *Population and Development Review* 11 (1985):193–245.

TABLE 5.9

Differentials in the Proportion Remarried* Within Specified Intervals After Separation from First Marriage, for Separations Occurring Between 1965 and 1979

Characteristics	Females				Males			
	Years After Separation				Years After Separation			
	2	5	10	N	2	5	10	N
TOTAL	20	46	64	6,407	22	57	78	5,139
RACE/ETHNICITY								
Non-Hispanic White	23	52	72	5,197	24	60	82	4,402
Mexican-American	15	36	53	202				162
Black	4	18	32	884	10	34	55	483
AGE AT SEPARATION								
<20†	27	59	78	815	25	63	83	1,708
20–24	21	50	69	2,281				
25–29	19	44	62	1,675	20	57	89	1,521
30–34	17	36	52	954	22	52	78	946
35+	10	27	40	682	21	47	63	962
EDUCATION								
<9	19	39	53	376	21	50	74	359
9–11	22	46	62	1,119	21	56	76	747
12	21	49	68	3,015	24	59	80	2,060
13–15	16	42	62	1,143	24	57	80	1,043
16	18	44	67	430	16	52	77	482
17+	10	32	57	314	18	57	79	441

*Life-Table Estimates.
†For men, under age 25.
SOURCE: June 1980 Current Population Survey.

not shown). Remarriage rates are higher for men than for women, but differentials are similar to those found for women.

As we would expect, the probability of remarriage declines steadily with increasing age at the time of separation. Among women who married and separated as teenagers, three-fifths were remarried within five years compared to one-quarter of those who were age 35 or over when the separation occurred. The differences by ten years following separation (78 versus 40 percent remarried) suggest that the proportion who never remarry increases markedly with age and may well be the dominant pattern for women whose marriages break up when they are beyond age 35 or so. The age differences are similar but not as pronounced among men. The differential in remarriage between men and women is greater at older ages, reflecting in part the tendency for men to marry women younger than themselves—which in turn creates an increasingly disadvantageous marriage market for women as they grow older. These age patterns are also unaffected by control for the other variables.

Educational differences in remarriage probabilities are less clearly patterned. The relationship is curvilinear, with the lowest rates of remarriage at the ends of the distribution, and with a depression in the middle for women who attended but did not complete college. These differences might be thought to reflect a relatively poor position in the remarriage market for those with the lowest education, and a greater ability to remain financially independent for the most educated. However, after the other variables are controlled, the major difference that remains is the lower remarriage rates of women who continued schooling beyond college graduation (data not shown).

Once again, we can examine differentials in more detail with census data, although we have only a crude measure based on the percent currently married (spouse present) among persons whose first marriage disrupted. We have selected all persons under the age of 45 who are no longer in an intact first marriage as the population base. This measure is only a rough indicator of levels of remarriage, because it does not hold constant exposure to risk in any precise sense, that is, the populations vary in their age distributions, as well as their ages at first marriage and ages at marital disruption. It is, however, useful for comparing remarriage levels among relatively small populations.

There is great variability among racial and Hispanic groups in remarriage as reflected in this measure (see Table 5.10). Among white women, 45 percent have been remarried by the time of observation. This is the highest rate among women. Very low rates of remarriage are found for blacks (18 percent) and Puerto Ricans (19 percent). Mexican-Americans and Cubans are intermediate, with rates of 34 percent. For most groups the rates of men are considerably higher than those of

TABLE 5.10

Remarriage Propensity, by Sex, for Racial and Hispanic Groups, 1980:
Percent of Persons Under 45 No Longer in First Marriage
Who Are Currently Married, Spouse Present

	Men	Women
Non-Hispanic White	52.6	45.9
Black	31.2	17.7
American Indian	47.4	39.6
Japanese	34.8	38.4
Chinese	36.0	35.2
Filipino	48.1	39.6
Korean	53.8	44.3
Asian Indian	45.8	40.0
Vietnamese	20.3	38.9
Hawaiian	44.5	37.2
Mexican	44.5	33.8
Puerto Rican	37.2	19.0
Cuban	51.3	34.0

women. (We would emphasize that this is not a measure of lifetime remarriage propensity since some of the individuals in the universe have only recently terminated their first marriage and will ultimately remarry in subsequent years.)

Using this same measure, we see that remarriage levels are similar from one education group to another. Among both white men and white women, the college-educated tend to have lower fractions remarried than persons with less education. The analysis of CPS data noted that this was not an artifact attributable to the older ages of these persons at disruption. Among blacks, on the other hand, remarriage tends to be slightly higher for college-educated men and women than for those with less education. All of these patterns have persisted since at least 1960.

The most interesting regularity observed in these data is the apparent drop in remarriage propensities between the 1960 and 1970 censuses and between the 1970 and 1980 censuses for both sexes, both racial groups, and all education groups.[13]

---

[13]Note that the census dates are the year of observation, not the year of the remarriage. Data in Table 5.7 are for the year of remarriage. The experience captured in this "remarriage rate" for 1980 occurred over the period of roughly 1955 to 1980, and was concentrated in the 1960s. This measure picks up longer-term trends, and is not sensitive to recent short-term trends.

TABLE 5.11

Remarriage Propensity, by Education, Sex, and Ethnicity, 1960–80:
Percent of Persons Under Age 45 No Longer in First Marriage
Who Are Currently Married, Spouse Present

	Years of Education			
	9	9–11	12	13+
NON-HISPANIC WHITE MALE				
1960	67.9	70.2	70.0	71.3
1970	62.2	66.1	64.4	58.2
1980	55.8	53.3	54.0	50.2
NON-HISPANIC WHITE FEMALE				
1960	66.0	65.9	63.3	60.8
1970	58.3	59.8	56.3	49.1
1980	48.7	50.4	47.1	40.9
BLACK MALE				
1960	51.2	48.6	45.0	53.3
1970	42.1	41.1	40.3	47.0
1980	26.7	27.7	31.3	35.4
BLACK FEMALE				
1960	37.7	33.5	35.0	36.7
1970	26.3	25.8	25.4	31.8
1980	13.9	15.3	18.3	20.5

Separation from Second Marriage

Table 5.12 shows life-table estimates of the cumulative proportion of second marriages ending in separation by the second, fifth, tenth, and fifteenth anniversaries by race/ethnicity, age at second marriage, and education. Consistent with previous studies,[14] these data indicate that second marriages have a somewhat higher level of separation than first marriages. Among women, 37 percent of second marriages are terminated within ten years in comparison to 30 percent of first marriages. Among men, the level is 31 percent versus 27 percent for first marriages. As for first marriages, the younger the person is when he or she enters

---

[14]James McCarthy, "A Comparison of the Probability of the Dissolution of First and Second Marriages," *Demography* 15 (1978):345–59.

TABLE 5.12

Differentials in the Proportion Separated Within Specified Intervals
After Second Marriage, Second Marriages Occurring Between 1965 and 1980*

	Females				Males			
	Years After Marriage				Years After Marriage			
Characteristics	2	5	10	N	2	5	10	N
TOTAL	11	23	37	3,588	9	20	31	3,340
RACE/ETHNICITY								
Non-Hispanic White	12	22	36	3,159	9	20	31	2,963
Mexican-American	10	24	34	99	7	14	23	111
Black	12	31	51	274	9	21	40	229
AGE AT SECOND MARRIAGE								
<20	20	34	51	166				
20–24†	11	26	42	1,021	13	29	45	572
25–29	11	22	36	1,186	8	19	29	1,049
30–34	10	18	31	738	8	16	27	836
35–39	11	21	28	477	8	17	26	883
EDUCATION								
<9	13	28	46	206	10	20	28	247
9–11	14	25	37	655	11	23	34	488
12	11	23	37	1,947	10	21	31	1,375
13–15	9	22	30	610	7	18	34	675
16	15	20	29	226	8	20	32	294
17+	2	8	20	138	5	11	23	259

*Life-Table Estimates.

†For men, under age 25.

SOURCE: June 1980 Current Population Survey.

a second marriage, the greater the probability that it will terminate. There is also a higher rate of disruption of second marriages, the lower the level of education, especially for women. Contrary to McCarthy, we find that the higher rate of marital disruption among blacks persists with respect to second marriages (51 percent versus 36 percent for majority whites separated within ten years).

Widowhood

Patterns of widowhood during the prime adult years are more difficult to describe than is divorce because widowhood is a much rarer event. The rate at which persons of a given age and sex are widowed is partly a function of the distribution of ages of their spouses. Women are more likely to be widowed than men both because they have lower mortality and because they are more likely to be younger than their spouses.

For a variety of reasons that are not fully understood, married persons have lower mortality than the unmarried, and this difference is much larger for men than for women. Thus it is not possible to simply use age-specific death rates of men and women to estimate rates of widowhood for the opposite sex. The best way to make estimates of widowhood is by multiple-decrement life tables. We have not prepared any original estimates of the incidence of widowhood because an excellent series has been prepared by Robert Schoen of the University of Illinois. In Table 5.13 we summarize some of his estimates.[15]

Approximately two in every 1,000 married women in their thirties are widowed each year. This increases with age to about one in 100 by the early fifties, and to above five in 100 among women in their late sixties. For men, the levels are much lower—the probability of a married man becoming a widower is only one-half to one-third as large as for a married woman at each age.

As the result of the decrease in male mortality, rates of widowhood fell at every age during each of the periods of the twentieth century shown in the table. Between 1910 and 1960 widowhood rates fell even more rapidly for men, since the rise in life expectancy was much greater for women than for men. Since 1960, however, male widowhood rates have increased slightly at many ages, but they remain very low.

[15]Schoen and his associates have published an interesting series of papers reporting analyses of cohort marital-status life tables from a variety of countries. See Robert Schoen et al., "Marriage and Divorce in Twentieth Century Cohorts," *Demography* 22 (1985):101–14; Robert Schoen and John Baj, "Twentieth-Century Cohort Marriage and Divorce in England and Wales," *Population Studies* 38 (1984):439–49; Schoen and Baj, "Cohort Marriage and Divorce in Twentieth-Century Switzerland," *Journal of Marriage and the Family* 46 (1984):963–69.

TABLE 5.13

Widowhood Rates (per 1,000 married persons), by Sex, 1910–80

	Women				Men			
	1910	1940	1960	1980	1910	1940	1960	1980
30–34	8	4	2	2	4	2	1	1
35–39	8	4	3	2	6	3	1	1
40–44	12	7	5	3	7	4	1	2
45–49	15	11	8	6	7	6	2	3
50–54	20	17	13	10	11	7	3	5
55–59	33	26	21	16	14	10	5	6
60–64	48	39	35	25	18	14	8	10
65–69	71	59	50	48	26	20	12	14
70–74	115	99	77	57	37	30	18	22
75–79	193	169	120	89	50	44	27	33
80–84	357	301	209	156	70	63	44	56
85+	449	388	386	178	106	112	104	98

SOURCE: Data provided by Professor Robert Schoen of the University of Illinois.

Racial, Ethnic, and Educational Differences in Widowhood

As noted earlier, we can measure the fraction of persons whose first marriage ended in widowhood with the decennial censuses of 1970 and 1980. From these data, we know when a person married, what his/her current marital status is, and, if the person is no longer in their first marriage, whether the first marriage ended in widowhood.

These data are used in Table 5.14 to compare levels of widowhood by age for the total and black populations. Among ever-married persons in 1980, about one man in 100 and about three women in 100 had been widowed by age 35–39. These fractions rise to 6 percent of the men and 17 percent of the women aged 55–59. By age 75–79, one man in four and five women in eight had had their first marriage ended by the death of their spouse. The figures for blacks are consistently higher, reflecting higher mortality and also the greater tendency for large age differences between spouses (see Chapter 2).

Mortality rates are inversely related to education.[16] Table 5.15 shows the education-specific fraction whose first marriage ended in wid-

[16]Evelyn Kitagawa and Phillip Hauser, *Differential Mortality in the United States: A Study in Socioeconomic Epidemiology* (Cambridge, Mass.: Harvard University Press, 1973).

TABLE 5.14

Percent of Ever-Married Persons Whose First Marriage Ended in Widowhood, by Age, Sex, and Race/Ethnicity, 1980

	Total		Non-Hispanic White		Black	
	Male	Female	Male	Female	Male	Female
25–29	0.3	1.0	0.2	0.8	0.7	1.9
30–34	0.5	1.7	0.5	1.5	1.1	3.8
35–39	0.9	2.7	0.8	2.3	1.8	5.6
40–44	1.5	4.4	1.3	3.7	3.2	9.0
45–49	2.4	7.1	2.1	6.3	5.1	13.2
50–54	4.0	11.6	3.6	10.5	8.0	20.0
55–59	6.0	17.4	5.6	16.5	11.1	25.2
60–64	8.8	26.3	8.2	25.4	15.6	34.3
65–69	13.2	37.4	12.4	36.5	22.0	45.7
70–74	18.9	49.7	17.8	49.0	30.8	55.2
75–79	27.3	63.3	26.0	62.9	39.3	67.1
80–84	37.3	75.9	36.2	75.9	48.6	75.9
85 +	54.6	85.2	54.2	85.5	57.3	80.8

TABLE 5.15

Percent of Ever-Married Persons Whose First Marriage Ended in Widowhood, by Education and Sex, for Selected Ages, 1980

Years of Education	Age			Age		
	45–49	55–59	65–69	45–49	55–59	65–69
	Non-Hispanic White Men			*Non-Hispanic White Women*		
<9	2.7	6.6	13.8	10.3	21.7	40.5
9–11	2.4	5.5	12.2	8.2	17.9	37.0
12	2.0	5.4	11.6	5.5	15.0	35.0
13–15	2.1	5.2	12.1	5.7	14.7	32.9
16 +	1.7	5.1	10.7	4.3	14.3	30.6
	Black Men			*Black Women*		
<9	6.5	12.8	23.6	18.0	29.7	48.8
9–11	5.2	12.1	20.2	15.3	24.3	43.0
12	4.9	8.7	20.4	11.0	22.4	40.5
13–15	3.0	8.1	14.8*	9.4	19.4	41.2
16 +	4.7	4.1	15.1*	8.5	18.7	36.6

*Less than 150 sample cases.

owhood at selected ages. There is a large education differential for both blacks and whites of both sexes. The levels vary with sex and race for the complex of reasons discussed above (including age differences between spouses as well as differential mortality). Education differentials are quite large; for example, for non-Hispanic white females at ages 65–69, 31 percent of the college-graduate women have been widowed, compared to 41 percent among women who did not complete high school. Recall that women who did not complete high school were found in Chapter 2 to be particularly likely to have married husbands more than five years older than themselves.

Summary

Conventional divorce rates, such as the number of divorces per 1,000 population or per 1,000 married couples, are extremely crude indicators of either trends or differentials in marital disruption. This is because rates of marital disruption vary markedly with duration of marriage and because there is great variability in the conditional probability of divorce given separation. Data from the vital statistics system are further limited because the Divorce Registration Area includes only thirty states, the content of the divorce certificate is very limited, and there is a high level of nonreporting on key characteristics. Census data are limited because dates of marital disruption and remarriage are not obtained. Hence we have used marital histories collected in June CPSs as the major data source in this chapter. Decennial census data are used as a supplementary source to examine differentials in marital disruption among relatively small population groups.

The crude divorce rate (divorces per 1,000 total population) has increased greatly over the last century from about 1 per 1,000 persons to 5 per 1,000 in 1980. Over this time it fluctuated considerably with peaks associated with the two World Wars and a trough associated with the Great Depression. There was a particularly sharp increase in divorce between 1965 and 1979 as the rate per 1,000 marriages more than doubled. When viewed from the perspective of successive marriage cohorts, the likelihood of lifetime divorce shows an accelerating increase from about 7 percent for marriages begun in the 1860s to a projected rate of about one-half for recent marriages.

The timing of divorces within marriage is only crudely indicated by the measure of the median duration of marriages that end in divorce in a given year (about seven years). This measure is influenced by the changing duration composition of marriages, and it provides no indication of how rates vary by marital duration. Timing is better seen in the pattern of duration-specific divorce rates. These rates are very high early in marriage and decline gradually thereafter—from 40 per 1,000 in the first five years to less than 10 per 1,000 after twenty-five years. Partially reflecting trends in fertility, the fraction of divorces in which children were involved increased by one-third between the 1920s and 1960, and then declined slightly from 60 percent to about 56 percent by 1980.

There are major differences in the likelihood of marital disruption depending on age at marriage and on education. The proportion of marriages disrupting within ten years varies from one-half among marriages in which the wife was under age 18 at marriage to about one-quarter among those where the wife was in her early twenties. Census and survey data provide conflicting results on whether the risk of disruption continues to decline with older age at marriage after the mid-twenties or whether it turns back up for older marriages. High school dropouts had considerably higher rates than other groups, and college graduates had considerably lower rates. Much of these educational differences appear to be due to differences by education in age at marriage.

First marriages of black women are twice as likely to disrupt within ten years (about one-half) as those of white or Mexican-American women. American-Indians, Puerto Ricans, and Hawaiians also have high levels of marital instability, whereas extremely low levels are found for Asian-Americans. Increases over the 1970s occurred at all educational levels among majority whites, but not among blacks. Education differentials in marital instability among blacks became more pronounced.

Three-fifths of separations are followed by divorce within a year, but there is a very large difference between whites and blacks in the rate of divorce after separation. For example, blacks are only half as likely to have divorced within two years of separation (42 versus 84 percent). Mexican-Americans are somewhat less likely than non-Hispanic whites to divorce after separation. Education is positively related to the probability of divorce after separation. This probability declines with age at separation after age 30. There appears to have been a modest trend toward a shortening of the interval between separation and divorce over the last two decades.

The rate of remarriage declined over the 1960s and 1970s for both sexes, both racial groups, and all educational levels. Among women age 25–44, the rate declined by one-quarter over the last decade. Differentials in remarriage among racial and Hispanic groups are very large. The proportion of women remarried within ten years of separation is almost three-quarters among majority whites, compared to one-half among Mexican-Americans and one-third among blacks. Not remarrying is the modal pattern for black women whose marriages disrupt. The probability of remarriage declines steadily with increasing age at the time of separation. The differential in remarriage between men and women increases with age. Educational differences are U-shaped, with the lowest rates of remarriage at the ends of the distribution.

Rates of widowhood are very low during the prime adult years and increase with age more rapidly for women than for men. Rates are higher among blacks, reflecting both higher mortality and the greater average age differences between spouses. There are large education differences in widowhood.

Appendix

Marriage History Data
from June 1980 Current Population Survey

Since the June 1980 Current Population Survey (CPS) asked the dates of marriage, separation, and divorce for the first, second, and last marriage, it is possible to estimate marital transitions from these data. While fourth or higher marriages are excluded, this is of little importance since less than 1 percent of women have had marriages of this order. These data have several clear advantages over other sources for the estimation of the incidence of marital dissolution and remarriage. They permit the use of separation rather than divorce as the measure of dissolution. In addition, from the individual records it is possible to establish the proper cohorts of entry to risk for the events of interest; that is, marriage cohorts for the analysis of separation, and separation cohorts for analysis of rates of divorce and remarriage. Being able to relate events to the proper cohort of entry to risk is essential. For example, when vital registration data are used, reports of the duration of marriage for divorces occurring in a given year confound the pace of divorce after marriage with the relative sizes of various marriage cohorts in that year, and their previous marital histories. A period with many marriages of short duration (reflecting past fluctuations in fertility and marriage) will have more divorces from marriages of short duration, other things being equal.

Offsetting these advantages is a concern about the quality of the retrospective reporting of the various events, and differentials in such quality. We know that the census substantially underestimates the proportion of marriage cohorts ever divorced when compared to vital statistics data, and it is likely that similar reporting biases would affect the CPS data. Indeed, we do find lower proportions divorced in these data as well, but the bias is not very large. The reported proportions divorced by successive years after marriage are as follows[17]:

| | | Years after marriage | | |
		3	5	10
1960 Marriages				
	CPS	3	7	13
	Vital Statistics	6	10	19
1965 Marriages				
	CPS	6	11	23
	Vital Statistics	7	12	25
1970 Marriages				
	CPS	8	14	
	Vital Statistics	9	16	

[17]National Center for Health Statistics, "Divorces by Marriage Cohort. Vital and Health Statistics," series 21, no. 34, 1979.

FIGURE 5.A

Marriage History Data in June 1980 Current Population Survey

18A. LINE NUMBER

0	0
1	1
2	2
3	3
4
5
6
7
8
9

18B. RELATIONSHIP TO REFERENCE PERSON

Reference Person WITH other relatives in household..... ○
Reference Person with NO other relatives in household ○
Husband............. ○
Wife............. ○
Own child............. ○
Parent............. ○
Brother/Sister............. ○
Other rel. of Ref. Person............. ○
Non-rel. of Ref. Person WITH OWN relatives in household..... ○
Non-rel. of Ref. Person with NO OWN relatives in household ○

18C. AGE

0	0
1	1
2	2
3	3
4	4
5	5
6	6
7	7
8	8
9	9

18D. MARITAL STATUS

Married – civilian spouse present..... ○
Married – Armed Forces spouse present..... ○
Married – spouse absent (Exclude separated) ○
Widowed............. ○
Divorced............. ○
Separated............. ○
Never married............. ○

18E. SEX AND VETERAN STATUS

Male (Also Mark Vet. Status) ○
Vietnam Era ○
Korean War ○
World War II ○
World War I ○
Other Service ○
Nonveteran ○
Female............. ○

18F. HIGHEST GRADE ATTENDED

E	H	C
1	1	1
2	2	2
3	3	3
4	4	4
5	5	5+
6	6
7	7
8	8
None ○

18G. GRADE COMPLETED

Yes ○
No ○

18H. RACE

1. White....... ○
2. Black....... ○
3. Amer. Indian, Aleut, Eskimo ○
4. Asian or Pacific Isl. ○
5. Other....... ○

18I. ORIGIN

0	0
1	1
2	2
3	3
4
5
6
7
8
9

(Fill 18I)

TRANSCRIPTION ITEM

18J. Month and Year of Person's birth
(c.c. Items 17a and 17c)
(Month)
J F M A M J J A S O N D
○ ○ ○ ○ ○ ○ ○ ○ ○ ○ ○ ○
(Year 19—)
0 1 2 3 4 5 6 7 8 9
0 1 2 3 4 5 6 7 8 9

34. When did . . . get married for the second time?
(Month)
J F M A M J J A S O N D
○ ○ ○ ○ ○ ○ ○ ○ ○ ○ ○ ○
(Year 19—)
0 1 2 3 4 5 6 7 8 9
0 1 2 3 4 5 6 7 8 9

42. When did . . .'s (most recent) marriage end in widowhood/divorce?
(Month)
J F M A M J J A S O N D
○ ○ ○ ○ ○ ○ ○ ○ ○ ○ ○ ○
(Year 19—)
0 1 2 3 4 5 6 7 8 9
0 1 2 3 4 5 6 7 8 9

48A. When was . . .'s (first) child born?
(Month)
J F M A M J J A S O N D
○ ○ ○ ○ ○ ○ ○ ○ ○ ○ ○ ○
(Year 19—)
0 1 2 3 4 5 6 7 8 9
0 1 2 3 4 5 6 7 8 9

48B. Is the child male or female?
Male ○   Female ○

48C. Where does the child live now?
(Fill one circle)
Child resides in this household ○
Child resides elsewhere:
– in (his/her) own household ○
– with relatives:
Father............. ○
Other............. ○
– with nonrelatives ○
Child deceased ○
Don't know............. ○

28A. INTERVIEWER CHECK ITEM
Persons 15–75 years of age and
Married......... ○ (Skip to 29)
Widowed......... ○
Divorced .... ○ (Skip to 28B)
Separated .... ○
Never married ..... ○ (Fill 28B)
All others .... ○ (End questions)

35. INTERVIEWER CHECK ITEM
(See Items 28A and 29)
Married twice and Currently:
Married ○ (Skip to 44)
Widowed ○
Divorced ○ (Skip to 37)
Separated ○ (Skip to 38)
Married 3+ times ○ (Ask 36)

43. When did . . . actually stop living with his/her (most recent) spouse?
(If widowed in 28A, skip to 44)
(Month)
J F M A M J J A S O N D
○ ○ ○ ○ ○ ○ ○ ○ ○ ○ ○ ○
(Year 19—)
0 1 2 3 4 5 6 7 8 9
0 1 2 3 4 5 6 7 8 9

(If "3" in 47, skip to 53, otherwise ask 51A—C)
51A. When was . . .'s fourth child born?
(Month)
J F M A M J J A S O N D
○ ○ ○ ○ ○ ○ ○ ○ ○ ○ ○ ○
(Year 19—)
0 1 2 3 4 5 6 7 8 9
0 1 2 3 4 5 6 7 8 9

51B. Is the child male or female?
Male ○   Female ○

51C. Where does the child live now?
(Fill one circle)
Child resides in this household ○
Child resides elsewhere:
– in (his/her) own household ○
– with relatives:
Father............. ○
Other............. ○
—with nonrelatives ○
Child deceased ○
Don't know....... ○

28B. INTERVIEWER CHECK ITEM

Male .... ○ } *End Questions*
Female, age 15–17 ○ } *(Skip to 47)*
Female, age 18+ .. ○ } *(Ask 30)*

29. How many times has ... been married?

1 ○ *(Skip to 40)*
2 ○ } *(Ask 30)*
3+ ○

30. When did ... get married for the first time?
(Month)
J F M A M J J A S O N D
○ ○ ○ ○ ○ ○ ○ ○ ○ ○ ○ ○
(Year 19—)
⓪ ① ② ③ ④ ⑤ ⑥ ⑦ ⑧ ⑨
⓪ ① ② ③ ④ ⑤ ⑥ ⑦ ⑧ ⑨

31. Did ...'s first marriage end in widowhood or in divorce?
Widowhood ○
Divorce .... ○

32. When did ...'s first marriage end in widowhood/divorce?
(Month)
J F M A M J J A S O N D
○ ○ ○ ○ ○ ○ ○ ○ ○ ○ ○ ○
(Year 19—)
⓪ ① ② ③ ④ ⑤ ⑥ ⑦ ⑧ ⑨
⓪ ① ② ③ ④ ⑤ ⑥ ⑦ ⑧ ⑨

33. When did ... actually stop living with his/her first spouse?
(If widowed in 31, skip to 34)
(Month)
J F M A M J J A S O N D
○ ○ ○ ○ ○ ○ ○ ○ ○ ○ ○ ○
(Year 19—)
⓪ ① ② ③ ④ ⑤ ⑥ ⑦ ⑧ ⑨
⓪ ① ② ③ ④ ⑤ ⑥ ⑦ ⑧ ⑨

---

36. Did ...'s second marriage end in widowhood or in divorce?
Widowhood ○
Divorce..... ○

37. When did ...'s second marriage end in widowhood/divorce?
(Month)
J F M A M J J A S O N D
○ ○ ○ ○ ○ ○ ○ ○ ○ ○ ○ ○
(Year 19—)
⓪ ① ② ③ ④ ⑤ ⑥ ⑦ ⑧ ⑨
⓪ ① ② ③ ④ ⑤ ⑥ ⑦ ⑧ ⑨

38. When did ... actually stop living with his/her second spouse?
(If widowed in 35 or 36, skip to 39)
(Month)
J F M A M J J A S O N D
○ ○ ○ ○ ○ ○ ○ ○ ○ ○ ○ ○
(Year 19—)
⓪ ① ② ③ ④ ⑤ ⑥ ⑦ ⑧ ⑨
⓪ ① ② ③ ④ ⑤ ⑥ ⑦ ⑧ ⑨

39. INTERVIEWER CHECK ITEM
(See item 29)
Married twice.......... ○ *(Skip to 44)*
Married 3+ times ..... ○ *(Ask 40)*

40. What was the date of ...'s *(most recent)* marriage?
(Month)
J F M A M J J A S O N D
○ ○ ○ ○ ○ ○ ○ ○ ○ ○ ○ ○
(Year 19—)
⓪ ① ② ③ ④ ⑤ ⑥ ⑦ ⑧ ⑨
⓪ ① ② ③ ④ ⑤ ⑥ ⑦ ⑧ ⑨

41. INTERVIEWER CHECK ITEM
(See item 28)
Currently married .... ○ *(Skip to 44)*
Currently widowed or divorced ...... ○ *(Ask 42)*
Currently separated ..... ○ *(Skip to 43)*

---

44. INTERVIEWER CHECK ITEM
(See items 28A–B and 29)
Male, currently married in 2nd or later marriage ○ } *(Ask 45A)*
Male, currently widowed, separated, or divorced . ○
Other male .... ○ } *(End questions)*
Female...................... ○ } *(Skip to 47)*

45A. Does ... have any children from a previous marriage who are less than 18 years old?
Yes ○ *(Ask 45B)*
No ○ *(End questions)*

45B. How many of these children usually live elsewhere?
None ○ } *(End questions for males)*
1 ○
2 ○ } *(Ask 46)*
3+ ○

46. Regarding the children who usually live elsewhere, during the past 12 months did ... provide financial support regularly, occasionally, seldom, or never?
Regularly .... ○ } *(End questions for males)*
Occasionally ○
Seldom....... ○
Never .... ○

47. How many babies has ... ever had, if any? *(Do not count stillbirths)*
None ○ *(Skip to 53)*
1 ○
2 ○
3 ○
4 ○
5 ○ } *(Ask 48A–C)*
6 ○
7 ○
8 ○
9 ○
10+ ○

(If "1" in 47, skip to 53, otherwise ask 49A–C)
49A. When was ...'s second child born?
(Month)
J F M A M J J A S O N D
○ ○ ○ ○ ○ ○ ○ ○ ○ ○ ○ ○
(Year 19—)
⓪ ① ② ③ ④ ⑤ ⑥ ⑦ ⑧ ⑨
⓪ ① ② ③ ④ ⑤ ⑥ ⑦ ⑧ ⑨

49B. Is the child male or female?
Male ○ Female ○

49C. Where does the child live now?
(Fill one circle)
Child resides in this household ○
Child resides elsewhere:
– in (his/her) own household ○
– with relatives:
 Father.............. ○
 Other............... ○
 – with nonrelatives ○
Child deceased .... ○
Don't know.............. ○

50A. When was ...'s third child born?
(Month)
J F M A M J J A S O N D
○ ○ ○ ○ ○ ○ ○ ○ ○ ○ ○ ○
(Year 19—)
⓪ ① ② ③ ④ ⑤ ⑥ ⑦ ⑧ ⑨
⓪ ① ② ③ ④ ⑤ ⑥ ⑦ ⑧ ⑨

50B. Is the child male or female?
Male ○ Female ○

50C. Where does the child live now?
(Fill one circle)
Child resides in this household ○
Child resides elsewhere:
– in (his/her) own household ○
– with relatives:
 Father.............. ○
 Other............... ○
 – with nonrelatives ○
Child deceased .... ○
Don't know.............. ○

(If "4" in 47, skip to 53, otherwise ask 52A–C)
52A. When was ...'s last child born?
(Month)
J F M A M J J A S O N D
○ ○ ○ ○ ○ ○ ○ ○ ○ ○ ○ ○
(Year 19—)
⓪ ① ② ③ ④ ⑤ ⑥ ⑦ ⑧ ⑨
⓪ ① ② ③ ④ ⑤ ⑥ ⑦ ⑧ ⑨

52B. Is the child male or female?
Male ○ Female ○

52C. Where does the child live now?
(Fill one circle)
Child resides in this household ○
Child resides elsewhere:
– in (his/her) own household ○
– with relatives:
 Father.............. ○
 Other............... ○
 – with nonrelatives ○
Child deceased .... ○
Don't know.............. ○

53. INTERVIEWER CHECK ITEM
Female, age 18–39 ○ *(Ask 54)*
All others ○ *(End questions)*

INTERVIEW WOMAN FOR HERSELF. IF NOT PRESENT, MAKE TELEPHONE CALLBACK (S).

54. Looking ahead, do you expect to have any (more) children?
Yes ○ *(Ask 55)*
No ○ } *(End questions)*
Uncertain ○

55. How many (more) children do you expect to have?
1 ○ 4 ○
2 ○ 5 ○
3 ○ 6+ ○

These data suggest that data for marriages before 1965 should be regarded with caution, but that we are not likely to be seriously misled by the data for more recent experience. Cherlin and McCarthy report that the CPS marriage history data are less satisfactory for men than for women.[18] For example, divorce rate estimates from the male data tended to be 10 to 20 percent lower than those estimated from the marital histories of females. For this reason we have restricted our estimates of trend to the data for women. Social and economic differentials are likely to be less affected by the underreporting by males so we have retained these, although this problem should be kept in mind.

When specific cohorts of entry to risk are under consideration, the estimation of the proportion with an event within specified intervals is straightforward. For example, with 1980 data we can follow the 1970 marriage cohort and record the proportion separated by the end of each year through 1979. However, when the sample is combined across marriage cohorts, respondents who may eventually separate will have been married varying numbers of years at the time they were interviewed. We need to include the experience of such cases in estimating the likelihood of separation up to specific durations of marriage, since they represent years of "exposure to risk" during which a separation did not occur. Life-table procedures are used to accomplish this in the tables in this chapter that are based on the CPS data. Put simply, life tables calculate the probability of a separation at any given duration of marriage for marriages that have experienced that duration. These duration-specific risks are then combined to provide an estimate of the cumulative proportion that would have become separated by each successive duration, if a marriage cohort were to live through the estimated sequence of duration-specific risks.

[18]Andrew Cherlin and James McCarthy, "Remarried Couple Households: Data from the June 1980 Current Population Survey," *Journal of Marriage and the Family* (February 1985): 23–30.

6

THE FORMERLY MARRIED

W E DISCUSSED the incidence of divorce, widowhood, and remarriage in Chapter 5. We turn now to the formerly married population.[1] At any point in time, this population is the outcome of complex patterns of inflow and outflow. One can be formerly married only by having first married and then having experienced separation, divorce, or widowhood; and one remains in this status only until reconciliation, remarriage, or death. Thus, trends over time and differentials among groups in the prevalence of the formerly married are the joint product of differences in these component processes. Many widowed, and most separated or divorced persons, are in a relatively brief transitional status that will soon be followed by remarriage, though this is much less so among blacks than among majority whites.

We begin with a discussion of the size and rate of growth of the formerly married population and then describe its characteristics—educational attainment, labor force status, income, presence of children, and poverty status. Finally, we examine the living arrangements of the formerly married. Throughout this chapter we disaggregate the formerly married population by sex, marital status, age, and presence of children. (Discussion of the population over age 60 is deferred to Chapter 8.)

---

[1]Persons who are classified as "Married, Spouse Absent–Other" are included in the formerly married population, even though they are currently married. The reasons for their inclusion here are discussed later in the chapter.

Prevalence

As noted in earlier discussions, concern with the prevalence of some component of the population can usefully focus on either the absolute number of persons or the proportion of the population with that characteristic. There were 17.0 million formerly married persons under age 60 in the United States in 1980, or 15 percent of all persons aged 18 to 59. Note that these are persons who are *currently* separated, widowed, or divorced; it does not include those persons who have been widowed or divorced but have remarried and are now living with a spouse. The fraction was higher for women than for men (19 versus 12 percent), so that three-fifths of all formerly married persons under age 60 were women. The sex difference is partially due to the higher mortality of men than women (there were 2.1 million widowed women and only 0.4 million widowed men under age 60), and to the higher remarriage rate of men. As we will discuss shortly, there is also some evidence that the number of formerly married men (especially separated and divorced men) is understated in census sources because of both differential underenumeration and misreporting of marital status.

The number of formerly married persons under age 60 rose about 24 percent between 1960 and 1970, from 9.2 to 11.4 million (see Table 6.1). This increase was more rapid for women than for men (26 versus 19 percent), and was due primarily to an increase in the number of divorced persons (57 percent among women compared to 48 percent among men). The number of separated men rose by 16 percent, while the number of separated women increased by 31 percent. In contrast to the trend in the 1960s, during the 1970s the number of the formerly married rose much more rapidly among men than among women (68 versus 39 percent). Again, the number of divorced persons increased at an extremely rapid rate (149 percent for men and 123 percent for women). The separated population also increased rapidly—61 percent for men and 36 percent for women.[2] The number of widows and "married, spouse absent—other" persons of each sex decreased.

In principle the total number of separated men and women of all ages that are enumerated in the census should be about the same. These numbers should be different only to the extent that an unequal number of separated husbands or wives are living outside of the United States.[3]

---

[2]While the recent differential trends by sex could reflect differential remarriage trends, it is more likely that they reflect changes in levels of underenumeration and misclassification of marital status. This is discussed below.

[3]Cohabitation and common-law marriages add confusion to the question. We have no idea how persons who end informal unions report their marital status. Whether or not they regarded themselves as "married" when in the union, they might reasonably regard

TABLE 6.1
Number of Formerly Married Persons Under Age 60, by Sex and Marital Status, 1940–80

	1940	1950	1960	1970	1980
			Number (thousands)		
MALES					
Divorced	526	889	1,026	1,516	3,782
Widowed	773	598	455	484	403
Separated	1,535†	700	710	821	1,321
MSA–O*		866	1,054	1,042	970
Total	2,834	3,053	3,245	3,863	6,476
FEMALES					
Divorced	758	1,236	1,556	2,438	5,447
Widowed	2,403	2,296	2,214	2,397	2,145
Separated	1,574†	1,053	1,187	1,553	2,107
MSA–O*		697	1,032	1,186	801
Total	4,735	5,282	5,990	7,575	10,500
			Percent Change		
MALES					
Divorced	+ 69		+ 15	+ 48	+149
Widowed	− 23		− 24	+ 6	− 17
Separated	+ 2†		+ 1	+ 16	+ 61
MSA–O*			+ 22	− 1	− 7
Total	+ 8		+ 6	+ 19	+ 68
FEMALES					
Divorced	+ 63		+ 26	+ 57	+123
Widowed	− 4		− 4	− 8	− 11
Separated	+ 11†		+ 13	+ 31	+ 36
MSA–O*			+ 48	+ 15	− 32
Total	+ 12		+ 13	+ 26	+ 39

*Married, Spouse Absent–Other (than separated).

†In 1940, Separated and MSA–O are combined into a single category because the distinction was not made in the 1940 census.

themselves as "separated" when the union is ended. Whether men or women are more likely to have this perception is unknown.

Another source of confusion is whether persons whose spouse dies during a period of separation report themselves to be separated or widowed. It would appear that the census scheme for marital status would have them classified as widowed, but this is not clearly specified anywhere.

There is, of course, no reason that numbers of divorced or widowed men and women should be identical. Men and women who are divorced can, and do, remarry in different numbers. And of course, the deceased spouse of a widowed person is not enumerated in the census.

In fact, the numbers of separated men and women are not identical. If we consider the total number of separated persons (of all ages, not just under the age of 60), the ratio of men to women was .682 in 1980. The ratio rose from .612 in 1970; in 1960, however, it was .695.

There are a number of reasons that this deficit of separated men may come about: (1) separated men may be disproportionately missed in the census; (2) separated (and divorced) men may report themselves as single more than women do; and (3) single women (with children) may report themselves as separated.[4] But all of this is speculation, since

[4]Why should there be fewer separated men than separated women? And why should the ratio have risen between 1970 and 1980? The reason for the differential probably involves both misreporting of marital status and a higher rate of underenumeration of separated men.

Misreporting of marital status—Even today there is a certain amount of social stigma associated with being separated or divorced. Acknowledging that you are separated or divorced may be regarded as an admission of a personal failing. Some separated and divorced persons probably represent themselves to others, including the census, as single (never married). This may be somewhat easier for men than for women because a much larger share of formerly married women have children living with them. For them to represent themselves as never-married would be to suggest that their children are illegitimate, which might be even more stigmatizing. Conversely, the difference may also be due to some never-married women with children reporting that they are separated to avoid admitting that they are a never-married parent.

No data are available that would help in assessing the degree to which this misreporting of marital status is occurring. In the program of evaluation of the 1960 and 1970 censuses there was a matching of cases enumerated in the Current Population Survey conducted during the same month. These studies show a high level of unreliability of classification of separated persons, that is, a low level of correspondence between census and CPS classification of separated persons of both sexes but very little net difference between the proportion classified as separated in the CPS and in the census. However, we do not know which, if either, of the two enumerations gives the true marital status. Also, if people are intentionally misrepresenting their marital statuses, they would probably do it in both the census and the CPS.

Underenumeration of Separated Persons—It is reasonable to expect that a disproportionate number of separated and divorced persons would be missed in the census. People missed in the census tend to be persons with unusual residences, those who are highly mobile, and those with weak or nonexistent ties to households, jobs, or the wider community. Separated or divorced men are probably less likely than women to be enumerated in the census for at least two reasons:

1. Men are less likely to have children living with them and thus more likely to have a lifestyle that would make them difficult to find and enumerate.

2. Men are also more likely to be without a stable residence and ties to the community; they are more likely to be homeless or drifting from one place to another.

Why should the ratio of men to women have increased between the 1970 and 1980 censuses? A great deal of effort was devoted in the 1980 census to improving the enumeration

there is no good evidence on any of these points. What is clear is that the coverage of separated men is seriously deficient, and it is likely that divorced men are also underrepresented.

The effect of the deficit of separated and divorced men on the aggregate characteristics of these populations is not clear. Although there is undoubtedly selectivity in the degree to which separated and divorced men are represented in the census, there is no way to assess it. Having expressed these reservations, we will, in the remainder of this chapter, report the census data as an adequate representation of the situation of the separated and divorced.

Divorced Persons

Table 6.2 shows the absolute and relative prevalence of divorced (and not remarried) persons in the United States population for each census year since 1890. At the turn of the century there were 200,000 divorced persons. By 1940 the number had increased to 1.4 million. Between 1940 and 1960 the number doubled to over 3 million, and by 1980 there was a further tripling to 10.8 million divorced persons. At the turn of the century, only about one adult in 300 was divorced. By 1930 it was about one in eighty, and by 1960, one in forty. Since 1960, and particularly during the 1970s, the divorced population grew rapidly, and by 1980 one woman in thirteen and one man in eighteen was divorced. In the mid-adult ages, nearly one out of ten adults is currently divorced. Women are more likely to be divorced than men at every age (see Table 6.3). For example, in 1980 at ages 30–34, 9 percent of the men and 11 percent of the women were divorced.

---

of population groups that have traditionally been difficult to enumerate. The evidence is that the overall rate of underenumeration decreased. This, then, should have resulted in better coverage of separated and divorced persons, especially males. In addition, one might suppose that the stigma of having experienced marital disruption decreased over the decade as the incidence of marital disruption increased. This might have had a similar effect on both men and women. To the extent that the deficit of separated men is due to never-married women with children reporting their marital status as separated, there were factors working in both directions during the 1970s. More never-married women have children, but the stigma associated with being never-married with children has probably decreased.

TABLE 6.2

Number of Currently Divorced Persons (in thousands)—All Ages, 1890–1980

	Male		Female	
	Number	Percent of Population 14 +	Number	Percent of Population 14 +
1890	49	0.2	72	0.4
1900	84	0.3	115	0.5
1910	156	0.5	185	0.6
1920	235	0.6	273	0.8
1930	489	1.1	573	1.3
1940	624	1.2	823	1.6
1950	1,071	2.0	1,373	2.4
1960	1,299	2.1	1,855	2.9
1970	1,958	2.7	3,069	3.9
1980	4,393	5.3	6,440	7.1

SOURCE: *1890–1970:* United States Bureau of the Census, *Historical Statistics of the United States, Colonial Times to 1970, Part 1,* series A, pp. 160–71, 1975. Persons whose marital status was not reported are distributed proportionately into marital status categories.

Separated Persons

Table 6.4 shows age-specific proportions separated for 1950 to 1980 (prior to 1950, separated persons were not distinguished from the currently married). The age-specific fractions separated have not increased much since 1950. For example, among 30–34-year-olds the fraction increased from 1.7 to 2.7 percent among men, and from 2.5 to 4.0 percent among women.

In 1950, there were about as many separated as divorced persons. The number of divorced persons rose much more rapidly than the number of separated persons, so that by 1980 three times as many persons were divorced as were separated. The ratio of separated to divorced persons has been lower in recent decades for at least two reasons: (1) the number of divorced persons has become larger and larger as the rate of divorce increased and the population grew. Even though remarriage and death depletes this population, it has "accumulated" more rapidly than the separated population, the members of which typically remain for a shorter duration; (2) more of those experiencing separation go on to become divorced, and those who divorce do so more quickly. Fewer of

TABLE 6.3

Percent Currently Divorced, by Age and Sex, 1890–1980

	20–24	25–29	30–34	35–44	45–54
MALES					
1890	0.0	0.2	0.2	0.3	0.4
1900	0.1	0.2	0.4	0.5	0.6
1910	0.1	0.4	0.5	0.7	0.8
1920	0.2	0.5	0.7	0.9	1.0
1930	0.4	1.0	1.4	1.6	1.6
1940	0.3	0.9	1.4	1.9	2.0
1950	0.9	1.7	2.2	2.5	3.0
1960	1.0	1.8	2.1	2.6	3.1
1970	1.4	3.0	3.3	3.6	3.8
1980	2.3	6.6	8.8	8.3	7.1
FEMALES					
1890	0.2	0.4	0.5	0.6	0.5
1900	0.4	0.6	0.7	0.7	0.6
1910	0.5	0.7	0.8	0.9	0.8
1920	0.6	0.9	1.0	1.1	1.0
1930	1.1	1.8	1.9	1.9	1.6
1940	0.9	1.8	2.4	2.7	2.2
1950	1.7	2.5	3.0	3.6	3.5
1960	1.8	2.6	3.1	3.8	4.3
1970	2.5	4.3	5.0	5.5	5.5
1980	4.2	9.0	11.1	11.4	9.4

SOURCES: *1890–1960*: U.S. Bureau of the Census, *U.S. Census of Population: 1960*, vol. 1, table 177. Washington D.C.: Government Printing Office, 1964. *1970*: U.S. Bureau of the Census, *Census of Population: 1970, Detailed Characteristics*, vol. D, table 203. Washington, D.C.: Government Printing Office, 1973; *1980*: Public Use Samples.

those whose marriages terminate spend the rest of their lives as separated persons. We argued in Chapter 5 that this is both because more persons wish to remarry following marital dissolution and because the law has become more complex; there are now more legal incentives for a separating couple to divorce, especially when there are children and/or substantial assets, even if neither spouse is contemplating remarriage. In the past, many separations resulted from one spouse (usually the husband) simply abandoning the other. There was often no reason to go to the trouble and expense of becoming divorced until one of the partners wished to remarry.

Reflecting the differential rate of remarriage noted in Chapter 5, a very different mix of separated versus divorced persons is found among

TABLE 6.4

Percent Currently Separated, by Age and Sex, 1950–80

	20–24	25–29	30–34	35–39	40–44	45–54
MALES						
1950	1.2	1.6	1.7	1.9	1.9	2.0
1960	1.1	1.5	1.7	1.7	1.7	1.8
1970	1.2	1.9	1.9	1.9	1.9	1.9
1980	1.3	2.6	2.7	2.6	2.8	2.2
FEMALES						
1950	2.3	2.5	2.5	2.7	2.6	2.4
1960	2.3	2.7	2.9	2.7	2.6	2.4
1970	2.6	3.3	3.5	3.4	3.2	2.7
1980	2.7	3.9	4.0	4.0	3.9	3.2

SOURCE: See Table 6.3.

majority whites, blacks, and Mexican-Americans. In 1980 there were about equal numbers of separated and divorced blacks, compared to about four times as many divorced as separated persons among non-Hispanic whites. Mexican-Americans are in between, with a ratio of three divorced to one separated person. These ratios are similar for men and women. Blacks are much more likely to remain separated for an extended period than are majority-white persons who experience marital disruption.

We know that most persons who separate become divorced within a fairly short time, and that remarriage often occurs shortly after divorce. It is unclear what this implies about the distribution of duration since separation of persons who, in the cross-section, are enumerated as separated or divorced. Most people who enter these statuses remain in them for only a short time. However, the minority who remain separated for long periods of time (or who divorce but do not remarry) may be heavily represented in the cross-section, as others rapidly enter and leave the separated or divorced population. With data from the June 1980 Current Population Survey, it is possible to look at this distribution. Table 6.5 shows the distribution by duration since separation for both the separated and the divorced populations of women. We classify the currently divorced as well as the currently separated by duration since separation.

Slightly over one-third of the currently separated women (under age 60) separated less than a year ago, and slightly under one-third separated

TABLE 6.5

*Distribution of Duration Since Separation
for Currently Separated and Divorced Women,
by Marital Status and Age, for All Women and Black Women, 1980*

	Years Since Separation							Total
	<1	1	2	3	4	5–9	10+	
TOTAL, ALL RACES								
Separated								
14–24	59.0	20.5	9.8	5.2	4.2	1.3	—	100.0
25–34	41.4	20.8	11.2	5.4	3.4	14.1	3.8	100.0
35–44	34.4	12.6	9.0	4.4	5.6	15.3	18.6	100.0
45–59	15.0	10.6	6.6	4.3	4.7	15.6	43.2	100.0
Total	35.0	16.0	9.2	4.9	4.4	13.1	17.4	100.0
Divorced								
14–24	22.6	28.3	22.2	10.8	7.5	8.5	—	100.0
25–34	8.8	15.6	15.8	12.3	11.7	29.8	6.0	100.0
35–44	5.8	9.8	9.9	9.6	8.2	32.4	24.3	100.0
45–59	3.6	5.2	5.8	6.1	6.0	28.0	45.3	100.0
Total	7.4	11.8	11.6	9.6	8.7	28.5	22.6	100.0
BLACK WOMEN								
Separated								
14–24	48.7	19.6	13.8	12.0	4.9	1.0	—	100.0
25–34	24.4	18.9	11.8	7.1	4.5	25.5	7.8	100.0
35–44	11.6	7.0	10.2	3.6	8.4	22.8	36.3	100.0
45–59	7.1	4.8	2.8	2.2	4.5	14.3	64.3	100.0
Total	17.4	11.2	8.6	5.0	5.6	19.1	33.3	100.0
Divorced								
14–24	20.7	21.8	10.1	16.2	7.4	23.8	—	100.0
25–34	4.8	10.2	11.7	9.4	8.9	39.0	16.0	100.0
35–44	3.1	6.8	4.7	5.6	6.0	31.5	42.2	100.0
45–59	2.0	4.6	2.2	2.3	4.5	17.9	66.4	100.0
Total	4.1	7.9	6.4	6.2	6.5	29.2	39.7	100.0

SOURCE: June 1980 Current Population Survey.

five or more years ago. Of course, these distributions vary by age; younger people are more likely to have recently separated, and older persons are more likely to have been separated for longer periods of time. Nearly three-fifths of separated persons under age 25, but only one-third of those aged 35–44, have been separated for less than a year.

Duration since separation is obviously longer among the divorced than among the separated population, since a segment of divorced time is included along with a segment of separated time. Nearly one of five currently divorced women separated less than two years ago; half separated five or more years ago.

Because of lower rates of transition from separation to divorce and lower rates of remarriage, currently separated and divorced black women have longer intervals since separation than the total population. For example, among separated women, 35 percent of the total, but only 17 percent of the black women, separated less than a year ago. Similarly, among divorced women, the fraction whose marriage ended five or more years ago is 30 percent for all women, and 52 percent for black women.

Separated and Divorced Persons

As we have just noted, separation is usually a temporary status before divorce. Therefore, in this section we combine the separated and divorced in order to examine this population in more detail. As discussed in Chapter 5, persons who are currently separated or divorced are only a subset of those who have ever experienced these events. From census data we do not know whether a currently married couple has been separated and "reconciled" in the past. We do know, however, if the first marriages of remarried persons ended in divorce. These data are summarized for men and women by age from the 1980 census in Table 6.6. "Persons known to have been separated or divorced" includes the currently separated and divorced, as well as currently married persons no longer in first marriages who report that their first marriage ended in divorce.

The currently separated and divorced comprise 47 percent of ever separated or divorced men and 56 percent of women. These fractions decrease with increasing age. Because blacks are less likely to remarry after separation or divorce (see discussion in Chapter 5), a much larger share of the ever-separated and divorced are currently in those marital statuses. For men at ages 35 and over, the ratio for blacks is around 60 percent, compared to about 40 percent for all men. About 70 percent of

TABLE 6.6

Currently Separated or Divorced Persons
as a Percent of Those Known to Have Been Separated or Divorced,
by Sex and Age, for Total and Black Population, 1980

Age	Total		Black	
	Male	Female	Male	Female
18–24	77.6	74.3	86.3	90.6
25–29	61.8	61.7	79.3	84.9
30–34	49.9	55.7	68.6	80.1
35–39	43.0	54.6	65.2	78.8
40–44	40.9	53.7	59.9	75.7
45–49	40.0	52.8	56.7	72.1
50–54	39.1	50.7	57.5	69.2
55–59	37.0	48.4	55.3	63.6
Total	46.6	56.2	64.3	76.8

ever-separated or divorced black women age 35 and over are in those statuses, compared to about 50 percent for all women.

Between 1970 and 1980 the number of currently separated and divorced persons rose at an extremely rapid rate at ages 25–44 (see Table 6.7). In 1980 there were three times as many separated and divorced men and 2.5 times as many separated and divorced women aged 25–34 as in 1970. At ages 35–44 there were 2.2 times as many separated and divorced men and nearly twice as many women than there were a decade earlier. Only a small portion of this increase can be explained by population growth (the larger baby boom cohorts reaching ages 25–44). There was a growth of 40 percent in the total number of 25–34-year-olds and of 10 percent in the total number of 35–44-year-olds of each sex, much less than the increase in the number of separated and divorced persons. Most of the increase of young separated and divorced persons is due to increased age-specific proportions separated and divorced.

It would be a mistake to think of the growth in the separated and divorced population as entirely among young adults. Table 6.8 shows the age components of growth in each of the two decades. In both periods more than one-third of the increase was contributed by 45–59-year-olds. About one-quarter was an increase in 35–44-year-olds, one quarter in 25–34-year-olds, and one-tenth in persons under age 25.

TABLE 6.7

Percent Increase in the Number of Separated and Divorced Persons,
by Age and Sex, for Total and Black Populations,
1960–70 and 1970–80

Age	1960–70		1970–80	
	Males	Females	Males	Females
TOTAL				
<25	87.6	77.6	44.9	55.9
25–34	51.2	53.0	209.1	157.3
35–44	22.3	29.5	121.4	92.6
45–59	29.5	43.1	59.2	54.1
Total	36.7	45.2	105.4	91.0
BLACK				
<25	46.8	40.9	16.0	1.5
25–34	10.3	24.5	153.1	83.8
35–44	3.6	26.3	76.5	51.5
45–59	27.1	46.4	47.6	52.7
Total	16.7	32.8	78.3	55.5

TABLE 6.8

Age Components of Growth*
in the Number of Separated and Divorced Persons
Under Age 60, by Sex, 1960–70 and 1970–80

Age	1960–70		1970–80	
	Men	Women	Men	Women
<25	7.4	10.7	10.1	13.1
25–34	23.1	24.4	25.6	25.7
35–44	29.1	29.6	26.1	26.4
45–59	40.4	35.3	38.3	34.8
Total	100.0	100.0	100.0	100.0

*Net increase in this age group as percent of total net increase.

Race and Ethnic Variation
in Prevalence of Separation and Divorce

Table 6.9 compares the age-specific prevalence of separation and divorce in 1980 among non-Hispanic whites, blacks, and Mexican-Americans. In the upper panel the base is the total population, while in the lower panel the base is the ever-married population. For non-Hispanic white males the prevalence of separation and divorce increases with age to a peak of about 13 percent of the ever-married population at age 25–29. Beyond that age it decreases to 7 percent at age 55–59. The pattern for Mexican-American men is very similar. However, for black men the prevalence is over 20 percent by age 25–29, and remains at about that level through age 55–59.

TABLE 6.9

Percent Separated or Divorced, by Age, Sex, Race/Ethnicity,
for Total and Ever-Married Population, 1980

	Male			Female		
	Non-Hispanic White	Black	Mexican-American	Non-Hispanic White	Black	Mexican-American
OF TOTAL POPULATION						
18–19	0.5	0.5	0.9	1.7	1.4	2.6
20–24	3.7	3.4	3.7	6.7	7.7	6.6
25–29	8.8	12.3	7.5	11.7	20.2	11.6
30–34	10.7	18.7	9.0	13.4	27.9	13.2
35–39	10.2	20.1	9.0	13.5	30.8	14.0
40–44	9.8	20.6	9.3	12.9	30.4	14.5
45–49	8.8	20.5	9.0	11.3	28.6	14.6
50–54	7.7	19.9	8.2	9.8	25.6	15.2
55–59	6.5	18.4	8.1	8.4	22.0	13.5
OF EVER-MARRIED PERSONS						
18–19	8.8	14.3	8.1	9.7	14.8	9.6
20–24	11.1	15.4	8.6	13.1	23.5	11.1
25–29	12.7	21.4	10.1	14.5	31.8	13.9
30–34	12.4	24.2	10.2	14.7	35.5	14.5
35–39	11.1	23.6	9.8	14.3	36.0	15.1
40–44	10.4	23.4	10.0	13.5	34.1	15.4
45–49	9.3	22.7	9.6	11.8	31.2	15.4
50–54	8.2	22.0	8.6	10.2	27.6	16.0
55–59	6.8	20.0	8.6	8.8	23.5	14.2

The age patterns for women are similar to those for men. The level peaks, at about 15 percent, at age 25–34 for ever-married non-Hispanic white women. For blacks, one-third of the ever-married women (30 percent of all women) aged 25–49 were currently separated or divorced in 1980. This is more than twice as high as for non-Hispanic white or Mexican-American women. These patterns are the outcome of age patterns of both marital separation and remarriage discussed in Chapter 5. The very high proportion separated and divorced among blacks results from both their high rates of marital separation and their low rates of remarriage.

Table 6.10 shows the fraction separated or divorced at age 35–44 for detailed racial and Hispanic subpopulations. This age range is selected for comparison because the prevalence of separation and divorce tends to be highest at these ages and because it is old enough not to be biased very much by subgroup differences in age at first marriage. Of all these groups, blacks have by far the highest fraction separated and divorced (31 percent of women). The groups with proportions of women separated or divorced higher than the 13 percent of non-Hispanic white women are American Indians (21 percent), Hawaiians (18 percent), and Puerto Ricans (28 percent). Groups with very low fractions of women separated or divorced are Asian Indians, Chinese, Filipinos, Koreans, and Vietnamese (all under 8 percent).

TABLE 6.10

Percent of 35–44-Year-Old Persons Who Are Separated or Divorced, by Sex, for Racial and Hispanic Groups, 1970 and 1980

	1980		1970	
	Men	Women	Men	Women
Non-Hispanic White	10.0	13.2	4.7	7.2
Black	20.3	30.6	13.2	23.3
Japanese	6.9	9.3	2.8	5.3
Chinese	4.2	5.4	3.0	3.2
Filipino	5.4	6.6	3.5	4.9
American Indian	16.1	21.1	8.7	14.4
Korean	3.7	6.8	NA	NA
Asian Indian	2.6	4.0	NA	NA
Vietnamese	6.6	6.9	NA	NA
Hawaiian	14.0	18.1	NA	NA
Mexican	9.2	14.2	4.9	10.3
Puerto Rican	13.9	28.5	7.3	19.8
Cuban	9.1	13.4	3.8	9.3

All groups for which 1970 data are available, even those with a relatively low level in 1970, show an increase in prevalence of separation and divorce during the decade.

Widowed Persons

Table 6.11 shows the age-specific percent of men and women under age 55 who were currently widowed at each census date since 1890. The prevalence of widowhood has declined with reduced mortality (see Chapter 5), and it has also been affected by trends in remarriage. At the turn of the century, about one man in thirty was a widower at age 35–44, and about one woman in twelve was a widow. By 1980, these fractions were one in 250 for men, and one in fifty for women.

TABLE 6.11

Percent Currently Widowed, by Age and Sex, 1890–1980

	20–24	25–29	30–34	35–44	45–54
MALES					
1890	0.2	1.0	1.8	3.3	6.0
1900	0.4	1.2	2.0	3.6	6.8
1910	0.4	1.1	1.8	3.2	6.4
1920	0.5	1.1	1.8	3.0	5.8
1930	0.3	0.8	1.3	2.5	5.2
1940	0.1	0.4	0.7	1.7	4.1
1950	0.2	0.3	0.4	0.9	2.8
1960	0.1	0.2	0.3	0.7	1.8
1970	0.2	0.3	0.3	0.7	1.7
1980	0.0	0.1	0.2	0.4	1.4
FEMALES					
1890	1.2	2.8	4.5	8.9	18.4
1900	1.4	2.9	4.6	8.6	17.6
1910	1.2	2.4	3.9	7.5	15.7
1920	1.4	2.6	3.9	7.2	15.3
1930	1.0	2.1	3.3	6.5	14.0
1940	0.6	1.3	2.5	5.9	13.1
1950	0.4	0.9	1.6	3.8	11.1
1960	0.3	0.7	1.2	3.0	8.8
1970	0.7	1.1	1.5	3.0	7.9
1980	0.2	0.5	0.9	2.2	7.0

SOURCE: See Table 6.3.

There are large education differentials in the prevalence of widow-hood, reflecting education differences in mortality, remarriage of wid-owed persons, and variations in age differences between spouses. To the extent that a large fraction of women in a group marry men who are much older than themselves, that group will tend to have a higher in-cidence of widowhood among women, but a lower incidence among men. (See Table 6.12.)

In 1980 very few women were widows at age 35–39 (3 percent of women with less than nine years of education and only 1 percent of the college-educated). At age 55–59, 19 percent of the women who did not attend high school were widows, compared with 16 percent of the high

TABLE 6.12

Percent of Persons Who Are Widows, by Age, Sex, and Education, for Total and Black Populations, 1980

| | Years of Education | | | | | | |
	<9	9–11	12	13–15	16	17+	Total
WOMEN							
Total							
35–39	3.2	2.5	1.4	1.4	0.8	0.6	1.6
40–44	4.9	4.0	2.5	2.3	1.9	1.8	2.9
45–49	8.6	6.9	4.1	4.4	2.6	3.5	5.1
50–54	13.6	10.4	7.4	7.3	5.6	5.6	8.8
55–59	19.2	15.9	12.1	11.4	11.0	10.4	14.0
Black							
35–39	6.6	5.0	3.5	3.0	2.6	1.5	4.0
40–44	9.5	8.1	5.8	4.7	4.6	3.3	6.7
45–49	14.3	12.1	9.0	7.6	5.6	6.0	10.6
50–54	21.0	17.9	14.2	12.9	10.2	9.7	16.9
55–59	26.7	22.7	19.5	18.4	16.3	14.8	22.8
MEN							
Total							
50–54	2.4	2.1	1.8	1.4	1.5	1.0	1.8
55–59	4.0	3.3	2.5	2.2	2.0	2.1	2.9
Black							
50–54	5.3	4.6	4.1	3.4	3.3	2.4	4.5
55–59	7.6	6.3	5.4	4.0	2.7	3.6	6.4

school dropouts and 12 percent of the high school graduates. There was no further decrease in the level of widowhood by education beyond high school graduation. Among blacks the levels of widowhood were much higher, but the education pattern was similar to that of whites.

As noted earlier, mortality rates are lower for women than for men, and in addition, widowed men are more likely than widowed women to remarry. Thus the proportion who are currently widowed is much lower for men. We show these percentages only for men aged 50–54 and 55–59. As for women, there is an inverse relationship of widowhood with education.

Married, Spouse Absent–Other Persons

The final marital status considered in this chapter is what is labeled in Census Bureau reports as "Married, Spouse Absent–Other" (MSA–O). This is a residual category of persons who report themselves to be "married" (and who do not report their marital status as separated, which legally is also "married"), and who are not living in the same household as their spouse at the time of the enumeration. The "other" in the label means "other than separated."[5]

The MSA–O category includes a great variety of situations, including:

1. married persons living in institutions such as prisons or mental hospitals;
2. persons living apart from their spouse in military barracks;
3. persons living apart because of the work requirements of one of the spouses;
4. the spouses of persons in the above categories.

Married persons who were not at home at the time of the census enumeration should not be included as MSA–O if the absence is temporary and of short expected duration (for example, traveling or in a short-stay hospital).

The definition (if enumerators or the enumerated persons bother to pay attention to it) of "separated" is "legally married, but living apart for reasons of marital discord." It is quite likely that some persons classified as MSA–O are in the process of becoming "separated" or are in

[5]In some Census Bureau tabulations the MSA–O and the Separated are combined with the Married, Spouse Present, into a category called "Married." This was especially true prior to 1950.

some sense "separated" but do not yet admit it to either themselves or others.

Table 6.13 shows the age-specific fractions of MSA–O persons in the population for each census year since 1950. For men in 1980, about 1.5 percent were MSA–O. The fraction is slightly higher at ages 20–24 and 25–29 and slightly lower at ages 45–54. The higher-than-average fraction of MSA–O persons in the age range 20–29 reflects armed forces participation, as well as a higher prevalence of men in jails and prisons. It may also be due to larger numbers living apart from their spouse for educational and work-related reasons. At the older ages, MSA–O persons are more likely to be in, or have spouses in, long-term care institutions. The fraction of persons who are MSA–O has generally been decreasing since 1950 or 1960. The large decrease between 1970 and 1980 at the young ages reflects the decrease in the number of men in the military, combined with a rise in the age at marriage.

The patterns for women are generally similar to those for men. At the younger ages, a large share of the women are the wives of men in the military. (As noted, there is a larger number of MSA–O wives of military men than there are married MSA–O military men, because those men who are overseas are not included in the census count.) The Current Population Survey (CPS) breaks the MSA–O women into two groups—those with husbands in the armed forces and others. In the CPS there were 275,000 fewer MSA–O with husbands in the armed forces in 1980 than in 1970; there was virtually no difference in the "Other" category. Hence, a large share of the decrease in the prevalence of

TABLE 6.13

Percent of Persons Who Are Married, Spouse Absent–Other, by Age and Sex, 1950–80

	20–24	25–29	30–34	35–39	40–44	45–49	50–54
MALES							
1950	1.7	2.4	2.2	2.1	2.1	2.2	2.3
1960	3.1	2.7	2.3	2.2	2.0	1.9	2.0
1970	3.1	2.3	2.1	2.0	1.8	1.7	1.7
1980	1.7	1.9	1.6	1.5	1.4	1.3	1.3
FEMALES							
1950	1.8	1.7	1.4	1.4	1.5	1.6	1.7
1960	3.4	2.4	2.0	1.8	1.7	1.7	1.8
1970	3.5	2.2	2.1	2.0	1.7	1.6	1.5
1980	1.5	1.4	1.1	1.1	1.0	1.0	1.0

MSA–O persons during the 1970s is a result of the decrease in the number of married men in the armed forces who live apart from their wives.

Formerly Married Women: Changing Characteristics and Activities

In the remainder of this chapter we discuss the changing characteristics and activities of the formerly married population under age 60 during the past five decades. (Data will be presented for each census since 1940, but we will emphasize the past two decades in this discussion.) This section will deal with formerly married women, while the section that follows discusses formerly married men in parallel, though somewhat less detailed, fashion.

TABLE 6.14

Marital Status Distribution and Percent with Own Children,
for Formerly Married Women, 1940–80

	1940	1950	1960	1970	1980
MARITAL STATUS DISTRIBUTION—TOTAL UNDER AGE 60					
Separated	32.1*	19.9	19.8	20.5	20.1
MSA–O		13.2	17.2	15.7	7.6
Widowed	51.5	43.5	37.0	31.6	20.4
Divorced	16.3	23.4	26.0	32.2	51.9
Total	100.0	100.0	100.0	100.0	100.0
PERCENT WITH OWN CHILDREN—TOTAL UNDER AGE 60					
Separated	34.9*	38.5	51.0	60.0	57.2
MSA–O		29.8	37.8	30.7	28.9
Widowed	31.9	24.4	28.2	31.3	28.4
Divorced	31.4	32.1	40.7	47.9	47.4
Total	32.8	29.7	37.6	42.4	44.1
PERCENT WITH OWN CHILDREN—AGE 35–39 ONLY					
Separated	37.5*	46.5	61.2	77.5	75.6
MSA–O		37.3	50.6	44.7	47.4
Widowed	55.4	56.1	67.8	72.2	75.1
Divorced	40.5	46.8	59.7	72.4	69.5
Total	47.6	47.7	60.2	69.7	70.0

*In 1940, Separated and MSA–O are combined.

229

Marital Status

In 1980, one-half of the formerly married women were divorced, and about one-fifth were separated. Thus, "marital discord" accounts for nearly three-quarters of the non-elderly, formerly married women. An additional one-fifth are widows, and about 8 percent are MSA–O (Table 6.14).

The fraction of the total who were divorced has risen over time. It was about one-eighth in 1940, one-quarter in 1960, one-third in 1970, and one-half in 1980. Widows comprised over half of the formerly married women in 1940, 37 percent in 1960, and only 21 percent in 1980.

Presence of Children

Separated women are most likely, and widowed and MSA–O women least likely, to have children present. This is in part due to differences in age structure. If we consider only women of a given age, for example, age 35–39, the differences are less pronounced: in 1980, 76 percent of the separated women, and 75 percent of the widows had children (bottom panel of Table 6.14). Sixty-nine percent of the divorced women and only 45 percent of the MSA–O had children. The very low proportion of MSA–O women with children is due to several factors, including the fact that some MSA–O persons are institutionalized; if there are any children, they are likely to be living with their other parent. In addition, couples who live apart for reasons of employment or other "voluntary" reasons may be selective of couples without children.

The probability that a formerly married woman has at least one own child in her household has risen over the past several decades, with most of the increase occurring during the 1950s and 1960s:

Year	Percent with Own Children
1940	32.8
1950	29.7
1960	37.6
1970	42.4
1980	44.1

The fraction of formerly married women with children present varies widely by age (Table 6.15). During the 1970s the fraction with children *declined* at all ages, particularly under age 35. At age 25–29, for example, 65 percent had children present in 1970, and 55 percent in

TABLE 6.15
*Percent of Formerly Married Women with Own Children,
by Age, 1940–80*

Age	1940	1950	1960	1970	1980
< 25	32.4	35.3	46.1	43.6	42.3
25–29	41.7	48.0	64.2	64.7	54.9
30–34	48.9	51.8	64.4	71.9	66.9
35–39	47.6	47.7	60.2	69.7	70.0
40–44	42.0	35.7	48.9	56.1	55.7
45–49	32.4	25.3	33.7	39.6	37.4
50–54	22.1	14.7	18.1	22.1	20.2
55–59	11.2	6.9	7.2	8.2	8.0
Total	32.8	29.7	37.6	42.4	44.1

1980. At age 30–34 the fraction was about 72 percent in 1970 and 67 percent a decade later. Hence the rise in the overall fraction with children was due to the changing age structure of the formerly married population.

Family Composition

Since 1960 a major change in the characteristics of formerly married mothers is the decrease in the number of large families and the increasing fraction of mothers with only one child. In both 1960 and 1970 about one in six formerly married mothers had four or more children. By 1980 this fraction had declined to 8 percent. In 1980, 45 percent of formerly married mothers had only one child, compared to 40 percent a decade earlier (see Table 6.16). These trends are even more pronounced when age is controlled. At age 35–39 the fraction with four or more children fell from 28 to 13 percent during the 1970s, while the fraction with two or fewer children rose from 52 to 68 percent.

The percentage distribution of formerly married mothers by age of youngest own child is shown in Table 6.17. In 1980, 15 percent of the mothers had children under age 3 and an additional 17 percent had a youngest child aged 3–5. Over the last two decades, the fraction of formerly married mothers with a preschool-age child has decreased from 42 percent in 1960 to 40 percent in 1970, and to 32 percent by 1980.

At every age formerly married black and Mexican-American women are much more likely than non-Hispanic white women to have own children. Blacks under age 35 have especially high proportions with chil-

TABLE 6.16

Distribution of Formerly Married Women Under Age 60, by Number of Own Children, 1940–80

Number of Own Children	All Formerly Married Women					Formerly Married Women with Children				
	1940	1950	1960	1970	1980	1940	1950	1960	1970	1980
TOTAL ALL AGES										
0	67.2	70.3	62.4	57.6	55.9	—	—	—	—	—
1	17.1	15.6	16.1	16.9	19.9	52.2	52.6	42.8	40.0	45.2
2	8.5	7.8	10.4	11.4	14.4	26.0	26.4	27.6	27.0	32.7
3	3.7	3.4	5.5	6.6	6.2	11.3	11.5	14.7	15.6	14.0
4+	3.4	2.9	5.6	7.4	3.6	10.5	9.6	15.0	17.5	8.1
Total	100.0	100.0	100.0	100.0	100.0	100.0	100.0	100.0	100.0	100.0
AGE 35–39										
0	52.4	52.3	39.8	30.3	30.0	—	—	—	—	—
1	20.4	20.5	20.2	17.3	21.9	42.9	43.0	33.5	24.8	31.3
2	13.2	13.2	17.0	18.6	25.4	27.7	27.7	28.2	26.7	36.2
3	6.5	6.9	11.1	14.0	13.7	13.7	14.4	18.4	20.0	19.6
4+	7.5	7.1	12.0	19.8	9.0	15.7	14.9	19.9	28.5	12.9
Total	100.0	100.0	100.0	100.0	100.0	100.0	100.0	100.0	100.0	100.0

TABLE 6.17

Distribution of Formerly Married Mothers,
by Age of Youngest Own Child, 1940–80

Age of Youngest Child	1940	1950	1960	1970	1980
0–2	12.6	21.1	25.6	21.0	15.2
3–5	13.6	17.8	16.3	18.5	17.2
6–8	15.1	15.4	13.9	16.9	17.4
9–11	17.0	13.7	14.2	15.2	18.3
12–14	20.8	16.0	15.3	14.7	16.1
15–17	20.9	16.1	14.7	13.6	15.8
Total	100.0	100.0	100.0	100.0	100.0

dren, while Mexican-Americans have higher proportions than blacks at ages 35 and over (see Table 6.18).

Formerly married black and Mexican-American mothers are much more likely to have several children and much less likely to have only one child than majority-white women. One-half of the non-Hispanic white women, and over one-third of the black and Mexican-American women have only one child (Table 6.19). One-sixth of the non-Hispanic white and one-third of the black and Mexican-American women have three or more children. There is relatively little difference between white and black mothers in the age distribution of youngest children. About one-third of each group have preschool age children. However,

TABLE 6.18

Percent of Formerly Married Women with Own Children, by Age,
for Non-Hispanic White, Black, and Mexican-American Women, 1980

Age	Non-Hispanic Whites	Black	Mexican-American
< 25	40.6	49.7	41.6
25–29	50.6	68.9	61.7
30–34	63.4	77.3	71.8
35–39	69.1	72.6	75.6
40–44	54.9	56.5	64.1
45–49	35.1	41.9	47.9
50–54	18.1	24.7	34.8
55–59	6.6	12.5	18.0
Total	41.2	51.7	52.7

TABLE 6.19

Distribution of Formerly Married Mothers,
by Number of Children and Age of Youngest Own Child,
for Non-Hispanic White, Black, and Mexican-Americans, 1980

	Non-Hispanic White	Black	Mexican-American
NUMBER OF CHILDREN			
1	49.8	35.4	35.4
2	33.6	30.7	30.8
3	11.8	18.6	18.5
4+	4.8	15.2	15.3
Total	100.0	100.0	100.0
AGE OF YOUNGEST CHILD			
0–2	13.8	16.2	23.5
3–5	17.0	17.1	19.9
6–8	17.5	17.6	16.5
9–11	18.7	18.0	16.1
12–14	16.3	16.7	12.8
15–17	16.7	14.4	11.3
Total	100.0	100.0	100.0

formerly married Mexican-American mothers are much more likely to have preschool age children (43 percent).

Education Composition

There has been a considerable upgrading in the education composition of the general population. This is also reflected in the education composition of formerly married women. Also contributing to the education composition of the formerly married are differential patterns of marital disruption and remarriage by education. These trends were discussed in Chapter 5. Table 6.20 presents the education composition of formerly married women in 1960, 1970, and 1980. The fraction of such women who had less than nine years of education decreased from over 32 percent in 1960 to 20 percent in 1970, and to 13 percent in 1980. The fraction of women who graduated from high school increased, from 40 percent in 1960 to 52 percent in 1970 and to 66 percent in 1980. In 1960 about 11 percent of all formerly married women had attended college. By 1980 this fraction had increased to 26 percent. The education trend of formerly married mothers parallels that of the total formerly married population.

TABLE 6.20

Education Distribution of Formerly Married Women Under Age 60,
for Total and Women with Own Children Under 18, 1960–80

	1960		1970		1980	
Education	Total	With Children	Total	With Children	Total	With Children
< 9	32.4	26.4	19.6	16.0	13.3	11.1
9–11	28.1	31.4	28.0	29.8	20.3	21.1
12	27.9	31.1	36.5	38.5	40.2	43.1
13–15	7.7	7.4	10.3	10.5	16.6	17.0
16 +	3.9	3.6	5.5	5.1	9.6	7.8
Total	100.0	100.0	100.0	100.0	100.0	100.0

Employment

Rates of employment vary by family situation and marital status. Table 6.21 summarizes employment rates of women by "life-cycle stage" and by marital status. Two-thirds of all formerly married women under age 60 were employed at the time of the 1980 census, compared to one-half of all currently married women under age 60. Comparing the last two columns (formerly married versus currently married women) shows that, except for young women without children, the employment rates of formerly married women are higher than those of currently married women. For example, among childless women aged 35–44, three-quarters of the formerly married and two-thirds of the currently married were employed. Among women with children under age 3, 43 percent of formerly married women worked compared to 37 percent of currently married mothers.

At all life cycle stages, divorced women had the highest rate of employment and separated women the next highest, with rates at least 10 points below those of divorced women. The lowest employment rates were for MSA–O women. Widows with children had rates that were 5 to 10 points below those of separated women. The employment rates of widows were below those of currently married women.

The rate of employment of formerly married black women is consistently lower than that of formerly married non-Hispanic whites (see Table 6.22). At most life cycle stages the differential is 10 points or more. Mexican-American women have employment rates similar to those of blacks. Some of the differential between minority women and majority-white women may be due to differences in employability and earning potential associated with differences in education. Table 6.23

TABLE 6.21

Employment Rates of Women Under Age 60,
by Family Status and Marital Status, 1980

	Separated	Divorced	MSA–O	Widowed	All Formerly Married	Married, Spouse Present
No Children						
Age <25	61.4	72.8	45.1	48.2	60.7	71.4
25–34	73.9	83.8	61.2	59.7	78.4	81.0
35–44	69.4	81.3	57.5	61.8	75.0	66.0
45–54	63.7	76.0	52.2	62.0	68.4	48.7
55–59	52.5	67.3	39.0	54.2	57.5	58.8
With Children						
Youngest 0–2	39.4	50.8	35.0	33.8	43.3	36.6
3–5	51.0	66.2	48.3	39.4	59.1	46.4
6–11	60.9	76.7	56.6	51.3	69.7	56.4
12–17	63.4	80.6	58.1	55.6	70.5	58.4
Total	59.1	75.4	50.2	56.0	66.2	49.5

TABLE 6.22

Employment Rates of Formerly Married Women, by Family Status,
for Non-Hispanic Whites, Blacks, and Mexican-Americans, 1980

	Non-Hispanic White	Black	Mexican-American
No Children			
Age < 25	65.6	44.6	52.1
25–34	81.7	66.0	66.7
35–44	78.4	68.2	67.5
45–54	71.4	61.0	56.3
55–59	60.3	49.2	43.6
With Children			
Youngest 0–2	47.0	40.3	38.3
3–5	64.1	51.2	52.7
6–11	74.8	61.2	61.8
12–17	75.2	61.4	62.3
Total	70.3	57.6	55.7

shows that educational differences in employment are extremely large among formerly married women. Among such women with preschool age children, about one-quarter of those with less than nine years of education are employed. The employment rate increases to one-third for high school dropouts, 58 percent for high school graduates, and 81 percent for college-educated women. Similar differentials are found for formerly married mothers of school age children.

Some of the differences among racial and ethnic groups may be due to differences in education composition. Among mothers of preschool age children, the differential between non-Hispanic whites and blacks is reduced from 10.5 to 7.3 points when education is controlled. The Mexican-American–Non-Hispanic white differential is reduced from 11.5 to 2.5 points. Education standardization also reduces the differentials in employment rates for mothers of older children—from 13.7 to 8.0 points

TABLE 6.23

*Employment Rates of Formerly Married Women,
by Education and Ethnicity,
for Women with Youngest Child Under 6 and 6–17, 1980*

Education	Non-Hispanic White	Black	Mexican-American	Total
Women With Children <6				
< 9	26.6	24.1	36.4	25.9
9–11	37.7	30.2	31.6	34.2
12	60.8	52.5	55.8	57.8
13–15	69.0	61.8	—	66.3
16+	82.2	75.0	—	80.9
Total				
Actual	56.4	45.9	44.9	51.7
Standardized*	54.4	47.1	51.9	51.7
Women With Children 6–17 Only				
< 9	45.4	38.8	48.3	40.0
9–11	61.8	49.5	60.9	56.6
12	78.6	69.2	79.0	76.2
13–15	82.8	75.8	—	81.0
16+	86.1	88.1	—	86.8
Total				
Actual	75.0	61.3	62.0	70.1
Standardized*	72.8	64.6	72.6	70.1

*Standardized on education distribution of total.

between black and majority-white women, and from 13.0 to 0.2 points differential between non-Hispanic white and Mexican-American women. Hence the lower employment rate of black mothers is partly due to a lower level of education, and the lower rate for Mexican-American mothers is primarily a consequence of their lower education.

Table 6.24 shows employment rates of formerly married mothers for the more detailed racial and Hispanic groups. The employment rates of Chinese, Japanese, Korean, and Filipino women are similar to those of non-Hispanic whites. The rates of American Indians are similar to those of black and Mexican-American women, while those of formerly married Puerto Rican women are extremely low, much less than one-half the rates of non-Hispanic white women.

These differentials in employment by "ethnicity" and education may be related to differential participation in the social welfare system. Many formerly married mothers are eligible to receive AFDC payments. The AFDC system has a work-disincentive feature to it. Women with limited employability and low earning capacity may be economically better off receiving AFDC than working.

Public Assistance and Poverty

In this section we look at the fraction of separated and divorced women with own children who received public assistance income in

TABLE 6.24

Employment Rates of Formerly Married Women with Children, by Age of Youngest Child, for Racial and Hispanic Groups, 1980

	Age of Youngest Child		
	0–5	6–11	12–17
Non-Hispanic White	56.4	74.9	75.2
Black	46.8	60.5	62.0
Japanese	57.4	70.8	79.2
Chinese	—	71.4	76.2
Filipino	66.2	75.4	76.3
American Indian	41.7	61.7	53.4
Korean	—	77.4	—
Hawaiian	44.1	—	—
Mexican	45.6	60.4	60.6
Puerto Rican	17.5	30.8	33.2
Cuban	52.2	62.9	69.2

—Less than 100 sample cases.

1979,[6] and the fraction who lived in families with income below the poverty line. The analysis is restricted to separated and divorced women rather than all formerly married women because most widows with children have access to a source of income (Social Security) that is not public assistance, while many MSA–O women are institutionalized or have absent husbands who may be providing economic support, or with whom they may be pooling their incomes. The poverty measure used here is an *after transfer* measure. It indicates the fraction in poverty after public assistance income, as well as earnings and all other sources of income, is received.

About one-quarter of all separated and divorced mothers received public assistance income (first column of Table 6.25). The proportion is highest (40 percent) for women with children under 3. It drops to 27 percent for mothers of children the youngest of whom is age 6–8, and to 17 percent for women with high school age children.

One-half of the mothers who did not attend high school received public assistance, compared to 41 percent of high school dropouts and to 22 percent of high school graduates. Less than one-tenth of mothers who have attended college received public assistance income. As noted earlier, women with higher levels of education are more likely to be able to adequately support themselves. Women with preschool age children often have child care expenses if they work, and many may prefer to care for their children than to work and arrange for alternative child care. They are also likely to have less work experience, and to be more recently separated from their spouses. The bottom panel of Table 6.25 shows that women with more children are more likely to receive public assistance. The more children, the greater the family economic needs as well as the greater the constraint on working.

The right panel of Table 6.25 shows the percent of separated or divorced mothers in poverty. Despite larger shares receiving public assistance, poverty is more prevalent among women with younger children, those with more children, and among low education mothers. The differences are extremely large—the proportion in poverty is 56 percent of mothers with children under age 3 compared to only 20 percent of women with youngest child in high school; more than half among women who did not complete high school compared to less than one-quarter of those who went to college; three-quarters of those with three or more children compared to one-quarter of women with only one child.

Twenty-one percent of non-Hispanic white separated and divorced mothers received public assistance income in 1979. This compares to 37

[6]Marital status, household composition, and education are measured in 1980, income during calendar 1979.

TABLE 6.25

Percent of Separated and Divorced Women with Children Who Received Public Assistance Income and Percent "In Poverty," by Age of Youngest Own Child, Education, and Number of Own Children, by Race/Ethnicity, 1980

	Percent with Public Assistance Income				Percent in Poverty			
	Total	Non-Hispanic White	Black	Mexican-American	Total	Non-Hispanic White	Black	Mexican-American
AGE OF YOUNGEST OWN CHILD								
0–2	40.3	35.0	49.2	42.2	55.8	49.2	64.6	63.0
3–5	31.5	26.7	40.2	40.7	43.0	37.1	53.7	51.6
6–8	26.6	21.8	35.2	35.6	37.2	31.3	47.2	52.2
9–11	21.7	16.1	33.8	22.7	30.0	23.4	44.4	36.7
12–14	20.4	14.0	33.2	29.2	27.0	19.7	41.6	33.7
15–17	17.4	11.9	29.1	22.9	19.6	14.5	32.2	24.3
EDUCATION								
< 9	49.9	45.0	57.0	40.9	63.0	57.8	68.9	59.5
9–11	41.2	34.8	50.7	43.1	53.0	45.6	63.7	52.9
12	22.5	19.4	31.0	25.6	30.7	26.6	42.0	34.6
13–15	15.6	12.4	23.3	18.1	23.8	20.0	32.0	31.5
16+	6.2	4.7	12.1	12.5	12.8	12.2	15.2	15.6
NUMBER OF CHILDREN								
1	18.1	15.2	25.4	23.1	24.2	21.1	31.4	28.0
2	26.4	22.1	34.4	29.6	34.9	30.5	42.0	44.1
3	38.0	31.2	45.8	44.5	53.5	46.1	62.1	60.8
4+	53.6	45.7	57.3	57.3	73.1	62.4	78.6	82.3
TOTAL	26.5	20.9	37.0	34.2	35.8	29.3	47.8	47.2

percent of black and 34 percent of Mexican-Americans. For all these groups, welfare participation declines with increasing age of youngest child. The education-specific rates are also consistently higher for blacks than for non-Hispanic whites. For example, among high school dropouts, 51 percent of the black women and 35 percent of the white women receive public assistance. Among college graduates the fractions are 12 percent of the blacks and 4 percent of the non-Hispanic whites. The education-specific fractions of Mexican-Americans receiving public assistance are lower than those of blacks. For women with less than nine years of education, the Mexican-American rates are even lower than for whites. Thus, education composition explains some of the difference in the receipt of welfare between majority whites and Mexican-Americans, but only a small part of the differential between whites and blacks.

The prevalence of poverty is very similar for formerly married Mexican-Americans and blacks. Forty-seven percent of the separated and divorced mothers in each group have family incomes that are below the poverty line. This compares to 29 percent for non-Hispanic whites. The differential is found at all ages of youngest child, education, and number of children categories. At each education level (except college graduate) the prevalence of poverty for Mexican-American women is between that of majority whites and blacks.

In Table 6.26 we show these same measures for detailed racial and

TABLE 6.26

Percent of Separated and Divorced Mothers
Receiving Public Assistance and Percent "In Poverty,"
for Racial and Hispanic Groups, 1980

	Percent Receiving Public Assistance	Percent in Poverty
Non-Hispanic White	21.1	29.7
Black	36.3	47.7
Japanese	15.1	24.8
Chinese	8.5	19.2
Filipino	20.6	24.2
American Indian	35.3	48.0
Korean	15.6	36.9
Vietnamese	32.4	43.5
Hawaiian	40.7	40.1
Mexican	33.5	47.2
Puerto Rican	62.5	70.5
Cuban	25.3	35.1

Hispanic groups. Receipt of public assistance income is extremely low among separated and divorced Chinese (8 percent), Japanese (15 percent), and Korean (16 percent) mothers. It is very high among American Indians (35 percent), Hawaiians, (41 percent), and Puerto Ricans (62 percent). The poverty level is highest for Puerto Ricans (70 percent) and also very high for blacks (48 percent), American Indians (48 percent), and Mexican-Americans (47 percent). The only groups with a poverty level below that of non-Hispanic whites (30 percent) are Chinese (19 percent), Filipinos (24 percent), and Japanese (25 percent).

Living Arrangements
of Formerly Married Women with Children

In this section we examine the living arrangements of formerly married women. It is important to appreciate that all of the data on living arrangements refer to a *cross-section* of the formerly married population.[7] A higher proportion would undoubtedly be found in the parental household for a short period following separation while they are in the process of rearranging their lives. It is likely that a large share of those living with parents and other relatives are recently separated persons who are living with relatives temporarily.

In 1980, 88 percent of formerly married women with children were maintaining their own households. Seven percent were residing in the households of their parents, 2 percent in the households of relatives, and 3 percent in households of nonrelatives.

TABLE 6.27

Distribution of Living Arrangements
of Formerly Married Women with Children, 1940–80

	Family Head	Child of Head	Other Relatives	Nonrelative	Total
1940	70.5	18.0	7.9	3.6	100.0
1950	67.0	21.9	8.3	2.8	100.0
1960	76.8	17.2	4.8	1.3	100.0
1970	84.5	11.4	2.8	1.2	100.0
1980	88.1	7.1	1.6	3.1	100.0

[7]See Maris A. Vinovskis, "The Historian and the Life Course: Reflections on Recent Approaches to the Study of American Life in the Past," *Life-Span Development and Behavior* 8 (1986): for a discussion of the relationship between observed cross-section living arrangements and the experience in the life course of individuals in historical perspective.

The major changes in living arrangements during the past four decades are:

1. The fraction who are living in the parental household declined from 17 to 7 percent between 1960 and 1980. It was 18 percent in 1940.

2. The fraction living with other relatives declined from about 8 percent in 1940 to 5 percent in 1960, and to less than 2 percent in 1980.

3. The fraction maintaining their own household rose from 70 percent to 77 percent between 1940 and 1960 and to 88 percent in 1980.

4. The fraction living in the household of a nonrelative decreased from 4 percent to 1 percent between 1940 and 1960, but rose to 3 percent between 1970 and 1980. The living arrangements represented by this category have likely changed over time. Historically it included a woman with a child who moved into the household of a "friend of the family," or who rented a room and boarded with someone in a small "rooming house." However, more recently, the majority of formerly married women classified as nonrelatives are persons who are living in a "cohabitation" relationship with a man who is the householder. Note that this would not include all cohabiting formerly married mothers. If the male partner moved into her household, or if the woman is regarded as the "head of the household" or "householder," she would be a family head, and he, a secondary individual (if he had no children), or a secondary family (if he had children with him). Cohabitation is discussed in greater detail in a later section of this chapter.

The living arrangements of mothers vary with both family and socioeconomic characteristics (Table 6.28). The younger the youngest child in the household, the lower the probability that a woman is living as family head and the higher the probability that she is living either in the parental household or in the household of another relative. Among formerly married women with children under age 3, 75 percent are family heads, 17 percent are living in the parental household, 4 percent are with other relatives, and 4 percent are living with nonrelatives. Among women who have children in their teens, about 94 percent are family heads, about 3 percent are living with their parents, and 1 percent are living with other relatives and nonrelatives.

This differential with respect to age of youngest child parallels differences by age. Between 94 and 97 percent of all formerly married mothers age 35 and over are living as family heads, and less than 5 percent are living in the households of their parents or other relatives. For-

TABLE 6.28

Living Arrangements of Formerly Married Women
with Children, by Selected Characteristics, 1980

	% Family Head	% Child of Head
AGE		
<25	62.7	25.9
25–29	79.8	11.4
30–34	89.3	5.9
35–39	93.7	3.7
40–44	96.1	2.1
45–49	97.1	1.7
50–54	97.4	0.9
55–59	97.1	0.4
AGE OF YOUNGEST CHILD		
0–2	75.7	17.3
3–5	82.3	10.5
6–8	88.0	6.1
9–11	91.4	4.3
12–14	93.9	3.0
15–17	96.8	2.2
NUMBER OF CHILDREN		
1	83.8	10.0
2	89.6	5.9
3	94.1	3.6
4+	96.5	1.7
RACE		
Non-Hispanic White	87.6	7.2
Black	89.8	7.0
Other	89.5	5.5
MARITAL STATUS		
Separated	87.3	8.4
MSA–O	72.9	18.0
Widowed	95.7	2.1
Divorced	88.1	6.7
EDUCATION		
<9 Years	90.8	4.7
9–11	85.6	8.4
12	87.1	8.0
13–15	89.9	6.0
16+	93.1	4.4
TOTAL	88.1	7.1

merly married mothers under age 25 have a family headship rate of 63 percent; 26 percent are living with their parents, 4 percent with other relatives, and 7 percent are with nonrelatives. The nonrelatives, who are primarily cohabitors, are most often under age 30.

The differences by age also reflect the recency of having entered the status of formerly married. Older women are more likely to have been in a formerly married status for a longer period of time and to have made a more permanent adaptation of their living arrangements. They are also selective of women who have not chosen to, or who have not had an opportunity to, remarry.

The greater the number of children, the higher the probability that the woman is living as a family head, and the lower the probability that she is living with her parents or other relatives. Similarly, women with only one child are more likely to be living with nonrelatives than women with more children

Widowed women with children are more likely to be family heads than are women in other marital statuses. Ninety-six percent of widows are family heads, in comparison to about 88 percent for separated and divorced women, and 73 percent for MSA–O women. MSA–O women with children are much more likely to be living in the parental household than women in other marital statuses: about 18 percent live with parents in comparison to about 7 percent of separated and divorced women and about 2 percent of widowed women. Similarly, MSA–O women are most likely to be living with other relatives (7 percent). Divorced women have the highest frequency of living with nonrelatives (4 percent). This reflects a higher prevalence of cohabitation among divorced women.

Living Arrangements
of Formerly Married Women with No Children

Like formerly married women with children, the majority of those without children maintain their own households (Table 6.29). One-half live alone or share a household with another unrelated person. About one woman in five with no own children under 18 is a family head. A large share of these are older women with one or more of their adult children in the household. One-tenth are living in the parental household, and nearly one-tenth are living with other relatives. Only 2 percent are in group quarters.

The changes that have occurred over the four decades include:

1. The proportion living in one-person households increased markedly between 1940 and 1960, and more gradually since then.

TABLE 6.29

Distribution of Living Arrangements
of Formerly Married Women with No Children, 1940–80

	In Family Household			In Nonfamily Household			
	Family Head	Child of Head	Other Relative	One Person Household	Other Nonfamily	Group Quarters	Total
1940	25.8	13.9	17.0	14.1	19.5	9.8	100.0
1950	22.7	13.8	15.7	21.7	16.2	10.0	100.0
1960	20.2	12.6	16.7	32.8	11.3	6.4	100.0
1970	20.6	13.7	13.2	37.5	11.5	3.5	100.0
1980	21.9	11.2	9.0	39.5	16.0	2.4	100.0

2. The fraction living with a nonrelative decreased between 1940 and 1960, and then returned to the 1940 level.

3. The proportion living in the household of their parents decreased.

4. The proportion living with other relatives decreased.

There are substantial age differences in the living arrangements of formerly married women with no children under 18 (Table 6.30). The proportion who are family heads increases with age. At ages 40–59, about one-third of all formerly married women with no children under 18 present are family heads. Most of these women are heading families that include an adult child. Similarly, there is a sharp decrease in age in the fraction living in the parental household. Among women under age 25, nearly 40 percent are living in the parental household. (This contrasts sharply with the 25 percent of this age group living in their parental household among formerly married women with children.) By age 35–39, only 8 percent are living in their parents' household. The fraction living with other relatives is highest at the youngest age (14 percent), while the fraction living in nonfamily households is greatest at age 30–34. At the older ages most childless formerly married women not living in families are living alone, while at the younger ages a larger share are living in two- or more-person nonfamily households.

A more detailed examination of the trend in living arrangements of formerly married women without children shows (data are not presented):

1. The fraction living in the parental household dropped considerably at the younger ages. For example, at ages under 25 the drop was from 50 percent in 1960 to 38 percent in 1980. At age 35–39 the decrease was from 19 percent in 1970 to 12 percent in 1980.

TABLE 6.30

Living Arrangements of Formerly Married Women
with No Own Children Under 18, by Age, 1980

| Age | Nonfamily Household | | Family Household | | | | |
	Alone	Other	Head	Child	Other Relative	Group Quarters	Total
<25	16.0	25.4	1.8	38.4	14.0	4.5	100.0
25–29	34.6	31.5	2.6	20.0	8.6	2.8	100.0
30–34	42.0	30.1	3.4	14.7	7.2	2.6	100.0
35–39	39.4	23.9	13.6	12.2	7.4	3.5	100.0
40–44	36.3	15.6	31.4	8.1	6.6	1.9	100.0
45–49	38.7	11.4	35.2	5.7	7.0	2.1	100.0
50–54	43.4	7.7	34.4	4.0	8.8	1.7	100.0
55–59	49.9	6.3	29.5	2.7	9.8	1.8	100.0
Total	39.5	16.0	21.9	11.2	9.0	2.4	100.0

2. The age-specific fractions who were "other relatives" decreased at all ages during the 1970s.

3. The fraction who were family heads increased during the 1970s at ages 40 and above. This seemingly anomalous trend occurred because these women are the parents of baby boom babies whose children have now reached adulthood. More of these women had given birth to more children, and by 1980, larger shares of these formerly married women had adult children still at home, and thus were classified as family heads.

4. The fraction of women under age 40 living in one-person households rose rapidly during both the 1960s and 1970s. The rapid increase in one-person households among women aged 45–59 occurred primarily during the 1960s, while the increase in 30–44 year old women living alone was most rapid during the 1970s.

5. Similarly there was a rise during the 1970s in the fraction in other nonfamily households. This rise occurred only among women under 40. As has been emphasized earlier, much of this was due to the increase in cohabitation.

6. Finally, there was a drop in the fraction of the formerly married population in group quarters, especially during the 1960s. This drop is largely a reflection of changing marital status composition. Separated and divorced persons constitute an increasing share of the total, while widows (who tend to be older) and MSA–O persons (a significant portion of whom are institutionalized) are a declining share of the total.

Cohabitation

In 1980, over 800,000 formerly married women under age 60 were cohabiting.[8] Table 6.31 shows the percent cohabiting by age and marital status (never-married women are also shown for comparison). The percent cohabiting is highest at ages 20–29, and drops off at older ages. It is highest among divorced women, although rates for widows and never-married women ages 20–35 are also quite high. Age-specific rates for separated women are only about half of those for divorced women. Reasons for this difference include:

1. The marriages of separated women have, on average, terminated more recently. They have not had as much time as divorced women to establish a new relationship and change their living arrangements.

2. Separated women may jeopardize their divorce settlement and may even lose custody of their children by cohabiting.

3. Persons who remain in a separated status for a long period of time without getting divorced may be selective of persons who are economically and educationally disadvantaged. They may also be selective of persons with less interest in establishing a new relationship.

Cohabitation of formerly married women varies by age, race, and presence of children (Table 6.32). Black women, particularly those under

TABLE 6.31

*Percent of Women Who Are Cohabiting,
by Age and Marital Status, 1980*

Age	Never-Married	Separated	Divorced	Widowed	MSA–O
18–19	3.0	7.7	11.2	—	2.5
20–24	7.5	9.4	19.0	17.5	3.8
25–29	10.3	9.0	18.3	14.2	4.5
30–34	7.4	8.1	14.2	11.4	4.6
35–39	4.4	5.1	8.9	5.7	4.4
40–44	2.6	3.9	6.8	3.2	3.1
45–49	2.6	3.8	5.8	3.4	3.1
50–54	1.6	3.7	4.8	2.9	1.4
55–59	1.2	3.2	4.3	2.3	2.9

—Less than 200 cases.

[8]A person is a cohabitor if he or she is an adult member of a two-adult household consisting of unrelated opposite sex adults who are not classified as married, spouse present. This definition misses cohabitors who live in households including more than two adults, and also misses couples in which one partner is under age 18.

TABLE 6.32

Percent of Formerly Married Women Cohabiting,
by Age, Presence of Children, and Race/Ethnicity, 1980

	With Children	No Children	Total
TOTAL			
18–24	10.9	13.5	12.4
25–34	10.0	18.3	13.2
35–44	4.3	10.5	6.6
45–54	2.0	5.0	4.2
NON-HISPANIC WHITE			
18–24	13.1	15.2	14.3
25–34	11.4	19.9	15.0
35–44	4.8	11.7	7.5
45–54	2.4	4.8	4.2
BLACK			
18–24	6.1	7.0	6.5
25–34	7.1	12.2	8.5
35–44	3.0	7.4	4.6
45–54	1.1	6.1	4.4

age 45, have a lower rate of cohabitation than white women. At age 25–34, 15 percent of non-Hispanic white women and 8 percent of black women are cohabiting. Women with children are less likely to cohabit than those with no children—10 percent compared to 18 percent at age 35–44.

Variation in Living Arrangements of Formerly Married Women Among Racial and Hispanic Groups

As summary measures of living arrangements of formerly married women without children, we have selected the percent of 25–44-year-old separated or divorced persons who live in nonfamily households, the percent living in the household of their parents, and the percent in group quarters (Table 6.33). The proportion living in the parental household is very high among Cubans (29 percent), somewhat higher than average among Mexican-Americans (17 percent) and blacks (16 percent), and very low among Chinese (5 percent). With these exceptions, about one-tenth of formerly married women live in the parental household. Three-quarters of the non-Hispanic white, Chinese, and Japanese

TABLE 6.33

Living Arrangments of 25–44-Year-Old
Separated and Divorced Women with No Own Children,
for Racial and Hispanic Groups, 1980

	Percent in Nonfamily Households	Child of Head	Group Quarters
Non-Hispanic White	73.2	11.8	1.4
Black	50.3	16.2	2.3
Japanese	80.7	9.1	0.4
Chinese	74.2	4.6	2.0
Filipino	64.0	9.2	1.2
American Indian	65.9	12.4	3.5
Mexican	55.2	16.9	2.1
Puerto Rican	57.1	9.6	2.3
Cuban	44.6	29.4	0.9

women live in nonfamily households. The fraction is much lower for blacks and the Hispanic groups. Very few women of any racial or Hispanic group live in group quarters.

There is not much variation in the living arrangements of separated and divorced women with children under 18 (data not shown). The great majority of all groups maintain their own households—90 percent of whites and blacks and 86 percent of Mexican-Americans. The range for other groups is from 84 percent (Filipinos and Hawaiians) to 96 percent (Puerto Ricans).

Formerly Married Men

In 1960 there were 3.25 million formerly married men under the age of 60. Between 1960 and 1970 the number increased to 3.86 million, or an increase of 19 percent over the decade. The rate of increase accelerated greatly in the 1970s and by 1980 there were 6.48 million formerly married men under age 60. For comparison, there were 10.5 million formerly married women under age 60 in 1980. In considering these numbers, our earlier discussion of these data should be kept in mind. We believe that there is a substantial undercount of separated men, and we also suspect a sizable undercount of divorced men. Since we do not know the magnitude of these undercounts, there is no choice but to report the census numbers, keeping these cautions in mind.

The number of formerly married men who had children living with them rose from 326,000 in 1960 to 543,000 in 1970, and to 695,000 in 1980. The fraction of all formerly married men with children was about 10 percent in 1960, rose to 14 percent in 1970, and declined to 11 percent in 1980. (Recall that there was also a modest decrease in the fraction of formerly married women under age 35 with children and little change in the fraction at ages 35 and over.) This suggests that there has probably not been much of a trend toward a larger share of fathers having custody of children following separation or divorce. The major reason that there is a much larger number of formerly married men with children in 1980 than previously is that there are more formerly married men, as a consequence of trends in divorce and remarriage, and not because of a large increase in the fraction of fathers with custody of their children following disruption. (The living arrangements of children are discussed in detail in Chapter 7.)

Characteristics of Formerly Married Men and Formerly Married Fathers

Marital Status and Presence of Children

In 1980, nearly three-fifths of the formerly married men were divorced and an additional one-fifth reported their marital status as separated (see Table 6.34).[9] Fifteen percent were classified as married, spouse absent (other than separated), and 6 percent were widowers. Twenty-two percent of widowed men have children present, in comparison to about 10 percent of men in each of the other marital statuses. At age 35–39, 40 percent of the widowers have children present, versus about 15 percent of men in the other marital statuses.

The proportion of formerly married men of each age who have children living with them is shown in Table 6.35. Overall, 11 percent of formerly married men have children. The fraction peaks at age 40–44, where 18 percent of formerly married men have own children present, while it is only slightly lower at the two adjacent age groups (35–39 and 45–49). The fraction of formerly married men with children present rose at every age during the 1960s, and decreased at every age during the 1970s.

---

[9]The section discusses formerly married men with own children living with them. There is another category of formerly married fathers not discussed here because adequate data are not available—formerly married men who have children under age 18 who are not living with them.

TABLE 6.34

Marital Status Distribution and Percent with Own Children,
for Formerly Married Men, 1940–80

	1940	1950	1960	1970	1980
Marital Status Distribution, Total Under Age 60					
Separated	51.4*	22.9	21.9	21.2	20.4
MSA–O		28.4	32.5	27.0	15.0
Widowed	29.5	19.6	14.0	12.5	6.2
Divorced	19.0	29.1	31.6	39.2	58.4
Total	100.0	100.0	100.0	100.0	100.0
Percent with Own Children, Total Under Age 60					
Separated	9.7*	6.8	7.6	9.3	10.0
MSA–O		6.3	9.8	20.1	8.3
Widowed	29.2	20.2	21.8	26.6	22.3
Divorced	7.6	6.2	6.8	8.5	10.5
Total	15.0	8.9	10.0	14.1	10.8
Percent with Own Children, Age 35–39 Only					
Separated	11.2*	9.6	10.1	13.4	14.5
MSA–O		7.1	13.6	31.9	14.0
Widowed	42.4	39.3	34.1	51.8	40.0
Divorced	11.2	3.4	10.5	14.5	16.1
Total	17.3	11.3	13.2	21.2	16.2

*In 1940, Separated and MSA–O are combined.

TABLE 6.35

Percent of Formerly Married Men with Own Children Present,
by Age, 1940–80

Age	1940	1950	1960	1970	1980
<25	4.4	3.9	5.0	5.0	5.0
25–29	8.9	6.7	8.8	12.6	7.3
30–34	14.8	9.5	12.1	17.0	10.9
35–39	17.3	11.3	13.2	21.2	16.2
40–44	19.9	12.7	13.6	20.3	17.7
45–49	20.2	10.9	12.2	18.5	13.6
50–54	15.4	9.0	9.5	12.8	9.6
55–59	12.6	6.7	6.2	8.0	6.0
Total	15.0	8.9	10.0	14.1	10.8

TABLE 6.36

*Percent of Formerly Married Men with Own Children Present,
by Age and Race/Ethnicity, 1980*

Age	Non-Hispanic White	Black	Mexican-American	Total
<25	4.2	5.0	4.9	4.4
25–29	7.3	8.0	5.9	7.3
30–34	10.6	11.2	14.0	10.9
35–39	17.3	12.1	17.2	16.2
40–44	19.3	12.3	19.2	17.7
45–49	14.3	10.9	12.5	13.6
50–54	10.4	6.8	13.0	9.6
55–59	6.0	5.6	10.6	6.0
Total	11.2	9.3	11.2	10.8

The probability that a formerly married man has own children liv-ing with him is slightly higher for non-Hispanic whites than for blacks, 11.2 versus 9.3 percent. At ages less than 35 the fraction of black for-merly married men with children is higher than that of whites. How-ever, at ages 35 and over the fraction is slightly higher for whites.

Size and Composition of Families of Formerly Married Men with Children

Between 1960 and 1970 there was not a great deal of change in the family size of formerly married fathers (Table 6.37). In 1960, 47 percent had only one child, and 25 percent had three or more. By 1970, families were somewhat larger (42 percent with one child and 30 percent with three or more children). However, as previously noted for mothers, there was a reduction in the average number of children during the 1970s, and by 1980, 56 percent of fathers had only one child and only 16 percent had three or more children.

Divorced fathers are slightly more likely than widowed or separated fathers to have only one child (data not shown). MSA–O men are least likely to have only one child. Similarly, the fraction with three or more children is higher for widowed and MSA–O men (over 20 percent for each group). This differential reflects the longer marriage duration of widowed and MSA–O men at the time of disruption, and perhaps a lower remarriage propensity of widowers with children in comparison to divorced men with children. In addition, the experience of widow-

TABLE 6.37

Distribution of Number of Children of Formerly Married Men with Own Children Under Age 18, Total, and Ages 35–39, 1940–80

	1940	1950	1960	1970	1980
ALL AGES					
1	52.2	51.4	46.6	42.4	56.0
2	26.0	26.4	28.4	27.8	28.5
3	11.3	12.4	13.5	14.7	10.1
4+	10.5	9.7	11.5	15.1	5.4
Total	100.0	100.0	100.0	100.0	100.0
AGES 35–39					
1	39.4	41.8	39.2	25.8	47.6
2	28.3	30.8	25.5	30.8	31.5
3	14.2	14.1	18.7	17.4	13.3
4+	18.1	13.3	16.6	26.0	7.6
Total	100.0	100.0	100.0	100.0	100.0

hood is probably more random with respect to family size than the joint experience of separation or divorce and the father's obtaining custody of the children.

Ages of Children

Forty percent of formerly married fathers have teenage children (Table 6.38). Only 28 percent of the men with children have preschool age children. During the 1970s there was a small drop in the fraction of formerly married fathers with preschool age children (32 to 28 percent),

TABLE 6.38

Distribution of Formerly Married Men with Own Children, by Age of Youngest Own Child, 1940–80

Age	1940	1950	1960	1970	1980
<3	8.9	15.2	18.0	16.2	14.2
3–5	12.4	14.6	16.0	16.1	13.7
6–8	14.6	16.1	13.9	16.9	14.7
9–11	18.6	16.3	15.5	15.8	16.9
12–14	21.5	18.2	18.8	17.4	17.8
15–17	24.1	19.2	17.8	17.6	22.7
Total	100.0	100.0	100.0	100.0	100.9

and a corresponding rise in the fraction with youngest child age 15–17 (18 to 23 percent). (In Chapter 7, the proportion of children of various ages living with fathers is examined.)

Living Arrangements of Formerly Married Men with Children

The overwhelming majority (90 percent) of men with own children present maintain their own households. Most of those who do not maintain their own households are residing in the household of their parents (an additional 7 percent). A very small minority live in the household of other relatives (1 percent) or of nonrelatives (2 percent). Even in 1940, more than three-quarters of formerly married men with children maintained their own households. Thirteen percent lived in the household of their parents and 7 percent in the household of other relatives.

At all ages of youngest child, the majority of fathers maintain their own household (Table 6.39), although the proportion rises with age of youngest child, from 81 percent for fathers of 3–5-year-olds to 93 percent for fathers of teenagers. About one-eighth of the fathers of children aged 3–5 live in their parents' household. Only about one in thirty are nonrelatives. For unknown reasons, fathers of 0–2-year-olds are more likely to have their own households, and less likely to be in their parents' household, than fathers of 3–5-year-olds.

Living Arrangements of Formerly Married Men with No Children Present

In 1980, over three-fifths of formerly married men with no own children present lived in a nonfamily household—40 percent were living alone and 23 percent in other nonfamily households—most of whom

TABLE 6.39

Living Arrangements of Separated and Divorced Men, by Age of Youngest Own Child, 1980

	0–2	3–5	6–11	12–17	Total
Family Head	87.3	80.9	89.4	93.0	89.3
Nonrelative	2.9	3.4	3.6	1.2	2.6
Child	7.7	13.2	6.0	4.5	6.7
Other Relative	2.1	2.5	1.0	1.2	1.5
Total	100.0	100.0	100.0	100.0	100.0

TABLE 6.40

*Living Arrangements of Formerly Married Men Under Age 60
with No Own Children Under 18, 1940–80*

| | In Family Household | | | In Nonfamily Household | | | |
	Family Head	Child of Head	Other Relative	One Person Household	Other Nonfamily	Group Quarters	Total
1940	11.4	15.8	10.4	15.1	24.6	22.7	100.0
1950	7.8	17.7	10.1	18.9	19.8	25.7	100.0
1960	7.0	16.1	13.3	25.6	14.3	23.6	100.0
1970	8.4	16.2	8.5	34.3	14.9	17.8	100.0
1980	6.5	14.6	7.1	39.8	22.8	9.1	100.0

were cohabiting (see Table 6.40). Fifteen percent lived in the household of their parents, 8 percent in the household of another relative, and 7 percent were heads of families (with, of course, no own children present). These latter men could be the head of a family including one or both of his parents, and an adult child or another relative. The remaining 9 percent are residents of group quarters.

The fraction of formerly married men living in nonfamilly households has risen during the 1970s, while the proportion living with parents or in the households of other relatives has decreased. About one man in twelve is a family head, and this has not changed much since 1960.

Living arrangements vary by age, with the fraction of formerly married men living with parents dropping from over one-third at ages under 25 to one-tenth by age 40–44 (see Table 6.41). Between ages 40–44 and 45–49 there is a rise in the proportion who are family heads, as a result of increasing numbers of men with children over 18. Nearly one-fifth of the formerly married men under 25 live in group quarters, primarily military barracks, but also prisons and other institutions. The fraction living in nonfamily households increases with age—by 30–34, two-thirds of the men are in nonfamily households. It remains at about this level at each of the older ages.

Variation in Living Arrangements Among Racial and Hispanic Groups

Virtually all formerly married men with children maintain their own households. This is true for all racial and ethnic groups. For the smaller of these groups there are too few sample cases to allow further

TABLE 6.41

Living Arrangements of Formerly Married Men
with No Own Children Under 18, by Age, 1980

Age	Nonfamily Household		Family Household			Group Quarters	Total
	Alone	Other	Head	Child	Other Relative		
<25	15.3	18.7	2.0	34.6	10.1	19.2	100.0
25–29	30.6	27.1	2.9	21.3	7.1	11.0	100.0
30–34	40.3	27.9	2.9	14.7	5.6	8.6	100.0
35–39	44.6	26.4	3.4	11.8	5.7	8.1	100.0
40–44	46.0	23.0	7.8	10.7	5.9	6.7	100.0
45–49	47.2	19.3	11.1	9.2	6.7	6.5	100.0
50–54	49.8	17.6	13.2	5.7	8.1	5.6	100.0
55–59	51.1	15.4	14.4	4.3	9.0	5.7	100.0
Total	39.8	22.8	6.5	14.6	7.1	9.1	100.0

consideration. However, there are sufficient cases of formerly married men without children (Table 6.42). For all groups the majority of men live in nonfamily households. Non-Hispanic whites (75 percent), Japanese (81 percent), and Chinese (75 percent) have very high fractions in nonfamily households. Lower fractions are found for Mexican-Americans (58 percent), Cubans (61 percent), blacks (61 percent), and Puerto

TABLE 6.42

Living Arrangements of 25–44-Year-Old
Separated and Divorced Men with No Own Children,
for Racial and Hispanic Groups

	Percent in Nonfamily Households	Child of Head	Group Quarters
Non-Hispanic White	74.9	14.5	3.8
Black	61.2	18.1	7.7
Japanese	80.7	12.8	1.4
Chinese	74.9	9.1	3.2
Filipino	63.9	11.0	6.9
Hawaiian	67.8	10.7	7.4
American Indian	66.6	12.8	10.8
Mexican	58.0	19.1	8.2
Puerto Rican	63.0	13.5	7.3
Cuban	60.6	19.3	4.4

TABLE 6.43

Percent of Men Who Are Cohabiting,
by Age and Marital Status, 1980

Age	Never Married	Separated	Divorced	Widowed	MSA–O
18–19	0.9	—	—	—	—
20–24	4.4	7.8	13.2	—	2.6
25–29	9.3	12.9	20.4	—	3.1
30–34	8.4	15.5	20.5	—	3.5
35–39	5.5	15.4	19.6	13.2	5.4
40–44	4.6	13.3	14.7	7.7	5.0
45–49	3.5	10.7	11.6	6.0	3.8
50–54	3.0	10.4	10.7	4.8	4.6
55–59	3.1	11.4	9.6	5.2	3.6

—Less than 200 sample cases.

Ricans (63 percent). Blacks, Mexican-Americans, and Cubans have about one-fifth living in the parental household.

Cohabitation

Table 6.43 shows the percent of formerly married men who are cohabiting by age and marital status. It shows patterns similar to those observed earlier for women, with peak levels of cohabitation at age 25–29. For women the peak prevalence was at age 20–24. Divorced men are more likely to be cohabiting than men in other marital statuses. Levels for separated men are lower than for the divorced, although the difference is not as large as observed for women. The levels of cohabitation for men are higher than for women. The reason for this is that there are more formerly married women than men. The total numbers of cohabiting formerly married men and women are almost identical.

Summary

The number of formerly married persons in the population has increased as a consequence of changing rates of marital disruption and remarriage. In 1980, there were 17 million formerly married persons under age 60: one-fifth of women and about 12 percent of men aged 18–59. In the 1960s this population grew more rapidly among women than among men, and the increase was primarily due to growth in the number of divorced persons. In the 1970s, formerly married men increased more rapidly than formerly married women, with large increases in the separated population as well. The higher measured rate among women reflects both lower remarriage rates of women and some unknown levels of underenumeration of men and of misreporting of marital status. Whereas the number of separated men and women should be about the same, there were one-third fewer separated men than women in 1980.

The proportion of the adult population that is currently divorced grew from about one in 300 at the turn of the century to one in forty in 1960. By 1980, one woman in thirteen and one man in eighteen was divorced. In the mid-adult ages, one of every ten adults was divorced. There were three times as many divorced as separated persons in 1980.

Slightly over one-third of the separated population stopped living with their spouses less than a year ago and slightly less than one-third had been separated for five or more years. Time since separation is of course longer for those who are currently divorced: one-fifth were separated less than two years ago, and for one-half, separation occurred at least five years ago. The time since separation is considerably longer among blacks because of their lower rates of remarriage.

Of persons who have had a marriage disrupted by separation or divorce, about one-half of the men and three-quarters of the women are currently separated or divorced. These ratios are higher among blacks than among whites, particularly among black men. Increases during the 1970s in the prevalence of separated or divorced persons were extremely rapid among persons age 25–34. Even so, one-third of the overall growth occurred at ages 45–59.

The proportion of ever-married persons who are currently separated or divorced peaks in the late twenties and early thirties and then declines thereafter; there is decline at subsequent ages among black females and almost none at all among black males. At ages 25–34, twice as high a proportion of ever-married black women was currently separated or divorced as among whites (30 versus 15 percent). There is a great deal of variation among racial and Hispanic groups in the proportion of ever-married women who are currently separated or divorced. Particularly high levels are found for Hispanics (especially Puerto Ricans), American Indians, and Hawaiians; lower values are found among Asian-Americans.

The prevalence of widowhood in the prime adult age has declined markedly since the turn of the century, for example, from about 9 to 2 percent among women 35–44. Education differences in the prevalence of widowhood reflect differences in mortality, remarriage, and age differences between spouses. Among women 55–59, 19 percent of those who did not complete high school were widows compared to 12 percent among those with at least high school graduation. Men are much less likely to be currently widowed—only 3 percent at ages 55–59 compared to 14 percent among women. Blacks have almost twice the average prevalence of current widowhood.

Less than 2 percent of the adult population falls into the residual category of those who are married and not living with their spouse, but who do not report their marital status as separated. This includes a diverse range of circumstances such as institutionalization and work related reasons. The proportion has declined over recent decades with fluctuations at the younger ages partially reflecting military-related absences.

Formerly married women are more likely than currently married women to be employed: two-thirds compared to one-half of women under age 60. At all life cycle stages, divorced women have the highest rate of employment. Formerly married women are less likely to be employed among blacks and Mexican-Americans than among majority whites. Some of this difference is attributable to differences in levels of education and large educational differentials in employment among formerly married women. There are also substantial variations in employment among racial and Hispanic groups.

About one-quarter of all separated and divorced mothers received public assistance income in 1980. This fraction varies from 40 percent among women with children under age 3 to 17 percent among those with high school age children. One-half of the formerly married mothers with a high school diploma received public assistance compared to less than one-tenth among those who have attended college. Blacks and Mexican-American formerly married mothers were much more likely to receive public assistance (37 and 34 percent, respectively) than were majority whites (21 percent).

Despite higher receipt of public assistance, poverty (after transfer payments) is more prevalent among those with younger children, more children, and low education. Almost one-half of formerly married Mexican-Americans and blacks have family incomes below the poverty line, compared to 29 percent among non-Hispanic whites. Education explains some of the differences in welfare receipt between majority whites and Mexican-Americans, but only a small part of the differential between whites and blacks.

Eighty-eight percent of formerly married women with children maintained their own households in 1980, 7 percent lived in the households of their parents, 2 percent lived with relatives, and 3 percent lived with nonrelatives. As for other subgroups, there has been a trend toward increased maintenance of one's own household and decreased living with relatives. Living with others is more likely among younger women, those with young children, those with fewer children, and the recently separated. Widowed women with children are more likely to be family heads than in the other marital status.

The majority of formerly married women without children maintain their own household, though they are less likely to do so than those with children: one-half live alone or share a household with an unrelated person. One-tenth are living in their parents' household and another one-tenth with other relatives. These patterns vary with age, so that among women under age 25 nearly 40 percent are living with their parents. There is considerable variation among racial and Hispanic groups in the percent of separated and divorced women without children who live in nonfamily households.

In 1980, over 800,000 formerly married women under age 60 were cohabiting. The percent cohabiting is highest at ages 20–29 (almost one in every five). Black women, especially under age 45, are less likely to be cohabiting than are majority-white women.

In general, patterns similar to those discussed for formerly married women are also found for formerly married men. A larger share of formerly married fathers have teenage children and fewer have children of preschool age. Most formerly married men with own children have only one child.

CHILDREN

T HE FAMILY experiences of children have been altered dramatically
by increases in separation, divorce, and nonmarital fertility.
These changes have been offset somewhat by the decreased likelihood of parental death[1]; nevertheless, there has been a marked increase in the proportion of children who spend part of their childhood
in a one-parent family. The life histories of individuals, and their family
relationships, have become much more complex. Only a minority of
persons spend all of their childhood living with both parents. And as
Cherlin has documented, kin relationships are more and more complex,
as parental divorce and remarriage creates step-parents, step-siblings,
and half-siblings, not to mention a multitude of grandparents, aunts,
uncles, and cousins.[2] Many children would have difficulty answering
the simple question, "Who are the members of your family?"

Experience of the late 1970s suggests that approximately one-half of
all first marriages will end in separation or divorce, and that about one-
half of all children will spend some time in a one-parent family.[3] Thus

[1]Mary Jo Bane, *Here to Stay: American Families in the Twentieth Century* (New
York: Basic Books, 1976).

[2]Andrew Cherlin, "Remarriage as an Incomplete Institution," *American Journal of
Sociology* 84 (1978):634–50; idem, *Marriage, Divorce, Remarriage* (Cambridge, Mass.: Harvard University Press, 1981).

[3]Mary Jo Bane, "Marital Disruption and the Lives of Children," *Journal of Social
Issues* 32 (1976):103–17; Larry L. Bumpass, "Children and Marital Disruption: A Replication and Update," *Demography* 21 (1984):71–82.

only a minority can be expected to have a simple family history over their lifetime.

The diversity of family experience that these patterns produce is even greater when we recognize that the timing and duration of these events vary. For some children, disruption of the parental marriage comes at an early age and is followed rapidly by the remarriage of the parent with whom they live; others may spend most of their childhood in a one-parent family; and for yet others, the disruption may come in the teenage years. Over one-half of the children who experience the breakup of their parents' marriage spend at least six years with only one parent. Further, although most of these children live in a second family following a remarriage, about one-half of those who do will experience another family disruption before they reach age 16. Experience in a one-parent family is the dominant pattern for black children: five of every six will spend some of their childhood with only one parent. Most of these will spend the majority of their childhood years in a one-parent family. These rates of family disruption are over twice what they were two decades ago.[4]

The cross-sectional distribution of living arrangements of children is presented in Table 7.1 for 1940 through 1980.[5] Because children enter one-parent families at different ages, and because the parent with whom they live often remarries, the proportion in one-parent families at any point in time is considerably lower than the proportion who live in such families at some time during their childhood. Reflecting the changes discussed above, the proportion of children living in two-parent families (including step-parents) declined from 87 to 77 percent over the last two decades, those with the simplest family (both parents married once) declined from 71 to 57 percent, while the proportion living with only their mother doubled from 8 to 17 percent.

The fraction of children living with fathers only is small, but has increased over the past two decades, from 1.1 to 2.1 percent, reflecting

---

[4]Bumpass, "Children and Marital Disruption."

[5]The data set used in this chapter includes all persons under age 18, except those who are currently married. The excluded persons are almost all aged 15–17. They constitute 0.2 percent of all children, and the following percentages of 15–17-year-old males and females.

Age	Males	Females
15	0.6	1.2
16	0.5	2.4
17	1.1	5.6

Children classified as living with two parents include all who are living with a currently married parent. Those classified as living with both biological once-married parents include all who were born after the date of this marriage; thus, adopted children who meet this definition are also included since they are reported as "own children."

TABLE 7.1

Distribution of Children Under 18,
by Detailed Parental Status, 1940, 1960, 1970, 1980

	1940	1960	1970	1980
Two Parents	85.1	87.2	82.8	76.9
Biological, Both Married Once	* / *	70.9	65.1	57.0
One Parent	9.9	9.2	13.7	19.3
Mother Only	7.5	8.0	11.8	17.0
Divorced	1.0	1.9	3.6	7.3
Separated	2.4	2.4	3.5	4.0
Widowed	3.9	2.0	2.4	1.8
MSA–O	*	1.4	1.1	0.7
Never Married	0.2	0.3	1.2	3.2
Father Only	2.4	1.2	1.9	2.3
Divorced	0.2	0.2	0.4	1.0
Separated	0.7	0.2	0.2	0.4
Widowed	1.4	0.4	0.4	0.3
MSA–O	*	0.4	0.7	0.3
Never Married	0.1	0.0	0.2	0.3
Neither Parent	5.0	3.7	3.6	3.9
Other Relative	3.3	2.5	2.4	2.9
Nonrelative	0.7	0.5	0.6	0.6
Group Quarters	1.0	0.7	0.6	0.4
Total	100.0	100.0	100.0	100.0

*Cannot be distinguished

a growing number of children with divorced and separated fathers. Slightly less than 4 percent of children lived with neither parent at each of the last three census dates—most living with relatives. It should be noted that those living with nonrelatives would include foster children as well as exchange students and children living in small group homes, while those living in group quarters include institutionalized children, children in larger group homes, and children who are living apart from their families while attending school.

The fraction living in two-parent familes was slightly lower in 1940 than in 1960. This was the case because in 1940 a larger share of children had experienced the death of a parent and were living with their widowed mother or father. Also, a larger proportion were living with neither parent. One suspects that many of these had also experienced the death of one or both parents.

The classification of living arrangements used in Table 7.1 has two important shortcomings. First, the classification of children living with their biological parents can only be approximated because only the date of first marriage is recorded in the census and because of classification problems relating to premarital and intermarital births. (See Bumpass, "Children and Marital Disruption," for a discussion of the latter issue.) Second, some children classified as living in a one-parent family were living with that parent and the cohabiting partner (1.6 percent of all children, but 8 percent of those classified as living with only one parent in 1980).

Table 7.2 provides distributions by children's age and by race/ethnicity, using a classification that reduces the marital detail but that identifies those children who are living with a parent and their cohabiting partner. In 1980, 63 percent of majority-white children were living with both once-married, biological parents, compared to 58 percent among Mexican-Americans and 29 percent among blacks. Fewer than one-half (46 percent) of black children were living with two parents in 1980, compared to 84 percent among majority whites and 78 percent among Mexican-Americans.

The patterns are closely mirrored by variation in the proportions of children living with only their mother, since this is the primary family situation of children who are not with two parents. This proportion varied in 1980 from 11 percent among majority-white children to 34 percent among blacks, with Mexican-Americans in between but much closer to the white levels (16 percent).

Living with a cohabiting parent was relatively rare in 1980 in spite of the rapid increase in the prevalence of cohabitation. The proportion of children in this arrangement varies from 1.3 percent among Mexican-Americans to 2.9 percent among blacks. Even when considered in relation to children not with both parents, cohabitation is a minor aspect of children's family experience (constituting about 7 percent of this base). Of course, the proportion of children who will ever live in this arrangement may be considerably higher than those doing so at a single point in time. Of the 1.6 percent living with a cohabiting parent in 1980, two-thirds were living with their mother and her partner. It is likely that most children living with their father and his partner are living, in fact, with both of their parents, while a smaller proportion of those with their mother and her partner are actually living with both biological parents.

Living in a father–child family is also rare (1.7 percent overall), and it varies rather little with ethnicity. More children live with neither

TABLE 7.2

Distribution of Children by Parental Status, by Age and Race/Ethnicity, 1980

	Total	0–2	3–5	6–8	9–11	12–14	15–17
TOTAL—ALL RACES/ETHNICITIES							
Two-Parents	76.9	80.3	78.0	77.4	77.0	75.8	73.8
Biological, Both							
Married Once	57.0	62.5	59.2	56.6	55.5	54.6	54.6
Cohabiting Parent	1.6	1.9	2.0	2.0	1.8	1.3	0.8
Mother Only	15.8	13.2	15.3	16.0	16.5	17.0	16.6
Father Only	1.7	0.9	1.3	1.4	1.6	2.1	2.5
Neither Parent	3.9	3.7	3.3	3.2	3.1	3.7	6.5
Total	100.0	100.0	100.0	100.0	100.0	100.0	100.0
NON-HISPANIC WHITE							
Two-Parents	83.8	88.3	85.4	84.3	83.5	82.4	80.0
Biological, Both							
Married Once	62.9	68.7	65.6	62.5	61.2	60.3	62.9
Cohabiting Parent	1.3	1.4	1.7	1.7	1.6	1.2	0.8
Mother Only	10.8	7.6	9.9	10.8	11.6	12.0	12.2
Father Only	1.5	0.7	1.1	1.3	1.4	2.0	2.4
Neither Parent	2.6	2.0	1.9	1.9	1.9	2.4	4.7
Total	100.0	100.0	100.0	100.0	100.0	100.0	100.0
BLACK							
Two-Parents	46.0	44.2	45.5	46.3	47.1	46.8	45.9
Biological, Both							
Married Once	29.0	32.7	30.0	28.2	27.9	27.8	29.0
Cohabiting Parent	2.9	4.1	3.7	3.5	3.0	2.3	1.4
Mother Only	39.0	38.4	39.3	39.5	39.4	39.5	38.1
Father Only	2.2	1.7	1.7	1.9	2.1	2.5	3.0
Neither Parent	9.9	11.6	9.7	8.8	8.4	8.9	11.6
Total	100.0	100.0	100.0	100.0	100.0	100.0	100.0
MEXICAN-AMERICAN							
Two-Parents	77.5	79.5	79.1	79.4	77.4	76.4	72.2
Biological, Both							
Married Once	58.4	63.8	60.5	59.0	56.5	55.4	54.0
Cohabiting Parent	1.4	1.9	1.7	1.4	1.6	1.2	0.8
Mother Only	14.6	12.8	14.1	14.3	15.8	15.6	15.6
Father Only	1.8	1.5	1.6	1.6	1.6	2.0	2.5
Neither Parent	4.7	4.3	3.6	3.2	3.5	4.9	8.9
Total	100.0	100.0	100.0	100.0	100.0	100.0	100.0

parent (3.9 percent) than live with their father alone. We will examine the composition of this category subsequently, but note here that this proportion living with neither parent varies from 2.6 percent among majority whites to 9.9 percent among blacks.

Age patterns must be seen as descriptive of the family circumstances of children of various ages rather than as an indication of how these arrangements change as children grow older. This is so, of course, because of the rapid increase in marital disruption—younger children have been exposed to higher rates of parental marital disruption than the older children were when they were at these young ages. In 1980 the proportion of children living with two parents declined from 80 percent among children under age 3 to 74 percent among those 15–17. Among blacks, the proportion living with two parents varies only slightly across ages. The small increase over the first twelve years reflects the high proportion that were born to women prior to their first marriage, and who begin to live in a two-parent family when their mothers marry.

Although the level is low, it is nonetheless interesting that the oldest children are nearly three times as likely as the youngest children to live with only their father. The age pattern of the proportion living with neither parent differs markedly by race. Living with neither parent is more likely for older children among whites; among blacks, this living arrangement declines with age from 12 percent at ages 0–2 to 8 percent at ages 9–11. It then increases again at the older ages. The difficulty of making aging inferences from these cross-sectional data must be kept in mind, but this U-shaped age pattern among blacks probably reflects nonmarital births that live initially with their grandparents or other relatives but who join their mothers at a later age.

Trends from 1960 to 1980 in age and racial differences in family composition are reported in Table 7.3. Similar trends are seen among children of all ages with the exception that the growth in the proportion living with a cohabiting parent was less marked among children over age 12. One percent of these older children, compared to 2 percent of the younger children, were living in such families in 1980. Changes in children's living arrangements were much more pronounced among blacks. Whereas the proportion living in mother–child families increased by 5 percentage points for white children (from 6 to 11 percent), it increased by 19 percentage points for black children (from 20 to 39 percent). Thus the marked racial differential in the proportions of children in one-parent families that existed in 1960 increased further over the two decades. (Note, however, that in relative terms the increases for blacks and whites were quite similar. The ratio of the 1980 to the 1970 percent in mother–child families was about 1.9 for both populations.)

TABLE 7.3

Distribution of Children by Parental Status,
by Race/Ethnicity and Age of Child, 1960–80

| Year | Two Parents | | Cohabiting Parents | One Parent | | | Total |
	Total	Both Married Once, Biological Parents		Mother	Father	Other	
TOTAL							
1960	87.2	70.9	0.2	7.8	1.1	3.7	100.0
1970	82.8	65.2	0.4	11.5	1.7	3.6	100.0
1980	76.9	57.0	1.6	15.8	1.7	4.0	100.0
AGE OF CHILD							
0–5							
1960	89.6	74.8	0.1	6.6	0.7	3.0	100.0
1970	84.6	68.4	0.4	10.8	1.2	3.0	100.0
1980	79.2	60.9	2.0	14.2	1.1	3.5	100.0
6–11							
1960	87.8	70.7	0.2	7.8	1.0	3.2	100.0
1970	83.3	65.1	0.4	11.5	1.7	3.1	100.0
1980	77.2	56.0	1.9	16.2	1.5	3.2	100.0
12–17							
1960	83.2	65.9	0.2	9.6	1.6	5.4	100.0
1970	80.5	62.3	0.3	12.3	2.2	4.7	100.0
1980	74.8	54.6	1.1	16.8	2.3	5.1	100.0
RACE/ETHNICITY OF CHILD							
Non-Hispanic White							
1960	90.7	75.0	0.1	6.0	0.9	2.4	100.0
1970	87.5	70.1	0.3	8.2	1.5	2.5	100.0
1980	83.8	62.9	1.3	10.8	1.5	2.5	100.0
Black							
1960	65.2	45.4	0.5	20.0	1.8	12.4	100.0
1970	57.2	38.4	0.7	29.8	2.7	9.6	100.0
1980	46.0	29.0	2.9	39.0	2.2	9.9	100.0
Mexican-American							
1960*	84.4	66.9	0.1	9.6	1.3	4.5	100.0
1970	80.8	62.5	0.3	12.2	2.3	4.5	100.0
1980	77.5	58.4	1.4	14.6	1.8	4.7	100.0

*Spanish surname in five southwestern states.

The increase in the proportion of children living with a cohabiting parent was also greater among blacks, and at the same time there was some reduction in the proportion of black children who were living with neither parent (from 12 to 10 percent).

Most children in one-parent families live with their mothers. In 1980, only 10 percent of such children lived with their fathers, a slight decline from 13 percent in 1970. Boys in one-parent families are more likely to live with their fathers than are girls (11 versus 8 percent) and the difference increases with age (Table 7.4). There is little difference among children under 3, but a rather large difference among teenagers. Black children in one-parent families are considerably less likely to live with their fathers (6 percent, versus 13 percent among majority whites), and there is little difference by sex of child among blacks. The pattern for Mexican-American children is more similar to that of white than that of black children.

Table 7.5 considers the marital status of the parents of children in one-parent families. The parent of about two-thirds of these children is separated or divorced. A widowed parent is more likely in father–child families: 15 percent, versus 11 percent among children living with only their mother. Since relatively few fathers have custody of their children following separation and divorce, widowhood plays a somewhat greater

TABLE 7.4

Percent of Children in One-Parent Families Who Live with Fathers, by Age, Sex, and Race/Ethnicity, 1980

	Total	0–2	3–5	6–8	9–11	12–14	15–17
TOTAL	9.5	6.5	7.6	8.1	9.0	10.9	13.1
Boys	10.6	6.8	8.1	8.6	10.2	12.3	15.2
Girls	8.4	6.2	7.1	7.5	7.8	9.5	10.9
NON-HISPANIC WHITE	12.5	8.6	9.8	10.6	11.1	14.3	16.5
Boys	14.1	8.9	10.4	11.4	13.0	16.2	19.2
Girls	10.8	8.2	9.2	9.7	9.1	12.4	13.6
BLACK	5.3	4.3	4.2	4.5	5.1	6.0	7.3
Boys	5.7	4.5	4.6	4.8	5.4	6.6	7.9
Girls	4.9	4.0	3.9	4.2	4.7	5.4	6.7
MEXICAN-AMERICAN	10.9	10.5	10.0	10.3	9.4	11.2	13.9
Boys	11.7	10.4	10.9	11.5	9.3	12.3	15.8
Girls	10.0	10.5	9.1	8.9	9.5	10.0	11.9

TABLE 7.5

Distribution of Children in Mother-Only and Father-Only Families by Marital Status of Parent, by Race/Ethnicity and Age of Child, 1980

	Mother Only						Father Only					
	Divorced	Separated	Widowed	MSA–O	Single	Total	Divorced	Separated	Widowed	MSA–O	Single	Total
ALL RACES/ETHNICITIES												
0– 2	21.5	23.2	3.5	7.0	44.7	100.0	23.7	15.6	4.2	27.1	29.5	100.0
3– 5	36.5	25.4	4.2	5.1	28.8	100.0	37.4	22.3	6.5	18.5	15.2	100.0
6–11	47.3	24.3	8.0	4.0	16.4	100.0	48.4	18.9	11.5	13.5	7.6	100.0
12–17	47.2	23.4	18.2	3.5	7.7	100.0	48.4	15.0	21.4	11.3	3.9	100.0
Total	42.3	24.0	10.8	4.4	18.6	100.0	45.0	17.1	15.3	14.1	8.5	100.0
NON-HISPANIC WHITE												
0– 2	34.3	27.4	3.5	9.0	25.9	100.0	30.6	17.8	4.3	28.6	18.8	100.0
3– 5	55.5	24.7	4.2	5.0	10.6	100.0	48.3	22.4	5.9	15.5	7.9	100.0
6–11	64.4	19.4	8.4	3.9	4.0	100.0	58.4	17.3	11.1	10.5	2.8	100.0
12–17	59.5	15.8	19.9	3.5	1.3	100.0	55.0	14.0	20.1	9.1	1.9	100.0
Total	57.9	19.5	12.1	4.4	6.1	100.0	53.5	16.1	14.9	11.5	4.0	100.0
BLACK												
0– 2	11.3	18.6	3.0	4.6	62.5	100.0	14.8	16.5	5.3	15.6	47.8	100.0
3– 5	17.1	24.6	3.7	4.2	50.3	100.0	19.3	21.0	7.2	15.5	37.1	100.0
6–11	26.8	29.7	7.4	3.2	32.9	100.0	26.2	23.8	15.4	13.7	20.9	100.0
12–17	30.4	33.4	15.8	2.7	17.7	100.0	25.5	23.0	28.6	12.2	10.7	100.0
Total	24.2	28.6	9.2	3.4	34.7	100.0	23.6	22.2	19.2	13.5	21.5	100.0
MEXICAN-AMERICAN												
0– 2	22.6	27.6	4.5	9.7	35.6	100.0	12.0	6.6	2.2	42.3	36.9	100.0
3– 5	34.9	29.6	5.8	7.2	22.5	100.0	27.5	17.5	5.7	32.5	16.8	100.0
6–11	44.0	27.7	10.0	6.2	12.1	100.0	37.6	15.2	11.0	26.4	9.8	100.0
12–17	45.6	23.8	19.3	5.3	6.0	100.0	40.5	13.7	19.7	21.2	4.9	100.0
Total	39.6	26.7	11.5	6.6	15.5	100.0	33.3	13.7	12.3	27.7	13.0	100.0

role in creating such families in spite of the higher widowhood rates of females. On the other hand, widowhood does not contribute much to one-parenthood even among fathers.

Only a small proportion of one-parent families are a consequence of spousal absences for reasons other than marital discord: 4 percent of mother–child families and 14 percent of father–child families (see discussion of married, spouse absent–other persons in Chapter 6). Again, the fact that this component is relatively larger for fathers reflects the lesser likelihood of their having custody of children after separation or divorce.

Because of the substantial levels of nonmarital fertility, it is not surprising to find that 19 percent of the mother–child families have a never-married mother. It is, however, surprising to note that 8 percent of the father–child families involve a never-married father. These are primarily children living with a cohabiting father whose partner is in many cases the mother of the child.

The major age and racial/ethnic variations in the marital status of parents of children in one-parent families involve differences in the proportion never-married—ranging from over one-third for mother–child families among blacks to 6 percent of these families among whites.

As we would expect, younger children in one-parent families are much more likely to have a never-married parent. This is true for both racial groups, although the decline with age is much sharper among whites (reflecting higher marriage rates among white never-married mothers). Very few majority-white children over age 12 in mother–child families have a never-married mother (1.4 percent), compared to one-sixth of black children in mother–child families.

The main difference by race/ethnicity among children living only with their fathers is with respect to the married, spouse absent–other category noted previously. Among both blacks and Mexican-Americans, about one-fifth of the father–child families involve a married, spouse-absent father. Among Mexican-Americans this component probably reflects migratory labor and immigration patterns that temporarily separate the mother from the household. However, the similarly high prevalence among black father–child families is not so easily understood. It should be kept in mind that less than 3 percent of these children are in father–child families.

In a similar fashion, Table 7.6 examines parental marital status for children living with a cohabiting parent. The patterns across age and ethnicity are similar to those discussed for one-parent families and hence will not be discussed. The major difference between Tables 7.5 and 7.6 is the higher proportion with never-married fathers among children with cohabiting fathers: this proportion reaches 52 percent among

TABLE 7.6

Distribution of Children Living with a Cohabiting Mother or Father by Marital Status of Parent, by Race/Ethnicity and Age of Child, 1980

	Mother Only						Father Only					
	Divorced	Separated	Widowed	MSA–O	Single	Total	Divorced	Separated	Widowed	MSA–O	Single	Total
TOTAL												
0– 2	32.1	15.1	4.3	1.7	46.9	100.0	28.7	14.8	1.0	3.8	51.6	100.0
3– 5	51.5	15.3	4.2	1.6	27.4	100.0	37.7	18.8	1.5	4.3	37.8	100.0
6–11	62.8	15.7	5.7	1.5	14.3	100.0	54.3	15.0	5.6	4.4	20.6	100.0
12–17	62.2	17.1	10.8	1.9	8.0	100.0	61.5	15.5	7.2	4.6	11.3	100.0
Total	56.0	15.9	6.4	1.6	20.0	100.0	45.9	15.7	4.0	4.3	30.2	100.0
NON-HISPANIC WHITE												
0– 2	42.9	16.6	4.6	1.8	34.2	100.0	39.6	15.2	0.7	3.6	40.9	100.0
3– 5	66.4	13.8	4.4	1.3	14.1	100.0	52.6	17.1	2.3	2.6	25.5	100.0
6–11	75.4	13.0	5.6	1.1	5.0	100.0	66.6	13.4	5.9	2.8	11.3	100.0
12–17	74.4	10.5	11.6	2.1	1.4	100.0	69.4	13.8	6.8	3.9	6.1	100.0
Total	69.2	13.0	6.7	1.5	9.6	100.0	59.1	14.5	4.4	3.3	18.7	100.0
BLACK												
0– 2	16.6	13.0	3.0	1.7	65.7	100.0	20.4	12.8	1.8	3.7	61.2	100.0
3– 5	20.5	17.3	3.2	1.6	57.3	100.0	20.8	19.8	1.8	4.2	53.4	100.0
6–11	30.9	20.9	6.2	2.1	39.9	100.0	31.7	23.5	4.4	5.0	35.4	100.0
12–17	37.6	27.3	10.6	2.2	22.3	100.0	36.0	25.6	9.8	7.5	21.1	100.0
Total	27.9	20.3	6.1	2.0	43.7	100.0	26.8	19.7	4.0	4.9	44.5	100.0
MEXICAN-AMERICAN												
0– 2	39.9	8.0	8.0	1.4	42.8	100.0	23.3	5.5	2.7	5.9	62.6	100.0
3– 5	49.7	15.1	2.7	2.2	30.3	100.0	29.0	14.0	0.9	10.5	45.6	100.0
6–11	65.5	13.6	4.9	1.6	14.4	100.0	36.6	6.9	3.4	12.4	40.7	100.0
12–17	61.6	15.3	14.8	0.9	7.4	100.0	50.0	11.5	8.3	14.6	15.6	100.0
Total	57.4	13.4	7.3	1.5	20.3	100.0	32.2	8.5	3.5	9.9	45.8	100.0

children under 3. This is consistent with our impression that most of the children living with their father and his partner are the offspring of that relationship.

Variations in children's family composition are presented for more detailed racial and Hispanic groups in Table 7.7. With the exception of the Vietnamese, all of the Asian groups (Indians, Koreans, Chinese, Japanese, and Filipinos) have higher proportions of children living with two parents than do majority whites. Asian Indians have the highest proportion, with 93 percent of children with two parents. The Vietnamese exception is easily understood in terms of the number of refugees in this population, but even so three-quarters of the children were living with two parents and only 12 percent were with neither parent. Among the Hispanic groups, Cubans and Mexican-Americans have patterns similar to those of majority whites. Puerto Ricans, however, are closer to blacks, with only 59 percent of children living with both parents and 32 percent living with mothers only. American Indians also have a low fraction living with both parents (63 percent), and a high fraction with mothers only (21 percent) and with neither parent (10 percent).

Number of Children in Household

We turn our attention in Table 7.8 to the number of other children in the household for each of the various family types. The number of

TABLE 7.7

Distribution of Children by Family Status, for Racial and Hispanic Groups, 1980

| | Two Parents | Cohabiting Parent | Single Parent | | Neither Parent | Total |
			Mother	Father		
Non-Hispanic White	83.8	1.3	10.8	1.5	2.5	100.0
Black	46.0	2.9	39.0	2.2	9.9	100.0
Japanese	87.6	0.9	7.6	1.3	2.6	100.0
Chinese	88.6	0.3	6.0	1.5	3.6	100.0
Filipino	84.9	0.9	8.8	1.6	3.8	100.0
American Indian	63.4	3.1	20.8	2.6	10.0	100.0
Korean	90.4	0.6	5.7	1.3	2.0	100.0
Vietnamese	74.3	1.1	9.6	2.8	12.2	100.0
Asian Indian	93.4	0.3	3.0	1.0	2.4	100.0
Hawaiian	68.1	3.8	19.0	2.1	7.0	100.0
Mexican	77.5	1.4	14.6	1.8	4.6	100.0
Puerto Rican	59.4	2.6	31.8	1.7	4.4	100.0
Cuban	81.4	0.9	12.6	1.2	3.9	100.0

other children in the family is an important aspect of children's family environment. Patterns of family interaction may be quite different depending on the number of children. There may also be substantial differences in available resources per child. Table 7.8 includes both siblings and other children, whether related or not, who are in the household. (A

TABLE 7.8

Distribution of Children by Number of Other Persons Under Age 18 in Household, by Parental Status and Race/Ethnicity, 1980

| | Number of Other Children | | | | | |
	0	1	2	3	4+	Total
TOTAL						
Two-Parent	18.3	38.1	25.2	11.2	7.2	100.0
Cohabiting Parent	27.5	33.2	21.5	10.5	7.4	100.0
Mother Only	21.8	32.1	22.4	12.5	11.2	100.0
Father Only	31.2	33.4	18.8	9.6	7.1	100.0
Neither Parent	29.2	26.6	19.2	12.0	13.0	100.0
Total	19.6	36.6	24.4	11.4	8.1	100.0
NON-HISPANIC WHITE						
Two-Parent	19.3	39.9	25.3	10.1	5.3	100.0
Cohabiting Parent	30.2	34.7	19.7	9.7	5.8	100.0
Mother Only	28.1	37.4	21.2	8.9	4.4	100.0
Father Only	35.2	36.2	17.1	7.5	3.9	100.0
Neither Parent	37.5	28.8	17.5	9.2	7.0	100.0
Total	21.0	39.3	24.5	9.9	5.3	100.0
BLACK						
Two-Parent	14.8	29.9	25.1	15.6	14.6	100.0
Cohabiting Parent	22.6	30.8	24.9	11.4	10.4	100.0
Mother Only	15.4	25.8	23.8	16.8	18.2	100.0
Father Only	23.8	28.0	20.8	13.7	13.7	100.0
Neither Parent	22.1	24.0	21.1	14.5	18.4	100.0
Total	16.2	27.7	24.1	15.8	16.2	100.0
MEXICAN-AMERICAN						
Two-Parent	11.9	27.3	26.0	17.1	17.8	100.0
Cohabiting Parent	25.2	30.1	20.2	12.6	12.0	100.0
Mother Only	16.7	26.9	23.2	16.6	16.7	100.0
Father Only	20.6	29.4	20.5	12.7	16.7	100.0
Neither Parent	24.8	24.5	20.0	14.1	16.5	100.0
Total	13.5	27.2	25.1	16.7	17.5	100.0

similar table based only on siblings is not shown because the results are almost identical.) One-fifth of the children are the only persons under 18 in the household, and nearly two-fifths are in families with only one other child. Less than one-fifth live in families with three or more other children. (Note that the unit here is children, not families.) The fraction of families with many children is much smaller than the fraction of children in families with many children. The difference, of course, simply reflects the different units of analysis. With children as the units of analysis, each child in a large family is "counted" separately; with families as the unit, the large family is "counted" only once. The proportion of only children varies from 13 percent among Mexican-Americans to 16 percent among blacks and 21 percent among majority whites. Conversely, 5 percent of white children but about one of every six black or Mexican-American children is living in a household with four or more other children. Children living with both parents are least likely to be only children, whereas those living with their father only, a cohabiting parent, or neither parent are most likely to be so. Even so, it is important to note that most children living in these circumstances share the household with other children, often several others.

These patterns vary by age (Table 7.9), with about one-quarter of the oldest and youngest age groups being only children, compared to only 12 percent among children ages 6–11. The youngest children are, of course, more likely to be in families in the earlier stages of family building, whereas the oldest ones will be more likely to have older siblings who have left home.

Grandparents and Other Relatives in Household

Table 7.10 shows the proportion of children who have grandparents or other relatives living in their household. We have distinguished among four situations: children with no relatives other than parents and siblings in the household,[6] those with grandparents present, those with no grandparents but other relatives age 18 or older, and those with other relatives under age 18 only. This latter category cannot be estimated for children living with neither parent because household members are classified by relationship to the householder, and it is difficult at best, and impossible at worst, to determine the relationship to other children in the household. Most of the other adult relatives are aunts and uncles and most of the other relatives under age 18 are cousins (data not shown).

[6]Adult brothers and sisters are not included here as "other relatives."

TABLE 7.9

Number of Other Persons Under Age 18,
by Age of Child, Parental Status, and Race/Ethnicity, 1980

	Age of Child							
	0–5				6–11			
	Number of Other Children				Number of Other Children			
	0	1–2	3 +	Total	0	1–2	3 +	Total
TOTAL								
Two-Parent	23.7	63.2	13.1	100.0	10.0	68.6	21.4	100.0
Cohabiting Parent	37.3	50.8	11.9	100.0	22.2	57.9	19.9	100.0
Mother Only	25.6	53.5	20.9	100.0	17.7	58.1	24.2	100.0
Father Only	30.9	51.5	17.6	100.0	22.8	57.5	19.7	100.0
Neither Parent	23.4	46.1	30.5	100.0	27.0	48.1	24.9	100.0
Total	24.4	60.9	14.8	100.0	12.3	65.8	21.8	100.0
NON-HISPANIC WHITE								
Two-Parent	24.7	64.5	10.8	100.0	10.4	71.5	18.1	100.0
Cohabiting Parent	42.5	48.0	9.5	100.0	24.5	58.5	17.0	100.0
Mother Only	33.8	55.0	11.2	100.0	21.6	64.2	14.2	100.0
Father Only	34.6	54.2	11.2	100.0	25.2	60.4	14.4	100.0
Neither Parent	31.4	49.6	19.0	100.0	34.2	49.1	16.7	100.0
Total	26.0	63.0	11.0	100.0	12.5	70.0	17.5	100.0
BLACK								
Two-Parent	19.7	58.6	21.7	100.0	10.6	57.2	32.2	100.0
Cohabiting Parent	31.0	54.9	14.1	100.0	17.7	57.6	24.7	100.0
Mother Only	18.7	51.9	29.4	100.0	13.9	50.8	35.3	100.0
Father Only	26.2	50.9	22.9	100.0	20.1	51.0	28.9	100.0
Neither Parent	17.5	44.0	38.5	100.0	21.9	46.5	31.6	100.0
Total	19.7	54.1	26.2	100.0	13.3	53.7	33.0	100.0
MEXICAN-AMERICAN								
Two-Parent	17.4	58.0	24.6	100.0	5.7	53.3	41.0	100.0
Cohabiting Parent	35.7	50.3	14.0	100.0	17.8	52.8	29.4	100.0
Mother Only	21.2	51.3	27.5	100.0	12.9	51.3	35.8	100.0
Father Only	20.4	52.5	27.1	100.0	13.1	50.9	36.0	100.0
Neither Parent	21.3	44.8	33.9	100.0	24.3	43.8	31.9	100.0
Total	18.4	56.4	25.2	100.0	7.7	52.7	39.6	100.0

TABLE 7.9 (*continued*)

	\ Age of Child \ 12–17 \ Number of Other Children			
	0	1–2	3+	Total
TOTAL				
Two-Parent	21.2	58.4	20.4	100.0
Cohabiting Parent	20.3	55.4	24.3	100.0
Mother Only	22.7	52.1	25.2	100.0
Father Only	36.3	49.3	14.4	100.0
Neither Parent	34.7	44.1	21.2	100.0
Total	23.0	56.0	21.0	100.0
NON-HISPANIC WHITE				
Two-Parent	22.7	60.3	17.0	100.0
Cohabiting Parent	22.6	56.7	20.7	100.0
Mother Only	30.1	56.1	13.8	100.0
Father Only	40.8	49.3	9.9	100.0
Neither Parent	42.5	43.0	14.5	100.0
Total	24.6	59.0	16.4	100.0
BLACK				
Two-Parent	14.5	50.1	35.4	100.0
Cohabiting Parent	14.7	53.9	31.4	100.0
Mother Only	14.0	46.5	39.5	100.0
Father Only	24.9	46.4	28.7	100.0
Neither Parent	26.9	44.9	28.2	100.0
Total	15.8	48.1	36.1	100.0
MEXICAN-AMERICAN				
Two-Parent	12.3	47.3	40.4	100.0
Cohabiting Parent	15.4	45.8	38.8	100.0
Mother Only	16.3	47.6	36.1	100.0
Father Only	26.8	47.2	26.0	100.0
Neither Parent	27.6	44.8	27.6	100.0
Total	14.2	47.2	38.6	100.0

TABLE 7.10

*Distribution of Children by Presence of Other Relatives and Whether
in Parental Household, by Parental Status and Race/Ethnicity:
All Children Under Age 3, 1980*

Presence of Other Relatives	All Children				
	Total	Two Parents	Mother Only	Father Only	Neither Parent
TOTAL					
None	88.0	93.2	78.5	76.0	18.6
Grandparents					
Parent's Household	3.8	2.3	2.6	4.0	N/A
Other*	2.0	0.6	8.8	8.4	42.5
Other Adult Relative					
Parent's Household	3.7	2.0	4.2	6.8	N/A
Other*	0.4	0.1	1.5	1.8	38.8
Other Relative Under 18	2.1	1.7	4.3	2.9	0.0
Total	100.0	100.0	100.0	100.0	100.0
NON-HISPANIC WHITE					
None	92.2	95.0	84.6	81.5	25.5
Grandparents					
Parent's Household	2.9	2.0	2.2	3.9	N/A
Other*	1.4	0.5	8.0	7.4	37.5
Other Adult Relative					
Parent's Household	2.2	1.3	2.5	4.8	N/A
Other*	0.2	0.1	1.1	1.0	36.9
Other Relative Under 18	1.1	1.1	1.6	1.4	0.0
Total	100.0	100.0	100.0	100.0	100.0
BLACK					
None	73.1	86.7	70.8	62.4	9.9
Grandparents					
Parent's Household	7.1	2.2	2.6	4.8	N/A
Other*	4.8	0.9	10.6	10.4	53.0
Other Adult Relative					
Parent's Household	7.9	4.0	5.8	12.9	N/A
Other*	0.9	0.2	1.9	2.4	37.0
Other Relative Under 18	6.2	6.0	8.2	7.1	0.1
Total	100.0	100.0	100.0	100.0	100.0
MEXICAN-AMERICAN					
None	81.7	87.1	72.6	65.8	17.0
Grandparents					
Parent's Household	4.5	3.0	3.4	5.0	N/A
Other*	2.7	1.2	11.0	10.2	35.5
Other Adult Relative					
Parent's Household	7.4	5.5	5.9	11.7	N/A
Other*	0.8	0.4	2.8	4.8	47.4
Other Relative Under 18	3.0	2.9	4.4	2.6	0.1
Total	100.0	100.0	100.0	100.0	100.0

*Subfamily or no parent present.

TABLE 7.10 (*continued*)

Presence of Other Relatives	Children < 3				
	Total	Two Parents	Mother Only	Father Only	Neither Parent
TOTAL					
None	86.1	93.4	62.3	57.0	12.1
Grandparents					
Parent's Household	3.6	1.6	1.8	4.4	N/A
Other*	5.0	1.6	26.6	19.8	56.8
Other Adult Relative					
Parent's Household	3.6	2.3	4.2	14.0	N/A
Other*	0.7	0.2	3.6	3.2	31.0
Other Relative Under 18	1.0	0.9	1.6	1.5	0.0
Total	100.0	100.0	100.0	100.0	100.0
NON-HISPANIC WHITE					
None	91.3	95.3	64.7	62.5	17.5
Grandparents					
Parent's Household	2.2	1.2	1.3	3.9	N/A
Other*	3.4	1.4	27.6	19.2	53.9
Other Adult Relative					
Parent's Household	2.0	1.4	2.6	9.9	N/A
Other*	0.4	0.1	3.1	3.3	28.6
Other Relative Under 18	0.6	0.6	0.8	1.4	0.0
Total	100.0	100.0	100.0	100.0	100.0
BLACK					
None	67.8	89.6	58.5	46.8	6.6
Grandparents					
Parent's Household	8.8	1.8	1.8	4.8	N/A
Other*	12.1	2.3	27.9	19.7	63.5
Other Adult Relative					
Parent's Household	7.5	3.9	5.2	22.7	N/A
Other*	1.9	0.4	4.3	3.6	29.9
Other Relative Under 18	1.9	2.1	2.3	2.4	0.0
Total	100.0	100.0	100.0	100.0	100.0
MEXICAN-AMERICAN					
None	78.3	85.2	57.1	54.4	10.9
Grandparents					
Parent's Household	4.6	2.5	2.4	4.0	N/A
Other*	6.2	3.0	27.6	16.8	53.3
Other Adult Relative					
Parent's Household	7.8	6.6	6.2	16.1	N/A
Other*	1.5	0.9	5.2	6.9	35.8
Other Relative Under 18	1.6	1.7	1.4	1.8	0.0
Total	100.0	100.0	100.0	100.0	100.0

While the presence in the household of other relatives was relatively rare among all children in the United States in 1980, it is higher than might have been expected (12 percent), and reaches substantial proportions among children in certain ages, family types, and racial/ethnic groups (Table 7.10). About one-quarter of all children in one-parent families, and nearly two-fifths of children under age 3 in such families, have other relatives present. This is true in both mother–child and father–child families, though the prevalence is somewhat higher in father–child families. Grandparents are in the household in about one-half of the instances where other relatives are present. Six percent of all children live in a household with a grandparent; this proportion is about one-quarter among children under age 3 who are in one-parent families.

Whether children with relatives present live in their own parents' household or in their relatives' household varies markedly by family type, age, and whether the other relative is a grandparent. Children and their parents are more likely to be in their own household if they are older, if they are living with two parents, and if the relative is other than a grandparent. When a grandparent is present, half of the very young children in two-parent families, and the vast majority of very young children in one-parent families, live in the grandparent's household. The great majority of children who are living with neither parent live in a household with other relatives (81 percent). Again, the proportion is higher among young children, 88 percent of whom live with other relatives (57 percent with grandparents).

Black children are considerably more likely to live in a household with other relatives (27 percent, compared to 8 percent among majority whites). Within family types the difference is largest among children living with neither parent, where 90 percent of black children, compared to 75 percent among white children, are living with relatives. However, the comparison among young children in mother–child families reveals less difference than we might expect. It is usually assumed that for non-married mothers, kinship networks are a more important source of support for blacks than for whites. This may be true, but it is not reflected in large differences in living arrangements. Among very young children in mother–child families, black children are somewhat more likely to have other relatives present, but the difference is not very large: 41 percent of blacks compared to 35 percent of majority whites. Hence, much of the black–majority-white difference in the presence of other relatives is a consequence of the higher prevalence of absent parents among black children. The presence of other relatives does, nonetheless, have the potential to reduce both economic and parenting strains experienced by single parents.

Mexican-Americans are intermediate between non-Hispanic whites and blacks with respect to the presence of other relatives: about 19 per-

TABLE 7.11

Distribution of Children by Presence of Other Relatives
and Whether in Parental Household, for Racial and Hispanic Groups, 1980

| | | Grandparents | | Other 18+ | | | |
	None	Parent's Household	Other	Parent's Household	Other	Other <18	Total
Non-Hispanic White	92.2	2.9	1.4	2.2	0.2	1.1	100.0
Black	73.1	7.1	4.8	7.9	0.9	6.2	100.0
Japanese	89.2	4.8	2.6	2.4	0.2	0.8	100.0
Chinese	79.2	11.0	1.5	6.7	0.8	0.8	100.0
Filipino	69.6	16.6	2.4	8.6	1.4	1.4	100.0
American Indian	77.6	5.8	3.3	7.7	0.7	4.8	100.0
Korean	85.3	9.1	0.9	3.9	0.4	0.4	100.0
Vietnamese	64.5	9.3	0.8	20.0	1.2	4.2	100.0
Asian Indian	82.7	5.8	0.6	9.1	0.9	0.9	100.0
Hawaiian	75.1	7.0	5.8	8.2	1.0	2.8	100.0
Mexican	81.7	4.5	2.7	7.4	0.8	3.0	100.0
Puerto Rican	84.8	4.7	1.6	6.1	0.4	2.4	100.0
Cuban	77.7	13.2	2.0	5.6	0.4	1.1	100.0

cent have other relatives present, compared to 8 percent of whites and 27 percent of blacks.

Table 7.11 reports the presence of other relatives for more detailed racial and Hispanic groups but without the breakdown by family type. The Japanese are very similar to non-Hispanic whites in having a low proportion with other relatives present (11 and 8 percent, respectively). Most other groups have considerably higher levels, ranging from 15 percent among Koreans and Puerto Ricans to 30 percent among Filipinos and 35 percent among Vietnamese. These latter two groups differ markedly in whether a grandparent or other adult relative is present. Filipinos are the most likely to have a grandparent present (one of every six Filipino children has a grandparent in the household), whereas the Vietnamese are most likely to have another adult relative present (20 percent).

Social and Economic Correlates

One of the major correlates of living in a mother–child family is economic deprivation. In Table 7.12 we observe the proportion of children in families with income below the poverty level and the proportion in families with income at least twice that level (the remainder, those

TABLE 7.12

Poverty Status of Children, by Family Status, Race/Ethnicity, and Age of Child, 1980

	Total		Non-Hispanic White	
	Poor	Adequate*	Poor	Adequate*
TOTAL				
Two-Parent	9.0	70.1	6.7	74.8
Cohabiting Parent	17.9	53.3	12.4	62.1
Mother Only	46.8	24.9	33.9	34.5
Father Only	17.7	59.8	10.9	70.2
Neither	27.9	43.3	15.6	58.0
Total	20.7	61.5	10.0	69.8
AGE >6				
Two-Parent	10.5	65.0	8.1	69.3
Cohabiting Parent	22.9	46.1	16.2	55.0
Mother Only	56.1	19.4	45.4	27.5
Father Only	24.3	49.6	15.7	61.7
Neither	30.4	40.8	15.4	58.3
Total	18.1	57.1	11.7	65.1
AGE 6–11				
Two-Parent	9.2	69.6	6.8	74.3
Cohabiting Parent	15.5	55.8	11.3	63.9
Mother Only	48.0	22.9	36.1	30.3
Father Only	18.9	57.9	12.0	67.8
Neither	28.5	43.7	16.1	60.0
Total	16.3	60.7	10.4	68.7
AGE 12–17				
Two-Parent	7.6	75.0	5.4	80.0
Cohabiting Parent	13.6	60.7	9.2	68.6
Mother Only	39.0	30.6	25.5	42.1
Father Only	14.3	65.1	8.8	74.3
Neither	25.6	45.0	15.3	56.6
Total	13.0	65.9	8.3	74.6

*"Adequate" means family income is at least twice the poverty standard.

TABLE 7.12 (*continued*)

	Black		Mexican-American	
	Poor	Adequate*	Poor	Adequate*
TOTAL				
Two-Parent	18.4	51.2	20.5	46.8
Cohabiting Parent	27.2	40.4	19.8	44.8
Mother Only	59.1	14.8	53.8	18.5
Father Only	32.6	37.3	27.4	41.6
Neither	41.5	27.6	27.9	38.1
Total	37.1	34.1	25.9	42.2
AGE >6				
Two-Parent	19.3	49.2	21.6	44.5
Cohabiting Parent	32.1	36.0	22.4	40.2
Mother Only	63.5	13.1	56.2	18.2
Father Only	36.0	32.4	29.1	34.8
Neither	43.3	25.8	29.7	38.7
Total	39.8	31.9	26.7	40.5
AGE 6–11				
Two-Parent	17.9	52.5	21.3	45.7
Cohabiting Parent	25.0	42.2	18.9	46.6
Mother Only	59.7	14.8	55.7	16.7
Father Only	33.4	37.9	28.2	42.2
Neither	41.0	28.4	29.3	37.8
Total	36.8	34.9	26.8	40.9
AGE 12–17				
Two-Parent	18.2	51.7	18.2	51.0
Cohabiting Parent	21.7	45.9	16.0	51.6
Mother Only	54.8	16.3	49.5	20.8
Father Only	30.3	39.6	25.4	46.4
Neither	40.1	28.7	26.0	38.0
Total	35.0	35.3	23.8	45.4

with poverty ratios of 1 to 1.9 are left out of the table for sake of brevity). While there is some modest improvement in economic well-being with age within family types, the major variation is between children in different family types. Children living in mother–child families are five times as likely to be in families with incomes below the poverty threshold as children living with both parents (47 versus 9 percent). Children in father–child families or those with a cohabiting parent are about twice as likely, and children with neither parent are about three times as likely to be below the poverty threshold as are those in two-parent families.[7] Thus, while children living with their fathers or other adults are much more likely to be in poverty than are two-parent families, they still do not suffer as severe an economic penalty as children who live only with their mothers. This, of course, in large part reflects the large differences between the earnings of men and women in our society.

The economic consequences of parental composition of children's families amplify differences by race in the economic well-being of children. Black children are much more likely to be below the poverty line even among two-parent families (18 versus 9 percent), but in mother–child families three of every five black children are in poverty compared to one-third of white children. The educational selectivity of single parents is very striking. It is not only sex differences in wages that produce the economic disadvantage of children living only with their mothers: patterns of fertility, divorce, and remarriage generate a concentration of one-parent families at low levels of education (Tables 7.13 and 7.14).

This is true for father–child families as well as for mother–child families, though the differences are somewhat smaller. While about one-quarter of the children in two-parent families had parents who had not completed high school, this proportion was 36 percent in father–child families and 39 percent in mother–child families. In part, this difference reflects the lower education and greater prevalence of one-parent families among blacks, but the differential is still large among majority whites (28 percent with the residential parent who was a high school dropout among children with only one parent, compared to 20 percent among those with two parents).

There are large differences by age in the educational selectivity of one-parent families. This selectivity is greatest among younger children. Among children under 6, those in mother–child families were twice as likely as those in two-parent families to have a mother who had not completed high school (31 percent versus 16 percent among non-His-

---

[7]In this analysis we have altered the census definition to include the income of the cohabiting partner in family income and have assigned children with neither parent to the poverty status of the householder.

TABLE 7.13

Education of Father, by Family Status, Race/Ethnicity, and Age of Child, for Children with Fathers Present, 1980

	Total		Non-Hispanic White		Black		Mexican-American	
	<12*	16†	<12	16+	<12	16+	<12	16+
TOTAL								
Two-Parent	25.0	21.4	20.4	23.8	40.3	8.8	56.3	7.1
Cohabiting Parent	40.0	7.6	34.2	9.6	42.0	3.7	56.3	4.4
Father Only	35.7	14.3	28.3	17.7	50.4	6.4	60.2	5.9
Total	25.4	21.2	20.6	23.6	40.7	8.6	56.4	7.9
AGE <6								
Two-Parent	20.3	22.9	15.9	25.4	29.2	10.5	51.9	7.5
Cohabiting Parent	40.9	5.0	37.0	6.5	38.3	3.9	55.6	1.5
Father Only	38.7	9.8	30.9	12.2	43.5	5.2	61.6	4.2
Total	20.8	22.5	16.2	25.2	30.0	10.1	52.1	7.4
AGE 6–11								
Two-Parent	24.1	21.9	19.5	24.2	37.9	9.5	56.6	7.3
Cohabiting Parent	38.1	9.3	32.2	10.1	43.1	3.3	57.9	4.8
Father Only	33.1	14.7	25.4	18.2	46.6	7.2	54.6	6.4
Total	24.2	21.6	19.7	24.0	38.3	9.3	56.5	7.2
AGE 12–17								
Two-Parent	30.1	19.7	25.1	21.9	51.6	6.9	61.4	6.2
Cohabiting Parent	40.8	10.6	32.8	13.4	50.2	1.4	56.3	5.2
Father Only	36.1	15.9	29.1	19.2	56.6	6.6	63.5	6.8
Total	30.3	19.5	25.2	21.8	51.9	6.9	61.4	6.3

*Father did not complete high school.
†Father completed college.

TABLE 7.14

Education of Mother, by Family Status, Race/Ethnicity, and Age of Child, for Children with Mothers Present, 1980

	Total		Non-Hispanic White		Black		Mexican-American	
	<12*	16+†	<12	16+	<12	16+	<12	16+
TOTAL								
Two-Parent	24.2	12.4	19.5	13.3	34.4	7.8	59.4	3.3
Cohabiting Parent	37.5	4.2	33.7	5.2	40.4	2.6	54.1	2.3
Mother Only	39.2	5.8	27.6	8.4	47.8	3.3	61.3	2.5
Total	26.9	11.2	20.6	12.7	40.6	5.7	59.6	3.2
AGE <6								
Two-Parent	20.9	15.0	16.5	16.3	26.0	9.5	54.6	3.9
Cohabiting Parent	39.7	2.5	38.6	2.8	39.5	2.2	55.7	0.6
Mother Only	40.9	4.0	31.4	5.6	44.9	2.7	59.0	2.0
Total	24.2	13.2	18.0	15.2	34.9	6.2	55.3	3.6
AGE 6–11								
Two-Parent	23.7	12.2	19.0	13.1	32.2	8.0	59.9	3.3
Cohabiting Parent	34.8	5.0	31.1	6.2	38.0	3.1	50.8	3.3
Mother Only	36.4	16.1	24.8	9.1	44.6	3.7	59.5	2.7
Total	26.0	11.1	19.8	12.6	37.9	5.9	59.7	3.2
AGE 12–17								
Two-Parent	27.7	10.1	22.7	10.8	43.6	6.3	64.6	2.7
Cohabiting Parent	39.1	5.2	31.9	6.6	45.6	2.5	57.4	3.2
Mother Only	40.6	6.6	28.6	9.4	53.1	3.4	65.4	2.7
Total	30.1	9.4	23.4	10.6	47.9	5.0	64.7	2.7

*Mother did not complete high school.
†Mother completed college.

panic whites). It is important to keep in mind that age differences in the cross-section reflect trends over time and patterns of moving into and out of one-parent families, as well as changes associated with growing older. Patterns of remarriage play a particularly important role.

Children with a cohabiting parent are about as likely as those living with only a single parent to have a parent with little education.

Table 7.15 considers variation by family status in the proportion of children whose mothers are employed full-time, part-time, or not at all, by age and race/ethnicity. Most of the family status variation in mother's employment is associated with full-time work. The differences are greatest among non-Hispanic white children, among whom 59 percent have mothers who are employed full-time if she is a single parent or cohabiting, compared with 36 percent when both parents are present. Although the proportion of children with mothers employed and the proportion employed full-time increases with a child's age, the relative differences by family status are similar across all children's ages. On the other hand, the difference is considerably smaller among Mexican-American children (47 versus 37 percent) and is in the opposite direction among blacks. In these comparisons the child is the unit of analysis. Patterns of employment of women in relation to their family composition are discussed in Chapter 4 (married women) and Chapter 6 (formerly married women).

Black children in mother–child families have mothers who are less likely to be employed and less likely to be employed full-time than black children with two parents present. This may reflect the marginal employability of many of these single mothers because of their limited education. We noted earlier that almost one-half had not completed high school. It also undoubtedly reflects labor market discrimination as well as residential concentration in areas with a limited number of suitable jobs.

A woman with limited earning potential may be economically better off receiving Aid to Families with Dependent Children (AFDC) and other forms of welfare, and refraining from working. This is because in many situations AFDC benefits are reduced nearly dollar for dollar by the amount of income earned, and also because eligibility for some in-kind programs such as food stamps or family medical care may be lost if the woman has more than nominal earnings. Many jobs that persons with limited education may find are extremely unstable. Even if a job that pays more than the welfare benefit level is available, a woman may be reluctant to take it because of the difficulty of regaining welfare benefits if the job is lost.

The research on the effects on children of experience in a one-parent family documents short-term trauma, but there is less evidence of

TABLE 7.15

Children by Employment Status of Mother, by Family Status, Race/Ethnicity, and Age, 1980

	Total				Non-Hispanic White			
	Full Time	Part Time	Not Working	Total	Full Time	Part Time	Not Working	Total
ALL AGES								
Two-Parent	35.6	21.0	43.4	100.0	33.2	22.8	43.9	100.0
Cohabiting Mother	56.6	14.8	28.6	100.0	58.9	16.6	24.4	100.0
Mother Only	50.4	14.3	35.3	100.0	58.6	16.3	25.1	100.0
Total	38.3	19.8	41.8	100.0	36.3	22.0	41.6	100.0
AGE <6								
Two-Parent	32.0	18.9	49.1	100.0	29.2	20.6	50.2	100.0
Cohabiting Mother	51.6	14.2	34.2	100.0	53.7	16.1	30.2	100.0
Mother Only	41.7	13.2	45.0	100.0	49.2	15.8	35.0	100.0
Total	33.7	18.0	48.3	100.0	31.2	20.1	48.6	100.0
AGE 6–11								
Two-Parent	34.9	21.9	43.2	100.0	32.1	23.9	44.0	100.0
Cohabiting Mother	58.4	15.6	26.0	100.0	60.2	17.4	22.4	100.0
Mother Only	52.6	14.5	32.9	100.0	60.6	16.6	22.8	100.0
Total	38.3	20.6	41.2	100.0	35.8	23.0	41.2	100.0
AGE 12–17								
Two-Parent	39.4	22.1	38.4	100.0	37.7	23.8	38.4	100.0
Cohabiting Mother	60.2	14.4	25.4	100.0	63.4	16.0	20.6	100.0
Mother Only	54.7	14.9	30.5	100.0	62.4	16.3	21.3	100.0
Total	42.4	20.7	36.9	100.0	41.1	22.8	36.1	100.0

TABLE 7.15 (continued)

	Black				Mexican-American			
	Full Time	Part Time	Not Working	Total	Full Time	Part Time	Not Working	Total
ALL AGES								
Two-Parent	52.5	14.3	33.2	100.0	36.6	13.2	50.1	100.0
Cohabiting Mother	53.0	11.9	35.1	100.0	55.6	13.1	31.3	100.0
Mother Only	43.2	12.9	43.8	100.0	46.8	12.6	40.6	100.0
Total	48.4	13.6	38.0	100.0	38.4	13.1	48.5	100.0
AGE <6								
Two-Parent	51.5	13.5	35.0	100.0	35.2	11.3	53.5	100.0
Cohabiting Mother	46.9	12.4	40.7	100.0	52.0	13.6	34.4	100.0
Mother Only	36.5	12.0	51.4	100.0	41.9	11.6	46.5	100.0
Total	44.6	12.8	42.6	100.0	36.3	11.4	52.3	100.0
AGE 6–11								
Two-Parent	54.2	14.4	31.4	100.0	36.8	14.1	49.1	100.0
Cohabiting Mother	56.7	11.2	32.1	100.0	56.0	11.4	32.6	100.0
Mother Only	46.3	12.6	41.1	100.0	48.6	12.6	38.8	100.0
Total	50.7	13.5	35.8	100.0	38.9	13.8	47.2	100.0
AGE 12–17								
Two-Parent	51.8	14.9	33.4	100.0	38.2	14.5	47.3	100.0
Cohabiting Mother	49.3	14.4	36.2	100.0	60.2	15.3	24.5	100.0
Mother Only	46.2	14.0	39.8	100.0	49.6	13.6	36.7	100.0
Total	49.3	14.4	36.2	100.0	40.3	14.4	45.3	100.0

TABLE 7.16

Proportion of 16–17-Year-Old Children
Who Are Not Attending High School, *
by Family Status and Race/Ethnicity, 1980

	Total	Non-Hispanic White	Black	Mexican-American
Total	8.4	7.6	9.2	17.4
Two-Parent	6.1	5.6	6.4	10.6
Cohabiting Parent	15.7	15.3	11.7	22.9
Mother Only	12.1	12.4	10.6	15.3
Father Only	13.9	13.4	10.8	22.9
Neither	25.1	26.5	15.7	43.7

*High school graduates are included as enrolled.

lasting consequences.[8] One area where there does appear to be a clear long-term effect is in high school completion. Teenagers in one-parent families are less likely to complete high school, and much of this effect appears to be attributable to the lower income of mother–child families.[9] This is an instance in which even transitory periods of economic adversity can translate into long-term negative effects.

We can examine this with the census data by looking at the enrollment status of 16- and 17-year-olds (Table 7.16). There is little difference between majority-white and black children with respect to the proportion who are high school dropouts (8 and 9 percent, respectively), but the proportion is twice as high (17 percent) among Mexican-American children. Majority-white children in mother–child families are twice as likely not to be enrolled in school as are those living with two parents. Similar, though somewhat smaller, proportional differences are found for minority children.

That almost one-quarter of the children living with neither parent are not enrolled in school may be both consequence and cause of this family status. The highly disruptive character of events that would cause children to live with neither parent may partially account for this high level of high school dropout. It is also probable that difficult children with problems leading them to drop out of high school are more likely to be living with foster families or in group homes because of

[8]E. M. Heatherington, K. Camara, and D. L. Featherman, "Intellectual Functioning and Achievement of Children in One-Parent Households," in J. A. Spense, ed., *Assessing Achievement* (San Francisco: W. H. Freeman, 1983); J. Wallerstein and J. Kelly, *Surviving the Breakup* (New York: Basic Books, 1980).

[9]S. McLanahan, "Family Structure and the Reproduction of Poverty," *American Journal of Sociology* 90 (1985):873–901.

those problems. This latter explanation would imply that "problem children" are a significant component of those living with neither parent. There is considerable variation by race/ethnicity, with high school dropouts constituting one-sixth of the black children with neither parent and almost one-half of the Mexican-American children in this family arrangement. The lower figure for blacks is consistent with a kin-oriented system in which living with other relatives is a less disruptive or unusual circumstance.

Summary

Experience of the late 1970s suggests that about one-half of all children will spend some time in a one-parent family. Family patterns are further diversified by variation in the timing and duration of disruption and second families. Over one-half of those whose parents' marriage disrupts spend at least six years with only one parent. Among those whose mother remarries, about one-half experience a second family disruption before age 16. Five of every six black children will spend some time in a one-parent family, and for most of these, this status will constitute the majority of their childhood years. These rates of children's experience of marital disruption doubled over the 1970s.

Because of their mothers' remarriage (or marriage, in cases where the child was born prior to the mother's first marriage), fewer children are living in a one-parent family at any point in time than the above estimates of lifetime experience. The proportion of children living in two-parent families (including those living with step-parents) declined from 87 to 77 percent over the last two decades, while the proportion living with only their mother doubled from 8 to 17 percent. The proportion living with both once-married parents declined during the 1970s from 71 to 57 percent. In 1980, this ranged from almost two-thirds of non-Hispanic white children to 58 percent of Mexican-American and less than one-third of blacks. The increase was larger for blacks than for majority whites.

Only about 2 percent of children live in a father-only family. Three percent of majority-white and 10 percent of black children live with neither parent. This living arrangement was most common at older ages among white children and at younger ages among black children. About two-thirds of the children in one-parent families are living with a separated or divorced parent. About one-fifth in mother-only families have a never-married mother—one-third among blacks and 6 percent among whites. Asian-American children are more likely than majority whites to be living with both parents; Hawaiian children have quite low proportions in two-parent families, though not as low as among blacks.

Three-fifths of the children in 1980 lived in households with one or two other children; about one-fifth were the only child in the household and another one-fifth were in households with three or more other children. The proportion of only children varies from 13 percent among Mexican-Americans to 16 percent among blacks and 21 percent among majority whites. Conversely, one in twenty white children but one in six black or Mexican-American children is living in households with four or more other children.

About 12 percent of the children have nonnuclear relatives in their household. Among children in one-parent families one-quarter have relatives present (nearly one-third among children under age 3). Grandparents are in the household in about one-half of the instances where other relatives are present.

Black children are much more likely to have other relatives present than majority-white children (27 versus 8 percent). Children of both races are more likely to have relatives present if they are in one-parent families. The Japanese are very similar to majority whites in having a low proportion with other relatives present, whereas most other ethnic groups have considerably higher levels.

Children living in a mother-only family are five times more likely to be in families with incomes below the poverty line than are children living with two parents (47 versus 9 percent). Children in father–child families or those with a cohabiting parent are about twice as likely, and those with neither parent about three times as likely, to be in poverty as those living with two parents. Within each family type, black children are much more likely than whites to be in poverty.

As a consequence of educational differences in fertility, divorce, and remarriage, there is a striking difference in the education of parents of children in one-parent compared to two-parent families. About one-quarter of the children in two-parent families had parents who had not completed high school. In contrast, this proportion was 36 percent in father–child families and 39 percent in mother–child families. This selectivity is particularly marked for young children. Low parental education is also found for the parents of children with cohabiting parents.

Majority-white children in mother–child families are twice as likely to not be enrolled in school as are those living with two parents (12 versus 6 percent among 16–17-year-olds). These differences are somewhat smaller among black children. Almost one-quarter of 16–17-year-old children living with neither parent are not enrolled.

Family type differences in mother's employment are greatest among majority-white children: of those living with only their mother or with their mother and her cohabiting partner, three-fifths have a mother who is employed full-time compared to slightly over one-third among children living with both parents. Black children in mother–child families have mothers who are less likely to be employed and less likely to be employed full-time than those with two parents present.

8

THE OLDER POPULATION

IN THIS chapter we turn our attention to the family and household situation of the older population of the United States. Persons age 60 and over are the focus; and when married couples are the unit of analysis, a couple is included if the husband is age 60 or more. Throughout the chapter we will divide this elderly population by age—typically in five-year intervals, with an upper interval of 85 and over.

We begin with a brief description of the size and growth of the elderly population. We then examine some of its characteristics, including its age and education composition, its health and disability status, and its work and retirement status. The major part of the chapter is devoted to an examination of the distributions of marital status and living arrangements of elderly persons (the degree to which the older population lives alone, with relatives, and in institutions, and how these living arrangements have changed during the twentieth century). We also discuss the level of homeownership by the elderly of different ages and marital statuses.

The final section discusses the changing prevalence of elderly households. We look at the composition and sources of the increase over recent decades in the proportion of households headed by a person age 60 and over.

Age Composition of the Older Population

Because of mortality, the number of persons decreases rapidly with increasing age. In 1980, for example, about three-tenths of men and one-quarter of women over 60 were aged 60–64 (Table 8.1). An additional one-quarter of each sex were aged 65–69. Eleven percent of the men and 17 percent of the women over age 60 were age 80 and above. Since 1960 there has been an increase in the fraction of the elderly who are very old. For men the fraction 80 and beyond rose from 9 to 11 percent between 1960 and 1980, and for women the rise was from 11 to 17 percent. The growth of the component of the population has been even more dramatic in absolute numbers. There were 1.1 million persons aged 80 and over in 1940, 2.3 million in 1960, 3.8 million a decade later, and by 1980 there were 5.1 million people over 80 years of age.

TABLE 8.1

Age Distribution of Persons Aged 60 and Over, by Sex, 1940–80

	1940	1950	1960	1970	1980
	Percent Distribution				
MEN					
60–64	34.9	34.2	32.0	31.9	31.4
65–69	28.0	27.5	26.9	25.3	26.0
70–74	18.8	18.4	19.9	18.7	19.0
75–79	10.5	11.4	12.3	12.8	12.3
80–84	5.3	5.7	5.8	7.1	6.8
85 +	2.5	2.7	3.1	4.3	4.5
Total	100.0	100.0	100.0	100.0	100.0
Number (000)	6,719	8,717	10,679	12,621	15,044
WOMEN					
60–64	33.5	31.7	29.7	28.0	26.4
65–69	27.7	27.2	26.1	24.1	23.7
70–74	18.6	18.8	20.1	19.2	19.1
75–79	11.1	12.1	13.1	14.1	14.2
80–84	6.0	6.5	6.8	8.7	9.3
85 +	3.0	3.6	4.2	5.9	7.3
Total	100.0	100.0	100.0	100.0	100.0
Number (000)	6,838	9,550	12,576	16,326	20,720

Education Composition

In earlier chapters on young singles and the formerly married we have repeatedly noted the significance of increased educational attainment from one cohort to the next. While the rate of intercohort change was most rapid for cohorts becoming adults since World War II, there has also been a significant educational upgrading in the elderly population. In 1940 more than three-fourths of persons aged 60 and over had not attended high school, and only about 6 percent had attended college. By 1980, only about two-fifths of each sex had not attended high school, and about one-fifth had been to college. This increased educational attainment is likely to have improved both the health and the economic status of the elderly population, quite apart from changes in medical technology and social institutions.

Similarly, there are very large differences among major racial/ethnic groups in the education composition of elderly persons. For example, the proportion of elderly men in 1980 who had not attended high school was 19 percent of non-Hispanic whites, 56 percent of blacks, and 68 percent of Mexican-Americans. Those with college experience constitute 21 percent of the majority whites, 8 percent of the blacks, and 4 percent of the Mexican-Americans.

Marital Status and Living Arrangements

The living arrangements of the elderly have changed significantly during the twentieth century as a consequence of both demographic and social and economic changes. Mortality levels have dropped sharply, especially for women. Declining fertility and population redistribution have reduced the access of the elderly to their adult sons and daughters, while some would argue that there have been fundamental changes in the obligations of children to their elderly parents as well as in the residential preferences of the elderly. In addition, the availability of Social Security and other pension programs has improved the economic position of the elderly, and has increased their economic independence from their sons and daughters.

Beresford and Rivlin argue that as incomes have risen, the elderly, as well as persons of other ages, have chosen to buy more "privacy" in the form of the "occupancy by an individual or a nuclear family of a separate dwelling unit not shared with other relatives or nonrelatives."[1] Similarly, with respect to the elderly, Chevan and Korson write that

---

[1] C. Beresford and A. M. Rivlin, "Privacy, Poverty, and Old Age," *Demography* 3 (1966):247–58.

"maintenance of an independent household is for many of the widowed the symbolic bastion within which they define their roles. To think of living any other way is abhorrent, entailing a loss of privacy as well as independence, and thereby threatening the integrity of personal adjustment."[2]

With the expansion in coverage and payment levels of Social Security and other pension programs, the elderly are increasingly able to afford to live on their own.[3] Michael et al. report that income differential among states accounts for a substantial share of the interstate variance in the proportion of elderly widows living alone.[4]

This section documents several important trends in the living arrangements of the elderly population of the United States during the twentieth century:

1. An increasing fraction of elderly persons, particularly men, at each age are married and living with their spouse.

2. An increasing proportion of the elderly live in their own households, and a decreasing proportion live with relatives.

3. An increasing proportion of the very old live in institutions.

4. There has been a rise in the rate of homeownership among the elderly.

Marital Status Distribution

The marital status distribution of the elderly population depends on a number of factors including the proportion who have never married; separation, divorce, and widowhood rates; and remarriage rates. At each age the fraction of women who are currently widowed is much higher than that of men (Table 8.2). This reflects the well-known sex differential in mortality as well as the age differential at marriage. At ages 60–64, 5 percent of American men and 23 percent of American women were widows. By ages 70–74 the fractions widowed were 11 percent of the men and 46 percent of the women, and by age 85 and over, 43 percent of men and 82 percent of the women were widowed. These fractions have decreased during the entire period, particularly for men (see Figure

---

[2]A. Chevan and J. H. Korson, "The Widowed Who Live Alone. An Examination of Social and Demographic Factors," *Social Forces* 51 (1972):45–54.

[3]Kingsley Davis and P. van den Oever, "Age Relations and Policy in Advanced Industrial Societies," *Population and Development Review* 7 (1981):1–18.

[4]Michael et al. "Changes in the Propensity to Live Alone," *Demography* 17 (1980):39–56. *See also* G. Carliner, "Determinants of Household Headship," *Journal of Marriage and the Family* 37 (1975):28–38.

TABLE 8.2

Marital Status Distribution of Persons Aged 60 and Over, by Age and Sex, 1980

	Married, Spouse Present	Widowed	Separated or Divorced	Never Married	MSA–O	Total
MEN						
60–64	82.1	4.6	6.6	5.3	1.4	100.0
65–69	79.9	7.3	5.8	5.4	1.6	100.0
70–74	76.5	11.3	5.0	5.4	1.9	100.0
75–79	69.3	17.6	4.8	5.4	2.9	100.0
80–84	59.9	26.8	3.8	5.4	4.0	100.0
85 +	41.2	43.4	2.8	5.9	6.7	100.0
WOMEN						
60–64	62.6	22.6	8.6	5.2	1.0	100.0
65–69	52.2	33.7	6.9	6.0	1.1	100.0
70–74	40.2	46.4	5.6	6.5	1.2	100.0
75–79	27.2	60.0	4.3	6.9	1.5	100.0
80–84	15.3	72.9	3.3	6.8	1.8	100.0
85 +	6.4	81.8	2.4	7.6	1.9	100.0

8.1). The proportions of men who are married are remarkably high. At ages 65–69, four of every five males have a spouse present (compared to one-half of women), and even at ages 80–84, three of every five men (compared to one of six women) are still married, spouse present.

Only a very small fraction of elderly persons are separated, divorced, or never-married. The category "Married, Spouse Absent–Other" accounts for an even smaller fraction, except among very old men. This is a census category for currently married persons who are not separated because of marital discord but whose spouse is not living in the same household. For the elderly population, MSA–O persons are primarily those who are themselves living in an institution, or whose spouse is living in an institution.

Elderly blacks are much less likely than elderly whites to be currently married. For example, 54 percent of black men aged 75–79 are currently married, compared to 71 percent of non-Hispanic white men (see Table 8.3). At these ages, 10 percent of black and 4 percent of white men are separated or divorced, and more than one-quarter of black men, but only one-sixth of non-Hispanic white men, are widowed. Similar differentials are found at the younger ages. The marital status distribu-

FIGURE 8.1

Percent of Women and Men Aged 60 and Over Who Are Widowed, by Age, 1940–80

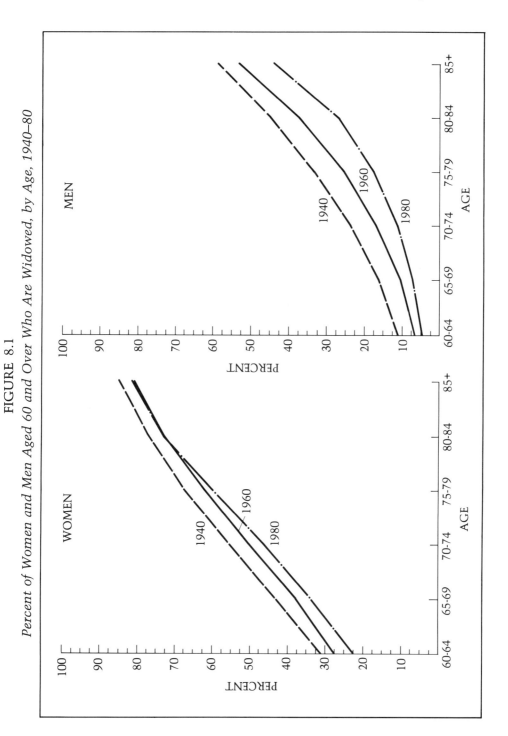

TABLE 8.3

Marital Status Distribution of Persons Aged 60–64 and 75–79,
by Sex and Ethnicity, 1980

	Age 60–64			Age 75–79		
	Non-Hispanic White	Black	Mexican-American	Non-Hispanic White	Black	Mexican-American
MEN						
Married, Spouse Present	84.2	63.8	77.1	71.3	54.1	60.4
MSA–O	1.1	2.5	4.4	2.7	2.9	4.6
Widowed	4.0	10.4	5.8	16.6	27.0	21.9
Separated or Divorced						
Never Married	5.6	16.2	7.8	4.1	9.9	6.6
	5.1	7.1	5.0	5.3	6.1	6.6
Total	100.0	100.0	100.0	100.0	100.0	100.0
WOMEN						
Married, Spouse Present	65.3	41.9	55.4	28.3	18.6	23.0
MSA–O	0.8	1.6	2.4	1.5	1.2	2.2
Widowed	21.5	32.2	23.7	59.2	66.8	64.6
Separated or Divorced						
Never Married	7.4	18.0	12.1	4.0	8.0	6.0
	5.1	6.2	6.5	7.0	5.4	4.2
Total	100.0	100.0	100.0	100.0	100.0	100.0

tions of elderly Mexican-Americans are intermediate between majority whites and blacks.

The contrasts between the marital status distributions of blacks and whites are even larger for women. At ages 60–64, 65 percent of white women, but only 42 percent of black women, are currently married. Nearly one-third of black women and one-fifth of white women are widows; one white woman in fourteen is separated or divorced, while for blacks it is about one in six.

It is important to realize that these differences in marital status distributions result from remarriage differentials as well as the differences in rates of separation and widowhood. Remarriage patterns will be discussed shortly.

The age-specific fractions of the total population who are widows have been decreasing since 1940, with a corresponding rise in the proportions married, spouse present (Figure 8.1). This change has been much less pronounced for blacks. At ages 70–74, for example, the pro-

FIGURE 8.2

Marital Status Distribution of Women and Men Aged 60 and Over, by Age, 1980

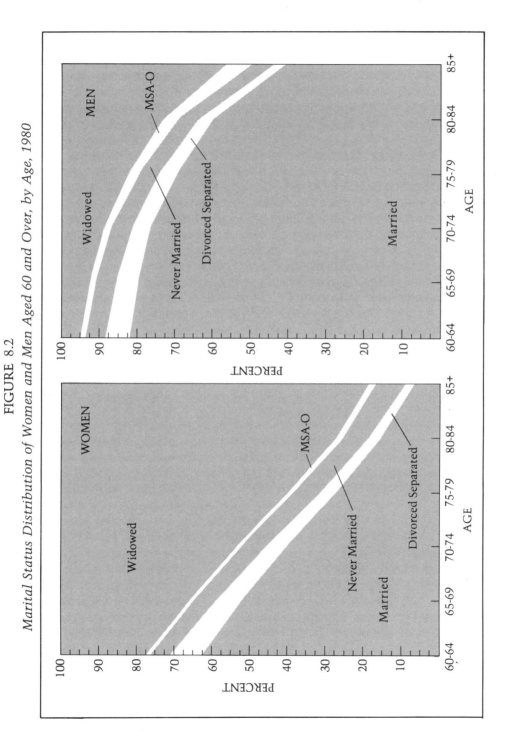

TABLE 8.4

Percent of Black Persons Aged 60 and Over Who Are Widowed and Who Are Married, Spouse Present, by Age and Sex, 1940–80

	Males					Females				
	1940	1950	1960	1970	1980	1940	1950	1960	1970	1980
PERCENT WIDOWED										
60–64	16.1	15.8	13.0	11.0	10.4	45.4	45.8	40.3	35.6	32.3
65–69	22.6	23.8	19.5	18.4	14.6	57.0	58.7	51.6	46.9	43.8
70–74	28.8	28.4	22.7	23.0	21.5	69.3	67.6	61.6	56.8	55.3
75–79	32.7	33.2	31.4	28.0	27.3	74.6	74.5	72.8	68.2	67.8
80–84	42.2	47.4	37.4	34.8	36.4	80.2	84.1	80.3	75.6	76.9
85+	44.6	53.6	57.2	36.2	48.1	89.2	88.2	86.9	80.3	83.0
Total	24.0	25.1	21.5	19.7	19.0	59.6	60.6	55.2	51.2	50.7
PERCENT MARRIED, SPOUSE PRESENT										
60–64	68.3	65.0	66.8	66.3	63.8	43.8	41.0	42.9	43.2	41.5
65–69	63.6	61.4	63.4	60.3	62.2	31.5	31.1	35.4	35.4	35.1
70–74	56.4	60.6	62.2	56.3	58.2	21.9	25.2	26.3	27.2	27.1
75–79	52.9	54.6	53.4	52.5	53.8	17.0	17.6	17.8	18.2	17.9
80–84	45.6	42.4	49.5	49.2	46.1	10.1	9.8	12.2	12.9	11.6
85+	40.3	40.4	32.3	36.5	35.0	4.7	5.5	6.2	7.3	6.0
Total	61.4	60.1	61.4	58.9	58.7	30.2	29.4	31.6	31.4	29.6

TABLE 8.5

Percent of 60–64- and 75–84-Year-Olds Who Are Widowed,
for Racial and Hispanic Groups, 1980

	60–64		75–84	
	Men	Women	Men	Women
Non-Hispanic White	4.0	21.5	20.0	64.6
Black	10.2	32.2	29.7	70.1
American Indian	8.8	30.0	27.5	69.9
Japanese	3.4	17.0	19.0	75.3
Chinese	2.8	24.3	19.9	73.8
Filipino	6.2	27.6	19.3	63.8
Korean	1.0	50.6	—	—
Asian Indian	7.1	27.1	—	—
Vietnamese	6.9	48.8	—	—
Hawaiian	8.6	31.7	—	70.8
Mexican	5.9	23.8	25.3	67.5
Puerto Rican	4.9	22.9	26.5	60.7
Cuban	3.5	18.4	12.7	60.7

portion of black men who were widowed dropped from 29 to 22 percent between 1940 and 1980, and almost all of this decrease occurred before 1960 (Table 8.4). For women the decrease was from 75 to 68 percent and was concentrated in the 1960s. The fraction of elderly black men and women who were married, spouse present, has not changed since 1940.

Table 8.5 presents the proportions who are widows at ages 60–64 and 75–84 for members of the more detailed racial and Hispanic groups. A very high prevalence of widowhood is found among blacks, American Indians, and Hawaiians. For women at ages 60–64, the highest rates are among Vietnamese and Koreans, probably reflecting war casualties and selective migration. Widowhood levels are low among Chinese, Japanese, and Cubans, as well as among non-Hispanic whites.

Remarriage

As we have discussed in Chapter 5, it is possible to make approximate comparisons of remarriage with data from the decennial census, in terms of the fraction of persons "known to have been widowed" who are currently married. From data in Table 8.6 it is clear that blacks who have been widowed have a much lower propensity to remarry than do whites. The differential is particularly pronounced among men, and at the younger ages. Hence, not only are blacks more likely to be widowed

TABLE 8.6

Percent of Persons "Known to Have Been Widowed"
Who Are Currently Married, Spouse Present,
by Age, Sex, and Race/Ethnicity, 1980

	Total	Non-Hispanic White	Black	Mexican-American
MEN				
60–64	43.7	47.0	28.8	40.0
65–69	40.6	42.9	28.4	31.0
70–74	36.6	38.6	26.6	27.7
75–79	31.4	32.7	25.9	24.7
80–84	24.3	24.5	23.1	18.6
85+	15.8	16.0	17.9	12.3
Total	33.0	34.4	26.0	26.9
WOMEN				
60–64	15.8	17.0	9.5	11.4
65–69	11.1	11.6	7.6	10.6
70–74	7.8	8.2	6.0	6.4
75–79	4.9	5.0	4.4	4.4
80–84	2.5	2.6	2.2	1.7
85+	0.9	0.9	1.2	1.6
Total	7.5	7.7	5.9	6.9

because of higher mortality and a larger proportion of couples with wide differences in ages between spouses, but they are also less likely to remarry after widowhood.

Distribution of Living Arrangements

We now turn to the family/household living arrangements of the total elderly population to provide the overall picture. After this, we will consider some aspects of the living arrangements of elderly widows and elderly married couples. Figure 8.3 summarizes the living arrangements of persons age 60 and over. Both sex and age differences are very large.

As already noted, men are much more likely than women to be married and living with their spouse because of higher male mortality and the age differential at marriage between husbands and wives. Three-quarters of the men and about two-fifths of the women are married, spouse present, and maintaining a household. On the other hand, one-

FIGURE 8.3

Distribution of Living Arrangements of Women and Men Aged 60 and Over, by Age, 1980

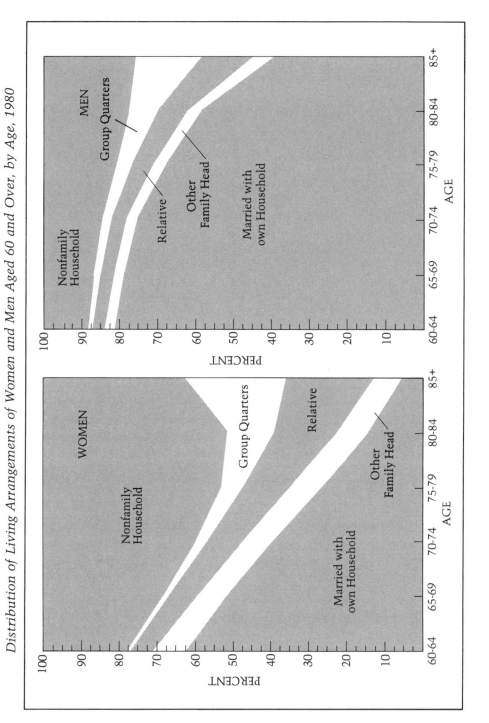

third of all elderly women are living alone or in other nonfamily households. Women are also more likely to be living in institutions or other group quarters. While only 5 percent of all elderly women and 3 percent of elderly men are in group quarters, among those aged 85 and over, 27 percent of the women and 18 percent of the men are in group quarters. About one elderly woman in twelve was the head of an "other family." This category includes persons who have their own adult sons and daughters, a brother or sister, or any relative (other than a spouse) living with them. This is much less common among men—about 2 percent— and it does not vary much with age for either sex. An elderly woman is about twice as likely as an elderly man to be living in the household of a relative—10 percent versus 5 percent. These proportions rise with age for both sexes, so among persons aged 85 and over, 14 percent of men and almost one-quarter of women are living in the household of a relative. While the proportions are much higher than those of persons in their early sixties, it bears emphasis that even among the oldest segment of the elderly population, only a minority shares the household of a relative. It is again important to emphasize that the patterns being described here are cross-sectional. A much larger share of persons who survive to age 75 and beyond will spend some time living in the household of a relative and/or in "group-quarters." We know of no data that adequately describe cohort living arrangements over the later years of life.

Blacks and Mexican-Americans

Elderly black persons are much less likely than whites to be married and living with a spouse in their own household (We have already compared the marital status distributions.) Among men, blacks are much more likely than whites to be living with relatives (8 versus 4 percent), to be living alone (18 versus 12 percent), to be a family head (6 versus 3 percent), and to be a nonrelative of householder (4 versus 1 percent) (see Table 8.7). Mexican-American men are as likely as blacks (8 percent) to be living with relatives or as other family heads (6 percent). The fraction who are currently married and living with a spouse is 67 percent of Mexican-Americans, in contrast to 58 percent of blacks and 77 percent of non-Hispanic whites.

Similar patterns exist for women. Only 29 percent of elderly black women are married and living with a husband in their own household. This compares to 43 percent for non-Hispanic whites. Elderly black women are much more likely to be "other family" heads (18 versus 7 percent) and relatives (14 versus 9 percent).

TABLE 8.7

Living Arrangements of Persons Aged 60 and Over, by Race/Ethnicity, 1980

	Men			Women		
	Non-Hispanic White	Black	Mexican-American	Non-Hispanic White	Black	Mexican-American
Married Couples with Own Household	76.9	58.2	66.7	43.4	29.4	38.3
Other Family Head	2.6	6.5	5.9	7.0	18.5	13.6
Alone	11.9	18.5	12.5	33.1	31.4	23.1
Head Nonfamily Household	0.6	2.0	1.0	0.9	2.1	1.0
Nonrelative	1.0	4.2	1.9	1.0	2.0	2.2
Relative	3.8	7.6	8.4	8.9	13.5	18.9
Group Quarters	3.2	3.0	3.5	5.7	3.2	2.8
Total	100.0	100.0	100.0	100.0	100.0	100.0

The major changes since 1940 include the following (see Table 8.8):

1. The probability that an elderly man is married and living in his own household has increased over the entire period since 1940 primarily as a result of the reduction in mortality levels of older women. The change has been quite small for women.

2. The probability that an elderly person is living in the household of a son or daughter has decreased. In 1940, 18 percent of all elderly women were living with their children; by 1980 it was only 7 percent.

3. The probability that an elderly person lives alone has risen sharply since 1950. It dropped between 1940 and 1950, at which time 3 percent of elderly men and 5 percent of elderly women lived alone. By 1980, one in eight men and one in three women lived alone.

4. There has been a drop in the fraction who are other family heads and also in the fraction living in rooming houses.

Despite the rapid changes in mortality as well as family and household structure, the distributions of the living arrangements of elderly black men have not changed very much since 1940. More are living alone: 10 percent in 1940, 13 percent in 1960, and 18 percent in 1980 (see Table 8.9). Fewer are roomers (7 percent in 1940, 6 percent in 1960, and 1 percent in 1980), and slightly fewer are living with their children (6, 4, and 3 percent, respectively). The changes for black women were larger. There has been a sharp drop in the fraction living with their chil-

TABLE 8.8

Living Arrangements of Persons Aged 60 and Over, by Sex, 1940–80

	1940	1950	1960	1970	1980
MALE					
Married, with Own Household	61.4	64.8	69.4	71.3	74.8
Other Family Head	8.0	6.5	4.4	3.8	3.0
Parent	7.8	11.9	5.0	3.1	2.4
Other Relative	3.7	4.8	3.4	2.8	2.1
Alone	7.5	3.0	10.4	12.7	12.5
Other Nonfamily Householder	1.5	1.2	1.0	1.0	0.8
Roomer	4.2	5.3	2.4	1.6	0.7
Other Nonrelative	0.6	0.6	1.1	0.7	0.6
Group Quarters	5.3	2.0	2.9	3.0	3.2
Total	100.0	100.0	100.0	100.0	100.0
FEMALE					
Married, with Own Household	37.7	37.9	40.7	40.5	41.9
Other Family Head	16.4	13.7	10.5	8.7	8.1
Parent	18.2	26.4	13.2	9.6	6.7
Other Relative	6.5	7.9	6.1	4.6	3.2
Alone	10.5	5.0	20.8	28.6	32.6
Other Nonfamily Householder	2.6	2.6	2.1	1.5	1.0
Roomer	2.6	3.3	1.8	0.9	0.4
Other Nonrelative	1.4	1.4	1.6	1.3	0.7
Group Quarters	3.9	1.7	3.2	4.3	5.4
Total	100.0	100.0	100.0	100.0	100.0

dren (22 percent in 1940, 14 percent in 1960, and 8 percent in 1980). The rise in the number of black women living alone was also great (9 percent in 1940, 18 percent in 1960, and 31 percent in 1980).

Living Arrangements of Widowed Persons

Much of the variation by age and sex and over time in the distribution of living arrangements of the elderly is the result of differences in marital status composition, particularly differences in the fraction currently married. The remaining variation is the result of differences in the marital status-specific distribution of living arrangements.

Although women are much more likely to be widowed (and not remarried) than are men, there is not much difference in the distribution of living arrangements of widowed men and women. Most widowed persons of either sex live alone. In 1980, 56 percent of elderly widowed men and 61 percent of elderly widowed women were living in one-person

TABLE 8.9

Living Arrangements of Black Persons Aged 60 and Over, by Sex, 1940–80

	1940	1950	1960	1970	1980
MALE					
Married, with Own Household	58.8	61.8	60.0	58.2	58.2
Other Family Head	7.6	7.3	6.3	5.7	6.5
Parent	6.3	9.5	4.4	2.8	3.0
Other Relative	3.6	5.4	4.6	4.8	4.7
Alone	9.7	3.2	12.6	17.6	18.5
Other Nonfamily Householder	2.1	2.0	2.4	2.4	2.0
Roomer	7.4	8.7	6.2	4.9	2.6
Other Nonrelative	0.8	0.6	1.1	1.0	1.5
Group Quarters	4.0	1.5	2.5	2.6	3.0
Total	100.0	100.0	100.0	100.0	100.0
FEMALE					
Married, with Own Household	28.4	26.7	30.9	31.1	29.4
Other Family Head	21.4	19.6	19.0	17.3	18.5
Parent	21.9	29.1	14.4	10.7	8.1
Other Relative	7.0	10.0	8.3	6.6	5.4
Alone	9.4	3.9	17.7	25.6	31.4
Other Nonfamily Householder	3.5	3.0	3.3	3.0	2.1
Roomer	4.3	5.5	3.1	2.1	1.0
Other Nonrelative	1.4	1.0	1.4	1.2	1.0
Group Quarters	2.7	1.2	2.0	2.5	3.2
Total	100.0	100.0	100.0	100.0	100.0

households. An additional 5 percent of the men and 3 percent of the women lived in other nonfamily household situations. About one-tenth lived in group quarters, and one-eighth were family heads.

Figure 8.4 shows the age patterns for men and women. Up to ages 80–84, a majority of both widowed men and widowed women live alone. Even at ages 85 and over, fully 40 percent are living alone. There is a gradual increase with age in the fraction living in the households of relatives—about one-tenth of the widows in their sixties and one-fifth of those in their eighties. The great majority of these persons are living with their sons or daughters. The fraction in institutions increases with age, from about 2 percent of widows in their sixties to about one-sixth at ages 80–84, and about one-quarter of widows at ages 85 and over.

The major trend in living arrangements of widowed persons during the past several decades has been a sharp decrease at all ages in fractions living in the household of relatives and a corresponding rise in the proportion living alone (Figures 8.5 and 8.6). For example, among widowed

FIGURE 8.4

Distribution of Living Arrangements of Widowed Women and Widowed Men Aged 60 and Over, by Age, 1980

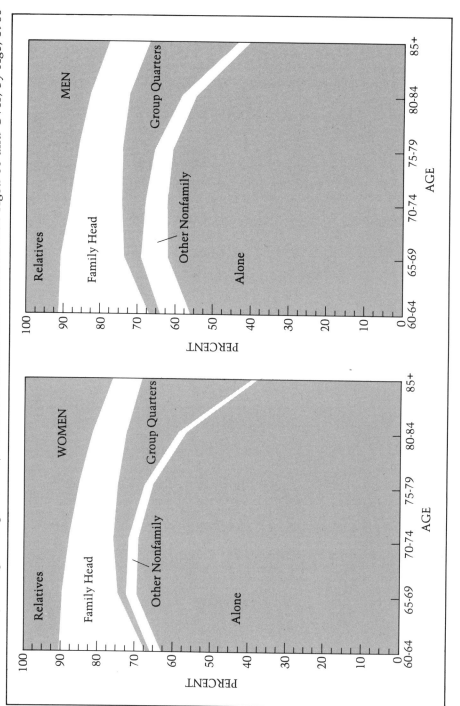

FIGURE 8.5

Percent of Widowed Women and Widowed Men Living with Relatives, by Age, 1940–80

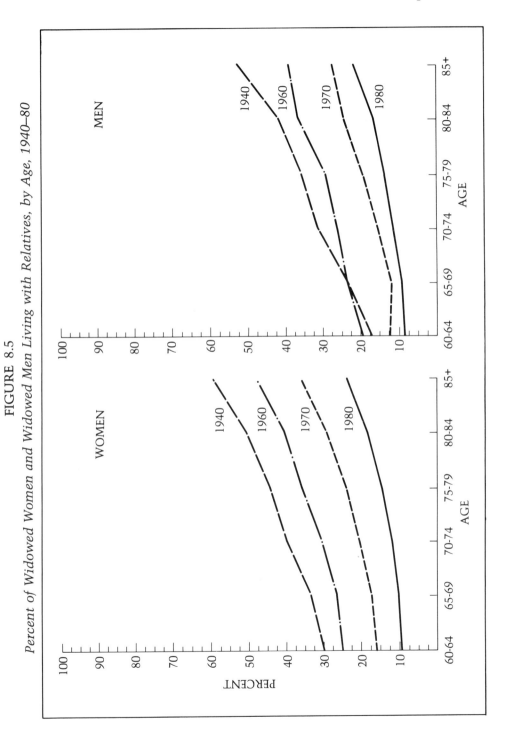

FIGURE 8.6

Percent of Widowed Women and Widowed Men Living Alone, by Age, 1940–80

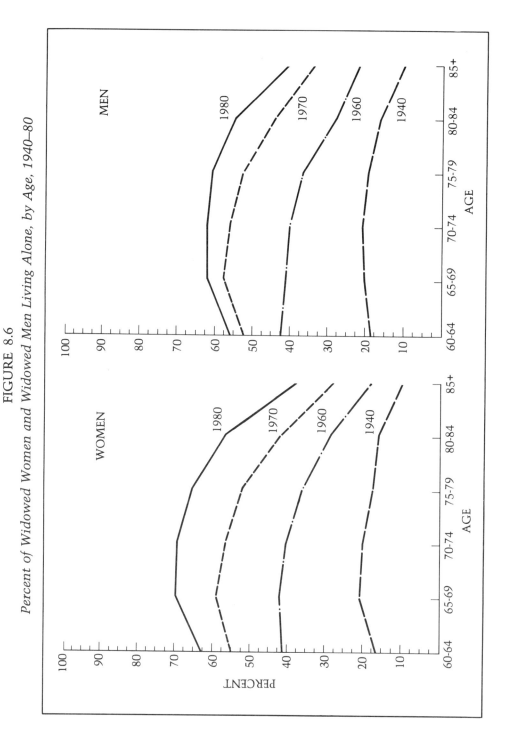

FIGURE 8.7

Percent of Widowed Women and Widowed Men Who Are Other Family Heads, 1940–80

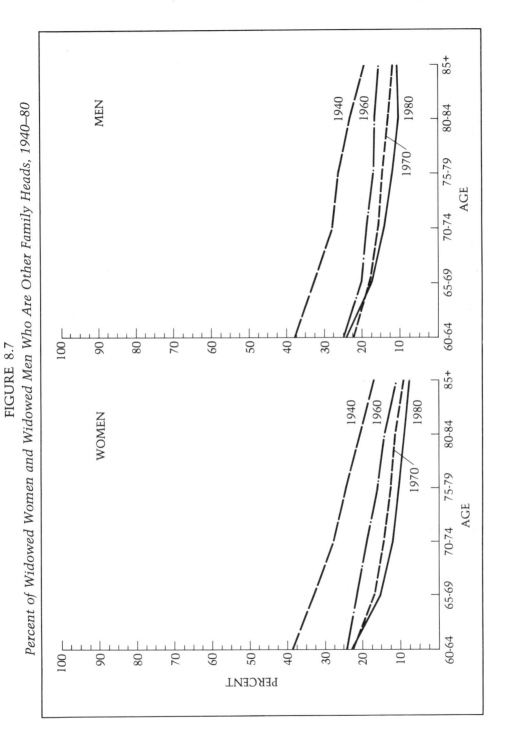

men ages 70–74, 31 percent lived in the household of a relative in 1940. By 1960 the proportion was 26 percent, and two decades later, in 1980, it was only 12 percent. Among widowed women of the same age, the fraction dropped from 40 percent in 1940 to 31 percent in 1960 and to 12 percent in 1980. All of this decrease in living with relatives was accounted for by a rise in the fraction living alone. Among 70–74-year-old widows, the fraction living alone rose from 21 to 40 to 62 percent among men and from 20 to 40 to 69 percent among women.

There has also been a decrease in the share of elderly widows who were family heads (Figure 8.7). This is part of the same social trend. Fewer older persons are living in the households of relatives, and fewer older persons have relatives living with them in their households. There was also a modest drop in the fraction who are nonrelatives of the householder. The fraction living in group quarters changed little except at the oldest age (85 and over). In 1980, 29 percent of the very old widowed women were living in group quarters. This is up from 23 percent in 1970 and 16 percent in 1960.

These trends for the 1940–80 period are a continuation of a longer-term trend. While we cannot make precise and detailed comparisons for 1900, the fractions of persons in a nonfamily household (including boarders, who were much more prevalent in 1900) increased between 1900 and 1940, from 27 to 32 percent among men and from 18 to 28 percent among women. There was a sharp drop between 1900 and 1940, particularly for women, in the fraction living with relatives (see Table 8.10).

TABLE 8.10

Distribution of Living Arrangements of Widows Aged 60 and Over, by Sex, 1900, 1940, and 1960

	1900		1940		1960	
	Men	Women	Men	Women	Men	Women
Family Head	33%	31%	30%	30%	19%	19%
Parent or Other Relative	35	49	31	39	28	32
Nonfamily Household (including boarder)	27	18	32	28	47	44
Group Quarters	4	2	7	4	6	5
Total	100	100	100	100	100	100

Variation in Living Arrangements of Widows Among Racial and Hispanic Groups

The living arrangements of the widowed elderly vary among the racial and Hispanic groups (see Table 8.11).

1. Elderly minority persons, especially women, are much more likely to be heading "other families," that is, to have relatives living in their household with them. About 13 percent of widowed majority-white men and women are other family heads;

TABLE 8.11

Living Arrangements of Widowed Persons Aged 60 and Over, by Sex, for Racial and Hispanic Groups, 1980

	Alone	With Children	Other Relative	Family Head	Nonrelative	Group Quarters	Total
WOMEN							
Non-Hispanic White	61.3	11.6	2.7	12.8	2.7	8.9	100.0
Black	45.2	11.9	5.5	27.5	5.6	4.3	100.0
American Indian	46.2	13.4	3.4	27.8	4.4	4.8	100.0
Japanese	38.1	38.1	2.6	12.9	2.1	6.2	100.0
Chinese	27.4	46.3	5.4	9.8	4.1	7.0	100.0
Filipino	8.5	69.9	6.8	10.4	3.4	1.0	100.0
Korean	13.6	74.1	3.6	5.3	2.1	1.3	100.0
Asian Indian	71.9	13.7	1.8	8.7	3.6	0.3	100.0
Vietnamese	11.1	66.0	11.8	6.2	4.2	0.7	100.0
Hawaiian	53.4	13.4	4.5	21.1	5.4	2.2	100.0
Mexican	40.0	23.4	4.6	23.8	3.6	4.6	100.0
Puerto Rican	38.6	27.8	4.3	22.8	2.5	4.0	100.0
Cuban	29.2	44.1	9.5	10.3	4.6	2.3	100.0
MEN							
Non-Hispanic White	58.4	10.4	2.5	13.1	4.6	11.0	100.0
Black	49.1	8.0	6.5	19.6	11.2	5.6	100.0
American Indian	45.4	10.8	3.5	25.1	5.3	9.9	100.0
Japanese	36.5	27.5	1.7	20.2	2.9	11.2	100.0
Chinese	40.3	23.5	4.1	16.8	5.6	9.7	100.0
Filipino	27.3	31.4	7.8	17.4	11.1	5.0	100.0
Mexican	41.8	17.8	5.2	22.8	5.4	7.0	100.0
Puerto Rican	47.8	21.0	3.1	15.8	7.5	4.8	100.0
Cuban	32.4	27.8	7.9	19.0	8.7	4.2	100.0

NOTE: There were too few sample cases, even in the 5 percent sample, of Korean, Asian Indian, Hawaiian, or Vietnamese men to compute reliable percentage distributions.

this compares with 20 percent of black and 23 percent of Mexican-American men, and 28 percent of black and 24 percent of Mexican-American women.

2. Mexican-Americans are more likely than majority whites to be living in the household of an adult son or daughter. There is no difference between blacks and whites. About one in ten elderly widowed black or non-Hispanic white persons is living with his or her children. It is one in six for Mexican-American men, and one in four for Mexican-American women.

3. Although living in the household of relatives other than sons and daughters is rare for all three groups, it is more common for blacks and Mexican-Americans than for whites.

4. Blacks and Mexican-Americans are much less likely to be living in nonfamily households. Specifically, they are less likely to be living alone. Sixty-one percent of widowed non-Hispanic white women live alone, compared to 45 percent of black and 40 percent of Mexican-American women. A similar pattern is found for men: 58, 49, and 42 percent, respectively.

5. Similarly, elderly black and Mexican-American persons are much less likely than majority-white persons to be living in group quarters. About one in ten widowed white persons is living in group quarters. This compares with one in twenty for blacks and Mexican-Americans.

Also in Table 8.11 are the living arrangement distributions of detailed racial and Hispanic groups. The highest fractions living with their adult sons and daughters are found among the Asian-American population (Korean, 74 percent; Filipino, 70 percent; Vietnamese, 66 percent; Chinese, 46 percent; and Japanese, 38 percent). A large proportion of elderly Cuban women (44 percent) live with their children. Mexican-American and Puerto Rican women are intermediate, and blacks, non-Hispanic whites, Hawaiians, and American Indians are very low. Groups with high fractions living with parents tend to have low fractions living alone.

There is large variation in the proportion of widowed women who are other family heads. Mostly these are persons who have adult sons and daughters living with them. This fraction is high among blacks (28 percent), American Indians (28 percent), Mexican-Americans (24 percent), Puerto Ricans (23 percent), and Hawaiians (21 percent). It is very low for Chinese (10 percent), Koreans (5 percent), Asian Indians (9 percent), and Vietnamese (6 percent).

FIGURE 8.8

Percent of Widowed Women and Widowed Men Living in Group Quarters, by Age, 1940–80

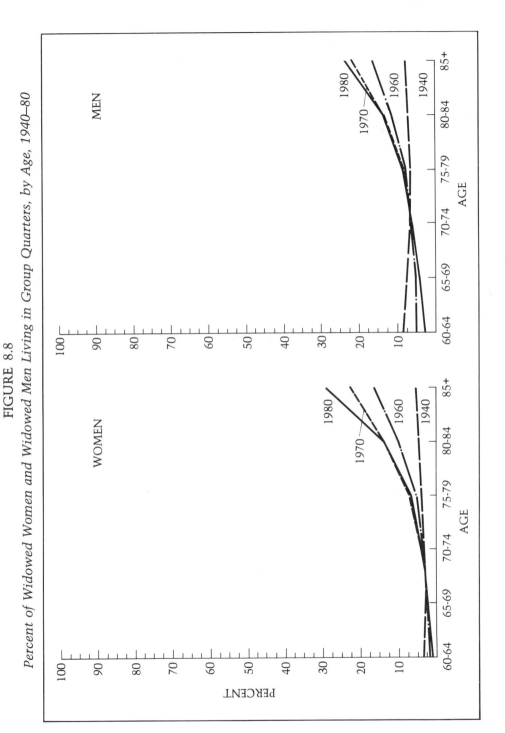

TABLE 8.12

*Percent of Elderly Married Couples Without Their
Own Household, by Age of Husband, 1900–80*

Age of Husband	1900	1940	1950	1960	1970	1980
60–64	2.6	2.7	3.3	1.0	0.7	0.6
65–69	4.1	3.5	4.1	1.5	1.0	0.8
70–74	7.5	4.7	5.3	2.4	1.3	0.8
75–79	8.8	6.7	7.2	3.4	2.0	1.2
80–84	12.2	9.2	9.7	5.0	2.4	1.7
85+	16.7	12.8	14.4	7.5	4.8	2.9

Living Arrangements of Married Couples

In contrast to widows, virtually all married couples maintained their own households in 1980 (Table 8.12). Even in 1900, the fraction of elderly couples living with their children or other relatives was not very high, and there was not much change between 1900 and 1940. In 1940 only about 13 percent of the very oldest married couples (with husbands aged 85 and over) did not live in their own household. By 1960, the fraction was below 8 percent, and by 1980, below 3 percent. At younger ages the fractions are much lower—at ages 65–69, for example, the percent of couples "doubling up" was 4 percent in 1940, 2 percent in 1960, and less than 1 percent in 1980.

Elderly black couples are only slightly less likely than elderly white couples to be maintaining their own households. However, Mexican-American couples are about three times as likely to be "doubled up" (see Table 8.13).

TABLE 8.13

*Percent of Elderly Married Couples Without Their
Own Household, by Age of Husband, 1980*

Age of Husband	Non-Hispanic White	Black	Mexican-American
60–64	0.4	0.6	1.4
65–69	0.6	0.8	2.3
70–74	0.6	0.9	3.3
75–79	1.0	1.2	4.1
80–84	1.5	2.0	3.2
85+	2.7	2.0	5.2
Total	0.7	0.9	2.5

Homeownership

Homeownership is another important aspect of the living arrangements of the elderly. Homeownership increases with age up to the retirement years, where a substantial share of elderly persons are homeowners; thereafter it stabilizes and then gradually declines with age (Table 8.14). In 1980, 84 percent of married couples with husbands aged 60 and over were homeowners. The fraction decreased slowly with age, from 87 percent of 60–64-year-olds to 75 percent of couples with husbands aged 85 and over. The fraction of elderly couples who are homeowners rose sharply between 1940 and 1960, did not change much during the 1960s, but increased during the 1970s, from 77 to 84 percent.

Levels of homeownership among elderly married couples are very high for blacks and Mexican-Americans, as well as for majority whites. About 86 percent of non-Hispanic white and about 75 percent of black and Mexican-American elderly couples are homeowners (see Table 8.15).

Widowhood is evidently associated with leaving owned housing, although exactly how the process works is not clear from these data. In contrast to the 87 percent who are homeowners among married couples with a husband aged 60–64, Table 8.16 shows that about three-fifths of the widowed persons of this age, both men and women, are homeowners. The fraction decreases with increasing age to about one-half of widowed persons in their seventies, and to about one-third of widows in their eighties and beyond. Homeownership is somewhat more common among the very old men than among the very old women. Over time the fraction of widowed persons who are homeowners has increased.

TABLE 8.14

Percent of Elderly Married Couples Who Are Homeowners,*
by Age of Husband, 1940–80

Husband's Age	1940	1960	1970	1980
60–64	62.1	74.6	78.3	86.8
65–69	63.4	76.2	76.9	85.3
70–74	66.4	76.2	76.0	83.1
75–79	66.5	76.0	75.0	80.6
80–84	65.5	74.4	74.1	77.4
85 +	64.3	68.7	69.6	75.1
Total	63.7	75.4	76.7	84.2

*Homeowner is defined as a couple who maintain their own household and live in a home that is owned. Homeownership is not available on 1950 census tape.

TABLE 8.15

Percent of Married Couples Who Are Homeowners,*
by Age of Husband, 1980

	Non-Hispanic White	Black	Mexican-American
60–64	88.2	76.6	77.8
65–69	86.8	76.3	74.2
70–74	84.4	73.7	72.5
75–79	81.9	72.6	—
80–84	78.6	69.9	—
85 +	75.9	73.8	—
Total	85.5	75.1	75.2

*Homeowner is defined as a couple who maintain their own household and live in a home that is owned.

The fraction of widows who are homeowners is the product of two components:

Percent of Widows Who Are Homeowners	=	Percent of Widows Who Are Householders	×	Percent of Widowed Householders Who Are Homeowners

The fraction of homeowners may change either because of a change in the householder rate or a change in the fraction of householders who are homeowners.

If we consider the homeownership of widows who maintain their own households, both the age differentials and the trend are greatly reduced (bottom panel of Table 8.16). About two-thirds of the widowed men and women who are householders own their own homes. The fraction decreases somewhat for women with age—66 percent at ages 65–69 to 59 percent at ages 85 and over—but is inconsistent with age for men.

Thus part, but not the majority, of the reduction in homeownership associated with widowhood is associated with the reduction in householder status as widowed persons move in with other relatives or into group quarters. The majority of the difference in homeownership between widows and married couples appears to be associated with housing transitions among those who then live alone.[5] Except at the

[5]Selective mortality may also be contributing to this differential by marital status. There is no way to separate this effect from the effect of housing change associated with widowhood.

TABLE 8.16

Percent of Widowed Persons Who Are Homeowners,
by Age and Sex, 1940–80

	1940	1960	1970	1980
Percent of All Widowed Persons Who Are Homeowners				
WOMEN				
60–64	36.8	44.0	49.8	60.1
65–69	36.9	42.8	47.5	55.9
70–74	34.1	40.1	44.8	52.2
75–79	31.4	35.1	40.7	47.4
80–84	28.8	29.4	33.4	39.4
85 +	21.4	20.3	23.4	27.4
Total	33.7	37.8	41.6	47.7
MEN				
60–64	35.1	41.6	44.7	57.8
65–69	35.1	38.6	44.0	55.1
70–74	33.2	39.7	45.9	53.5
75–79	34.5	36.9	44.8	49.2
80–84	31.0	32.5	39.2	44.6
85 +	24.0	27.2	31.6	37.0
Total	33.4	36.8	42.1	49.2
Percent of Widowed Householders Who Are Homeowners				
WOMEN				
60–64	61.2	63.2	62.3	69.8
65–69	63.2	62.8	60.4	65.9
70–74	65.7	63.7	60.5	63.7
75–79	67.3	62.8	60.4	61.9
80–84	71.1	63.5	59.9	59.0
85 +	69.7	64.0	59.6	59.0
Total	64.6	63.2	60.7	63.7
MEN				
60–64	58.0	59.1	57.5	68.9
65–69	61.4	59.5	56.2	66.6
70–74	62.7	63.9	61.8	67.5
75–79	69.5	64.5	64.3	65.6
80–84	72.5	68.6	65.7	66.3
85 +	75.5	67.5	66.0	70.2
Total	63.8	63.1	61.6	67.3

TABLE 8.17

Percent of Widows Aged 60 and Over Who Are Homeowners,
by Age, Sex, and Race/Ethnicity, 1980

	Men			Women		
	Non-Hispanic White	Black	Mexican-American	Non-Hispanic White	Black	Mexican-American
ALL						
60–64	64.4	37.6	45.4	64.0	45.6	43.9
65–69	59.5	38.7	47.5	58.9	45.1	44.7
70–74	57.1	38.0	49.8	54.0	43.8	41.7
75–79	52.3	37.8	37.7	49.1	39.8	38.3
80–84	45.4	40.3	39.2	40.1	36.6	33.3
85 +	36.2	36.7	33.7	27.6	27.5	26.4
Total	51.6	38.2	42.4	49.2	41.3	39.6
HOUSEHOLDERS ONLY						
60–64	73.6	49.5	60.0	72.8	54.0	60.3
65–69	70.9	50.0	65.1	68.1	54.8	62.0
70–74	70.8	50.9	66.5	65.0	54.8	60.8
75–79	68.5	52.6	57.1	63.3	53.6	59.4
80–84	67.7	58.5	64.8	59.5	55.3	58.0
85 +	69.6	63.8	70.4	59.4	55.1	60.1
Total	70.1	52.6	63.4	65.2	54.5	60.4

very oldest ages, widowed black and Mexican-American persons have much lower rates of homeownership than majority-white persons (see Table 8.17).

Access to Vehicles

One aspect of the access by elderly persons to services and to their friends and relatives is the degree to which they have access to automobiles. Data collected in the 1980 housing census concerning the ownership of cars and trucks are summarized in Table 8.18. The measure used is the percent of persons living in a household in which someone owns a car or a truck. At ages 60–64, 94 percent of the men and 87 percent of the women have access to a vehicle. By ages 70–74 this fraction drops to 90 percent of the men and 73 percent of the women, and by age 85 and over, only two-thirds of these men and one-half of the women have access to a vehicle.

TABLE 8.18

Percent of Persons Age 60 and Over with Access to a Vehicle,*
by Age, Sex, and Living Arrangement, 1980

	Total		Living Alone	
	Male	Female	Male	Female
60–64	93.8	87.3	75.4	66.1
65–69	92.2	81.0	73.9	59.4
70–74	89.5	72.9	71.1	51.1
75–79	84.4	62.9	67.8	41.2
80–84	76.1	52.2	58.0	28.4
85 +	65.0	49.5	45.2	16.4
Total	89.2	74.4	68.8	47.9
Married, with Own Household	93.2	92.2		
Other Family Head	83.8	73.1		
Alone	68.8	47.9		
Other Householder	76.4	69.4		
Relative	87.8	86.8		
Nonrelative	77.6	78.4		

*Living in household that reported having a car or truck.
NOTE: Persons not living in households are excluded from this sample.

The fraction with access to a vehicle varies by living arrangements. Persons who are married and living in their own households have a high rate of access to a vehicle, as do people living with relatives. People living alone, especially women, have much lower access. About two-thirds of the men and one-half the women living alone have a vehicle. This proportion varies by age with, for example, two-thirds of the women aged 60–64, one-half at ages 70–74, and one-quarter at ages 80–84 having access to a vehicle.

Work and Retirement

In the census we can identify who is working and who is not, but it is more difficult to identify who is "retired." Generally we think that an older person is "retired" if he or she is no longer working regularly at the kind of work they had been doing earlier in their lives. Typically in the contemporary industrial world, they are receiving income from a pension or from Social Security. Many retired persons continue working, often on a part-time basis, and often in a different occupation than they had worked in prior to retirement. The situation of older women is more ambiguous, since many women now in their sixties or seventies did not work regularly when they were younger. Hence, it would not be strictly correct to think of them as "retired." Some, however, may receive Social Security or pension incomes as surviving spouses, or on the basis of work experience earlier in their lives.

In the remainder of this section we will look at the prevalence of working and receipt of pension income by age, sex, and marital status.

Nearly three-fifths of men and one-third of women aged 60–64 were employed during the census week (see Table 8.19). (This compares with 78 percent of men and 46 percent of women aged 55–59.) The employment rate drops off substantially by ages 65–69 where 28 percent of the men and 14 percent of the women were working. At ages 80–84 the employment rates were 8 and 2 percent for men and women, respectively.

At each age the employment rate of widowed men is lower than that of married men. However, for women the reverse is true. A widowed woman is more likely than a married woman to be working.

TABLE 8.19

Percent Employed, by Age, Sex, and Marital Status, 1980

	Married, Spouse Present	Widowed	Separated or Divorced	Never Married	MSA–O	Total
MEN						
60–64	60.8	45.3	45.6	43.7	54.0	58.2
65–69	28.9	19.6	24.7	23.2	25.7	27.7
70–74	18.8	13.3	16.6	15.6	16.5	18.0
75–79	12.5	8.7	12.6	11.9	9.4	11.8
80–84	8.1	6.5	6.3	8.2	5.3	7.6
85 +	6.1	4.1	6.9	6.0	7.0	5.4
Total	34.3	15.5	29.1	25.5	25.4	31.5
WOMEN						
60–64	27.1	38.3	50.0	49.6	29.1	32.7
65–69	11.0	16.4	24.0	20.8	15.2	14.3
70–74	5.1	8.0	11.8	11.2	7.8	7.2
75–79	2.8	4.5	8.4	6.9	1.7	4.3
80–84	2.0	2.4	4.3	4.8	—	2.5
85 +	3.1	1.7	5.2	2.3	9.0	2.0
Total	15.1	11.9	29.0	20.8	14.4	14.9

NOTE: Data refer to population living in households. Residents of group quarters are omitted from the sample.

TABLE 8.20

Percent of Persons Aged 60 and Over with Social Security Income and "Other Income," for All Persons and Persons Who Are "Relative of Householder," by Age and Sex, 1980

	Social Security Income	"Other Income"	Either Source
All Persons			
MEN			
60–64	28.7	30.2	45.4
65–69	76.8	39.2	83.2
70–74	86.3	36.9	91.4
75–79	88.9	31.7	93.2
80–84	88.7	32.7	93.5
85 +	87.2	31.2	92.1
Total	65.9	34.2	74.9
WOMEN			
60–64	36.7	14.1	43.4
65–69	79.5	18.2	82.0
70–74	84.0	19.3	86.6
75–79	83.7	19.9	86.8
80–84	84.0	19.3	87.1
85 +	82.6	15.6	86.0
Total	69.7	17.5	73.6
Persons Who Are "Relative of Householder"			
MEN			
60–64	34.7	26.4	49.3
65–69	68.2	28.5	74.4
70–74	75.9	25.6	80.8
75–79	80.0	25.9	84.0
80–84	83.5	27.2	88.4
85 +	84.6	30.8	89.8
Total	67.9	27.3	75.1
WOMEN			
60–64	39.6	16.0	47.5
65–69	70.8	17.9	74.2
70–74	77.7	17.8	80.6
75–79	78.6	18.2	82.2
80–84	80.2	17.8	84.0
85 +	79.0	13.8	82.3
Total	71.4	16.9	75.5

From data not shown in the tables, it is clear that the majority of elderly persons of every age who work are working regularly. Even at the oldest ages, a large fraction of those persons who worked during the previous year worked at least 40 weeks. This is true for both men and women. Of elderly men who are working, the fraction working full-time (thirty-five or more hours per week) is slightly more than one-half at ages 65–69, and about 40 percent at older ages. For women it is 40 percent at ages 65–69, and about one-third at older ages (data not shown).

In 1980 the great majority of persons aged 65 and over were receiving Social Security and/or pension income. These data are summarized in Table 8.20. At ages 65–69, over three-quarters of men and women received Social Security. At older ages, between 85 and 90 percent of the men and between 80 and 85 percent of the women received Social Security income. The average amount received per recipient per year was about $3,700 for men and $2,800 for women. About one-third of the men aged 60–64 received other pension income—compared to one-fifth of women at these ages. The average amount of other pension income received per recipient is about $5,300 for men and about $3,400 for women. These differences in amount reflect at least three separate things: men are likely to have worked for longer periods of time than women in jobs qualifying them for pensions; they are likely to have earned more while working; and women are more likely to be surviving spouses who are typically entitled to smaller benefit levels than they were as a couple when the other spouse was alive.

Data in Table 8.20 speak, indirectly at least, to the question of whether elderly persons living in the household of relatives are less likely to have pensions and Social Security income, that is, to the hypothesis that persons adapt to economic need by moving in with their relatives. At each age from 65–69 and beyond, persons who are living in the household of a relative have somewhat lower fractions with Social Security and pension incomes. However, even among persons living with relatives, over 80 percent of both men and women have income from Social Security or pensions.

Disability

The 1980 census asked three questions concerning disability:

Does this person have a physical, mental, or other health condition which has lasted for six or more months and which . . .

a. *Limits* the kind of or amount of work this person can
do at a job   Yes   No

b. *Prevents* this person from working at a job   Yes   No

c. *Limits or Prevents* this person from using public transportation   Yes   No

None of these questions is ideally suited for classifying the disability status of the elderly. Questions on work limitation are confusing with respect to persons who are retired. For example, a person who worked all his life as a construction worker but at age 85 does not have the energy he had at 50, is limited in the kind or amount of work he can do, but may not be disabled. How he should answer the second question is not clear. The person living in an area without a public transportation system might be confused by the third question, as might a person with a car who has no need for public transportation. Despite these limitations, the questions concerning inability to work or difficulty using public transportation would seem to be useful in classifying the disability status of the elderly. For each the percent disabled increases with age. There is a tendency for women to report a higher prevalence of disability than men, particularly limitations in the use of public transportation, and particularly at ages 70 and above. We will use the question concerning public transportation as an indicator of disability status.

To what extent does the fraction of persons with a disability vary by household status? If elderly persons who become ill or disabled often moved in with relatives, and/or if the duration of these living arrangements were long, persons living with relatives should have a higher disability rate than those living alone. Table 8.21 shows that married persons living in their own households have a disability level of about 9 percent; those living with relatives have a level of 17 percent. Much of this overall difference, however, is due to differences in age distribution. Within a given age group, married persons with their own households are somewhat less likely than those without to report a disability. Similarly, among nonmarried persons, one-quarter of those living with relatives report a disability compared to slightly over one-eighth of persons living alone. In the bottom panel of Table 8.21 is the prevalence of disability by age for nonmarried persons who were classified as relative of head. The fraction rises with age from about one in six at ages 65–69 to one in four at ages 75–79, and to nearly half for persons aged 85 and beyond (39 percent for men and 50 percent for women). These levels are not much higher than for all persons of the same age.

The striking thing about these comparisons is, however, not the differential in disability between persons living with relatives versus those living on their own but the fact that the great majority of elderly persons living with relatives do not have a disability severe enough that they report being limited in their use of public transportation.

TABLE 8.21

*Percent of Persons Aged 60 and Over Reporting a Disability
That Restricts Use of Public Transportation,
by Age, Sex, and Living Arrangements, 1980*

	Men	Women
Married Spouse Present		
With Household	8.5	9.2
Without Household	16.3	17.9
Other Family Householder	13.0	16.0
Relative of Householder	23.2	27.9
One-Person Household	12.1	17.9
Other Nonfamily Householder	12.7	15.1
Nonrelative	16.5	21.0
Group Quarters	72.2	78.6
Total	11.8	17.4
Relative of Householder		
60–64	16.0	12.4
65–69	16.8	16.2
70–74	19.9	20.7
75–79	23.4	28.3
80–84	32.3	38.1
85+	38.6	50.0
Total	23.2	27.9
Total—All Persons		
60–64	6.1	7.2
65–69	8.8	10.6
70–74	11.6	15.0
75–79	16.4	22.4
80–84	24.3	33.6
85+	38.1	52.4

Elderly Households

In 1980 there were 22.3 million households in the United States in which the "householder" was age 60 or older. The significance of this population is evident from the fact that they constitute over one-quarter of all households. The distribution of elderly households by type is shown in Table 8.22 for 1940 through 1980.

We will examine marital status in more detail subsequently, but for now it is important to recognize that one-half of the elderly households are married couples; the other one-half consists primarily of one-person households (30 percent females and 8 percent males), as well as family households not including a married couple (8 percent female- and 2 percent male-headed).

TABLE 8.22
Distribution of Elderly Households, by Type, 1940–80

	As Percent of Elderly Households					As Percent of All Households				
	1940	1950	1960	1970	1980	1940	1950	1960	1970	1980
Married Couples	56.6	57.2	55.8	51.3	50.2	11.8	12.9	14.0	14.2	13.9
Other Family Household										
Male Householder	7.4	5.3	3.6	2.9	2.2	1.6	1.2	0.9	0.8	0.6
Female Householder	15.4	12.1	10.0	7.9	7.6	3.2	2.7	2.5	2.2	2.1
Nonfamily Householder										
Male—One Person	6.9	7.7	8.4	9.0	8.3	1.5	1.7	2.1	2.5	2.3
Male—Two + Person	1.4	1.2	0.8	0.7	0.4	0.3	0.3	0.2	0.2	0.1
Female—One Person	9.9	13.4	19.5	26.7	30.3	2.1	3.0	4.9	7.4	8.4
Female—Two + Person	2.5	2.9	2.0	1.4	1.1	0.5	0.7	0.5	0.4	0.3
Total	100.0	100.0	100.0	100.0	100.0	21.1	22.6	25.1	27.7	27.7
Number (000)	7,412	9,896	13,298	17,548	22,264					

Although the number of elderly households rose rapidly, there was not a great change in their relative prevalence. (The percentage increase was 34 percent during the 1940s, 34 percent in the 1950s, 32 percent in the 1960s, and 27 percent in the 1970s.) Elderly households constituted 21 percent of all households in 1940, and 28 percent in 1970 and 1980. One reason that the rapid growth in the number of elderly households did not increase their relative prevalence during the recent decade was that one-person households composed of young single and divorced persons were also increasing very rapidly (see Chapter 10).

The proportion of elderly households that were married couples declined from about 56 percent in 1940 and 1960 to about 50 percent in 1970 and 1980. The major change in the composition of elderly households was the growth in single-person female households, from 10 percent in 1940 to 20 percent in 1960, and to 30 percent of all elderly households in 1980. Between 1940 and 1980 there was a drop in the fraction of "other families," from 23 percent to 14 percent of elderly households.

It is instructive also to look at the age distribution of elderly householders in 1980. This is shown in Table 8.23. Slightly over one-half of elderly householders are in their sixties—three-fifths of the married householders and two-fifths of the unmarried householders. Thirteen percent are aged 80 and over—8 percent of the married householders and 19 percent of the unmarried householders.

The growth in the population of elderly households results from three factors: (1) changes in the number of elderly persons; (2) changes in the age and marital status-specific propensities of the elderly to maintain their own households; and (3) shifts in the age- and marital-status

TABLE 8.23

Distribution of Elderly Households, by Age of Householder,* 1980

	Married Couple	Other	Total
60–64	34.3	20.1	27.3
65–69	27.7	21.9	24.8
70–74	19.3	21.0	20.1
75–79	11.1	17.7	14.4
80–84	5.2	11.8	8.5
85 +	2.3	7.5	4.9
Total	100.0	100.0	100.0
Number (000)	11,179	11,090	22,269

*Married couples are classified by age of husband.

TABLE 8.24

*Components of Growth in the Number of Elderly Households,
1960–70 and 1970–80*

	1960–70		1970–80	
	Rates	Composition	Rates	Composition
MALE				
60–64	2.1%	6.9%	0.7%	7.8%
65–69	2.1	3.8	0.6	7.7
70–74	2.4	2.8	0.3	5.0
75–79	1.8	3.6	0.2	2.1
80+	1.6	4.7	0.9	3.0
Total	10.0	21.8	2.8	25.6
FEMALE				
60–64	4.4	10.7	2.7	10.9
65–69	4.8	9.1	3.1	11.9
70–74	4.9	8.4	4.1	10.2
75–79	4.3	8.3	4.1	8.4
80+	3.8	9.5	5.5	10.8
Total	22.2	46.0	19.4	52.2
Grand Total	32.2%	67.8%	22.3%	77.8%
		100%		100%

composition of the elderly population. An example of this last component is that an increase in the proportion widowed would be expected to increase the number of households, since about 70 percent of widows maintain their own households, whereas there is an average of less than one household for every two married persons.

According to a procedure described by James A. Sweet,[6] the growth in the number of elderly households is decomposed into the effects of changes in composition by age and marital status, and changes in rates of household headship (Table 8.24). During the 1960s, 68 percent of the growth in elderly households was due to population growth and change in the age and marital status composition, and 32 percent to increased propensities to form households (increased headship). During the 1970s, three-quarters was due to growth and composition, and 22 percent was due to increased propensities. Thus, while most of the change was attributable to demographic factors, there was also an increase in category-specific headship rates among the elderly over both decades. During

[6]James A. Sweet, "Components of Change in the Number of Households: 1970–1980," *Demography* 21 (1984):129–40.

both decades the preponderance of both rates and composition components occurred for women. In fact, during the 1970s, 90 percent of the
rate component resulted from increases of the rates of household headship of women, and two-thirds of the composition component was a
result of changes in the number and age/marital status composition of
women.

Summary

Reflecting the sharp rise in mortality with age, the age distribution
of the older population is concentrated in the sixties and early seventies.
Almost three-fifths of the men and one-half of the women over age 60
are under age 70. At the same time, the proportion over age 80 has increased over the last two decades: from 9 to 11 percent for men, and
from 11 to 17 percent for women. There has been a significant educational upgrading of the older population for all major racial/ethnic
groups.

The fraction of the elderly that is widowed has declined over recent
decades, and is much higher at each age for women than for men: for
example, 46 versus 11 percent at ages 70–74. Three-quarters of the men
and one-half of the women aged 70–74 are married and living with a
spouse. Among the elderly, blacks are much less likely, and Mexican-
Americans somewhat less likely than non-Hispanic whites to be currently married. These differences result from differentials in both mortality (rates of widowhood) and remarriage rates.

There have been major changes in the living arrangements of the
elderly since 1940: a large increase in the proportion of elderly men married and maintaining their own household; a reduction in the proportion
of elderly living with a son or daughter; and a large increase in the proportion living alone.

Overall, three-quarters of elderly men and two-fifths of elderly
women maintain their own household with their spouse. One-third of
all elderly women and one-eighth of elderly men are living alone or in
other nonfamily households. Only 5 percent of the women and 3 percent of the men are living in institutions or other group quarters, but
these fractions rise to one-quarter and one-sixth at ages 85 and over. The
proportion living in the household of a relative also rises at these older
ages, to 14 percent of males and almost one-quarter of females. Elderly
blacks and Mexican-Americans are about twice as likely as elderly majority whites to be living with relatives or as other family heads.

Although women are more likely to be widowed than men, there is
not much difference in the living arrangements of widowed women and

men: the proportions living in one-person households in 1980 were 61 and 56 percent, respectively, in 1980. Even at ages 85 and over, 40 percent of the widowed are living alone. The fraction living with relatives increases with age from about one-tenth of those in their sixties to one-fifth of those in their eighties. Similarly, the proportion in institutions increases from about 2 percent in the sixties to about one-quarter at ages 85 and over. The trends and race/ethnic differences observed for the elderly overall are particularly marked among the widowed population. Asian-American widows are particularly likely to be living with their children: two-thirds to three-quarters in some populations, compared to 12 percent among majority whites.

In contrast to widows, virtually all married couples maintained their own households—only 3 percent did not in 1980. Elderly black couples are only slightly more likely than non-Hispanic whites to be sharing another's household, but Mexican-Americans are about three times as likely to be doing so. Homeownership reaches its highest level at the retirement ages, stabilizes, and then gradually declines with age. Five of every six elderly married couples owned their own home in 1980; the proportion was three-quarters among couples with husbands who were 85 and older. This fraction rose sharply between 1940 and 1960, did not change much in the 1960s, but then increased further during the 1970s. Levels of homeownership are lower, but still very high, among elderly black and Mexican-American couples. Widows are less likely to be homeowners, partially because of the higher proportions living with relatives or in group quarters. About two-thirds of widowed persons own their own homes. Access to a vehicle declines with age, particularly among the elderly who are living alone.

Nearly three-fifths of men and one-third of women aged 60–64 were employed during the census week in 1980. The fraction employed drops by more than one-half by ages 65–69 and approaches zero by the eighties. Widowhood is associated with lower employment rates among men but with higher rates among women. Even at the oldest ages, a large fraction of those who worked in the preceding year worked at least forty weeks.

In 1980 the great majority of persons aged 65 and over were receiving Social Security and/or pension income. About one-third of the men and one-fifth of the women aged 60–64 received other pension income. At each age 65 and over, the receipt of Social Security and pension income is less likely among persons living in the household of a relative, although the proportion receiving such income is still over 80 percent.

Reported disability is lower among elderly men than among elderly women, and among married persons in their own household than among persons living with relatives. Even among unmarried elderly living with relatives, the proportion reporting disabilities that would limit the use of public transportation is relatively low and rises to only about one-half in the oldest age group.

The 22 million elderly households in the United States in 1980 constituted over one-quarter of all households. About one-half of the elderly households are maintained by a married couple; the other half consists primarily of persons living alone (three-quarters of whom are female). Although the number of elderly households rose rapidly, their relative prevalence did not change greatly because of the rapid increase of one-person households among younger single and divorced persons. The major change in the composition of elderly households was the tripling in the proportion that were one-person female households: from 10 to 30 percent between 1940 and 1980. The majority of the growth in elderly households was due to growth and changes in the marital-status composition of the elderly population. At the same time, there was a substantial increase in category-specific headship rates among the elderly over both decades, most of which occurred for women.

9

HOUSEHOLDS

THE TERM "household" is used almost identically in the United States Census as in everyday language. It refers to all of the people who live together in the same housing unit.[1] In almost all cases the identity and composition of a household is very clear. For example, a household might include a husband, wife, and their children; a divorced woman and her child; or three college students sharing an off-campus apartment. A single person living alone would also be a separate household, and is included in the census count of households.

There are, on occasion, ambiguous cases. For example, if two married couples and their children share a single house, do they constitute

---

[1]A housing unit is a house, apartment, mobile home or trailer, group of rooms, or single room occupied as a separate living quarter. Separate living quarters are those in which the occupants live and eat separately from any other persons in the building and that have direct access from the outside of the building or through a common hall. The occupants may be a single family, one person living alone, two or more families living together, or any other group of related or unrelated persons who share living arrangements.

The first Census of Housing in 1940 established the "dwelling unit" concept. Although the term became "housing unit" and the definition has been modified slightly in each succeeding census, the 1980 definition is essentially comparable to previous censuses. In 1970, the definition of a housing unit required that the occupants live and eat separately and have either direct access or complete kitchen facilities. For 1980, direct access is required; the alternative of complete kitchen facilities has been dropped. Also in 1970, units with five or more unrelated persons living together were classified as group quarters; for 1980 that requirement was raised to ten or more unrelated persons.

one or two households? In the census definition, the character of their housing unit rather than of the relationship among the occupants is the crucial test. If they have living quarters that are clearly separated, that is, have separate direct access, they would constitute two households. Otherwise they would be a single household. Another ambiguous case might be a family with an unrelated person, such as a lodger or employee. If the unrelated person shares the same living quarters as the family, he or she would be included as part of the household. If not, the unrelated person would constitute a separate household.

Households can be divided into two types: family households and nonfamily households. Family households are those including relatives of the household head or "householder." A family household may also include nonrelatives in addition to family members. Nonfamily households, on the other hand, are those households that do not contain any relatives of the household head or householder. Nonfamily households are primarily one-person households, but groups of two or more unrelated persons sharing a housing unit are also included. During the 1970s one form of nonfamily household, the cohabiting couple, has become more common than in earlier years.

Not everyone in the population lives in a household. Some people live in "group quarters." Group quarters include such places as college dormitories, prisons, workers' barracks, hospitals, and other institutional living arrangements. Another type of group quarters is a housing unit containing ten or more persons who are unrelated to the person in charge. (In earlier censuses the number was five or more unrelated persons.) This would include rooming houses with ten or more residents, as well as various kinds of communal groups, the members of which are not related to one another.

The overwhelming majority of the population lives in households. At the time of the 1980 census, there were 220.8 million persons in households and 5.7 million persons in group quarters. Hence, about 97.5 percent live in households and only 2.5 percent of the population live in group quarters. In 1970 there were 5.8 million persons in group quarters. This constituted about 2.9 percent of the total population.

Household Head and Householder

Another census concept that is crucial to understanding the material presented in this chapter is the "household head" or "householder." Traditionally the census interview began with the enumerator asking, "Who is the head of the household?" Information on the characteristics of head of the household was collected first. All other persons in the household were asked their "relationship" to the person designated as head of the household. Historically, the notion of "household head" had a clear meaning in everyday language, and in the overwhelming majority of situations there was no ambiguity as to what was meant by "head of the household."

A married woman living with her husband could not be shown on the census as the head of a household. Whenever such a woman was listed as the household head, the entry was changed by computer edit to make her husband the household head.

The household head concept has caused increasing difficulty in recent years, both in married couple households and in nonfamily households. The expression "head of the household" is no longer commonly used, and in a growing share of households its meaning would be unclear. With increasing fractions of married couples viewing their marriage as an egalitarian partnership, "headship" has become an increasingly foreign concept. In addition, many nonfamily households consisting of two or more persons involve co-equal parties who are simply sharing housing.

This increasing inappropriateness and ambiguity led to the abandonment of household head as a concept. Beginning with the 1980 census, it has been replaced by the "householder" concept. The census schedule begins with the instruction: "Start in this column with the household member (or one of the members) in whose name this home is owned or rented. If there is no such person, start in the column with any adult household member." This person is the "householder," and the "reference person" for the "relationship" question asked of all other members of the household.

The change in concept from household head to householder complicates comparisons between 1980 and earlier years. However, apart from the change in the treatment of married women, it appears to have had little effect on comparability. Some data on the prevalence of married, spouse present, female householders are presented in Appendix 9.1.

We know of no published effort to systematically assess the effect of this change. We have examined distribution of household status and relationship in the 1979 Current Population Survey, which used the headship concept, and the 1980 CPS which first used the householder concept. We could see no difference in these distributions.

We will use the terms "household head" and "householder" interchangeably, and make comparisons between the 1980 and earlier censuses using these two concepts as if they were identical. We do not use the household head concept when discussing married couple households; rather, such couples are classified by characteristics of the husband or of the wife.

Both this and the next chapter are concerned with the population of households, that is, the units of analysis are households and families, not individual persons. We begin with a discussion of the growth in the number of households over time, and then discuss the distribution of households by type. We also examine changes in the "life cycle" composition of households, in an attempt to relate these patterns to changing population structure and changing marriage and reproductive patterns.

The following chapter describes the characteristics of households of each major type—female-headed families, other male-headed families, and nonfamily households. (Married couple families are not discussed here, since they were the subject of Chapter 4.) The population living in group quarters or in sub- and secondary families is also considered.

Growth in the Number of Households

Table 9.1 shows the number of households (and the total population) enumerated in 1790 and in each decennial census since 1850. During each decade of the twentieth century the number of households in-

TABLE 9.1
Total Number of Households, 1790–1980

Decennial Census	Households	Percent Change	Population*	Percent Change
1790	558		3,929	
1850	3,598	N/A	23,192	N/A
1860	5,221	45.1	31,443	35.6
1870	7,579	45.2	38,558	22.6
1880	9,946	31.2	50,189	30.2
1890	12,690	27.6	62,980	25.4
1900	15,964	25.8	76,212	21.0
1910	20,183	26.4	92,228	21.0
1920	24,467	21.2	106,021	15.0
1930	29,997	22.6	123,203	16.2
1940	34,553	15.2	132,165	7.3
1950	43,863	26.9	151,326	14.5
1960†	52,998	20.8	179,323	18.5
1970	63,444	19.7	203,302	13.4
1980	80,533	27.0	226,546	11.4

*Includes population not in households (group quarters).
†Series includes for the first time Alaska and Hawaii 780,000 persons; 225,000 households
SOURCE: *1790–1930:* U.S. Bureau of the Census, *Historical Statistics of the United States, Colonial Times to 1970,* part 1, series A-349-355, 1975; *1940–1980:* Public Use Samples.

creased by between one-sixth and one-quarter. The slowest rate of growth in the number of households was in the 1930s, when the number increased by 15 percent. Until the 1970s, the most rapid increase in the number of households in this century was in the first decade, when there was a growth rate of 26 percent. The rate of growth was slower thereafter except in the 1940s, and again in the 1970s, when the increase was 27 percent. During the entire period the number of households increased more rapidly than the population, reflecting a long-term decline in average household size (a topic we will discuss in more detail in a later section). While population growth had slowed to about 11 percent in the 1970s, the number of households increased more than twice as rapidly.

Change in the Composition of the Population of Households

Historically, the great majority of households were family households, and most family households involved married couples.[2] In 1910, 80 percent of all households included married couples.[3] This fraction gradually decreased to 74 percent in 1960, and then declined to 70 percent by 1970 and to 61 percent by 1980. Beginning in 1940 the data also permit the computation of the percent of all households that were family households. This fraction decreased from 90 percent in 1940 to 85 percent in 1960. There was a further decrease to 81 percent in 1970, and then a more rapid decrease to 74 percent in 1980.

The Inventory of Households: 1980

Table 9.2 (last column) shows the distribution by type of the 80.5 million households in the United States in 1980. Slightly less than three-quarters of all households were family households and one-quarter were nonfamily households. Of the 59.3 million family households, 49.0 million were married couple households. Married couple households constituted 61 percent of all households, or 82 percent of all family households. About one-half of all married couple households included children under the age of 18.

[2]A family household is a household in which at least one member is related to the head or householder. A married couple household is one in which the head or householder is a married person living with his or her spouse.
[3]The year 1910 was the first for which the data permit any classification of households by type; 1940 was the first census year in which detailed type was available.

TABLE 9.2

Distribution of Households, by Type, 1940–80

	1940	1950	1960	1970	1980
Family Households					
Married Couples					
No Children <18	33.4	34.7	30.5	30.5	30.2
With Children <18	42.9	42.3	44.3	38.5	30.7
One Parent Families					
Mother with Children	3.2	2.7	3.5	4.8	6.2
Father with Children	1.1	0.6	0.6	0.9	1.0
Other Family Household	9.4	7.8	6.2	5.6	5.6
Nonfamily Households					
Persons Living Alone					
Men	3.7	4.0	5.0	6.3	8.8
Women	4.1	5.8	8.4	11.3	13.8
Other Nonfamily Households	2.2	2.2	1.7	2.1	3.8
Total	100.0	100.0	100.0	100.0	100.0
Number (000)	34,553	43,863	52,998	63,444	80,533

An additional 7 percent of all households consisted of one parent and minor children (and perhaps other relatives as well). The great majority of these (5.0 out of a total 5.7 million) were mother–child households. There were in addition 4.5 million family households that did not include a married couple or a parent–child (under age 18) combination. These "other families" include, for example, two sisters sharing a household, as well as households comprised of a parent and their adult (aged 18 and over) child.

Only two-fifths of all American households have children (under age 18) in them—31 percent are married couples with children, 6 percent are parent–child families, and a small number are other families. In 1940 and 1960, about half of all families included children.

In 1980 there were 21.3 million nonfamily households. Eighty-six percent of these nonfamily households were one-person households. There were only 3.1 million nonfamily households consisting of two or more individuals.

Change in the Distribution of Households by Type

Between 1940 and 1960 there was not much change in the distribution of households by type (see Table 9.2). About three-quarters were married-couple families, but, because of the baby boom, the proportion with no children dropped between 1950 and 1960. The prevalence of other families declined slightly from 9 percent in 1940 to 6 percent in 1960, while, correspondingly, nonfamily households increased from 10 percent to 15 percent.

It was during the 1960s that the composition of households began to change markedly. Married couple households fell from 75 to 69 percent of all households. All of this decrease involved a decrease in married couples with children. There was a rise from 15 to 20 percent in the prevalence of nonfamily households.

Between 1970 and 1980 the number of households in the United States increased by 27 percent, implying a compound growth rate of 2.4 percent per year. Table 9.3 shows the percentage change for each type of household over the decade. There was great variation in the growth rate of different types of households. The major increases were in non-family households (70 percent versus 16 percent for family households)

TABLE 9.3

*Percentage Change in the Number of Households,
by Type, 1940–50 to 1970–80*

	1940–50	1950–60	1960–70	1970–80
Family Households				
Married Couples				
No Children <18	32.1	6.0	19.9	25.6
With Children <18	25.0	26.5	4.0	1.3
One-Parent Families				
Mother with Children	6.0	56.6	64.4	62.1
Father with Children	−31.4	18.3	90.9	35.1
Other Families	5.3	−4.0	8.1	26.9
Nonfamily Households				
Persons Living Alone				
Men	35.2	51.8	50.8	78.2
Women	79.0	73.3	62.2	54.6
Other Nonfamily Households	24.7	−6.3	47.8	132.7
Total	26.9	20.8	19.7	27.0

and in one-parent households (58 percent). Married couple households grew by about 12 percent. There was a 29 percent increase in the number of married couples with no children present but only a 2 percent increase in the number of married couples with children under age 18. Other kinds of family households grew by 27 percent over the ten-year period.

There was an extremely rapid increase of 78 percent in the number of men living alone (in one-person households), and the number of women in one-person households also grew rapidly—by 55 percent. The number of other nonfamily households, that is, those comprised of two or more unrelated persons, grew by 133 percent. There were 1.3 million such households in 1970 and 3.1 million in 1980. As we will discuss in a later section, a large share of this growth was an increase in unmarried couples living together.

The number of one-person households grew very rapidly in each of the earlier decades, especially among women. There was also a rapid increase in mother–child families during both the 1950s and the 1960s. However, there was very little increase in the number of married couple families with children in either the 1960s or the 1970s.

In Table 9.4 we show how the net household growth in each decade was distributed by household type. In the 1970s there was a growth of 17.1 million households, equally divided between family and nonfamily

TABLE 9.4

Components of Growth in the Number of Households,
1940–50 to 1970–80

	1940–50	1950–60	1960–70	1970–80
Family Households	81.0	70.2	56.8	48.6
Married Couples, No Children	39.7	10.0	30.8	29.0
Married Couples, with Children	39.9	53.8	9.1	1.9
Mother–Child Families	0.7	7.3	11.5	11.1
Father–Child Families	−1.2	0.5	2.6	1.2
Other	1.9	−1.4	2.9	5.5
Nonfamily Households	18.9	29.7	43.2	51.4
One-Person—Male	4.8	9.8	12.8	18.1
One-Person—Female	12.1	20.5	26.4	23.0
Other Nonfamily Households	2.0	−0.6	4.1	10.3
Total	100.0	100.0	100.0	100.0
Increase in Number of Households (millions)	9.3	9.1	10.4	17.1

households. Most of the growth in family households (29 of the 49 percent) was due to an increase in the number of married couples with no children. (Note that this includes young couples who have not (yet) had any children and couples who have been and will be childless throughout their marriages, as well as older married couples whose children have left home). Most of the remainder of the increase (11 percent) was of mother–child families.

In earlier decades, much more of the net household growth involved family households, particularly married couples with children. In the 1940s, four-fifths of the growth was an increase in family households— almost all a growth in the number of married couples. Among nonfamily households, the great majority of the increase before 1970 was in women living alone (mostly elderly widows).

Family Life Cycle Distribution of Households

Classifying households by the "life cycle stage" of the householder or household head provides a more detailed view of the distribution of households, and offers a clearer picture of the underlying dynamics of changing household structure. The same classification is used here as was used in earlier chapters for individuals, but in this case the unit of analysis is the household. The first five columns of Table 9.5 show the inventory of households by family life cycle stage of the householder for each census year. The right side of the table shows the percentage growth of each household type for each decade.

Households headed by never-married persons under 30 were only 1 percent of all households in 1940 through 1960, whereas such households constituted 2.4 percent of all households by 1970, and 6.8 percent by 1980. In 1940 through 1960, about 10 percent of households were headed by formerly married persons who were not elderly. This increased to 12 percent in 1970, and to 15 percent in 1980. The major category that decreased in relative size was married couples with children. Such households were 44 percent of all households in 1960, 38 percent in 1970, and only 30 percent in 1980. The fraction of households with elderly heads increased gradually from 17 percent in 1940 to 24 percent in 1980.

Households of formerly married persons with children constituted 4 percent of all households in 1940, and in spite of the rapid increase in divorce, such households represented only 6 percent of the total in 1980. Formerly married persons with no children were 6 percent of all households in 1940, and two-thirds of these were headed by persons aged 45–

TABLE 9.5

Distribution of Households and Percent Increase in Number of Households,
by Life Cycle Stage of Householder, 1940–80

Family Life Cycle Stage of Household Head	Percent Distribution					Percent Change			
	1940	1950	1960	1970	1980	1940–50	1950–1960	1960–1970	1970–80
Never Married									
Age <30	1.1	0.8	1.2	2.7	6.8	1.6	76.7	162.8	214.1
30–44	1.7	1.3	1.5	1.5	2.6	−3.7	36.4	22.0	121.2
45–59	1.8	1.5	1.7	1.5	1.2	6.5	35.9	8.8	2.7
Married Couple With Children									
Youngest < 6	21.3	25.2	24.7	18.8	14.0	50.4	18.7	−9.0	−5.6
6–11	11.7	9.8	11.0	11.3	8.9	6.0	35.7	23.2	−0.1
12–17	9.7	7.2	8.6	8.4	7.7	−6.7	44.6	17.2	17.2
Married Couple With No Children									
Age <30	6.3	5.2	3.2	4.5	4.7	4.7	−25.6	67.0	34.1
30–44	7.6	7.3	4.5	2.8	3.1	21.7	−26.2	−25.0	38.6
45–59	12.2	13.9	13.3	13.0	11.7	44.8	15.4	17.0	14.6
Formerly Married With Children									
Youngest < 6	0.7	0.9	1.3	1.8	1.7	55.8	82.4	56.5	21.0
6–11	1.3	1.0	1.2	1.8	2.1	−6.0	47.0	81.2	49.9
12–17	1.9	1.2	1.4	1.7	2.1	−17.7	36.1	46.9	54.1
Formerly Married With No Children									
Age <30	0.3	0.4	0.3	0.7	1.3	70.9	−8.0	161.9	135.4
30–44	1.6	1.7	1.4	1.5	2.8	38.2	1.8	22.9	144.2
45–59	4.1	4.5	4.2	4.5	4.7	37.7	13.3	27.8	33.5
Elderly (Age 60 +)									
Never Married	1.4	1.4	1.7	1.9	1.5	19.3	48.6	34.7	2.4
Married Couple	7.5	8.4	9.5	10.2	10.8	43.0	36.4	29.3	33.6
Formerly Married	7.7	8.3	9.3	11.4	12.2	36.4	35.9	47.0	35.8
Total	100.0	100.0	100.0	100.0	100.0	26.9	20.9	19.7	27.0
Total Number of Households (thousands)	34,553	43,863	52,998	63,444	80,533				

59. Their fraction did not change much until 1980, when it was 9 percent. Even in 1980, the majority of these had householders over age 45.

A somewhat different perspective on these same data is provided by the right panel of Table 9.5, where the rate of growth of each type of household is shown. In the 1940s, because of the baby boom, the number of married couples with children increased by 50 percent. Other rapidly growing types were formerly married persons aged 45–59 with no children (45 percent), formerly married persons with preschool children (56 percent), and young formerly married persons with no children. In the 1950s young never-married households rose by 77 percent, and formerly married persons with preschool children by 82 percent. During the 1960s very rapid rates of increase occurred for single persons under age 30 (163 percent), young childless couples (67 percent), formerly married persons with children of all ages, and childless formerly married persons under age 30 (162 percent).[4]

The 1970s were a continuation of trends from the previous decade. The number of households of never-married persons under age 30 more than tripled, and there was also very rapid growth in the number of households of single persons aged 30–44. This very rapid growth reflects the increased size of baby boom cohorts reaching these ages, as well as the delay of marriage and the increased propensity of single persons to live on their own.

There was a *decrease* in the number of married couple households with children under age 12, reflecting the delay in childbearing and the decrease in the number of children per couple. Childless couple households of all ages increased during the 1970s, but especially at ages under 45.

The number of households of formerly married persons with children continued to increase, especially those with children age 6 and over, where the increase was about 50 percent for the decade. A more rapid increase occurred for households of formerly married persons with no children. There was a 135 percent rise for ages under 30, and a 144 percent rise at ages 30–44.

Elderly households also continued to increase—both married couples and households of formerly married (primarily widowed) elderly. In each decade the number of each of these types rose by between 30 and 50 percent.

[4]Many of these decade-to-decade changes involve large percentage increases—as high as 214 percent. These are relatively small groups within the population. These estimates are statistically reliable, but may be deceiving if not considered in the context of the relative size of the subgroup involved. The significance of the percentage changes and relative subgroup size reported in Table 10.5 to total growth in the number of households is reflected in data on the components of increase in number of households reported in Table 9.6.

Finally, in Table 9.6 the net growth in the number of households in each decade is allocated by life cycle stage of householder. We will comment only on the growth of the 1970s, during which time there was an increase of 17.1 million households. About 29 percent of the total growth in households consisted of households with never-married, non-

TABLE 9.6

*Components of Increase in the Number of Households,
by Life Cycle Stage of Householder, 1940–50 to 1970–80*

Family Life Cycle Stage of Household Head	1940–50	1950–60	1960–70	1970–80
Never Married				
Age <30	0.1	3.1	10.3	21.7
30–44	−0.2	2.3	1.7	6.8
45–59	0.4	2.6	0.8	0.2
Married Couple with Children				
Youngest < 6	39.8	22.6	−11.3	−3.9
6–11	2.6	16.7	12.9	0.0
12–17	−2.4	15.3	7.5	5.3
Married Couple with No Children				
Age <30	1.1	−6.4	10.9	5.7
30–44	6.2	−9.2	−5.7	4.0
45–59	20.3	10.2	11.4	7.0
Formerly Married with Children				
Youngest < 6	1.5	3.5	3.9	1.4
6–11	−0.3	2.2	4.8	3.3
12–17	−1.3	2.1	3.3	3.4
Formerly Married with No Children				
Age <30	0.8	−0.2	2.7	3.6
30–44	2.2	0.1	1.6	7.8
45–59	5.8	2.9	5.9	5.6
Elderly (Age 60+)				
Never Married	1.0	3.2	3.0	0.2
Married Couple	11.9	14.6	14.1	12.8
Formerly Married	10.4	14.3	22.2	15.2
Total	100.0	100.0	100.0	100.0
Total Increase in Number of Households (thousands)	9,296	9,149	10,446	17,088

aged heads. Of this, 22 percent involved households with heads under age 30 and almost all of the rest consisted of households with heads aged 30–44. About 17 percent of the total increase was growth in the number of non-aged married couples with no children. This was about equally distributed among the three age groups. The decrease in the number of married couples with preschool-age children was offset by the growth in the number of married couples with teenage children. The increase in households of non-aged, formerly married persons accounts for about one-fourth of the growth in the total. Households headed by formerly married persons with children contributed about 8 percent of the total growth, while those of non-aged formerly married persons without children accounted for 17 percent of the growth. More than one-quarter of the growth involved an increase in the number of households of elderly persons. This growth was about equally distributed between married couple households and households of widowed persons.

Household Size

In 1980 the average household consisted of 2.75 persons, a decline from 3.11 persons in 1970. This decrease is a continuation of a trend of decreasing household size going back to at least 1850. Table 9.7 shows average household size at each decennial census since the mid-nineteenth century and the percentage change from the preceding census. During the early part of this century the average household size was decreasing by about 5 percent per decade, from 4.93 people in 1890 to 4.11 persons in 1930. Between 1930 and 1950, average household size continued to drop to 3.38 persons. The decrease was more rapid during those decades than earlier in the century. In the 1950s the rate of decrease in household size slowed to 2.7 percent, primarily because of the growth in the number of children during the baby boom. The decrease was 5.5 percent in the 1960s, and in the 1970s the rate of decline accelerated to about 12 percent.

There are several factors contributing to the very rapid decline in household size in the 1970s. The most significant is the decrease in the number of children per household, resulting from the decline in the birth rate, which began in the early 1960s but which had its maximum cumulative effect on household size during the 1970s. In addition, there was a marked increase in the fraction of all households that were nonfamily households, most of which are one-person households.

TABLE 9.7

Average Household Size, 1790–1980

Year	Average Household Size	Percent Change from Previous Decade
1790	5.79	
1850	5.55	
1860	5.28	− 4.9
1870	5.09	− 3.6
1880	5.04	− 1.0
1890	4.93	− 2.2
1900	4.76	− 3.4
1910	4.54	− 4.6
1920	4.34	− 4.4
1930	4.11	− 5.3
1940	3.65	−11.2
1950	3.34	− 8.5
1960	3.30	− 1.1
1970	3.11	− 5.8
1980	2.75	−11.6

SOURCE: See Table 9.1.
NOTE: Prior to 1940, average household size is the total population divided by the total number of households. From 1940 to 1980 it is the number of people in households (i.e., total population less group quarters population) divided by the number of households. In 1940 the total population divided by household measure was 3.77, and in 1950, 3.52. The percent change for 1930–40 is computed from the population per household measure. That for 1940–50 is computed from the persons in households per household measure.

Distribution of Households by Size

Table 9.8 shows the distribution of households by size for censuses from 1790 to 1980. In 1790, more than one-third of all households included seven or more members, and less than one-quarter had three or fewer members. A century later, nearly one-quarter of the households had seven or more members, and one-third had three or fewer. The fraction of households with many members dropped gradually during the twentieth century, while the fraction with few members increased. By 1950, only 5 percent of all households had seven or more members, and over 60 percent had three or fewer members. By 1980, the concentration of households in the one-to three-person range was even greater, including over 70 percent of all households; only 2 percent of households had seven or more members. There were two large changes in this distribution during the 1970s. There was an increase of 64 percent in the number of one-person households from 17 percent of all households in 1970 to 22 percent in 1980. Households of five or more persons decreased

TABLE 9.8

Distribution of Households, by Size, 1790–1980 (percent distribution)

Number of Persons	1790	1890	1900	1930	1940	1950	1960	1970	1980
1	3.7	3.6	5.1	7.9	7.8	9.8	13.2	17.6	22.6
2	7.8	13.2	15.0	23.4	24.6	28.4	28.1	29.6	31.3
3	11.7	16.7	17.6	20.8	22.3	22.7	18.9	17.2	17.4
4	13.8	16.8	16.9	17.5	18.2	18.2	17.2	15.3	15.4
5	13.9	15.1	14.2	12.0	11.5	10.2	11.1	9.8	7.8
6	13.2	11.6	10.9	7.6	6.8	5.2	5.9	5.4	3.2
7 or more	35.8	23.0	20.4	10.9	8.6	5.4	5.5	5.0	2.2
Total	100.0	100.0	100.0	100.0	100.0	100.0	100.0	100.0	100.0

SOURCE: See Table 9.1.

TABLE 9.9

Distribution of Family and Nonfamily Households,
by Size, 1940–80

Number of Members	1940	1950	1960	1970	1980
	Family Households				
2	25.8	30.6	31.6	34.9	38.4
3	24.3	25.3	21.9	21.0	22.9
4	20.1	20.6	20.1	19.1	20.7
5	12.8	11.5	13.0	12.1	10.6
6	7.5	5.9	6.9	6.7	4.4
7 or More	9.5	6.2	6.5	6.3	3.0
Total	100.0	100.0	100.0	100.0	100.0
Number (000)	31,077	38,596	45,044	50,973	59,282
	Nonfamily Households				
1	78.0	81.8	88.8	89.4	85.5
2	14.5	12.1	8.5	8.0	11.6
3	4.7	3.8	1.9	1.7	2.0
4	1.9	1.5	0.6	0.7	0.7
5 or More	0.9	0.7	0.2	0.2	0.3
Total	100.0	100.0	100.0	100.0	100.0
Number (000)	3,476	5,244	7,955	12,474	21,251

dramatically during this period: from 21 percent of all households in 1970 to only 13 percent in 1980.

Table 9.9 shows separately the size distributions of family and of nonfamily households. In 1980, 38 percent of all family households were two-person households. The great majority of these were married couples with no children present. Eighteen percent of all family households had five or more members in 1980, compared to 26 percent in 1960.

Nonfamily households, as we have already shown, are predominantly one-person households. In 1970, 89 percent of all nonfamily households were one-person households, but by 1980 this fraction decreased to 86 percent. This decrease reflects a rise in the proportion with two persons, from 8 percent to 12 percent of all nonfamily households. Only 3 percent of all nonfamily households have three or more members. This proportion did not change much during the 1970s.

The great majority of the decrease in average household size during the 1970s was due to a decrease in the average number of children per household (see Table 9.10). Of the drop of .36 persons per household, .30

TABLE 9.10

Average Number of Children and Adults per Household,
by Household Type, 1940–80

	All Ages	<18	18–59	60+
All Households				
1940	3.65	1.15	2.13	0.37
1950	3.34	1.06	1.88	0.40
1960	3.30	1.22	1.67	0.42
1970	3.11	1.10	1.57	0.44
1980	2.75	0.80	1.53	0.42
Married Couple Households				
1940	3.98	1.34	2.32	0.33
1950	3.66	1.25	2.08	0.35
1960	3.75	1.47	1.91	0.37
1970	3.64	1.36	1.88	0.40
1980	3.35	1.04	1.87	0.44
Other Family Households				
1940	3.55	0.91	2.08	0.56
1950	3.31	0.89	1.81	0.61
1960	3.19	1.13	1.48	0.59
1970	3.28	1.38	1.43	0.47
1980	3.12	1.23	1.54	0.35

was accounted for by the decline in the average number of children. This was true for both married couple and other family households. In earlier decades, more of the decrease in average household size was due to a decrease in the average number of adults. For example, during the 1940s, average household size dropped by .31 persons—.09 children and .22 adults.

Variation in Household Size by Type of Household

It is instructive to examine the components of this recent decrease in average household size from a life cycle stage perspective (Table 9.11). During the 1970s there was virtually no change in the size of households of never-married persons, of married couples or formerly married persons without children, or of elderly persons. The only significant decreases were in the households of married couples and formerly married persons with children under the age of 12, reflecting, of course, the decline in fertility.

Table 9.12 shows the average household size that would have prevailed in 1970 and 1980 had there been no change in the composition of households by life cycle stage. If the 1970 population composition remained constant through 1980, average household size would have decreased from 3.16 to 2.98 persons per household. This would have been a decrease of 5.7 percent compared to the actual decrease of 11.6 percent; hence, somewhat more than one-half of the overall decline in average household size was due to a change in the composition of households by life cycle stage. Almost all of the decrease associated with changing category-specific average household size was among married couples and formerly married persons with children under the age of 12. During the 1960s, however, almost all of the 6 percent decrease in average household size was due to changing life cycle composition. There was only a 1 percent decrease during the 1960s that was not a product of changing life cycle composition.

Distribution of Black and Mexican-American Households

In 1980, 10.5 percent of all households in the United States had black householders, and 2.6 percent had Mexican-American householders. An additional 4.2 percent had householders who were members of other nonwhite races or other Hispanic groups. Black households in

TABLE 9.11

Average Household Size, by Life Cycle Stage of Householder, 1940–80

Family Life Cycle Stage of Household Head	Average Household Size					Change			
	1940	1950	1960	1970	1980	1940–50	1950–60	1960–70	1970–80
Never Married									
Age < 30	2.17	2.10	1.77	1.79	1.72	−.07	−.33	+.02	−.07
30–44	2.08	1.98	1.70	1.78	1.69	−.10	−.28	+.08	−.09
45–59	1.97	1.83	1.61	1.59	1.56	−.06	−.22	−.02	−.03
Married Couple with Children									
Youngest < 6	4.99	4.62	4.94	4.73	4.22	−.37	+.32	−.21	−.51
6–11	4.93	4.53	4.59	4.94	4.53	−.40	+.06	+.35	−.41
12–17	4.30	4.14	3.92	4.08	4.20	−.36	−.22	+.16	+.12
Married Couple with No Children									
Age < 30	2.25	2.16	2.10	2.07	2.07	−.09	−.06	−.03	.00
30–44	2.62	2.50	2.43	2.48	2.48	−.12	−.07	+.05	.00
45–59	3.17	2.83	2.54	2.52	2.59	−.34	−.29	−.02	+.07
Formerly Married with Children									
Youngest < 6	5.08	4.40	4.55	4.33	3.64	−.68	+.15	−.22	−.69
6–11	4.53	4.05	3.86	4.17	3.60	−.48	−.19	+.31	−.57
12–17	3.89	3.53	3.14	3.25	3.34	−.36	−.39	+.11	+.09
Formerly Married, No Children									
Age < 30	1.82	1.56	1.39	1.42	1.43	−.26	−.17	+.03	+.01
30–44	2.04	1.77	1.54	1.51	1.47	−.27	−.23	−.03	−.04
45–59	2.47	2.12	1.72	1.62	1.67	−.35	−.40	−.10	+.05
Elderly (Age 60+)									
Never Married	1.79	1.72	1.50	1.42	1.35	−.07	−.22	−.08	−.07
Married Couple	3.10	2.76	2.42	2.27	2.26	−.34	−.34	−.15	−.01
Formerly Married	2.43	2.05	1.63	1.40	1.35	−.38	−.42	−.17	−.05
Total	3.65	3.34	3.30	3.11	2.75	−.31	−.04	−.19	−.36

TABLE 9.12

Average Household Size Standardized on Life Cycle
Stage Distribution, 1960–70 and 1970–80

Actual 1980	2.75	Actual 1970	3.11
Actual 1970	3.11	Actual 1960	3.30
Standardized* 1980	2.96	Standardized 1970	3.26

	Percent Change *1970–80*	*Percent Change* *1960–70*
Actual	−11.6	−5.8
Standardized	− 5.7	−1.2

*If distribution by life cycle stage had not changed. Only the life cycle stage-specific average household size changed.

1980 were as likely as majority-white households to be families—73 percent for each group (Table 9.13). However, Mexican-American households were more likely to be families (84 percent). On the other hand, the distribution among types of family households is very different. Only 42 percent of black households were married couples, compared with 63 percent of majority-white, and 67 percent of Mexican-American households. Nearly half of all Mexican-American households were married couples with children. This is twice the fraction of black households (27 percent), and much higher than the fraction of non-Hispanic

TABLE 9.13

Distribution of Black, Mexican-American,
and Non-Hispanic White Households, by Type, 1980

	Non-Hispanic White	Black	Mexican-American
Married Couple			
No Children	32.6	17.2	17.8
With Children	30.6	24.2	48.9
Mother–Child Families	4.3	18.6	9.1
Father–Child Families	0.8	1.8	1.8
Other Families	4.8	10.8	6.6
Nonfamily Households			
One-Person Male	8.6	10.8	6.6
One-Person Female	14.4	13.0	5.6
Other	3.8	3.6	3.6
Total	100.0	100.0	100.0
Number (000)	66,672	8,413	2,154

white households (30 percent). In comparison to majority whites, black households were much more likely to be one-parent families (20 percent) and other families (11 percent). Mexican-American households were also disproportionately one-parent and other families, but not nearly to the degree of black households. In comparison to both blacks and whites, Mexican-Americans were underrepresented among nonfamily households, especially those with only one member.

Between 1970 and 1980 there was a rapid growth in the number of households headed by black persons. In 1970 there were 6.2 million black households. By 1980 there were 8.4 million. This growth of 36.0 percent over the decade is considerably more rapid than the 26.9 percent for the total population.

The size of the total black population living in households increased by 17 percent during the 1970s. This is a considerably faster growth than for the entire population of all races (12 percent). The num-

TABLE 9.14

Change in the Number of Black and Mexican-American Households, by Type, 1970–80

	Percent Change in Number of Households		Components of Growth in Number of Households	
	Black	Mexican-American	Black	Mexican-American
Family Households				
Married Couple				
No Children Under 18	10.8	105.8	6.3	17.7
With Children Under 18	5.4	86.9	4.6	44.1
One-Parent Household				
Mother with Children	75.5	133.4	30.2	10.1
Father with Children	44.0	102.2	2.0	1.8
Other Family Households	55.8	114.3	14.5	6.8
Nonfamily Households				
Persons Living Alone				
Men	77.5	160.1	17.8	7.9
Women	62.5	136.6	18.8	6.3
Other Nonfamily Households	72.2	342.6	5.7	5.4
Total	36.1	106.6	100.0	100.0

ber of black adults increased by 31 percent, in contrast to 23 percent for the total population. The number of black children decreased by about 1 percent, in comparison to a decrease of 8 percent for children of all races. Average household size fell more rapidly for blacks (by 14 percent) than for the total population, although it continues to be somewhat larger for blacks (3.05 versus 2.75). In 1970 there were 3.54 persons per black household. Both the average numbers of children and adults decreased and, as for the total population, most of the overall decrease in average household size was due to decreased number of children. Of the total decrease of .49 persons per household, .08 was a decrease in adults, and .41 a decrease in children.

The number of black married couple households—both with and without children—increased very slowly during the 1970s, while the number of other family households, especially mother–child families, rose more rapidly (see Table 9.14). There were 75 percent more mother–child families in 1980 than in 1970. The rate of growth of nonfamily households was also quite rapid, with about 75 percent more in 1980 than 1970. About three-fifths of the growth in black households was due to an increase in family households—half of which was growth in mother–child families, one-quarter to "other" families, and one-sixth to married couple families.

The number of Mexican-American households more than doubled during the 1970s. All types of households experienced a rapid increase. The category growing at the slowest rate (87 percent) was married couples with children. The number of mother–child households grew by 134 percent, while one-person households increased by about 150 percent.

Trends and Variations in Household Structure of Smaller Racial and Ethnic Groups

In this section the household characteristics of smaller racial and Hispanic groups,[5] such as Chinese Americans, Japanese Americans, American Indians, Puerto Ricans, and Cubans, are contrasted with

---

[5]There are several possible alternatives for classifying married couples or families by ethnic status. In an analysis of differential fertility [Ronald R. Rindfuss and James A. Sweet, *Postwar Fertility Trends and Differentials in the United States* (New York: Academic Press, 1977)], *couples* were considered to be part of an ethnic group if either husband or wife was a member. Thus, a couple consisting of a black husband and an Indian wife fell in both the black and Indian populations. This procedure could be extended to households or families by including a person or family as a member of a group if any member of the household was a member. An alternative is to use the ethnic status of the household head (householder) to classify the household. We have chosen the latter approach, largely because of computing convenience and to maximize comparability between the published census reports (which generally follow this practice) and our estimates made from the Public Use Samples.

blacks and majority whites. There was great variability in the distribution of households by type in 1980 (see Table 9.15). Sixty-three percent of non-Hispanic white households were husband–wife families, and 52 percent of the husband–wife families had children present. Blacks (41 percent), Puerto Ricans (49 percent), Hawaiians (54 percent), and American Indians (56 percent) had a lower prevalence of married couples. The other groups had between 60 and 70 percent married couple households. However, there was considerable variation in the fraction of married couple households with children present.

About 4 percent of majority-white households were mother–child families. This fraction was considerably higher for most other groups except for the Asian American groups. The highest prevalence of mother–child families was found among blacks (19 percent), Puerto Ricans (23 percent), American Indians (12 percent), Mexican-Americans (9 percent), and Vietnamese (9 percent).

An additional 6 percent of non-Hispanic white households were "other families" (including father–child families). The fraction of "other families" was very high for blacks (13 percent), Vietnamese (14 percent), and Hawaiians (10 percent).

TABLE 9.15

Distribution of Households, by Type, for Racial and Hispanic Groups, 1980

	Percent of All Households That Are:					Percent of Married Couple Households with Own Children
	Married Couples	Mother–Child Families	Other Families*	Nonfamily Households	Total	
Non-Hispanic White	63.2	4.3	5.6	26.8	100.0	48.4
Black	41.4	18.6	12.5	27.4	100.0	58.4
Japanese	59.7	3.9	7.1	29.3	100.0	48.6
Chinese	66.6	2.8	7.1	23.6	100.0	59.4
Filipino	69.2	5.7	8.2	16.9	100.0	71.5
Korean	72.0	5.6	5.5	17.0	100.0	78.2
Asian Indian	67.1	1.6	4.6	26.6	100.0	72.6
Vietnamese	60.4	8.7	14.2	16.7	100.0	83.6
Hawaiian	53.7	10.2	10.5	25.7	100.0	65.1
American Indian	55.5	12.2	9.1	23.2	100.0	65.4
Mexican	66.7	9.1	8.4	15.8	100.0	73.4
Puerto Rican	49.1	22.7	8.7	19.4	100.0	69.2
Cuban	66.5	5.0	8.5	19.9	100.0	50.2

*Includes father–child families.

TABLE 9.16
Mean Household Size of Racial and Hispanic Groups, 1980

	Husband–Wife Families	Other Family Households	Nonfamily Households	Total
Non-Hispanic White	3.24	2.85	1.18	2.65
Black	3.91	3.65	1.17	3.08
Japanese	3.35	2.81	1.23	2.67
Chinese	3.78	3.20	1.29	3.14
Filipino	4.37	3.51	1.36	3.74
American Indian	4.03	3.65	1.25	3.31
Korean	4.05	3.18	1.20	3.47
Asian Indian	3.68	2.99	1.15	2.94
Vietnamese	5.32	4.19	1.50	4.43
Hawaiian	4.18	3.72	1.31	3.35
Mexican	4.36	3.70	1.34	3.77
Puerto Rican	4.01	3.56	1.22	3.33
Cuban	3.52	3.01	1.19	2.99

Slightly over one-fourth of non-Hispanic white and black households were not families. Similar proportions are found for Japanese, Chinese, American Indians, Asian Indians, and Hawaiians. Mexican-Americans (16 percent), Filipinos (17 percent), Koreans (17 percent), and Vietnamese (17 percent) had the lowest prevalence of nonfamily households.

Non-Hispanic whites had an average household size of 2.65 persons overall and of 3.24 for husband–wife families (see Table 9.16). All groups considered here had larger average household sizes than those of majority whites. For example, husband–wife families averaged 5.32 persons among Vietnamese, 4.36 among Mexican-Americans, and 3.91 among blacks. Asian Indians and Japanese had household sizes most similar to majority whites, 3.68 and 3.35, respectively, among husband–wife families.

Table 9.17 presents the average number of adults (persons aged 18 and over) per household for husband–wife and other family households. Among non-Hispanic whites, husband–wife families include an average of 2.27 adults. This is smaller than any other group shown. The largest number of adults per husband–wife family are found for Vietnamese (2.78), Filipinos (2.74), Chinese (2.59), and Cubans (2.55). Blacks have an average of 2.49 adults per husband–wife family.

Non-Hispanic white "other families" have an average of 1.87 adults, only 0.40 adults fewer than husband–wife families. For all other groups

TABLE 9.17

*Average Number of Persons Aged 18 and Over per Family,
by Type, for Racial and Hispanic Groups, 1980*

Racial-Ethnic Group	Husband–Wife Families	Other Families
Non-Hispanic White	2.27	1.87
Black	2.49	1.91
Japanese	2.45	2.08
Chinese	2.59	2.38
Filipino	2.74	2.37
American Indian	2.38	1.89
Korean	2.47	2.06
Asian Indian	2.31	2.22
Vietnamese	2.78	2.51
Hawaiian	2.53	2.03
Mexican	2.47	2.04
Puerto Rican	2.40	1.63
Cuban	2.58	2.16

TABLE 9.18

*Average Number of Children per Household, by Household Type,
for Racial and Hispanic Groups, 1980*

	All Families		Families with Own Children	
	Husband–Wife	Other Families	Husband–Wife	Other Families
Non-Hispanic White	0.97	0.98	1.96	1.77
Black	1.42	1.74	2.28	2.34
Japanese	0.90	0.73	1.81	1.57
Chinese	1.19	0.82	1.95	1.79
Filipino	1.63	1.14	2.22	1.95
American Indian	1.65	1.76	2.42	2.30
Korean	1.58	1.12	2.00	1.79
Asian Indian	1.37	0.77	1.87	1.79
Vietnamese	2.54	1.68	3.00	2.52
Hawaiian	1.65	1.69	2.42	2.36
Mexican	1.89	1.66	2.51	2.36
Puerto Rican	1.61	1.93	2.27	2.35
Cuban	0.94	0.85	1.79	1.72

except Puerto Ricans the number of adults per "other" family is higher than that for whites.

Although there is variation in the number of adults per household, most of the overall variation in household size of both husband–wife and other families is due to variation in the number of children per household. This can be seen from Table 9.18. The average number of children per husband–wife family varies from 0.90 for Japanese to 2.54 for Vietnamese. Mexican-American married couple families have an average of 1.89 children, and blacks, 1.42. This variation reflects both differences in the age structure of married couple families and differences in fertility. If the comparison is restricted to married couple families with children under 18, the differences are primarily due to fertility variation. Non-Hispanic white families have just under two children per married couple family with children. Larger numbers of children are found for Vietnamese (3.00), Mexican-Americans (2.50), Hawaiians (2.42), and American Indians (2.42).

Summary

In this and the following chapter, the focus shifts from persons to households as the units of analysis. Reflecting the long-term decline in household size, the number of households has increased more rapidly than the population in every decade since 1850. In the 1970s the number of households increased at over twice the population growth rate of 12 percent. The proportion of households that included married couples decreased from 80 percent in 1910 to 61 percent by 1980.

Thirty-one percent of all households were married couples with children under age 18, and an additional 7 percent included a single parent with children under age 18. About 6 percent of all households were family households that included neither own children nor a married couple. Within family households, growth shifted from an equal contribution of those with and without children, to a greater increase in households with children in the 1950s, to an increasing predominance of growth in family households without children. In the 1970s, over 90 percent of the growth in family households was in those without children. There was a *decrease* in the number of married couple households with children under age 12, reflecting the delay in childbearing and the decrease in the number of children per couple. The number of households of formerly married persons with children continued to increase, and an even more rapid increase occurred for households of formerly married persons with no children.

Whereas only 10 percent of households were nonfamily households in 1940, this fraction had increased to a quarter by 1980. Eighty-six percent of these nonfamily households were one-person households. Nonfamily households thus became an increasing component of growth in the number of households, particularly after 1960.

The average size of households has declined over this century, first at a decreasing rate and then at an accelerating rate. Fertility fluctuations and increases in one-person households have been major contributors to this trend. The prevalence of one-person households grew continuously from 4 percent in 1890 to 10 percent in 1950, reaching 23 percent by 1980. Conversely, the proportion of households with more than three persons in 1980 was one-quarter below the levels of 1940–60, and less than one-half those of 1900 and earlier. Five-sixths of the decline in average household size over the 1970s was a consequence of a decline in the average number of children.

Mexican-American households are more likely to be family households than either black or majority white households (84 versus 73 percent). The distribution among family types differs markedly by race and ethnicity. The percent of households with married couples was only 42 percent among black households, compared to 63 percent among majority-white, and 67 percent among Mexican-American households. One-half of Mexican-American married couple households had children, compared to 30 percent among majority whites and 27 percent among blacks. Black households were four times as likely to be one-parent families than majority-white households (20 versus 5 percent). Mexican-American households were less likely than others to be nonfamily households

During the 1970s minority households increased more rapidly than majority-white households: 36 percent among blacks and 107 percent among Mexican-Americans, compared to a 27 percent increase overall. In spite of a more rapid decline in average household size, black households in 1980 were still somewhat larger than among majority whites (3.08 versus 2.65). The growth in mother–child families and in nonfamily households was particularly rapid among blacks. Average household size was much larger among Mexican-Americans (3.77), and all types of Mexican-American households experienced rapid increase during the 1970s, though the slowest growth was among married couples with children (87 percent).

10

OTHER TYPES OF HOUSEHOLDS: GROWTH AND CHARACTERISTICS

IN THIS chapter we will examine in greater detail the size and characteristics of three subtypes of households: (1) female-headed families; (2) male-headed families other than married couples; and (3) nonfamily households. In addition, the final section will describe the population living in group quarters and secondary and subfamilies. These sections will describe both the prevalence and the characteristics of each of these family or household types.

Female-Headed Families

Between 1940 and 1970 the number of female-headed families increased from about 3.2 million to 5.6 million, but their relative prevalence remained at about 10 percent of all families (Table 10.1). During the 1970s the number of female-headed families increased from 5.6 to 8.2 million, from 11 to 14 percent of all families. The change has been less dramatic among whites than among blacks. In 1970, 9 percent of white families were female-headed; by 1980 the fraction had increased to 11 percent. Among blacks, on the other hand, 28 percent of all families were female-headed in 1970, and 37 percent in 1980. Mexican-American families are more likely to be headed by a woman then white

TABLE 10.1

Number of Female-Headed Families, by Presence of Children, 1940–80

	Number (000)	% of All Families	% With Own Children <18	Percent Change		
				Total	No Children	With Children
1940	3,229	10.4	34.7			
1950	3,494	9.1	34.0	+ 8.2	+ 9.3	+ 6.0
1960	4,154	9.2	44.8	+18.9	− 0.6	+56.6
1970	5,589	11.0	54.7	+34.5	+10.4	+64.4
1980	8,239	13.9	60.2	+47.4	+29.7	+62.1

families, but less likely than blacks. In 1970, 13 percent of Mexican-American families were female-headed, and by 1980 this fraction had increased to 17 percent.

As we have discussed earlier, change in the number of female-headed families is the outcome of a number of separate processes. There have been many attempts to decompose the process into its component parts.[1] Among the more recent of these is the study by Smith and Cutright. They find that during the 1970s, 45 percent of the increase in the number of white female-headed families (headed by ever-married women)[2] with children was due to the increase of proportions in disrupted marriages. This component combines trends in marital disruption and remarriage. An additional 20 percent was due to the increase in the propensity of mothers in disputed marriages to maintain their own households, and 18 percent was due to the sheer growth in the number of ever-married women. During the 1960s the growth in the proportion of women in disrupted marriages played a more dominant role (nearly 60 percent).

[1]See, for example, Heather Ross and Isabel Sawhill, *Time of Transition: The Growth of Families Headed by Women* (Washington, D.C.: The Urban Institute, 1975); P. Cutright, "Components of Change in the Number of Female Family Heads Aged 15–44: United States, 1949–1970," *Journal of Marriage and the Family* 36 (1974):714–21; R. S. Cooney, "Demographic Components of Growth in White, Black, and Puerto Rican Headed Families: A Comparison of the Cutright and Ross/Sawhill Methodologies," *Social Science Research* 8 (1979):144–58; James A. Sweet, "Components of Change in the Number of Households, 1970–1980," *Demography* 21 (1984): 129–40; Irwin Garfinkel and Sara McLanahan, *Female Headed Families and Public Policy: A New American Dilemma?* (Washington, D.C.: The Urban Institute, 1986).

[2]Smith and Cutright consider only female family heads aged 15–44 with children under age 18.

Among nonwhite women during the 1970s, the increased propensity to form households accounted for 45 percent of the increase. (Smith and Cutright considered nonwhites rather than blacks because they were relying on data published from 1940 to 1980, and in earlier years blacks were not separately identified.) Population growth and the increased proportion of women in disrupted marital statuses each accounted for about one-quarter of the growth. For both whites and nonwhites the decline in the proportion of women with children ever born resulted in only a slight decrease in the number of female-headed families.

Smith and Cutright also decomposed the growth in the number of families headed by never-married women. They found that the increase in the number of never-married women, the increased proportion of never-married women with children ever born, and the increased propensity of never-married mothers to maintain their own households all played important roles in the growth of families headed by never-married women.

Presence of Children

It is a mistake to equate female-headed families with mother–child families. In fact, from 1940 to 1960 less than one-half of all female-headed families included own children under 18 (column 3 of Table 10.1). Between 1960 and 1970 the number of female-headed families with children increased by over 60 percent, from 1.9 to 3.0 million, and the fraction of all female-headed families with children rose from 45 to 55 percent. During the 1970s there was a further increase from 3.0 to 5.1 million (an increase of 62 percent). By 1980, three-fifths of the female-headed families included own children under 18. About two-thirds of those without children under 18 include adult children of the householder. Only 1.2 million of the 8.2 million female-headed families did not include a son or daughter (of any age) of the householder.

Marital Status

There are several ways that a woman can become a family head. Historically, the majority of female family heads were widowed women who were rearing their children after the death of their husband. In fact, even in 1980 three-tenths of all female family heads were widows, although only a minority of them had dependent children. Forty percent

TABLE 10.2

Percent Distribution and Growth Rate of Female-Headed Families, by Marital Status of Head and Presence of Children Under 18, 1940–80

	Percent Distribution					Percent Increase in Numbers			
	1940	1950	1960	1970	1980	1940–50	1950–60	1960–70	1970–80
With Children <18	34.7	33.9	44.8	54.7	60.2	+ 6	+ 57	+ 64	+ 62
Never Married	0.8	0.8	1.8	4.6	10.2	+20	+156	+238	+225
Separated*	9.4	6.9	10.7	14.0	12.8	+28	+ 83	+ 76	+ 35
Divorced	4.4	7.4	11.8	18.1	27.7	+80	+ 90	+106	+126
Widowed	20.1	14.6	14.4	13.6	7.4	−21	+ 17	+ 2	− 20
MSA–O*	—	4.2	6.1	4.5	2.1	—	+ 72	0	− 32
No Children <18	65.2	66.0	55.2	45.3	39.8	+ 9	− 1	+ 10	+ 30
Never Married	10.1	9.8	9.7	7.8	6.1	+ 5	+ 18	+ 8	+ 15
Separated*	5.7	3.7	3.2	2.9	2.9	+17	+ 2	+ 21	+ 48
Divorced	2.9	4.6	5.0	5.7	8.1	+69	+ 29	+ 54	+110
Widowed	46.5	45.4	35.7	27.5	22.0	+ 6	− 12	+ 4	+ 18
MSA–O	—	2.5	1.6	1.4	0.7	—	− 21	+ 15	− 29
Total	100.0	100.0	100.0	100.0	100.0	+ 8	+ 19	+ 35	+ 47
Number (000)	3,229	3,494	4,154	5,589	8,239				

*1940 MSA–O and Separated are combined.

of female family heads in 1980 were separated or divorced women with children under 18 (see Table 10.2). Single women with children constituted one-tenth of the total.

Among female householders with children under age 18, the majority are separated and divorced (42 percent are divorced and 24 percent are separated); 17 percent are never-married, and 13 percent are widows. Four percent are married women living apart from their husbands for reasons other than separation. The marital status distribution of female householders with no children present is quite different. Fifty-six percent are widowed, 26 percent separated or divorced, 16 percent single, and 2 percent married, spouse absent, other (MSA–O).

There has been a very rapid increase in the number of female householders with children who were never married—76,000 in 1960, 258,000 in 1970, and over 800,000 by 1980. The number of separated and divorced women with children rose from about 900,000 in 1960 to 1.8 million in 1970, and to 3.3 million in 1980. A much larger share of black female family heads have children present, and a larger share are never married women. Over time the share of black female family heads who are never married has risen sharply to almost 30 percent in 1980, the great majority (five-sixths) of whom have children under age 18. Comparisons of the marital status distributions of non-Hispanic white, black, and Mexican-American female family heads are in Tables 10.3 and 10.4.

Number of Children of Female Householders

The average number of children in female-headed families has decreased over time. This decrease is primarily the result of the decrease in marital fertility. In 1980, 45 percent of all female-headed families with children under 18 included only one child. An additional 32 percent had two children, 14 percent had three, and 9 percent had four or more children (see Table 10.5). The distribution by number of children changed markedly during the 1970s. In 1970, only 36 percent had one child and 19 percent had four or more children.

Black and Mexican-American female family heads are much less likely than majority whites to have only one child and much more likely to have several children. In 1980, one-half of the white women, 38 percent of the black women, and 36 percent of the Mexican-American women had only one child. About one-sixth of the white women and one-third of the black and Chicano women had three or more children.

TABLE 10.3

Percent Distribution of Female-Headed Families, by Marital Status of Head and Presence of Children Under 18, by Race/Ethnicity, 1940–80

	Non-Hispanic White					Black				
	1940	1950	1960	1970	1980	1940	1950	1960	1970	1980
With Children <18										
Single	0.5	0.4	0.7	2.0	3.6	2.4	3.1	6.0	12.4	23.7
Separated*	8.2	4.8	7.1	9.7	9.5	15.7	17.2	23.6	26.6	18.5
Divorced	4.7	7.8	12.9	20.0	32.7	2.7	4.6	7.1	11.9	17.3
Widowed	19.1	14.2	14.7	14.0	7.4	25.2	16.1	12.7	11.9	7.3
MSA–O*	—	4.2	6.1	4.6	1.8	—	3.7	5.4	3.7	1.9
Total	32.5	31.3	41.6	50.3	55.0	46.0	44.7	54.9	66.6	68.7
No Children <18										
Single	11.1	11.1	11.3	9.1	6.7	5.0	3.8	4.1	3.9	4.5
Separated	5.2	2.7	2.1	2.1	1.8	8.8	9.3	7.5	5.4	5.3
Divorced	3.1	4.8	5.2	6.3	9.2	1.9	3.4	4.2	4.0	6.0
Widowed	48.2	47.5	38.0	30.8	26.7	38.4	36.6	27.8	18.8	14.9
MSA–O*	—	2.5	1.6	1.4	0.6	—	2.2	1.5	1.3	0.5
Total	67.6	68.6	58.3	49.7	45.0	54.1	55.3	45.1	33.4	31.3
Total	100.0	100.0	100.0	100.0	100.0	100.0	100.0	100.0	100.0	100.0
Number (000)	2,723	2,864	3,202	4,064	5,183	459	558	838	1,341	2,278

TABLE 10.3 *(continued)*

	Mexican-American				
	1940	1950	1960	1970	1980
With Children <18					
Single	0.3	1.3	2.7	6.6	13.3
Separated*	19.0	13.6	17.6	19.1	17.3
Divorced	6.2	11.3	15.1	21.7	27.5
Widowed	29.0	20.7	18.5	14.2	9.6
MSA–O*		7.6	7.4	6.0	3.5
Total	54.5	54.4	61.2	67.6	71.1
No Children <18					
Single	5.4	5.7	5.5	5.2	6.0
Separated*	5.4	3.4	3.0	3.2	3.2
Divorced	3.0	4.0	4.2	4.5	6.4
Widowed	31.7	29.8	24.7	18.9	12.4
MSA–O*		2.6	1.5	0.8	0.9
Total	45.5	45.6	38.8	32.5	28.9
Total	100.0	100.0	100.0	100.0	100.0
Number (000)	37	110	82	120	274

*1940 Separated and MSA–O are combined.

TABLE 10.4

Percent Change in Number of Female-Headed Families with Children,
by Marital Status of Head and Race/Ethnicity, 1960–70 and 1970–80

	Non-Hispanic White		Black		Mexican-American	
	1960–70	1970–80	1960–70	1970–80	1960–70	1970–80
Never Married	+256	+132	+230	+225	+259	+361
Separated	+ 72	+ 26	+ 80	+ 18	+ 61	+106
Divorced	+ 96	+109	+170	+146	+112	+188
Widowed	+ 21	− 33	+ 50	+ 4	+ 14	+ 53
MSA–O	− 4	− 50	+ 9	− 15	+ 20	+ 35
Total	+ 53	+ 40	+ 94	+ 75	+ 63	+140

Poverty Status and Public Assistance

Female-headed families with children are disproportionately poor, and because the welfare system is oriented to supporting families with children, a large share of such families receive public assistance income. Thirty percent of all female-headed families with children received public assistance income during 1979; 41 percent had total family income below the poverty line (Table 10.6). Note that this is a post-transfer measure of poverty. In the classification of poverty status, income from public assistance is included along with earnings and all other income.

Higher rates of poverty and higher rates of receipt of public assistance occur in families with young children (see Table 10.7). Over two-thirds of female-headed families with children under 3 were poor; one-half were receiving public assistance. One-quarter of the female-headed families with teenage children were poor, and one-fifth were receiving public assistance. Poverty levels are higher for families with never married, separated, and MSA–O mothers than for families with divorced or widowed mothers. This is true at all ages of youngest child.

Similarly, the greater the number of children in a female-headed family, the greater the proportion receiving public assistance. One-fifth of the families with one child and one-half of the families with four or more children received public assistance income. Thirty percent of the female-headed families with one child and over three-quarters of those with four or more children were "in poverty."

Table 10.8 compares the proportions of black, Mexican-American, and majority-white female-headed families who were receiving public assistance income and who were in poverty. Both minority groups had

TABLE 10.5

Distribution of Number of Children in Female-Headed Families with Children, by Race/Ethnicity, 1940–80

Number of Own Children Under 18	1940	1950	1960	1970	1980
Total					
1	46.9	47.8	40.5	37.6	44.8
2	26.9	27.1	27.6	26.9	32.0
3	13.0	12.9	15.1	16.5	14.4
4+	13.2	12.1	16.8	19.1	8.7
Total*	100.0	100.0	100.0	100.0	100.0
Number (000)	1,121	1,188	1,861	3,059	4,958
% of all Female-Headed Families with Children	34.7	34.0	44.8	54.7	60.2
Black					
1	40.2	38.4	28.9	28.7	37.9
2	24.7	25.8	23.9	24.2	30.4
3	13.8	14.9	16.8	17.3	17.6
4+	21.3	20.8	30.4	29.8	14.2
Total	100.0	100.0	100.0	100.0	100.0
Number (000)	211	249	460	893	1,565
% of all Female-Headed Families with Children	46.0	44.7	54.9	66.6	68.7

Number of Own Children Under 18	1940	1950	1960	1970	1980
Non-Hispanic White					
1	48.9	51.0	45.0	41.8	49.7
2	27.5	27.5	28.9	28.2	33.3
3	12.8	12.2	14.5	16.0	12.1
4+	10.9	9.3	11.6	14.0	4.9
Total*	100.0	100.0	100.0	100.0	100.0
Number (000)	884	900	1,333	2,042	2,850
% of all Female-Headed Families with Children	32.4	31.4	41.6	50.3	55.0
Mexican-American†					
1	33.3	36.6	28.1	31.4	36.6
2	24.4	25.7	25.7	23.1	29.1
3	14.4	16.1	17.3	17.6	18.7
4+	27.9	21.7	28.9	27.9	15.7
Total	100.0	100.0	100.0	100.0	100.0
Number (000)	20	60	50	81	195
% of all Female-Headed Families with Children	54.5	54.4	61.2	67.6	71.1

*Total includes other nonwhite and Hispanic groups.
†1960: Spanish surname.

TABLE 10.6

Percent of Female-Headed Families Receiving Public Assistance
Income and Percent with Incomes Below the Poverty Line,
by Number of Children and Race/Ethnicity, 1980

Number of Own Children Under 18	Total	Non-Hispanic White	Black	Mexican-American
	Percent with Public Assistance Income			
No Children	11.9	7.7	23.2	21.7
With Children (total)	30.1	21.6	41.4	37.0
1	22.4	17.1	31.2	29.5
2	30.2	22.2	42.0	33.2
3	40.1	29.5	49.4	44.5
4+	52.6	43.0	57.1	52.5
Total	22.9	15.4	35.7	32.6
	*Percent With Income Below Poverty Line**			
No Children	13.2	8.1	27.0	21.0
With Children (total)	41.4	31.3	54.8	52.6
1	30.0	23.6	41.0	36.4
2	40.7	32.4	52.4	48.3
3	58.0	47.1	67.5	66.8
4+	75.8	62.9	81.3	81.6
Total	30.2	20.8	46.1	43.5

*All sources of income included.

higher percentages receiving public assistance income than majority whites at every marital status and every age of youngest child. For most categories the level was higher for blacks than for Mexican-Americans. The minority-majority differential was much smaller for never-married women than for women in any of the other categories.

Similarly, poverty levels were higher for the minority groups than for non-Hispanic whites. For all groups except widows and families with teenage children, the differential between blacks and Mexican-Americans was small: for those two categories blacks had a higher poverty level than Mexican-Americans.

Male-Headed Families

In 1980 there were 2.0 million families headed by men who were not married and living with their wives. This constituted 3.6 percent of all families. The prevalence of these male-headed families is much

TABLE 10.7

Percent of Female-Headed Families with Children Receiving Public Assistance Income and Percent with Family Income Below the Poverty Level, by Marital Status of Householder and Age of Youngest Own Child, 1980

Age of Youngest Child	Never Married	Separated	Divorced	MSA–O	Widowed	Total
	Percent with Public Assistance Income					
< 3	60.4	48.4	40.4	23.2	30.5	48.7
3– 5	52.3	40.4	29.4	20.7	23.8	36.8
6–11	41.8	33.0	21.5	14.4	22.6	26.4
12–17	36.8	29.4	15.4	8.4	19.7	20.0
Total	51.1	36.7	22.7	16.3	21.5	30.1
	*Percent with Income Below Poverty Line**					
< 3	73.6	73.1	58.3	73.8	51.9	68.4
3– 5	62.8	59.5	40.9	64.1	42.8	51.3
6–11	50.6	51.4	28.8	54.2	33.1	37.5
12–17	45.2	38.2	18.8	38.8	21.4	25.0
Total	62.0	54.0	30.5	57.3	28.0	41.4

*All sources of income included.

smaller than the prevalence of female-headed families. For every male-headed family, there are four female-headed families.

The number of male-headed families has remained relatively constant over time (Table 10.9). It was 1.5 million in 1940, and about 1.3 million from 1950 through 1960, and has increased to 2.0 million since 1960. As a percent of all families, the relative prevalence of male-headed families has tended to decrease, with some slight upturn in recent years. Male-headed families constituted 5 percent of all families in 1940, about 3 percent from 1950 to 1970, and about 4 percent in 1980. The recent increase in the absolute and relative prevalence of male-headed families undoubtedly reflects the upturn in the number of divorces, perhaps a downturn in the probability of remarriage of divorced and widowed men with children, and an increased propensity to maintain one's own household rather than living with other relatives. We have discussed each of these trends in previous chapters.

Most male-headed families are father–child families. Compared with married couple and female-headed families with children, the children in male-headed families tend to be older. Seven percent of all male-headed families have children under age 3. An additional 5 percent have

TABLE 10.8

Percent of Female-Headed Families with Children Receiving Public Assistance Income and Percent with Income Below the Poverty Line, by Marital Status of Householder and Age of Youngest Child, 1980

	Percent Receiving Public Assistance			Percent in Poverty		
	Non-Hispanic White	Black	Mexican-American	Non-Hispanic White	Black	Mexican-American
MARITAL STATUS						
Never Married	47.7	50.5	51.9	50.2	63.7	64.0
Separated	25.8	44.8	42.9	46.5	58.4	62.0
Divorced	19.5	31.0	32.0	26.3	41.7	44.3
MSA–O	9.0	26.4	18.6	54.3	59.5	65.0
Widowed	16.0	30.9	26.3	18.2	46.8	39.3
AGE OF YOUNGEST CHILD						
< 3	40.4	55.8	47.5	61.3	73.0	71.9
3– 5	28.5	46.0	44.8	41.8	61.5	61.2
6–11	19.2	36.4	31.2	28.8	49.8	47.0
12–17	13.4	32.0	27.1	16.9	40.8	33.0
TOTAL	21.6	41.4	37.0	31.3	54.8	52.6

youngest child aged 3–5, and a total of 36 percent have youngest child under the age of 18. Twenty-two percent of all male-headed families consist of a man and his adult child or children. Thus, three-fifths have a son or daughter present, although only about one-third have a child under age 18. The remaining 40 percent are households with other relatives, such as parents, or brothers or sisters, living with them.

TABLE 10.9

Number of "Other" Male-Headed Families, by Presence of Children, 1940–80

	Number (000)	Percent of All Families	Percent With Own Children <18	Percent Change		
				Total	No Children	With Children
1940	1,488	4.8	24.6			
1950	1,355	3.5	18.5	− 8.9	− 1.6	−31.4
1960	1,290	2.9	23.0	− 4.8	−10.1	+18.3
1970	1,620	3.2	35.0	+25.6	+ 6.0	+90.9
1980	2,006	3.6	38.2	+23.8	+17.8	+35.1

Nearly one-third of the male family heads are never-married men (Table 10.10). About one-fifth are widowed, and 40 percent are divorced or separated. Among those with children under 18, about three-fifths are separated and divorced, 15 percent are never-married (many of whom are cohabitors), and about 13 percent are widowed. Among male family heads with no children present, the modal marital status is never-married (44 percent). An additional 24 percent are widows, and 26 percent are separated or divorced men.

TABLE 10.10

Marital Status Distribution of Heads of Other Male-Headed Families, by Presence of Own Children Under 18, 1940–80

| | Total | | | | |
	1940	1950	1960	1970	1980
Never Married	31.1	33.5	35.3	29.7	32.7
Separated	15.3*	5.7	6.3	6.8	10.0
Divorced	4.4	7.3	10.1	13.7	30.3
Widowed	49.2	43.4	35.1	28.1	20.0
MSA–O	*	10.1	13.2	21.7	7.1
Total	100.0	100.0	100.0	100.0	100.0
Number (000)	1,488	1,355	1,290	1,620	2,006

| | With Children Under 18 | | | | |
	1940	1950	1960	1970	1980
Never Married	3.4	1.2	3.7	7.9	14.2
Separated	27.3*	10.6	12.9	11.4	15.4
Divorced	7.5	13.8	17.8	19.4	47.7
Widowed	61.8	49.9	35.8	25.3	13.2
MSA–O	*	24.3	29.8	35.9	9.5
Total	100.0	100.0	100.0	100.0	100.0
Number (000)	366	251	297	567	766

| | No Children Under 18 | | | | |
	1940	1950	1960	1970	1980
Single	40.1	40.9	44.8	41.4	44.1
Separated	11.4*	4.5	4.3	4.3	6.6
Divorced	3.4	5.8	7.8	10.6	19.6
Widowed	45.1	41.9	34.9	29.6	24.1
MSA–O	*	6.9	8.2	14.1	5.6
Total	100.0	100.0	100.0	100.0	100.0
Number (000)	1,123	1,104	993	1,053	1,240

*Separated and MSA–O cannot be distinguished in 1940 data.

Nonfamily Living Arrangements

We have discussed the distribution of living arrangements of specific subgroups in earlier chapters. Here we examine the prevalence of living in one-person households and other nonfamily living arrangements for the life cycle categories used earlier. Obviously, only those persons without children present are considered, since only they can live in nonfamily situations. As a review and summary of earlier discussions of the living arrangements of specific subgroups, Table 10.11 shows the percent of each life cycle category living in each of four nonfamily living arrangements—one-person households, head or householder of a two- or more-person household, nonrelative, and resident of group quarters.

Of young single persons, only about one in nine lives alone. As we have shown earlier, most of the rest live in the household of their parents. About one-quarter of young, formerly married persons live in a one-person household. The proportion living alone is higher for older persons—over 40 percent of 30–44-year-old and 50 percent of 45–59-year-old formerly married persons. Nearly three-fifths of formerly married persons aged 60 and over live alone.

When persons under age 30 live in nonfamily households, they are less likely to be living alone, and more likely to be living with roommates (cohabitating partners as well as same-sex roommates). In the last column of Table 10.11 is the proportion living alone of all those in nonfamily households. This proportion is 38 percent for never-married women and 42 percent for never-married men under age 30. It increases with age. For never-married or formerly married women aged 45–59, about four-fifths of those living in nonfamily households live alone. Among elderly formerly married women, 95 percent live alone.

These differentials by age undoubtedly reflect primarily differing economic situations. Young, unmarried persons tend to have low incomes. Older persons are more likely to be homeowners, and are likely to remain in housing that they shared with their former spouse and children. In addition, young never-married persons are likely to have never lived alone, and may be more able to tolerate the lack of privacy of sharing a household.

Nonfamily Households

As shown in the previous chapter, the number of nonfamily households rose rapidly, from only 3.5 million in 1940, to almost 8 million in 1960. There was a further increase of 57 percent to over 12 million in 1970, and an additional 70 percent increase to 21 million in 1980.

TABLE 10.11

Percent of Persons Who Are Not Living in Families, by Living Arrangement, Sex, and Life Cycle Stage, 1980

	Living Alone	+ Other Nonfamily Householder	+ Nonrelative	= Total in Nonfamily Household	+ Group Quarters	= Total Not in Family	Living Alone as % of All in Nonfamily Households
MEN							
Never Married							
18–29	11.9	6.5	9.7	28.1	12.4	40.5	42.3
30–44	36.0	8.2	10.2	54.4	6.2	60.6	66.2
45–59	39.2	4.8	6.8	50.8	8.8	59.6	77.2
Formerly Married, with No Own Children							
18–29	25.1	11.1	13.0	49.2	14.4	63.6	51.0
30–44	43.1	11.5	14.7	69.3	8.0	77.3	62.2
45–59	49.4	6.7	10.8	66.9	5.9	72.8	73.8
Elderly							
Never Married	44.3	3.3	6.2	53.8	15.5	69.3	82.3
Formerly Married	52.8	3.2	4.8	60.8	12.2	73.0	86.8
WOMEN							
Never Married							
18–29	10.9	5.4	12.4	28.7	10.1	38.8	38.0
30–44	30.9	5.7	10.1	46.7	3.2	49.9	66.2
45–59	33.8	3.4	6.6	43.8	7.2	51.0	77.2
Formerly Married, with No Own Children							
18–29	26.2	7.2	22.0	55.4	3.7	59.1	47.3
30–44	39.2	6.4	16.8	62.4	2.6	52.2	62.8
45–59	45.3	3.2	4.6	53.1	1.8	54.9	85.3
Elderly							
Never Married	43.8	2.4	4.7	50.9	15.5	66.4	86.1
Formerly Married	58.0	1.7	1.5	61.2	8.5	69.7	94.8

The great majority of nonfamily households consists of only one person. In 1970, 89 percent of nonfamily households were one-person households, 8 percent were two-person households, and only about 3 percent were three- or more-person households. By 1980 the fraction of two-person households increased, while that of one-person nonfamily households decreased—86 percent were one-person and 12 percent were two-person households. The growth in the number of two- or more-person nonfamily households resulted primarily from an increase in the number of cohabiting couples (see Table 10.12). Of the 1.76 million increase in nonfamily households with more than one member, 1.01 million was an increase in cohabiting couples. In 1980, 59 percent of these households were cohabitors, up from 35 percent in 1970.

Between 1970 and 1980 the age distribution of nonfamily householders shifted from a concentration at older ages toward the younger ages. It remains, however, a fairly old population. In 1960 and 1970 over half of the nonfamily householders were aged 60 and over. By 1980, this fraction had dropped to about 40 percent, while the proportion under age 40 had increased from 21 to 38 percent (see Table 10.13).

The marital status distribution of nonfamily householders also changed considerably during the 1970s. Thirty percent of nonfamily householders were never-married persons in 1970, compared to 37 percent in 1980. There was also an increase in the prevalence of separated and divorced nonfamily householders, rising from 21 to 26 percent. Widows decreased in relative prevalence, from 46 percent of all nonfamily householders in 1977 to 35 percent in 1980. There are large differences by sex in the marital status of nonfamily householders: one-half of the males, but only one-quarter of the females, were single (never-married) persons. About one-sixth of the male, but over one-half of the female nonfamily householdes, were widowed.

TABLE 10.12

Number of Nonfamily Households, 1940–80 (in thousands)

	One Person	Two + Persons	Total	Cohabitors
1940	2,710	766	3,475	not computed
1950	4,289	955	5,244	not computed
1960	7,060	895	7,955	248
1970	11,151	1,323	12,474	343
1980	18,172	3,079	21,251	1,349

NOTE: It appears that the number of cohabitor households in 1960 and 1970 is overstated, due to the erroneous classification of an unknown number of boarders and lodgers as cohabitors. These were a larger share of the cohabitor households in 1960 than in 1970. By 1980 it was an insignificant portion.

TABLE 10.13

Distribution and Growth of Nonfamily Households,
by Age and Marital Status of Householder, 1940–80

	1940	1950	1960	1970	1980	Percent Change	
						1960–70	1970–80
AGE							
<25	4.1	3.6	4.5	8.7	13.2	+203	+158
25–39	16.9	13.5	12.6	12.9	25.5	+ 61	+236
40–59	35.7	35.2	31.3	25.1	19.1	+ 26	+ 30
60–74	32.6	35.1	37.0	35.2	26.0	+ 49	+ 26
75+	10.7	12.7	14.6	18.1	16.2	+ 94	+ 52
Total	100.0	100.0	100.0	100.0	100.0	+ 57	+ 70
MARITAL STATUS							
Never Married	36.6	26.3	28.8	29.6	36.7	+ 61	+111
Separated/Divorced	20.6	18.5	19.3	21.1	26.2	+ 71	+112
MSA–O		8.1	4.3	3.0	2.0	+ 10	+ 9
Widowed	42.8	47.1	47.5	46.3	35.1	+ 29	+ 53
Total	100.0	100.0	100.0	100.0	100.0		
Number (000)	3,475	5,244	7,955	12,474	21,251	+ 57	+ 70

One-Person Households

We have shown that, in 1980, one-person households were about 86 percent of nonfamily households and more than one-fifth of all households. The distributions of one-person households by life cycle stage of the householder are presented in Table 10.14 for each decade from 1940 to 1980. In 1980, nearly one-half of the persons who lived alone were elderly, almost all of whom were widowed. An additional 25 percent were formerly married persons under age 60, primarily ages 45–59. Sixteen percent were never-married persons under age 30, with another 11 percent never-married persons between ages 30 and 59.

Over time, the fraction of one-person households who were young singles and young formerly married persons has increased, while the fraction elderly has dropped (Table 10.14, bottom panel). Overall, the number of one-person households increased by about 60 percent in each of the last two decades. The number of never-married persons under age 30 living alone increased by 188 percent during the 1960s, and by 218 percent in the 1970s. Also more than doubling during the 1970s were 30–44-year-old singles, formerly marrieds under age 30, and formerly married persons aged 30–44. The number of one-person households of

TABLE 10.14

Distribution and Growth of One-Person Households,
by Life Cycle Stage of Householder, 1940–80

Life Cycle Stage	1940	1950	1960	1970	1980
			Percent Distribution		
Never Married					
<30	5.6	3.5	5.0	8.2	16.0
30–44	9.8	6.1	6.6	5.2	7.5
45–59	10.9	7.9	7.6	5.5	3.6
Formerly Married					
<30	2.3	2.9	1.8	2.9	4.0
30–44	9.1	10.0	7.2	5.8	8.6
45–59	17.3	20.7	18.9	16.2	12.8
Elderly					
Never Married	9.8	7.6	8.3	7.6	5.1
Formerly Married	35.3	41.2	44.6	48.7	42.4
Total	100.0	100.0	100.0	100.0	100.0
Number (000)	2,170	4,289	7,059	11,148	18,172

	Percent Increase			*Components of Total Increase in One-Person Households*	
	1960–70	1970–80		1960–70	1970–80
Never Married					
<30	188	218		13.8	28.5
30–44	25	133		2.9	11.0
45–59	13	8		1.8	0.7
Formerly Married					
<30	157	123		4.9	5.7
30–44	26	143		3.2	13.1
45–59	35	29		11.4	7.5
Elderly					
Never Married	45	9		6.4	1.1
Formerly Married	72	42		55.7	32.4
Total	58	63		100.0	100.0

formerly married elderly persons increased by 72 percent during the 1960s, and by only 42 percent during the 1970s.

During the 1970s the increase in young singles accounted for 28 percent of the growth in one-person households. Older singles (30–44) accounted for an additional 11 percent, and nonelderly, formerly married persons accounted for about one-quarter of the growth. Formerly married elderly persons accounted for the remaining one-third of the growth in the 1970s. (They had accounted for three-fifths of the growth in one-person households in the 1960s.)

Two- or More-Person Nonfamily Households

Nonfamily households of two or more members are disproportionately the households of young adults. Thirty-six percent are headed by a person under age 25, 40 percent by a person aged 25–39, and only 11 percent by a person over age 60. Sixty-five percent of the heads are single, and an additional 27 percent are separated or divorced. As noted previously, nearly three-fifths are cohabiting couples. There are several distinct types of nonfamily households—cohabiting couples, persons who are "roommates" sharing a house or apartment, and homosexual couples (the number and characteristics of which are unknown). The cohabiting population tends to be concentrated in the young ages as are the "roommates," many of whom may prefer to live alone but cannot afford to. They choose to share a dwelling with one or more roommates, as an economically viable alternative, perhaps in preference to living with their parents. It is, of course, impossible to distinguish between "roommates" and homosexual couples. The two groups together numbered about 1.25 million in 1980.

Group Quarters

In 1980, 5.75 million persons or about 2.5 percent of the total United States population lived in group quarters rather than in households. Residents in group quarters are normally unrelated to one another.[3] There are two major subgroups of group quarters populations—institutional and noninstitutional. Institutions provide care for resi-

---

[3]Another population, a large share of which is living in group quarters, is not covered in these census data—the military stationed overseas (497,000 persons in 1980). We do not know the fraction of this population living in group quarters.

TABLE 10.15

Distribution of the Adult Group Quarters Population, by Type, 1980

	Total	Black
INMATES	42.4	46.0
Mental Institutions		
Age 18–64	3.2	4.3
65+	0.9	0.8
Homes for the Aged		
Age 18–64	3.4	3.1
65+	22.5	8.6
Correctional Institutions	8.3	25.5
Other Institutions		
Age 18–64	3.1	3.0
65+	1.0	0.7
NON-INMATES	57.5	53.8
Military Barracks	11.8	20.1
College Housing	36.0	25.3
Rooming Houses		
Age 18–64	2.3	2.4
65+	0.6	0.3
Other Group Quarters		
Age 18–64	5.0	5.3
65+	1.7	0.4
Total	100.0	100.0
Number (000)	5,480	762

dents, or maintain custody of them. Residents of institutions are referred to as inmates.[4]

About two-fifths of the group quarter population are in institutions, and over half of those are residents of homes for the elderly (see Table 10.15). The majority of noninstitutional residents of group quarters are living in college housing. There are relatively more residents of correctional institutions and military barracks among blacks.

[4]Users of data from the Current Population Survey will notice a large discrepancy in the number of persons enumerated in group quarters in the CPS compared to the decennial census. In the March 1980 CPS there were only 618,000 persons in group quarters. There are three major differences:

a. The Current Population Survey samples only the "noninstitutional" population. Thus persons in prisons, mental hospitals, and nursing homes are not covered.

b. Most unmarried college students are enumerated as members of the households of their parents in the CPS. Thus, very few people are shown as dormitory residents in the CPS. CPS dorm residents would, in principle, include only foreign students and persons who have no parental household in which to be enumerated.

c. The Current Population Survey excludes virtually all of the military population living in military barracks.

TABLE 10.16

Percent of All Persons in Group Quarters,
by Age, Sex, and Type of Group Quarters, 1980

	All Group Quarters		Institutions		Other Group Quarters	
	Male	Female	Male	Female	Male	Female
0– 4	0.1	0.1	0.0	0.0	0.1	0.0
5–13	0.3	0.1	0.2	0.1	0.1	0.0
14–17	1.6	0.7	1.0	0.4	0.6	0.3
18–19	15.8	13.4	1.2	0.2	14.6	13.2
20–24	9.6	4.9	1.6	0.3	7.9	4.7
25–29	2.8	0.7	1.5	0.3	1.4	0.4
30–34	1.8	0.4	1.1	0.3	0.7	0.2
35–44	1.3	0.4	0.8	0.3	0.5	0.2
45–54	1.1	0.6	0.7	0.4	0.4	0.2
55–64	1.3	0.9	0.9	0.7	0.4	0.3
65–74	2.1	2.3	1.8	1.9	0.3	0.4
75–84	5.5	8.9	5.1	8.1	0.5	0.8
85 +	16.7	27.1	15.8	25.7	0.9	1.3

Table 10.16 shows the percent of the total population of each age and sex who are residents of each of the two types of group quarters. Only one child in 1,000 is living in group quarters. Among adolescents the fraction rises to about 1 percent—higher for boys (1.6 percent) than for girls (0.7 percent).[5] At ages 18 and 19, about one person in seven is living in group quarters. This fraction drops off very quickly at older ages and then begins to rise rapidly at ages 65 and beyond.

Table 10.17 shows the age distribution of both types of group quarters population. About one-half of all group quarter residents, and about four-fifths of the noninstitutional population are between ages 18 and 24. This reflects the concentration of both college dorm and military barracks residents at these ages. The institutional population is concentrated at the older ages. Fifty-three percent are ages 65 and older.

Slightly more than 3 percent of the adult non-Hispanic white population are living in group quarters. This compares with 4.5 percent of blacks and 2.6 percent of Mexican-Americans. These differences can be better understood if the population is disaggregated by age and sex and into institutional and other group quarters (see Table 10.18). Blacks have a higher percentage in institutions at all ages under 65 for both men and

[5]Note that there is some ambiguity in classification of group homes providing foster care for children. Many of these are small, and if they consist of fewer than ten residents including resident staff, they may be classified as households. There is a "halfway house" category, but the number of juvenile residents enumerated appears to be too small.

TABLE 10.17

Age Distribution of Group Quarters Population, 1980

Age	All Group Quarters	Institutions	Other Group Quarters
0– 4	0.2	0.2	0.3
5–13	1.1	1.9	0.5
14–17	3.2	4.6	2.1
18–19	22.2	2.6	37.2
20–24	26.9	8.1	41.5
25–29	5.9	6.7	5.3
30–34	3.4	4.9	2.3
35–44	3.9	5.6	2.7
45–54	3.3	5.0	2.0
55–64	4.1	6.7	2.1
65–74	6.0	11.6	1.7
75–84	10.3	21.7	1.6
85 +	9.3	20.4	0.8
Total	100.0	100.0	100.0
Number (000)	5,738	2,492	3,246

women. The difference is extremely large for men at ages 18–24. Nearly 5 percent of black men aged 20–24 are in institutions, compared to 2 percent for Mexican-Americans and 1 percent for non-Hispanic whites. As shown in Chapter 3, this difference is due to the very large fractions of young, single black men in correctional institutions. At the oldest ages non-Hispanic whites are much more likely to be in institutions. This is especially true for women. Whites are more likely to be in homes for the aged—probably because of differential affluence and perhaps because of differences in family structure.

Mexican-Americans in the young adult ages are much less likely to be in "other group quarters" than whites or blacks—much less likely to be living in either college dorms or in military barracks. Black men and women are less likely to be in college dorms, but more likely to be living in military barracks.

Secondary and Subfamilies

Thus far, the "families" we have considered have been families that comprise separate household units. There are other "families" that do not have their own households but rather share the household of another person or family. In order to talk about these units we must define two more census concepts: subfamilies and secondary families. A

TABLE 10.18

Percent of Adult Population Living in Group Quarters, by Age, Sex, Ethnicity, and Type of Group Quarters, 1980

	All Group Quarters			Institutions			Other Group Quarters		
	Non-Hispanic White	Black	Mexican-American	Non-Hispanic White	Black	Mexican-American	Non-Hispanic White	Black	Mexican-American
MEN									
18–19	16.4	17.0	8.2	0.9	3.2	1.5	15.5	13.8	6.7
20–24	8.9	15.2	6.4	1.1	5.1	2.0	7.9	10.2	4.4
25–34	1.6	6.7	3.2	0.8	4.8	1.5	0.8	1.9	1.6
35–44	1.4	3.4	2.2	0.6	2.5	1.0	0.8	1.0	1.2
45–64	1.0	2.2	1.9	0.7	1.6	0.8	0.3	0.6	1.1
65–74	2.0	2.7	2.1	1.7	2.3	1.5	0.3	0.3	0.6
75+	7.9	6.1	5.5	7.4	5.9	5.2	0.6	0.2	0.3
WOMEN									
18–19	15.0	10.6	3.1	0.2	0.4	0.2	14.8	10.2	2.9
20–24	5.2	4.8	1.8	0.2	0.4	0.2	5.0	4.3	1.6
25–34	0.5	0.8	0.4	0.2	0.5	0.2	0.3	0.4	0.3
35–44	0.4	0.5	0.6	0.3	0.3	0.2	0.2	0.1	0.4
45–64	0.8	0.7	0.6	0.5	0.6	0.3	0.2	0.2	0.3
65–74	2.4	2.1	1.7	2.0	2.0	1.4	0.4	0.2	0.4
75+	14.1	7.5	7.2	13.1	7.3	6.7	1.0	0.3	0.5

subfamily is a married couple with or without children, or a parent and one or more children under the age of 18, who are living in the household of a relative. The two most common types of subfamily are young married couples sharing the household of a parent, and formerly married persons, with children sharing the household of their parents.

A secondary family consists of two or more related persons who are living in the household of a nonrelative. The secondary family concept was abandoned in the decennial censuses of 1970 and 1980, but continues in the Current Population Survey. However, in recent years the CPS has begun calling secondary families "unrelated subfamilies." We will, however, use the older terminology.

The number of secondary families has decreased over time (Table 10.19). It increased from about 675,000 in 1940 to 830,000 in 1947, reflecting the severe housing shortage during and after World War II. The number of secondary families then decreased to a low of about 118,000 in 1965. Since 1965, the number has again begun to rise, and by 1980 there were 348,000 secondary families.

The last three columns of this table show the number of secondary families by family type. Up through 1955, more than one-half were hus-

TABLE 10.19

Number of Secondary Families, by Type, 1940–80
(in thousands)

	Total	Husband-Wife	Other Male Head	Other Female Head
1940	675	400	69	206
1947	830	599	57	174
1950	465	365	15	85
1955	219	127	11	81
1960*	207	75	47	85
1965	118	60	14	44
1970	130	27	11	91
1980	348	19	36	294

*Includes Alaska and Hawaii for first time.

SOURCE: U.S. Bureau of the Census, *Historical Statistics of the United States, Colonial Times to 1970, Part 1*, series A-288–319, 1975.

NOTE: Except for 1940, data shown are from Current Population Survey. Secondary family concept was not used in the 1970 or 1980 decennial census. The 1960 decennial census found only 101,000 secondary families, less than one-half the number enumerated in the March 1960 CPS (1960 Census, U.S. Summary, Table 186).

band-wife families. The prevalence of "doubling up" (married couples without their own household) is discussed in Chapter 4. Since 1955 there has been a decrease of husband-wife secondary families, and by 1980 there were virtually none. There have never been very many male-headed secondary families apart from husband-wife families. The number was small in 1940, and continues to be very small in 1980. Never has it risen above 75,000.

The number of female-headed secondary families decreased dramatically from over 300,000 in 1940 to 44,000 in 1965. Since 1965 there has been an increase, and by 1980 there were 294,000. This seeming anomaly is quite easily explained in terms of the increase in cohabitation since 1970. If a woman and her child live in the household of a man to whom she is not married, the mother and child are classified as a secondary family. As we have seen in Chapters 3 and 6, the prevalence of such couples with children present has increased dramatically. Not all cohabiting couples with children present are included among secondary families. If a man lives with a woman and her child in her household, the household is classified as a female-headed family with an unrelated member, and there is no secondary family. It is only when a parent and child live in the household "headed" by the nonparent that a secondary family exists. It is likely that virtually all of the increase in female-headed secondary families is associated with increased cohabitation.

In Table 10.20 we show the number of subfamilies enumerated at various points in time since 1940. In 1940 there were 2 million subfamilies. By 1947 this number had increased to over 3 million. However, since that time there has been a continuous decrease in the number of subfamilies to slightly over 1.3 million by 1980.

The number of subfamilies enumerated in the 1980 CPS is considerably smaller than the number enumerated in the decennial census. This is probably because until 1982–83 the "relationship to householder" was not coded in enough detail to permit the reliable identification of parent–child dyads for other than the householder. A revision of CPS procedure in 1982–83 resulted in a large increase in the number of subfamilies: primarily mother–child subfamilies.[6]

In 1940, three-quarters of all subfamilies were married couples. Gradually this fraction has decreased and the fraction of other female-headed subfamilies has increased. By 1980, 38 percent of all subfamilies

---

[6]This change is discussed in U.S. Census Bureau, "Marital Status and Living Arrangements, Current Population Reports, P-20, no. 399, p. 8.

TABLE 10.20

Number of Subfamilies, by Type, 1940–80

(in thousands)

		Total	Husband-Wife	Other Male Head	Other Female Head	Husband-Wife as Percent of Total
1940		2,062	1,546	52	464	75.0
1947		3,123	2,332	83	708	74.7
1950		2,402	1,651	113	638	68.7
1955		1,973	1,178	69	726	59.7
1960*	CPS	1,514	871	115	528	57.5
	Census	1,424	832	77	515	58.4
1965		1,293	729	72	492	56.4
1970	CPS	1,150	617	48	484	53.7
	Census	1,265	582	65	617	46.1
1975		1,349	576	69	705	42.7
1980	CPS	1,115	567	55	494	50.9
	Census	1,342	506	74	762	37.7

*Includes Alaska and Hawaii for first time.

SOURCES: U.S. Bureau of the Census, *Historical Statistics of the United States, Colonial Times to 1970*, Part 1, series 288–319; idem, *U.S. Census of Population: 1960*, vol. I, *Characteristics of the Population*, table 185; idem, *Census of Population: 1970, Detailed Characteristics*, table 206, idem, *Census of Population 1980, Detailed Population Characteristics*, table 267.

were married couples, 57 percent were mother–child subfamilies, and the remaining 5 percent had other male heads. Blacks are overrepresented among subfamilies (29 percent of all subfamilies and 42 percent of mother–child subfamilies). Sixty-five percent of black subfamilies are mother–child subfamilies, and only 26 percent are married couple subfamilies. Among whites, 40 percent are mother–child subfamilies and 56 percent are married couple subfamilies.

About one-half of the married couple subfamilies include children, and most of those with children have only one child. Most of the children are under age 3. Similarly, the great majority of mother–child and father–child subfamilies include only one child. In mother–child subfamilies the child is likely to be under age 3 and the mother is likely to be never married, while in father–child subfamilies the child is more likely to be older, and the father, separated or divorced.

TABLE 10.21
Selected Characteristics of Subfamilies, 1980

	Total	Non-Hispanic White	Black	Mexican-American
TYPE OF SUBFAMILY				
Married Couple	37.7	46.7	13.1	44.8
Father–Child	5.5	5.6	5.0	6.1
Mother–Child	56.8	47.7	81.9	49.1
Total	100.0	100.0	100.0	100.0

	Total	Type of Subfamily		
		Married Couple	Father–Child	Mother–Child
NUMBER OF CHILDREN				
0	21.5	54.8	—	—
1	53.5	26.8	66.1	71.1
2	18.5	13.1	24.0	21.7
3	5.0	4.1	7.6	5.4
4+	1.5	1.0	2.3	1.8
Total	100.0	100.0	100.0	100.0
AGE OF YOUNGEST CHILD				
0– 2	39.0	26.8	25.0	48.4
3– 5	17.1	7.9	23.4	22.7
6–11	15.3	6.9	27.6	20.0
12–17	7.1	3.6	24.1	8.9
None	21.5	54.8	—	—
Total	100.0	100.0	100.0	100.0
MARITAL STATUS OF HEAD				
Separated	10.3		18.8	16.4
MSA–O	5.2		14.7	7.7
Widowed	1.9		5.9	2.8
Divorced	17.2		39.5	26.4
Never Married	27.6		21.1	46.7
Married, Spouse Present	37.7		—	—
Total	100.0		100.0	100.0

TABLE 10.22

Distribution of Subfamilies, by Age of Head and Subfamily Type, 1980

	Married Couple	Father–Child	Mother–Child
<20	6.3	6.1	19.8
20–24	24.0	15.8	32.8
25–29	19.1	22.2	21.9
30–34	11.0	22.8	12.5
35–39	9.6	24.3	9.9
40–44	7.4	5.4	2.4
45–54	7.8	2.7	0.6
55–64	8.3	0.5	0.1
65+	6.7	0.1	0.1
Total	100.0	100.0	100.0

Summary

Several types of households are examined: female-headed families, male-headed families other than married couples, and nonfamily households. In addition, attention is given to secondary and subfamilies and to the population in group quarters.

The number of female-headed families grew faster than other types of families during the 1970s, increasing from 11 to 14 percent of all families. The change was particularly large among blacks (from 28 to 36 percent of all families). The proportion of female-headed families with children increased from less than one-half in 1940 and 1960 to three-fifths in 1980. About two-thirds of those without children under 18 include adult children of the householder.

Three-tenths of all female family heads in 1980 were widows, 40 percent were separated or divorced, and 10 percent were never-married. Among female-headed families with minor children, two-thirds were separated or divorced, 17 percent were never-married, and 13 percent were widowed. The proportion of female householders who are never-married with children has risen very rapidly, especially among blacks. The number of children in female-headed families has decreased. For example, the proportion with more than two children decreased from 36 to 23 percent during the 1970s. Black and Mexican-American female family heads have more children in the household than do majority whites.

Thirty percent of all female-headed families with children received public assistance income during 1979 and 41 percent had total family income below the poverty line. Over two-thirds of female-headed families with children under age 3 were poor and one-half were receiving public assistance. These figures are lower among female-headed families with a divorced head and are higher among families with more children and among minorities.

Male-headed families (other than married couples) are only about one-quarter as common as female-headed families. The proportion of all families that were male-headed was only about 4 percent in 1980. One-third of these male family heads are never-married, one-fifth are widowed, and 40 percent are divorced or separated. Three-fifths of these families have at least one son or daughter present, although only about one-third have a child under age 18. Of those with a minor child, about three-fifths are headed by separated or divorced men.

The number of nonfamily households has increased at an accelerating rate since 1940; during the 1970s there was a 70 percent increase to 21 million in 1980. Most of these households consist of only one person, although this proportion decreased over the 1970s from 89 to 86 percent as the number of cohabiting couples increased. Between 1970 and 1980 the distribution of ages of nonfamily householders became younger, and there was also a change in the marital status distribution of nonfamily household heads, with increases in the proportions never-married and separated or divorced, and decreases in the proportion widowed.

In 1980, nearly one-half of the persons who lived alone were elderly, and the other half was evenly divided between never-married and formerly married persons. Elderly persons living alone accounted for a lower proportion of the growth in one-person households during the 1970s than during the 1960s.

About 2.5 percent of the total United States population lived in group quarters in 1980. About two-fifths of this population were in institutions (over half of these were residents of homes for the elderly). About one-half of all group quarter residents, and about four-fifths of the noninstitutional population were between ages 18 and 24. The majority of noninstitutional residents of group quarters live in college housing (one-third of total group quarters population).

Blacks are more likely and Mexican-Americans are less likely than majority whites to live in group quarters. Relatively large proportions of blacks in group quarters are in correctional institutions and military barracks. The differences are largest among men at ages 18–24, where 5 percent of black males are in institutions, compared with 2 percent of Mexican-Americans and 1 percent of majority-white men.

The number of subfamilies peaked in 1947 at 3.1 million and has since declined to 1.3 million in 1980. Most subfamilies are either young couples or formerly married persons with children who live with their parents. The proportion of married couples has declined markedly from three-quarters in 1940 to less than one-tenth in 1980. About one-half of the married couple subfamilies include children, and most subfamilies with children have only one child. Female-headed subfamilies with children are most likely to be never-married mothers, and the children are likely to be under age 3. Most of the father–child subfamilies are a formerly married father and an older child.

A secondary family consists of two or more related persons who live in a household headed by a nonrelative. The number of secondary families also peaked in 1947 and has declined subsequently. However, since 1965 the number of such families has tripled, with most of the growth occurring in the 1970s. Less than 1 percent of all families in 1980 (348,000) were secondary families. Since 1955 the proportion of these families that are married couples has declined from more than half to 5 percent. Female-headed secondary families have more than doubled as a proportion of all secondary families since 1960, reflecting the increasing cohabitation of women with children.

11

IMPLICATIONS FOR THE FUTURE

A S STATED at the outset, this book has been designed to make much detailed information easily accessible to a broad community of scholars interested in family and household issues. In the attempt to provide such a reference work, we have intentionally kept very close to the information being provided and have not engaged the large theoretical and social policy issues that appear at almost every turn. This concluding note reflects on the interpretation and implications of the seemingly radical changes in American family and household experience. Since substantive summaries can be found at the end of each chapter, that detail will not be repeated here.

Marriage and family relationships seem to be occupying a shrinking space in our lives. Marriage rates before age 25 have declined markedly, so that young people spend a much larger proportion of their adult lives before adopting marital obligations; it is possible that a significant proportion may never do so. Parenthood is also being delayed, so that an increased proportion of the early years of marriage is being spent in lifestyles that are not defined in terms of the family roles that children bring. Again, a substantial proportion of today's youth may never become parents at all. The vast majority will marry and have children, but over half of those who do will experience the breakup of that marriage. Persons who are not currently married—the young, the separated or divorced, and the widowed elderly—have progressively chosen to live alone, rather than with other family members.

How are we to understand these changes? It may be useful to identify two prevalent perspectives in order to distinguish our position. The first is captured well in both the title and the content of Mary Jo Bane's book, *Here to Stay* (1976). By this view the family remains a healthy and dominant institution; its resilience is demonstrated in the very changes under consideration, as adaptations to a changing social environment. The second perspective is not inconsistent with the former, but it emphasizes specific factors in the changing social environment that may be regarded as "causes" of altered family patterns. Examples are the emphasis placed on changing roles of women, particularly labor force participation, in the interpretations of the Chicago economist Gary S. Becker, *A Treatise on the Family* (1981) or of Andrew Cherlin in his book *Marriage, Divorce, Remarriage* (1981). Both of these perspectives contain insights, but we feel that the historical continuity of the underlying processes deserves greater emphasis. This is much more in line with Charles F. Westoff's interpretation in his essay "Some Speculations on the Future of Marriage and Fertility" (1978) and, as he concludes, may lead to a less sanguine assessment of the future success of family roles as they compete with other lifestyles.

Because changes are so much more rapid now than they were, say, thirty years ago, we are misled into thinking that they must have been caused by something that has happened recently. William J. Goode, in *World Revolution and Family Patterns* (1968), has noted how family changes tend to get compared to a fictional golden past. The truth of the matter is that accelerating change stretches into the distant past.

Consider three critical dimensions of family change: marriage and marital stability, childbearing and parenting, and the roles of women. Each of these is closely interrelated with the others, but the critical point is that changes in all three have deep historical and cultural roots. The shrinking dominance of family roles in the lives of men and women reflects the relative value our society places on these roles in comparison with other adult roles. This, in turn, is a continuation of the reduction of family functions over several centuries that has occurred with the transformation of our economy, and with an associated increasing cultural value on individualism.

Marriage and Marital Stability

We have seen that marriage is occurring later and lasting for a much smaller proportion of adults' lifetimes. This has greatly altered the context and expectations of family life as well as the "texture" of social life more generally. Marriage and sex have been effectively separated. While marriage is being delayed, sexual relationships begin at increasingly earlier ages. The proportion of unmarried 19-years-olds sexually active increased from 46 to 69 percent between 1971 and 1979,[1] and the norms have accommodated by becoming increasingly approving.[2] It is in this context that cohabitation has become common over the decade. Social disapproval of "shacking up" must have rested largely in its proclamation that an unmarried couple was sexually intimate. That objection has been effectively destroyed by the knowledge that such relationships are common in any event. So, at the same time that marriage is being delayed, the meaning of marriage is becoming more ambiguous. We know very little about how couples view marriage and cohabitation differently, but it seems likely that a major dimension has to do with commitment and a sense of permanence. But then, it is at this very point that marriage has undergone such dramatic change.

The majority of recent first marriages are not likely to avoid separation and divorce. More than half of recent marriages involved at least one partner who had been previously married, and in one of four both had been married before. These changes may have feedback effects in that everyday observation blatantly contradicts normative presumptions that marriages should be "until death," and that a formerly married person is not an appropriate marriage match for a never-married person. There are further feedback implications as well, which relate to our subsequent discussion of childbearing and parenting, in that the investment persons are willing to make in a relationship is likely to be hedged to the extent that the permanence of the relationship is seen as an open question.[3] Put simply, insecurity about the viability of relationships may lead to behavior that, in turn, lowers the prospects that the relationship will last.

We have noted that the overwhelming social concern with increasing marital instability relates to its effects on the lives of children. When no children are involved, it may be a rather trivial matter that one or both partners have had previous partners; they may well have gained from the experience in learning how better to relate to their partner, or at least to shop more carefully for the new one. There is a substantial literature that quite rightly emphasizes the collective gains to marital happiness that come from being able to trade in unhappy relationships for happy ones. But the matter is quite different from the point

[1]Melvin Zelnik and John F. Kantner, "Sexual Activity, Contraceptive Use and Pregnancy Among Metropolitan Area Teenagers: 1971–1979," *Family Planning Perspectives* 12 (1980): 229–33.

[2]Arland Thornton and Deborah Freedman, "Changing Attitudes Toward Marriage and Single Life," *Family Planning Perspectives* 14 (1982):297–303.

[3]Gary S. Becker, *A Treatise on the Family* (Cambridge, Mass.: Harvard University Press, 1981).

of view of children. What may maximize their parents' happiness has quite a different consequence for them. Research documents considerable emotional strain on children involved in divorces and remarriages, and we are now finding lasting effects for many in their adult lives. Having lived in a mother-only family is associated with higher rates of high school dropout, teenage marriages, teenage childbirth, unmarried motherhood, and divorce in one's own marriage. This is not to say that all children who experience a family breakup face these consequences, but rather that the risks are higher for these children. One major social policy concern is the high poverty rate of one-parent families, half of whom are in poverty compared with less than one-tenth of two-parent families. This in itself is a major route through which marital disruption affects the lives, and the life chances, of children of divorce—though we have found that economic deprivation is not the whole explanation.

More than half of today's young children will spend some time in a one-parent family. We may think of this as a short-term transition, and for some it is, but the average child who enters this status lives in a family without a father for six years; for many this is the remainder of their childhood.[4] For those whose mothers do remarry there are the complications of family life involving stepparenting and often children from the new marriages as well. We are only beginning to study the complexities of remarriages, but recent work makes it clear that, with or without remarriage, the biological father typically disappears altogether from the lives of most children of disrupted marriages.[5]

Differing ages of children at disruption, differing durations in one-parent families and differing ages at parental remarriage combine to create an enormous diversity in the family experience of children. It is simply not possible to talk about *the* American family, and, indeed, many children might have difficulty answering the simple question "who is in your family." Note further the even greater diversity in family experience that is generated over lifetimes when childhood and adult risks of marital disruption are combined. Only a minority are likely to grow up in a stable family and have a stable marriage of their own.

Can factors such as the increased employment of wives and mothers be regarded as the underlying causes of these trends? Could policies perhaps reverse the trend by altering the costs and benefits of such behaviors? The figure showing the proportions of marriages ending in divorce for marriages since 1860 (Figure 5.1) is extremely informative on

---

[4]Larry L. Bumpass, "Children and Marital Disruption: A Replication and Update," *Demography* 21 (1984): 71–82.

[5]Frank F. Furstenberg and Christine Winqueist Nord, "Parenting Apart: Patterns of Childrearing After Marital Distruption," *Journal of Marriage and the Family* 47 (1985):893–905.

this point. While annual rates of divorce have fluctuated with wars and the economy, the likelihood that marriages occurring in a given year would ultimately divorce has increased in a steady, accelerating curve, from 7 percent in 1860 to the current expectation of over one-half. At some point the trend must obviously plateau at some high level, but where we are now lies very much on the long-term trend line. Divorce rates have plateaued for the moment, with rates of the early 1980s no higher than those of the late 1970s. Some may be quick to interpret this as the beginning of a downturn; however, a similar plateau seen for those marrying in the late 1940s suggests that we should not be too quick to reach such a conclusion, given the experience that followed. This trend seems to us to be compelling evidence that the roots of current patterns of marital instability are much deeper than just recent changes in other domains. Rather, it seems most likely that the decreasing dominance of family roles is tied to the evolution of our culture and economy in a way that is shared with other areas (such as fertility, sex-role attitudes, or female employment) but that then is reinforced by interactions among those areas.

Childbearing and Parenting

Childbirth and parenting are core aspects of our notion of family. Indeed, for most of our cultural history marriage has been indistinguishable from parenthood except for those few who were sterile. On the other hand, the number of children that a couple has, and the centrality of parenting in contrast to other adult roles, have been declining over the last couple of centuries in the United States. Much research on the "demographic transition," from high mortality and fertility to low mortality and fertility, has demonstrated the complexity of understanding these declines. There is no single simple explanation such as education, industrialization, or urbanization.[6] But there is agreement that the costs of children have systematically increased and the benefits systematically decreased with the transformation of the society following the industrial revolution. This transformation and its effect on the relative costs of parenting is a continuing process rather than a past event.

The baby boom was a peculiar blip on that long-term trend that we are not likely to see again. Many observers, for either theoretical reasons or out of concern for financing the retirement of "baby boomers," alter-

---

[6]Ansley J. Coale, "Fertility Trends in the Modern World: The Decline of Fertility in Europe from the French Revolution to World War II," in *Fertility and Family Planning: A World View*, ed. S. J. Behrman, Leslie Coras, and Ronald Freedman (Ann Arbor: University of Michigan Press, 1969).

nately predict or announce the next baby boom. A full engagement of these arguments would take us too far from our main theme. We simply agree with observations of Westoff, among others, that both historical and international evidence shows that today's situation, not the baby boom, lies on the long-term trend line with respect to fertility.

Let us briefly summarize current low levels of childbearing. Age-specific fertility rates are below levels consistent with long-run stability of the population—they imply an average family size of 1.8 children per woman, and have been at this level for over a decade. We have more births than deaths simply because the baby boom produced an unusual age composition. This circumstance will quickly disappear as the baby boomers age out of the reproductive years. Indeed, quite a few Western European countries, with much smaller versions of the postwar baby boom, are already experiencing natural decrease. There seems little reason to think that we have reached some natural equilibrium around two children per woman. The process that underlies this long-term decline is far from exhausted. To illustrate with a point to which we will return in a minute, true equality of opportunity for women is far from reality—and yet motherhood does not compete well for a woman's time even with alternative roles constrained by inequality.

However, the most important aspects of our current low fertility are not obvious from the low average number of children per woman. The first of these is the transformation of parenthood from an ascribed (and dominant) role for women to a matter of choice. Parenthood is now truly an option in a way that is quite different from several decades ago. Modern contraceptives and sterilization, backed up by abortion, place far more emphasis on a decision process than used to be the case. Indeed, one of us has been so rash as to suggest that values surrounding parenthood may have been in some respects rationalizations of the inevitable.[7] Among women in the later years of childbearing in the late 1960s, over three-quarters had experienced at least one accidental pregnancy and one-third had given birth at least once after they thought they were through with having children. Cultural values that prescribe motherhood as the central role around which other activities must be organized helped to make such a circumstance tolerable. When accidental childbirth is much less likely, and no longer necessary, it is also a much less tolerable intrusion into women's lives. The change in the fertility control setting now requires that the costs and benefits of childbearing be explicitly weighed.

---

[7]Bumpass, "Is Low Fertility Here to Stay?" *Family Planning Perspectives* 5 (1973):67–9.

Our cultural heritage regarding parenthood is resilient, so that it is still difficult for a couple to admit to themselves and others that, all things considered, they choose to remain childless. For many the process is one of delaying motherhood until intervening events, or age, make it clear that the option has been foregone.[8] Nonetheless, it is likely that perhaps one-quarter of today's young women will remain childless.[9] So, in the competition with other adult options, parents are having fewer children, and many men and women will simply never become parents at all.

A second aspect, not obvious from just the low level of fertility, has direct links with our earlier concerns with divorce and single-parent families. In 1980 one of every five births occurred to an unmarried mother. While unwed motherhood has been much higher among blacks than among whites, it is striking that rates have declined among black women at the same time that they have increased by over one-quarter since 1977 among white women of all reproductive ages.[10] Sociologists and anthropologists have long emphasized the critical role of family relationships in providing a clearly defined set of obligations for the support and socialization of the new entrants into the social system. Taboos against illegitimacy have undoubtedly found much of their strength in this concern. The trends in marital stability discussed earlier make it clear that marriage provides little guarantee that a child will have a stable parental environment throughout childhood. The recognition of this fact may well be loosening the conviction that it is essential for a woman to be married to have a child.[11] All the problems aside, there is ample evidence that mothers do cope in the absence of a husband; and a single pregnant young woman may well ask what benefit is to be derived from marrying the father and divorcing a few years later. This is yet another interaction among changes in family domains, loosening the linkage between marriage and childbearing, and in so doing perhaps reducing further the competitive advantages of either in contrast to other adult alternatives.

[8]J. E. Veevers, *Childless by Choice* (Toronto: Butterworth & Co., 1980).

[9]David Bloom and James Trussell, "What Are the Determinants of Delayed Childbearing and Permanent Childlessness in the United States?" *Demography* 21 (1984): 613–23.

[10]National Center for Health Statistics, "Monthly Vital Statistics Report," "Advance Report of Final Natality Statistics," Vol. 33, No. 6, 1984.

[11]Bumpass, "The Changing Linkage of Nuptiality and Fertility in the United States," in *Nuptiality and Fertility: Proceedings of the International Union for the Scientific Study of Population Seminar*, held in Bruges, 8–11 January 1979, ed. Lado T. Ruzicka (Liege, Belgium: IUSSP, 1980).

Changing Roles of Men and Women

This brings us quite directly to the changing character of gender roles. This too is a process that began with the transformation of a farm economy. We have emphasized that marriage and motherhood are decreasing in their dominance in women's lives. "A wife and mother" used to be a sufficient, and proud, definition of a woman's adult roles. The shrinking competitive advantage of these roles for women is surely related to their increased participation in alternatives, most particularly the labor force. Economists speak explicitly of the increased opportunity costs of children, and of home time more generally, as the wage a woman could earn in other pursuits increases. This is surely an important part of the story, and it has been accentuated by equality of educational attainment of women, a shifting industrial structure away from heavy manual jobs and toward occupations requiring those educational skills,[12] and family economic pressures associated with particular stages in the family life cycle.[13]

While the roles of women are most dramatically altered by these changes, men's lives are directly affected as well. There has been only a modest increase in shared household tasks, but the role definition of "breadwinner" is progressively shared. Hence men's claim to home services in exchange for this role is weakened at the same time that wives' labor force participation reduces the amount of time women spend in home tasks and increases the substitution of purchased services (from cleaning to meals eaten out). These changes in the complementarity of marital roles are likely to affect how the advantages of marriage are perceived[14] and the qualities sought by men and women in the marriage market.

There is an additional critical factor underlying changing family life. This is an ideological aspect related to the long-term structural changes in our society—the flowering of individualism. This is a strong value in our cultural heritage; we share it with Europe, but it has grown vigorously in the fertile soil of American democracy.[15] With the development of an industrial economy in conjunction with the rise of the modern nation-state, the functions performed by the family have diminished—focusing progressively on volatile social-emotional relation-

---

[12]Valerie K. Oppenheimer, *The Female Labor Force in the United States: Demographic and Economic Factors Governing Its Growth and Changing Composition* (Westport, Conn.: Greenwood Press, 1970).

[13]Oppenheimer, *Work and the Family* (New York: Academic Press, 1982).

[14]Becker, *A Treatise on the Family.*

[15]Ron Lesthaeghe, "A Century of Demographic and Cultural Change in Western Europe," *Population and Development Review* 9 (1983):411–36.

ships.[16] We have already commented on the relevance of this shrinkage in our discussion of changing marital stability and childbearing. The dimension we would call attention to here is the group of others whose interests must be considered when decisions are being made. When needs and interests conflict, as they do in any collectivity, how much weight must the individual give the interests of other persons in contrast to his or her own, and how large a circle of others must be considered? Over the centuries this circle has narrowed from a broader group of extended kin, to the nuclear family, and increasingly to the individual.

Divorce is a clear case where the interests of children and adults in the family may be very different. Should a couple stay together for the sake of the children? The proportion of persons answering "no" increased from 51 to 81 percent between 1962 and 1982.[17] We have already noted that about 2 million children each year are involved in a marital breakup.

Or consider the employment of women. The importance of a mother's full-time care for a young infant has been built into our value system and reinforced by major sources of advice on child care. In 1970, three-quarters of American women said that they thought that a mother's working was harmful to a preschool child.[18] Yet in the years since, the proportion of mothers of children under age 5 who are employed has doubled to over one-half. The evidence on the effects of working mothers on children is mixed, but our point is that this trend occurred *despite* the belief that it was somehow harmful. Again we note that the increasing employment of women is not a new factor on the scene. Rather, it has been a continuous process over the century,[19] with the increases among mothers of young children a lag induced by the strong cultural values against such employment. The dissonance between cultural prescription and behavior may well be a factor in the declining psychological well-being of women. Recent research by Sara McLanahan finds that such declines are concentrated among working mothers of young children.[20]

[16]William J. Goode, *World Revolution and Family Patterns* (New York: Free Press, 1963).

[17]Thornton and Freedman, "The Changing American Family," *Population Bulletin* 38 (1983):1–44.

[18]Sandra Retert and Larry L. Bumpass, "Employment and Approval of Employment Among Mothers of Young Children," University of Wisconsin, Center for Demography and Ecology, Working Paper 74-4, 1974.

[19]Kingsley Davis, "Wives and Work: Consequences of the Sex Role Revolution," *Population and Development Review* 10 (1984):397–417.

[20]Sara McLanahan, "Family Structure and the Reproduction of Poverty," *American Journal of Sociology* 90 (1985):873–901.

Thus, when parenting competes with other adult interests and roles, we increasingly acknowledge the legitimacy of self-interest as the decision criterion. The declining birthrate, and especially the increasing proportion of women who will never become mothers, are straightforward consequences of the competition of motherhood roles, as prescribed by our culture, with alternative opportunities for individuals, in which the individual interests win out. The proportion of American adults who say that all couples should have children has been cut in half in the last two decades, from 84 to 43 percent.

While we emphasize the deep historical and cultural roots of these major trends, the linkages among them clearly give further impetus to the processes of change. We have noted several such connections in the preceding discussion, such as the possibility that changing gender roles within marriage may be reducing the advantages gained from a domestic division of labor and hence the net benefit of marriage. The prevalence of premarital sexual relations makes delayed marriage less burdensome (which is another way of saying that it, too, reduces the net benefit of marriage). It is clear that both attitudes and behavior regarding marriage are changing markedly. This is evident not only in the increased prevalence of cohabitation but also in delayed marriage and in attitudes about the importance of marriage.[21]

Delayed parenthood exposes both men and women to lifestyles that may compete more directly with future childbearing, and further, the role hiatus provided by delayed marriage allows young women to experience adult role identities not directly dependent on either marriage or motherhood.[22] At the same time, increased employment and earnings of women compete directly with childbearing, and make it possible for women to leave unhappy marriage relationships in which they might otherwise have been trapped.[23]

The uncertainty about marital stability is likely a factor in both women's employment and reduced fertility. Young women in the current context are well advised to develop and nurture labor market skills capable of providing adequate support in the absence of a husband. The costs and benefits of having children are clearly altered by divorce—for both men and women. Marriage may well be a short-term contract, but parenthood is not. For women, the possibility of marital breakup means that childbearing brings with it a substantial risk of the difficulties and

[21]Thornton and Freedman, "The Changing American Family."

[22]Karen O. Mason, "Women's Labor Force Participation and Fertility: Final report 21U 662, prepared for the National Institutes of Health, 1974.

[23]Michael Hannan, Nancy Tuma, and Lyle P. Groeneveld, "Income and Independence Effects on Marital Dissolution: Results from the Seattle and Denver Income-Maintenance Experiments," *American Journal of Sociology* 84 (1978):611–33.

economic hardships of single parenting. For men, the likelihood of divorce reduces the prospective cost-benefit ratio of parenthood,[24] since relationships between biological fathers and their children frequently become minimal within a few years of marital disruption.[25] It is possible that increasing divorce has also reduced pronatalist pressure from the older generation, since the grandparent generation risks losses and obligations with respect to grandchildren when divorce occurs. In one study, only 12 percent said that it would bother them a great deal if they did not have grandchildren.[26]

The trends outlined are still very much in process and will likely continue for the foreseeable future. Take, for example, equality of opportunity for women. From only 6 percent of married women in the labor force in 1890, long-term trends imply that there will be no difference in the employment rates of men and women in little more than a decade.[27] Yet the occupational distribution and wages of women are far from equality. Whatever effects women's employment has on marital and childbearing decisions, it has occurred *in spite of* very substantial inequality. The same forces we have been considering will move us irresistibly toward greater equality of opportunity for women. Note also that the pressures of a slow, or even negative labor force growth are likely to open new opportunities for women as a matter of necessity.

What then are the implications of these reflections for future trends in family and household patterns? They are, quite simply, that one would be seriously misguided to treat the present as if it were some kind of new equilibrium state. Rather, the same forces that have given rise to the long-term trends are likely to continue into the future. Surely there will be period variations associated with economic or even attitudinal fluctuations, but we should not be too eager to interpret plateaus or reversals as turning points in processes with such deep historical roots. That the family is adaptive, and that family relationships continue to play a very important role in the lives of Americans, are incontrovertible. At the same time, it seems likely that the relative dominance of these relationships in competition with other adult roles is likely to continue to dwindle over the foreseeable future.

[24]Yoarm Weiss and Robert J. Willis, "Children as Collective Goods in Divorce Settlements," *Journal of Labor Economics* 3 (1985):258–92.

[25]Furstenberg and Nord, "Parenting Apart."

[26]Thornton, "The Influence of the Parental Family on the Attitudes and Behavior of Children," Presentation at the Family and Household Structure Workshop, National Institute of Child Health and Human Development, 1983.

[27]Davis, "Wives and Work."

Bibliography

Alba, Richard D., and Mitchell B. Chamlin "Ethnic Identification Among Whites." *American Sociological Review* 48(1983):240–247.

Bancroft, Gertrude *The American Labor Force: Its Growth and Changing Composition.* A volume in the 1950 Census Monograph Series. New York: Wiley, 1958.

Bane, Mary Jo *Here to Stay: American Families in the Twentieth Century.* New York: Basic Books, 1976a.

—— "Marital Disruption and the Lives of Children." *Journal of Social Issues* 32(1976b):103–117.

——, **and D. T. Ellwood** "Single Mothers and Their Living Arrangements." Harvard University, mimeo, March 1984

Becker, Gary S. *A Treatise on the Family.* Cambridge, Mass.: Harvard University Press, 1981.

Beresford, C., and A. M. Rivlin "Privacy, Poverty, and Old Age." *Demography* 3(1966):247–258.

Bloom, David, and James Trussell "What Are the Determinants of Delayed Childbearing and Permanent Childlessness in the United States?" *Demography* 21(1984):613–623.

Bowen, William, and T. Aldrich Finegan *The Economics of Labor Force Participation.* Princeton, N.J.: Princeton University Press, 1969.

Bumpass, Larry L. "Is Low Fertility Here to Stay?" *Family Planning Perspectives* 5(1973):67–69.

—— "The Changing Linkage of Nuptiality and Fertility in the United States." In Lado T. Ruzicka, ed., *Nuptiality and Fertility: Proceedings of the International Union for the Scientific Study of Population Seminar Held in Bruges, 8–11 January 1979.* Liege, Belgium: IUSSP, 1980.

—— "Children and Marital Disruption: A Replication and Update." *Demography* 21(1984):71–82.

—— "Recent Trends in Women's Education After Marriage." University of Wisconsin, Center for Demography & Ecology Working Paper 85–28, Madison, Wisconsin, 1985.

——, **and James Sweet** "Differentials in Marital Instability." *American Sociological Review* 37(1972):754–766.

Cain, Glen *Married Women in the Labor Force: An Econometric Analysis.* Chicago: University of Chicago Press, 1966.

Carliner, G. "Determinants of Household Headship." *Journal of Marriage and the Family* 37(1975):28–38.

Carter, Hugh, and Paul C. Glick *Marriage and Divorce: A Social and Economic Study.* Cambridge, Mass.: Harvard University Press, 1976.

Cherlin, Andrew "Remarriage as an Incomplete Institution." *American Journal of Sociology* 84(1978):634–650.

―――― "Postponing Marriage: The Influence of Young Women's Work Expectations." *Journal of Marriage and the Family* 42(1980):355–365.

―――― *Marriage, Divorce, and Remarriage.* Cambridge, Mass.: Harvard University Press, 1981.

――――**, and James McCarthy** "A Note on Maritally-Disrupted Men's Reports of Child Support in the June 1980 Current Population Survey." *Demography* 20(1983):385–389.

―――― Final Report, Demographic Analysis of Family and Household Structure. Center for Population Research Contract No.1-HO-12802, 1984.

―――― "Remarried Couple Households: Data from the June 1980 Current Population Survey." *Journal of Marriage and the Family* 47(1985):23–30.

Chevan, A., and J. H. Korson "The Widowed Who Live Alone: An Examination of Social and Demographic Factors." *Social Forces* 51(1972):45–53.

Coale, Ansley J. "Fertility Trends in the Modern World: The Decline of Fertility in Europe from the French Revolution to World War II." In S. J. Behrman, Leslie Corsa, and Ronald Freedman, eds., *Fertility and Family Planning: A World View.* Ann Arbor: University of Michigan Press, 1969.

Cooney, R. S. "Demographic Components of Growth in White, Black, and Puerto Rican Headed Families: A Comparison of the Cutright and Ross/Sawhill Methodologies." *Social Science Research* 8:(1979):144–158.

Cutright, P. "Components of Change in the Number of Female Family Heads Aged 15–44: United States, 1949–1970." *Journal of Marriage and the Family* 36(1974):714–721.

Das Gupta, Prithwis "Future Fertility of Women by Present Age and Parity: Analysis of American Historical Data, 1917–1980. United States Census Bureau. *Current Population Reports*, Special Studies Series P-23, 1985.

Davis, Kingsley "Wives and Work: Consequences of the Sex Role Revolution." *Population and Development Review* 10(1984):397–417.

――――**, and P. van den Oever** "Age Relations and Policy in Advanced Industrial Societies." *Population and Development Review* 7(1981):1–18.

Davis, Nancy, and Larry Bumpass "The Continuation of Education after Marriage among Women in the United States." *Demography* 13(1976):351–370.

Durand, John The Labor Force in the United States: 1890 to 1960. New York: Social Science Research Council, 1948.

Easterlin, Richard A. "The American Baby Boom in Historical Perspective." National Bureau of Economic Research Occasional Paper #79 (a portion of which appeared in the *American Economic Review*, December 1961), 1962.

―――― "Relative Economic Status and the American Fertility Swing." In Eleanor Bernert Sheldon, ed., *Family Economic Behavior: Problems and Prospects.* Philadelphia: Lippincott, 1973.

―――― *Birth and Fortune: The Impact of Numbers on Personal Welfare.* New York: Basic Books, 1980.

Ermisch, J. F. "Economic Opportunities, Marriage Squeezes and the Propensity to Marry: An Economic Analysis of Period Marriage Rates in England and Wales." *Population Studies* S35(1981):347–356.

Espenshade, T. "Marriage Trends in America: Estimates, Implications and Underlying Causes." *Population and Development Review* 11(1985):193–245.

Farley, Reynolds *Growth of the Black Population.* Chicago: Markham, 1970.

Furstenberg, Frank F., Jr., and Christine Winqueist Nord "Parenting Apart: Patterns of Childrearing After Marital Disruption." *Journal of Marriage and the Family* 47(1985):893–905.

Garfinkel, Irwin, and Sara McLanahan *Female Headed Families and Public Policy: A New American Dilemma?* Washington, D.C.: The Urban Institute, 1986.

Glick, Paul *American Families.* New York: John Wiley & Sons, 1957.

———— "Updating the Life Cycle of the Family." *Journal of Marriage and the Family* 39(1977):5–13.

———— "Marriage, Divorce, and Living Arrangements: Prospective Changes." *Journal of Family Issues* March (1984a):7–26.

———— "American Household Structure in Transition." *Family Planning Perspectives* 16(1984b):205–211.

————, **and Arthur Norton** "Frequency, Duration, and Probability of Marriage and Divorce." *Journal of Marriage and the Family* 33(1971):307–317.

Glick, Paul, and Graham Spanier "Married and Unmarried Cohabitation in the United States." *Journal of Marriage and the Family* 42(1980):19–30.

Goldman, Noreen, Charles F. Westoff, and Charles Hammerslough "Demography of the Marriage Market in the United States." *Population Index* 50(1984):5–25.

Goode, William J. *World Revolution and Family Patterns.* New York: Free Press, 1963.

Hajnal, John "European Marriage Patterns in Perspective." In D. V. Glass and D. E. C. Eversley, eds., *Population in History.* London: Edward Arnold Publishing Co., 1965.

Hannan, Michael, Nancy Tuma, and Lyle P. Groeneveld "Income and Independence Effects on Marital Dissolution: Results from the Seattle and Denver Income-Maintenance Experiments." *American Journal of Sociology* 84 (1978):611–633.

Heatherington, E. M., K. Camara, and D. L. Featherman "Intellectual Functioning and Achievement of Children in One-Parent Households." In J. A. Spense, ed., *Assessing Achievement.* San Francisco: W. H. Freeman, 1983.

Jacobson, Paul H. *American Marriage and Divorce.* New York: Rinehart & Co., 1959.

Kitagawa, Evelyn, and Phillip Hauser *Differential Mortality in the United States: A Study in Socioeconomic Epidemiology.* Cambridge Mass.: Harvard University Press, 1973.

Lesthaeghe, Ron "A Century of Demographic and Cultural Change in Western Europe." *Population and Development Review* 9(1983):411–436.

Marini, Margaret Mooney "Women's Educational Attainment and Parenthood." *American Sociological Review* 49(1984):491–511.

Mason, Karen O. "Women's Labor Force Participation and Fertility: Final Report 21U-662," prepared for the National Institutes of Health under contract #NIH 71-2212, 1974.

McCarthy, James "A Comparison of the Probability of the Dissolution of First and Second Marriages." *Demography* 15(1978):345–359.

McFalls, Joseph "The Impact of VD on the Fertility of the Black Population, 1880–1950." *Social Biology* 20(1973):2–19.

McLanahan, S. "Family Structure and the Reproduction of Poverty." *American Journal of Sociology* 90(1985):873–901.

Michael, Robert, Victor Fuchs, and Sharon Scott "Changes in the Propensity to Live Alone." *Demography* 17(1980):39–56.

Morgan, S. Philip "Parity-Specific Fertility Intentions and Uncertainty: The United States, 1970 to 1976." *Demography* 19:(1982):315–334.

National Center for Health Statistics "Trends in Illegitimacy: United States— 1940–65. Vital and Health Statistics, Series 21, No. 15, 1968.

——— "Divorces by Marriage Cohort." Vital and Health Statistics, Series 21, No. 34, 1979.

——— "Duration of Marriage Before Divorce." Vital and Health Statistics, Series 21, No. 38, 1981.

——— "Monthly Vital Statistics Report: Advance Report of Final Natality Statistics, 1982" Vol. 33, No. 6, 1984.

——— "Changes in Mortality Among the Elderly: United States, 1940–78." Vital and Health Statistics, Series 3, No. 22a, 1984.

——— "Monthly Vital Statistics Report, Births, Marriages, Divorces and Deaths for January 1985." Vol. 34, No. 1, 1985a.

——— "Monthly Vital Statistics Report: Births, Marriages, Divorces and Deaths for March 1985." Vol. 34, No. 3, 1985b.

——— "Monthly Vital Statistics Report: Annual Summary of Births, Marriages, Divorces, and Deaths: United States, 1984." Vol. 33, No. 13, 1985c.

Norton, Arthur "The Influence of Divorce on Traditional Life-Cycle Measures." *Journal of Marriage and the Family* 42:(1980):63–69.

Oppenheimer, Valerie K. *The Female Labor Force in the United States: Demographic and Economic Factors Governing its Growth and Changing Composition.* Westport, Conn.: Greenwood Press, 1970.

——— *Work and the Family.* New York: Academic Press, 1982.

Pratt, William F. "A Study of Marriages Involving Premarital Pregnancies." Ph.D. dissertation, University of Michigan, 1965.

Preston, Samuel, and John McDonald "The Incidence of Divorce Within Cohorts of American Marriages Contracted Since the Civil War." *Demography* 16(1978):1–25.

Retert, Sandra, and Larry Bumpass "Employment and Approval of Employment Among Mothers of Young Children." University of Wisconsin, Center for Demography & Ecology Working Paper 74-4, Madison, 1974.

Rindfuss, Ronald R., and Larry L. Bumpass "Age and the Sociology of Fertility." In Karl Taeuber, Larry Bumpass, and James Sweet, eds., *Social Demography.* New York: Academic Press, 1978.

———**, and Craig St. John** "Education and Fertility: Implicatons for the Roles Women Occupy." *American Sociological Review* 45(1980):431–447.

———, "Education and Timing of Motherhood: Disentangling Causation." *Journal of Marriage and the Family* 46(1984):981–984

Rindfuss, Ronald R., and James A. Sweet *Postwar Fertility Trends and Differentials in the United States.* New York: Academic Press, 1977.

Rockwell, Richard "Historical Trends and Variations in Educational Homogamy." *Journal of Marriage and the Family* 38(1976):83–96.

Rodgers, Willard L., and Arland Thornton "Changing Patterns of First Marriage in the United States." *Demography* 22(1985):265–79.

Ross, Heather, and Isabel Sawhill *Time of Transition: The Growth of Families Headed by Women.* Washington, D.C.: The Urban Institute, 1975.

Ryder, Norman B. "Components of Temporal Variations in American Fertility." In Robert W. Hiorns, ed., *Demographic Patterns in Developed Societies,* Vol. 19, Symposia of the Society for the Study of Human Biology. London: Taylor & Francis, 1980.

Schoen, Robert, and John Baj "Cohort Marriage and Divorce in Twentieth-Century Switzerland." *Journal of Marriage and the Family* 46(1984a):963–969.

————, "Twentieth-Century Cohort Marriage and Divorce in England and Wales." *Population Studies* 38:(1984b):439–449.

Schoen, Robert, and William Urton "Marriage, Divorce and Mortality: The Swedish Experience." *Proceedings of the General Conference of the International Union for the Scientific Study of Population in Mexico City* 1(1977):311–332.

———— "A Theoretical Perspective on Cohort Marriage and Divorce in Twentieth Century Sweden." *Journal of Marriage and the Family* 41(1979).

Schoen, Robert, William Urton, Karen Woodrow, and John Baj "Marriage and Divorce in Twentieth Century American Cohorts." *Demography* 22(1985):101–114.

Shryock, Henry S., and Jacob S. Siegel *The Methods and Materials of Demography.* Condensed edition, ed. Edward G. Stockwell. New York: Academic Press, 1976.

Smith, D. P. "A Reconsideration of Easterlin Cycles." *Population Studies* 35(1981):247–264.

Smith, Herbert L., and Phillips Cutright "Components of Change in the Number of Female Family Heads Ages 15 to 44, An Update and Reanalysis: United States, 1940–1983." *Social Science Research* 14(1985):226–250.

Smith, Peter "Asian Marriage Patterns in Transition." *Journal of Family History* 5(1980):58–97.

Smith, Ralph E., ed. *The Subtle Revolution: Women at Work.* Washington, D.C.: The Urban Institute, 1979.

Smuts, Robert *Women and Work in America.* New York: Columbia University Press, 1959.

Spitze, Glenna D. "Role Experiences of Young Women: A Longitudinal Test of the Role Hiatus Hypothesis." *Journal of Marriage and the Family* 40 (1978):471–479.

Sweet, James A. *Women in the Labor Force.* New York: Seminar Press, 1973.

———— "The Timing and Duration of the 'Empty Nest' Stage of the Family Life Cycle." University of Wisconsin, Center for Demography & Ecology, Working Paper 81–25, 1981.

———— "Work and Fertility." In Greer Litton Fox, ed., *The Childbearing Decision: Fertility Attitudes and Behavior.* Beverly Hills, Calif.: Sage Publications, 1982.

———— "Components of Change in the Number of Households: 1970–1980." *Demography* 21(1984):129–140.

————, **and Larry Bumpass** "Differentials in Marital Instability of the Black Population: 1970." *Phylon* 35(1974):323–331.

Taeuber, Irene, and Conrad Taeuber *People of the United States in the 20th Century.* Washington, D.C.: U.S. Bureau of the Census, 1971.

Thompson, Warren S., and P. K. Whelpton *Population Trends in the United States.* New York: Gordon & Breach, 1969.

Thornton, Arland "Fertility and Income, Consumption Aspirations, and Child Quality Standards." *Demography* 16(1979):157–176.

———— "The Influence of the Parental Family on the Attitudes and Behavior of Children." Presentation at the Family and Household Structure Workshop, National Institute of Child Health and Human Development, 1983.

————, **and Deborah Freedman** "Changing Attitudes Toward Marriage and Single Life." *Family Planning Perspectives* 14(1982):297–303.

———— "The Changing American Family." *Population Bulletin* 38(1983):1–44.

Thornton, Arland, and Willard L. Rodgers "Changing Patterns of Marriage and Divorce in the United States." Final Report, Contract NO1-HD-02850, National Institute for Child Health and Human Development, 1983.

—— "The Influence of Individual and Historical Time on Marital Dissolution,"*Demography* 24 (February 1987):1-24.

United States Bureau of the Census *Historical Statistics of the United States, Colonial Times to 1970, Part 1,* 1975.

—— "Household and Family Characteristics: March 1975." *Current Population Reports,* Series P-20, #291, 1976.

—— "Child Support and Alimony." *Current Population Reports,* Special Studies P-23, #112, 1978.

—— "Child Support and Alimony (Advance Report)." *Current Population Reports,* Special Studies P-23, #124, 1981.

—— "Child Support and Alimony." *Current Population Reports,* Special Studies P-23, #141, 1983a.

—— "Population Characteristics. Fertility of American Women: June 1981." *Current Population Reports,* Series P-20, #378, 1983b.

—— "Childspacing Among Birth Cohorts of American Women: 1905–1959." *Current Population Reports,* Series P-20, #385, 1984.

—— "Fertility of American Women: June 1985." *Current Population Reports,* Series P-20, #406, June 1986.

United States Department of Health and Human Services National Estimates of Marriage Dissolution and Survivorship: United States. Vital and Health Statistics, Series 3, No. 19, National Center for Health Statistics Publication No. (PHS) 81-1403.

Veevers, J. E. *Childless by Choice.* Toronto: Butterworth & Co., 1980.

Vinovskis, Maris A. "The Historian and the Life Course: Reflections on Recent Approaches to the Study of American Family Life in the Past." *Life-Span Development and Behavior* 8(1986):33–60.

Wallerstein, J., and J. Kelly *Surviving the Breakup.* New York: Basic Books, 1980.

Weed, James "National Estimates of Marriage Dissolution and Survivorship: United States." DHHS Publication (PHS) 81–1403, Series 3, No. 19, November 1980.

Weiss, Yoarm, and Robert J. Willis "Children as Collective Goods in Divorce Settlements." *Journal of Labor Economics* 3(1985):258–292.

Westoff, Charles F. "Some Speculations on the Future of Marriage and Fertility." *Family Planning Perspectives* 10(1978):79–83.

—— "The Decline in Unwanted Fertility 1971–76." *Family Planning Perspectives* 13(1981):70–71.

——, **and Norman B. Ryder** *The Contraceptive Revolution.* Princeton, N.J.: Princeton University Press, 1977.

Zelnik, Melvin, and John F. Kantner "Sexual Activity, Contraceptive Use and Pregnancy Among Metropolitan Area Teenagers: 1971–1979." *Family Planning Perspectives* 12(1980):229–233.

Name Index

A

Alba, Richard D., 30*n*15

B

Baj, John, 201*n*15
Bancroft, Gertrude, 146*n*21
Bane, Mary Jo, 262*n*1, 262*n*3, 392
Becker, Gary S., 49*n*22, 392, 393*n*2, 398*n*14
Behrman, Samuel J., 395*n*6
Beresford, John C., 296*n*1
Bloom, David, 132*n*16, 397*n*9
Bowen, William, 146*n*21Bumpass, Larry L., 30*n*12, 102*n*15, 131*n*15, 156*n*25, 174*n*1, 175*n*2, 182*n*8, 184*n*10, 184*n*11, 262*n*3, 263*n*4, 394*n*4, 396*n*7, 397*n*11, 399*n*18

C

Cain, Glen, 146*n*21
Camara, Kathleen, 290*n*8
Carliner, Geoffrey, 297*n*4
Chamlin, Mitchell B., 30*n*15
Cherlin, Andrew, 57*n*3, 176*n*3, 178*n*6, 210*n*18, 262*n*2, 392
Chevan, Albert, 297*n*2
Coale, Ansley J., 395*n*6
Cooney, Rosemary S., 362*n*1
Coras, Leslie, 395*n*6
Current Population Reports (CPR), 133, 136
Current Population Survey (CPS), 32*n*17, 33, 380*n*4, 384
Cutright, Phillips, 362*n*1, 362*n*2

D

Davis, Kingsley, 297*n*3, 399*n*19, 401*n*27
Davis, Nancy, 156*n*25
Durand, John, 146*n*21

E

Easterlin, Richard A., 126*n*4
Ermisch, John F., 126*n*5
Espenshade, Thomas, 195*n*12
Eversley, David E. C., 30*n*13

F

Farley, Reynolds, 130*n*13
Featherman, David L., 290*n*8
Finegan, T. Aldrich, 146*n*21
Fox, Greer Litton, 131*n*15
Freedman, Deborah, 393*n*2, 399*n*17, 400*n*21
Freedman, Ronald, 395*n*6
Fuchs, Victor, 297*n*4
Furstenberg, Frank, 394*n*5, 401*n*25

G

Garfinkel, Irwin, 362*n*1
Glass, David V., 30*n*13
Glick, Paul, 141*n*19, 184*n*11
Goldman, Noreen, 44*n*20
Goode, William J., 392, 399*n*16
Groeneveld, Lyle P., 400*n*23

H

Hajnal, John, 30*n*13
Hammersough, Charles, 44*n*20
Hannan, Michael, 400*n*23
Hauser, Phillip, 202*n*16
Hauser, Robert M., 5
Heatherington, E. Mavis, 290*n*8
Hiorns, Robert W., 2*n*1, 126*n*6

J

Jacobson, Paul H., 177

Subject Index